Roman Literary Culture

Ancient Society and History

ELAINE FANTHAM

Roman Literary Culture

From Cicero to Apuleius

The Johns Hopkins University Press
Baltimore and London

© 1996 The Johns Hopkins University Press
All rights reserved. Published 1996
Printed in the United States of America on acid-free paper

Johns Hopkins Paperbacks edition, 1999
9 8 7 6 5 4 3 2 1

The Johns Hopkins University Press
2715 North Charles Street
Baltimore, Maryland 21218-4363
www.press.jhu.edu

Library of Congress Cataloging-in-Publication Data will be found
at the end of this book.

A catalog record for this book is available from the British Library.

Frontispiece: Funerary relief of Avita, probably from early third century
A.D. Found in Rome, the relief is inscribed in Greek and carved in
marble from Asia Minor, reflecting the dominance of Greek verbal and
artistic culture. British Museum Sculpture 649.

Contents

Contents

Preface and Acknowledgments

Let me start with a demurral. This book does not try to be a literary history; that would demand a rare combination of synoptic vision and intimate understanding of widely different generic traditions and individual creative minds. Even those most gifted with critical talents have voiced their concerns about the difficulty of such an ambitious enterprise, in which the divergent aims of tracing historical development and providing critical tools and evaluations often conflict, and writers often meet uneven treatment. Fortunately, English-speaking students and teachers now have available an enlightened, consistently organized, analytical survey of Roman literature by a distinguished critic. The publication of an updated and expanded English-language version of Gian Biagio Conte's *Latin Literature: A History* is a powerful justification for my refusal to attempt what he has done so well.

Instead I have tried to offer a companion volume, which I hope will be useful to college and university students familiar with the main Latin authors and the outline of Roman history: more ambitiously, perhaps, I hope to offer some new perspectives to students of other literary periods and to general readers seriously interested in Latin literature and its social contexts. I. A. Richards and the pioneers of Practical Criticism would certainly not approve: but their greatest contribution to literary criticism lay in interpreting lyric poetry and poetry written over the past two centuries. Classicists have always practiced "close reading," a process not very different from Practical Criticism, but have usually recognized the need for context to help them across the millennia. In the current renewal of interest in historical context ("the New Historicism"), a social history of Roman literature may seem less strange. Even when we feel sufficiently intimate with the great poetic and prose texts to form our own aesthetic judgments, knowledge of social and cultural context can modulate or sharpen our appreciation of the individual work: hence, my theme is the world in which this literature developed from maturity around 50 B.C. to decline in the generation after A.D. 150.

Such a book could have been organized thematically—with separate chapters to consider bilingualism or oral communication or patronage across the two centuries. Instead it operates chronologically, moving from one generation to the next, and paying special attention to individual canonical authors in successive chapters. It seemed likely that many students would turn to the book to give an extra dimension to their study of Virgil or Ovid, Seneca, Pliny the Younger, or Apuleius, and this format would enable them to close in on their target. But there is a stronger reason to move in this way: almost every aspect of Roman society was undergoing such rapid change. Thus the reality of, say, Ovid's world depended on a conjunction of changes: the growth of public libraries, the absorption of oratory into the schools of declamation, the expansion (in terms of age, sex, and geography) of the readership of personal poetry, and the withering away of patronage outside the imperial house.

What do we understand by Roman literature? The second, Latin, volume of the *Cambridge History of Classical Literature* clearly felt that literature was primarily creative or imaginative writing whether in verse or (less often at Rome) in prose: in terms of space, it privileged poetry and the novel over history (though Roman historical writing often comes closer to creative fiction than to objective record) and over works of geography, law, natural science, or literary history. It also wasted no time on discussing Greek writers and teachers at Rome, although these men exercised such extraordinary influence over both writers and their public. But that element, like many others, would be fully and splendidly conveyed by the late Elizabeth Rawson's *Intellectual Life in the Later Roman Republic.*

Today, in Russia or Italy or Holland, the bookstalls are full of translated American fiction and works of politics or philosophy from France or Germany; this is what people are reading, just as young Americans now study fiction translated from the Spanish of Argentina or Mexico and students of drama everywhere study Ibsen and Strindberg. It would be unrealistic to judge modern American or Russian writers as if they had not read these foreign models and been affected by their innovations of form and content. There may have been few literal translations of Greek writing at Rome, but to the extent that well-educated Romans understood Greek, their literary experience was shaped by Greek texts, Greek teachers, and Greek performers, and for at least part of the second century of our era Greek seems to have renewed its hegemony over Latin. So a recurring feature of this "social history" will be the issue of bilingualism and the role played by living Greeks in the Roman literary world.

I have also been inclusive in another way: *Roman* literature suggests the literature written and read in Rome or Italy, the next concentric circle of its citizenship and culture. But Roman literature began and continued to be written by men from outside the inherited cultural boundaries: by the Greek-speaking Livius Andronicus and Ennius, by Plautus from Umbria, by Catullus and Virgil from Cisalpine Gaul, north of Italy proper, and as Rome expanded, by Seneca and Martial and Quintilian from Spain and Fronto and Apuleius from Africa. No one doubts that Seneca was a Roman writer because he made his career and died at Rome. Apuleius seems a different case: he had some education at Rome and returned there later in life, but he shows more evidence of his Athenian education. Rome itself was no longer the most vigorous center of Latin literature, so that a study of Roman literary culture in Apuleius's time becomes a study of Latin literary culture where it was most highly developed—in Africa and its social and intellectual capital, Carthage. Yet given the near silence of pagan Latin literature for two centuries after Apuleius's death and Christianity's increasing dominance as the theme of African eloquence, it seems fair to end with the cultural world of Apuleius. More Roman than Hadrian's society, more vital than Juvenal's bitter satiric image of the capital, Apuleius's world offers an exuberant coda—pointing to a society still too little explored.

My aim, then, has been to throw light on the changing society in which Roman writers wrote and found their public, to evoke the cultural equipment and expectations with which audience or reader first experienced authors or texts, and, where appropriate, to explain the rise and fall of different genres by social and political change. With such a large theme, and a wealth of exciting new publications dealing with individual authors and periods, I have had to make a personal sample, and this will be most apparent in the two chapters discussing the complex public and private cultures of the Augustan age; still, readers may turn to other recent studies for greater detail on this canonical period.

Many colleagues and students have helped this book to take shape. I owe too much to too many friends, living and dead, to do them justice, but I would like to voice particular thanks to Ted Champlin, for his careful reading of Chapters 6 and 7; to Maud Gleason, for giving her expert eye to my brief account of the Second Sophistic; and especially to Gian Biagio Conte, for sharing with me his enhanced treatment of many authors in *Latin Literature* before its publication and, more recently, for our time spent discussing his ideas on Neronian literary culture as seen (and *preso in giro*) by Petronius—but above all for sustaining my morale in difficult times.

I am also grateful to many institutions: to Princeton, my own university, for leaves in 1991 and 1995, and support from the Humanities Research fund, to Pembroke College and the Faculty of Classics at Cambridge for their hospitality and wonderful working environment, to the Dipartimento di Studi Classici of the University of Pisa for its warm welcome of an unofficial guest, and to the American Academy for the glorious privilege of living on the green summit of Monteverde, sharing its community, and enjoying the peace of its library. The words are stale but the memories are fresh and a source of continuing delight.

Finally I would like to thank Ingo Gildenhart and Andrew Zissos for their help in indexing and proofreading this manuscript. I owe much to their high standards and good humor.

Roman Literary Culture

Introduction: Toward a Social History of Latin Literature

Whether we consider the brief period between 50 B.C. and the death of Cicero in November 43 as the last years of the Roman Republic or the first years of autocracy, this is effectively the first time in Roman history when there is abundant contemporary evidence for the education, attitudes, and circumstances of individual authors. Thanks to the unparalleled insights provided in Cicero's letters, the daily record of this final phase of the "free" republic enables us to perceive both the political and the literary transformations in process. First come political changes brought about by the advent of autocratic rule; then literature undergoes the more subtle domination of models of perfection that determine the literary viewpoints of generations of successors. From this time writers will struggle self-consciously not to be postclassical, mere imitators falling away from the high point of creativity and confidence reached during the Augustan age.

So my task is limited both in time and in theme. Passing over two of the critical divisions that shape Horace's treatment of the *Art of Poetry*,[1] those of literary artistry and its product (*ars* and *opus*), this book must renounce analysis and interpretation of individual works, leaving literary criticism for other, more specific, discussions. But my theme includes more than can be assumed under the third rubric of the Hellenistic and Horatian division—more than the study of *artifex*, the writer himself. We now recognize for all literature the importance of circumstance and context, considered by Aristotle and the classical critics only for their study of rhetoric.[2] We know that literature is molded not only by the composer-performer but also by its audience and the manner of its communication. My interest has been to extend Aristotle's approach, because I see as important aspects of any literary work its author in his social and political setting, its recipients and their culture, and the medium or nature of its presentation.

Author, Audience, and Medium

Let me expand on each of these three categories. First, of course, the author. What do we need to know about him? (For the author in Roman culture is usually, however regrettably, male: neither the memoirs of the younger Agrippina nor any other significant work by women has survived from our period, although some female poets can be named and briefly considered.)[3] The author at Rome was in many genres and most periods both composer and performer. He designed his work and controlled its realization, whether as the director of a mime troupe or, more formally, as an orator in court, Senate house, or public assembly; as a poet or grammarian too he would present his work, or discuss the work of others, in oral performance, and as a rhetorician he would be expected to demonstrate his technique in action, and do so not only to his pupils and their fathers, but to large audiences who came to enjoy the display.

It is also important to understand the author's background: his social class—senatorial, or from the wealthy and established equestrian order—or civil status. He might be an outsider, a noncitizen of free birth like the Calabrian Ennius, or the Greek Archias, who were rewarded with citizenship by their Roman patrons, or an Italian with citizen rights like the comic dramatist Plautus from Sarsina in Roman Umbria. As a third possibility the poet or author might be freeborn and enslaved through kidnapping or as a prisoner of war; such prisoners of war sometimes lived as privileged slaves, like the

Augustan librarian Gaius Melissus,[4] but most often earned their freedom. We can assume that the third-century Livius Andronicus of Tarentum, the first poet to translate Greek drama into Latin plays, or Terence, the "African" whose comedies were staged between 166 and 160 B.C., was freed by his aristocratic master. This practice became the expected pattern, especially for freeborn citizens of Greek states such as the scholars Tyrannio of Amisus and Parthenius of Nicaea, taken prisoner in the wars against Mithridates of Pontus during Cicero's youth.[5] If there is no obvious case of a slave or ex-slave author born in the first century of our era or later, it is because more and more of the civilized world was now part of the Roman Empire; it has been plausibly suggested that the fable writer Phaedrus had been a slave, but this cannot be verified.

Senatorial and equestrian authors may have needed no patronage; certainly anyone of senatorial origin could spread his works through his friends and family connections directly to the most influential members of society. But equestrian status is more ambiguous. Horace is now thought to have reached equestrian rank despite the loss of his inherited property in the civil wars, yet he certainly appreciated the security and public standing offered to him by the very wealthy Maecenas, himself a mere *eques*.[6] Virgil must have quickly reached an equestrian fortune, thanks to the support of Maecenas and the protection of Augustus, yet he needed their support and protection. One may fairly wonder whether any writer of the imperial age up to the time of Marcus Aurelius was not equestrian, in the sense of meeting the minimum census or property rating. Inflation and devaluation may have reduced the required property qualification to a level that produced a barely adequate income without some remunerative employment. It would not be surprising to find that Statius, Martial, and even the self-pitying Juvenal were all technically equestrian. But for Statius and Martial at least patronage was essential, not so much to provide them with meals and good-quality cloaks (a favorite poetic motif) as to give them an entrée to society—an audience and a reputation.[7]

One aspect that will significantly affect any author's work is his education—the extent of his knowledge of literature and the biases that came with the type of training he received. Cicero's education

3

was both rhetorical—acquired from Greek rhetoricians like Apollonius Molo of Rhodes and polished by imitation of Roman orators like Licinius Crassus—and philosophical. Indeed, he studied with philosophers from three of the contemporary schools: with the Stoic Diodotus, the Academic skeptic Philo of Larissa, and the reforming Neoacademic Antiochus of Ascalon.[8] Virgil, like the Neoteric poets before him, seems to have studied both rhetoric and Greek poetics. Both are attested in the poem from the youthful collection attributed to him, in which he dismisses the too familiar "rhetoricians' bombast" (*rhetoron ampullae*) and even at one stage renounces the muses of poetry for the sake of pursuing Epicurean philosophy. Twenty-five years later we can contrast Ovid's education in the declamatory schools where Seneca the Elder observed and reported his early achievements.[9] There is no hint that Ovid learned the art of verse from any source but the Greek and Latin poetic texts, yet his verse technique was already refined in his earliest work. If Ovid, like his predecessor Cornelius Gallus, had a Parthenius to instruct him,[10] he has suppressed the fact, but in his poetic autobiography[11] Ovid acknowledges his youthful experience listening to Propertius recite his verse, and he has clearly read Virgil and Tibullus many times.

Two generations later the education of Papinius Statius is very different, since he grew up in the Greek culture of Naples, trained in the school of his father, a Greek *grammaticus* and professional poet, on an intensive diet of Hellenistic poetry.[12] In the last generation of our study the commonplace books of the cultured gentleman Aulus Gellius report his training in the traditional dyad of rhetoric and philosophy, but also show that he studied the texts of archaic and classical Latin literature in a way not too different from nineteenth-century students in Europe. His teachers too were cosmopolitan and bilingual, with mixed cultural allegiance, like the Gallic Favorinus of Arles who wrote and spoke in Greek, the consular Fronto, an eloquent Latin orator from Roman Africa, and the Asiatic Greek philosopher Taurus.

Bilingualism is another crucial element in assessing an author, and bilingualism can vary immensely. I read and appreciate five languages beyond my own: the living French, German, and Italian, and the "dead" Latin and Greek, but with unequal facility. I was late in learning Greek and still find non-Attic dialects and the language of lyric and erudite Hellenistic poetry a challenge. After learning French at school for eight years I still could not follow the sound of spoken French or speak with fluency until I went to live in France for half a year; German I learned at school, revived at university, and constantly experience passively in reading academic books and articles, but I cannot compose a correct letter, still less a lecture. Italian, in my case self-taught and practiced by reading Italian scholarship and novels, I still do not know well enough to write for others; yet I can talk after a fashion in all three languages. This must have been the level of Greek known by many Romans, but with some additional complication and specialization.

The Roman learned only one language beside his own—Greek—but he learned it at a very early age, by hearing the poetry of Homer. As a child he must have copied out texts, but would not possess his own reading text of the *Iliad* or the *Odyssey*. It is not clear that he was trained to listen to Greek prose, but in the republican period the young man who went on to rhetorical training would receive it from Greeks communicating in Greek, and would at least have composed exercises in Greek to match. Those who read or listened to philosophy did so exclusively in Greek, until Cicero created a Roman corpus, and most would-be philosophers continued to write in Greek in the first and second centuries of our era.

Cicero loved Greek and used it whenever possible outside his public career; he included sophisticated Greek phrases in his letters to intimates such as Atticus or his brother Quintus, he made speeches in Greek to the Greeks of Sicily, and he read technical Greek authors on geography, astronomy, and philosophy. He not only had Greek teachers; he even brought some to live with him, no doubt talking in their language when in private. When he wanted the great Posidonius to compose a history of his consulship, he himself provided a Greek outline so elegant—and perhaps *over*elegant— that Posidonius claimed he could not improve on it and excused himself from the unnecessary task.[13] I doubt whether any other

5

Roman writer had such a full knowledge of Greek literature before the Greek-educated Statius, for whom Greek may have been the natal and Latin the acquired culture.

The bilingualism of a Virgil or an Ovid was manifestly rich, entailing the power to read and understand the most complex Hellenistic poetry and to study Greek scholarly commentaries on Homer and later poets; they knew the scholiasts on Homer, and probably those of Callimachus, Theocritus, Apollonius, and others. Seneca's command of Greek was probably more philosophical in orientation, but as a tragic dramatist he shows familiarity with Euripides and Sophocles, and his nephew Lucan seems to have known Apollonius as well as he knew Homer. As for Nero, his knowledge of Greek was up to the minute, less a study of the classics than an immersion in contemporary popular Greek song and stage works.[14]

So it is not enough to record that a Roman poet or writer was bilingual; we must reconstruct his education in Greek culture alongside his upbringing in the growing tradition of Roman rhetoric, history, and poetry.

With class and education comes motivation; but this will vary as much with the genre practiced as with the social circumstances of the writer; despite his own ironic claim, we can hardly believe that Horace was driven to write poetry by need for money,[15] since poetry brought no direct economic reward. For poetry as for prose, social acceptance, even fame, will have been a primary motive, varying with the esteem accorded to a given genre by different classes and generations. And while rhetorical prose always served a political end, and history or autobiography might often do so, philosophical writing may have sprung from cultural or literary motives, like those of Cicero, or it may have been driven by missionary fervor. Lucretius's passionate advocacy of Epicureanism is perhaps unique among Roman poetry in its subordination to a message. Although Roman commanders took over from Alexander and the Hellenistic rulers the tradition of encouraging second-class poets who lived by celebrating the powerful,[16] for most of the poets whose work has survived their poetry must have been its own motive and fulfillment.

More difficult to define is each author's changing perception of Latin literature and his own place in its development. From the time of Virgil on there was a Latin canon, soon to be dominated by Virgil himself, but, like Virgil, his contemporaries Propertius and Horace also worked with a perception of their generic inheritance. Propertius saw himself as successor to Catullus, Calvus, and Gallus,[17] Horace as successor in satire to Lucilius[18]—and both were proud of their success in adapting Greek models, whether of elegy or lyric. But at this time there can have been no Roman poet or historian who did not measure himself against a Greek model, and seek to appropriate one who had not yet been matched in Latin writing; along with the notion of becoming the Roman Demosthenes or Archilochus, Mimnermus, or Callimachus, came the boast of primacy: *primus ego,* "I was the first."

There was an inherited apparatus of consecration for poets, equipped with advice from Apollo or the muses, and poetic attributes like the pipes of Hesiod, the lute of Orpheus or Linus, and the pure spring of Hippocrene. There was a similar *auctoritas* for writers of prose genres, rhetoric, history, and philosophy, but the latter do not so much claim to be the Roman Plato or Demosthenes as to be their followers. Quintilian calls Cicero *Platonis aemulus* (10.1.123). While Cicero is too proud to acknowledge this explicitly, he certainly speaks of contemporary orators as emulating Thucydides, Lysias, or Demosthenes. For the understanding of both prose and verse artists we need to know whom they looked to as masters in their genre, both Greek and Roman, and how they saw the history of their genres up to their own time. Our assessment of Pliny's oratory should take into account the eclecticism with which he blended in a single (lost) speech the stylistic qualities of Demosthenes, Calvus, and Cicero.[19] It helps us to understand Pliny's attitude to literary composition to know that he took even his erotic verses seriously and subjected them to criticism and revision, justifying himself by a long line of honorable practitioners of occasional erotic verse (*Ep.* 5.3).

Let me move on to the audience or public of literature at Rome. No single word for the recipients of literature is without its limiting implications. An *audience* implies listening or watching without

7

access to a text, so that the experience is single and linear, without possibility of review; a *readership* implies access only through a text; and a *public* implies distribution to a wide group outside the circle of the poet or writer. In early Latin literature, public and occasion go together, as they often will. The literature was for performance rather than for reading, and the question is largely of the context in which performance would take place. A dramatic script would normally be sold by the author to the public officials who financed its first performance, and one could expect that there would be some cooperation between author and master of the stage troupe— but scripts were clearly vulnerable to subsequent actors' modifications. Again the stage author could to some extent introduce and justify his innovations in the dramatic prologue. Epic poetry, on the other hand, would normally be recited by its author, and might be prefaced or followed by the poet's own interpretation. Suetonius reports in his *Lives of Critics and Teachers of Rhetoric* that the very first poets at Rome, Livius and Ennius, also served as critics, giving and interpreting readings of their own and other men's work (*Gramm.* 1).

With the development of formal education and increase in private libraries, a reading public can be assumed among the elite in Cicero's day, but most works of this period will have had both an immediate audience and a subsequent readership. Cicero's speeches delivered in the Senate, assembly, or open courts of the Forum were first prepared in writing, then delivered from memory, then remodeled and reedited for circulation to others who could not be expected to know the full circumstances of the case. Indeed several of Cicero's greatest "speeches," like those of Isocrates, were never delivered in court, but were designed to be self-explanatory literary texts. These range from the five speeches representing the second action against Verres in 70 B.C., to the defense of Milo in 52 and the second Philippic speech against Antony in 43. Influenced by Demosthenes' corpus, Cicero also reorganized and rewrote the speeches of his consulship three years later to serve as a reminder of his political services. But even at this relatively early time he may have intended them as a model for future students of oratory, just as he himself had used his teacher Crassus's great speech against the repeal of the Servilian Jury Law as a model in his youth.[20]

Cicero's philosophical works were designed to fill a void and give Rome a philosophical corpus written with a style as rich and memorable as Plato's;[21] his comments on the writing of history show that if he had been free to compose a Roman history, it would have been as much to provide Roman youth with elegant historical texts as to commemorate the events of his own day. Even poetry was seen as a proper medium of self-advertisement, and Cicero commemorated his consulship and subsequent political martyrdom in both oratory and narrative verse. Later generations mocked his three books *de consulatu suo*,[22] but in the republic poetry played as important a role in immortalizing historic events as women in the upbringing of a family (the image is mine, not Cicero's). We think of the function of poetry as aesthetic and cannot see any merit in versified military campaigns, but at Rome it found an audience, and probably a larger audience than prose *commentarii*, like Caesar's masterpieces.

There are other considerations in estimating an author's chosen audience. Although the primary audience of Cicero or Caesar was his own class, and to some extent his own age group, both men must have aimed to influence the next generation. From its beginning Roman prose writing affirmed its purpose as either the instruction of the young or the satisfaction of a friend's request. This often took the form of a dedication, and such dedications are a useful source of understanding about the social function or pretexts of literature. Most of Cicero's later work was dedicated to his bicultural friend Atticus or to Brutus, the spiritual heir he so longed to convert, but two works, one on rhetoric, the other on social obligations (*De Officiis*), were dedicated to his son. In this he was following an old tradition, but in each case the choice of addressee reflects the nature of the work and of the reader's understanding.

Cicero's correspondence from the years of Caesar's political supremacy shows that there were many literati among the wealthy leisured class who would listen to works of prose or verse at dinner gatherings, and it is only a step to infer that they would be specifically invited to private recitations of history, tragedy, and various poetic forms. The public recitation seems to have become official in the triumviral period, since it is credited to Asinius Pollio, the consul of 40 B.C. This was also the time when public declamation began to be fashionable. It may amaze the modern reader that Augustus, Agrippa, and Maecenas, as well as the historian Livy, found time to attend declamatory performances on hackneyed and fictitious themes by Porcius Latro or Cestius or Haterius, but in Rome the art of language and its manipulation was second only to the arts of government and warfare; as these were withdrawn into imperial hands, the time available for the art of words increased and came to dominate social life.

Ovid's audience must have been quite different in age, sex, and class. Elegy even before Ovid is explicit in speaking of young men and women in love who seek in the supposed experience of the poet a mirror for their own. Even though the *Metamorphoses*, with the formal scale and features of epic, might reach a more mature audience, it would I think be right to assume as many female as male readers of this text. For it is preoccupied with the sorrows of women, with love and various forms of sexuality. But the public for sophisticated poetry must have included both those able to listen and appreciate the performed text—those from the inner circles of Roman society—and others further away who had to depend on reading what had been performed at Rome. Literary histories always undervalue the provinces, but the provinces produced poets as Rome never did. Residents of, say, Iowa City cannot attend a live performance of *Die Walküre*, but will still be eager to buy compact disks and enjoy the sound of Wagner. So from the time of Horace onward we hear of readers in Africa or Spain[23] who eagerly awaited the arrival of texts "published" at Rome. The very distance from fashionable recitations may have accelerated the growth of a book trade, more necessary in Gaul or Spain than in Rome itself. How else did Martial acquire his culture in far away Bilbilis, or Quintilian in Calagurris, or Tacitus in his Gallic childhood, or Gellius and Apuleius in North Africa?

This brings me to the third component in the sociology of our literature: the locus of performance or the medium of textual diffusion. Latin literature began with performance for a mass public— the tragedies and comedies of Livius Andronicus, adapted from the Greek and financed by the Roman magistrates for public games to celebrate the victory over Carthage in 240 B.C. One aspect of these public games is that such plays were performed only once, as part of the celebration, and did not have time to build up a reputation that would bring new audiences. Excuses could be found for repeating a performance, and Lily Ross Taylor shrewdly suggested that the desire to see a second showing of a successful play provoked the many recorded occasions when a religious flaw required a second presentation.[24] Yet the Roman theater, so wasteful of its own products, survived for some 150 years before it began to live on revivals and display performances full of spectacle or stage business. For more than a century, from 240 B.C. to the time of Lucilius (around 125), the poetic record is almost exclusively of drama (for the masses) and epic (for the ruling class), and it is the members of the ruling class who commission the plays performed for the games, reward poets with citizenship, or establish colleges of dramatic poets and temples of the muses.[25]

Ennius and Cato, Two Early Writers

Rome's earliest literary culture can be exemplified in the intersecting careers of two famous men, born within five years of each other, Q. Ennius (239–169) and M. Porcius Cato (234(?)–149). Between them they wrote in every known genre of Latin prose and verse, and their long lives—Ennius reached seventy and Cato either eighty-five or ninety—witnessed the full expansion of Roman imperial conquest and both public and private wealth. Cato was born into a family of Sabine landowners and owed his early career to the patronage of a noble family. He met Ennius when he was returning from his quaestorship (he would be about thirty years old) and brought the poet back to Rome.[26] While the Calabrian Ennius was trilingual, in Greek, Oscan, and Latin, and a professional poet, the Sabine Cato is said to have learned Greek late in life (but "late" might only mean after the age of formal education), and turned to writing only after he had carried his political career to the summit of the censorship.

Ennius, who affirmed his artistic standards by claiming the Greek title of *poeta* or "maker," wrote successful tragedies and less successful comedies, but achieved his lasting fame for his national epic of Rome, the *Annales* or "Chronicles." This was originally intended to cover Rome's history from Romulus to the defeat of Hannibal, but was continued by the poet into the wars of his own maturity. He is known to have written not only the public poetry of the drama but the lesser genres of fashionable epigram and a didactic poem on gastronomy adapted from the work of a Sicilian Greek, Archestratus of Gela. He wrote a kind of verse called *satura* on miscellaneous topics, without the social criticism or invective of Lucilian or Horatian satire; he is even credited with adapting into Latin prose the debunking history of the Olympian gods by Euhemerus, but evidence for this sophisticated product is insecure. In later life Ennius found other patrons, the Scipios (both Africanus and Nasica) and Fulvius Nobilior, the conqueror of Aetolia, whose son bestowed Roman citizenship on the poet.[27] This was a man who gave learned readings and interpretations of poetry, who lived in his own house on intimate terms with the Cornelii Scipiones, and received a statue in their family monument.

The other, complementary, side of Roman literature was developed by his former patron, Cato, who after Ennius's death composed the first history of Rome and Italy in Latin. Cato included in his history some of his own political speeches on major foreign and domestic issues, and left behind him separate texts of some 150 published speeches of every kind.[28] He even composed a manual of agriculture for his own class and an encyclopedia written in large letters for the education of his son. Each of the works I have mentioned might be said to have a different audience, according to its genre, but in their persons these two extraordinary men provided Rome with the full range of literature, omitting only philosophy and prose fiction.

New Genres of Literature, from Lucilius to Apuleius

A quick survey of the growth of literature in the mid-republic will show the social dimension of each genre. To the new educated members of the upper class of the second century, even their own daily life, their gossip, and prejudices were of importance, and so the first personal poetry was written by the wealthy and politically inactive Lucilius, perhaps to be sent as letters to his friends, but certainly for afterdinner entertainment. His verse was treated by the Romans as the beginning of satire, a genre they claimed to have invented, but not, perhaps, so very different in its early themes and function from the sympotic elegies and iambi of Greek private occasions.

As public presentations of straight tragedy and comedy began to recede in the age of Sulla, their place was taken first by literary mime, then by unscripted forms of dramatic entertainment, whose importance in contemporary society must have been far greater than our text-based studies might suggest. Nor was mime simply the entertainment fodder of the uneducated. The emperor Augustus himself, as he lay dying, chose mime as the model of his life, asking his friends "whether he had performed the mime of life nicely," and adding the Greek envoi of such shows, "then since it has been a good show, applaud, and send us cheerfully upon our way" (Suet. *Aug.* 99).

The upper class developed for itself a literature of politics: political autobiography, contemporary history, and political oratory, the sort of texts distributed by the authors to their own circle. Thus we hear of several autobiographical works from the period around the turn of the second century: memoirs of Aemilius Scaurus and Lutatius Catulus the Elder, and Greek memoirs written by the exiled Rutilius Rufus and later by the dictator Sulla.[29] The younger generation of the same class begins to try its talent in occasional poetry, first as an educational exercise or a social game, then with increasing standards of perfectionism. Influenced by Hellenistic theory and poetic models, the leisured and educated young men around Catullus produce miniature epics that take nine years to refine— like the *Zmyrna* of Cinna—and can be read only by those of equal erudition.[30] With this generation the emphasis is on a restricted audience of the initiated, a small refined public, defined by exclusion of men like Suffenus from the circles of these cultured dandies. This attitude will persist in Horace's pride as a lyric poet, excluding the profane from his refined poetry. Both his opening ode with its

13

appeal to his patron and his muse, and the great prefatory ode to the third book revel in rejection of the crowd:

> I have no use for secular outsiders
> I bar the gross crowd: give me reverent silence.
> I am the Muses' priest:
> I sing for maidens and for boys grave verse unheard before
> (*Odes* 3.1.1–4 trans. Michie)

Horace uses the language of initiation, as if his odes were religious hymns that could only be sung by pure virgins and youths. On one unique occasion, the Secular Games of 17 B.C., he was commissioned by his emperor to compose such a hymn. It is generally supposed that this hymn was heard by the public, but it is far more likely that it was confined to the select magistrates and attendants participating in the successive cult acts on the Palatine, and made known to the public only by subsequent inclusion among his published works.

So one aspect of our interest in the changing Roman audience must be its access to literature, if not its place of assembly. At a republican dinner party, readers or comic actors might perform new works as well as old, Latin works as well as Greek, to an audience who came for other reasons. With the Augustan age comes some rather ambiguous evidence suggesting poetic competitions perhaps in the official libraries created by the princeps.[31] The existence of such libraries is itself a factor in the literary education of both writers and readers, and they must not be forgotten as places for both invited and uninvited recitation and literary discussions. Libraries remained an imperial concern, and after the destruction of the Capitoline libraries during the siege of Rome in A.D. 69, Domitian is found sending to Alexandria for replacements of rare Greek texts.

So far I have said little of the book-selling industry. In Cicero's time, at least, it does not seem to have been significant for the dissemination of works of Latin prose, the bulk of which was still composed by senatorial writers wealthy and important enough to diffuse their work among those who mattered. Yet surely commercial copying and book selling must have been needed for the public purchasers of manuals, such as Columella on agriculture, Vegetius on military tactics, or Celsus on medicine and the other arts. Men have always bought manuals, even when they were indifferent to imaginative literature. And precisely this kind of book was most likely to be circulated in the form of garbled lecture notes or given a kind of pirate publication. Quintilian uses this kind of unofficial anticipation to justify entrusting the *Training of the Orator* to the bookseller Trypho for publication. With conventional authorial modesty he claims that he had wanted to hold back the manuscript but was forced to hurry on its completion since "there were already two volumes of the art of rhetoric circulating under my name, which I had neither published nor prepared," due apparently to the overenthusiasm of his students taking and circulating notes from his lectures. Yet the existence of such pirated publications surely suggests that there was profit as well as the satisfaction of curiosity in the reproduction of such works.

There were also rich book collectors, and both Tacitus's *Dialogus* and Gellius's stories of the book trade suggest an antiquarian market for works of the great departed, especially if they could be passed off as written by the author's own hand.[32] What did the wealthy Seneca do if he wanted his own copy of a literary text? He quotes in *Letters* 88 from Cicero's *Republic*—where did he find the text? In this case it seems more likely that he searched it out in a public or private library than in the possession of a bookseller. But with no copyright, he could perhaps simply have sent an educated slave to make a copy in the public library, or borrowed it for copying at home. There is no evidence for ancient regulations confining texts to the libraries and much to suggest that wealthy men could circumvent any inconvenient rules.

Again, booksellers and copyists were presumably the same people and could use one skill to supplement the other. When a text was not immediately available, we can imagine that a would-be buyer might commission a bookseller to track it down and copy it for an extra charge.

At the same time we should not forget that much of the young man's education or the older man's culture was imparted orally—in Seneca's case by the Roman philosopher Papirius Fabianus, and later by his spiritual mentors Attalus and Demetrius the Cynic. Seneca's father praises Papirius as an accomplished declaimer, and it is quite likely that he used the same form and style in his oral sermons as a philosopher that are illustrated by the elder Seneca from his declamations.[33] We are so accustomed to privilege written over oral sources that we forget the ancient world had no such snobbery and probably regarded the words of Demetrius or his interpretation of Chrysippus's teaching as more valuable than a text that could not explain its own ambiguities or answer questions arising from its doctrine.[34]

Poetry was another matter. Its relative brevity made it suitable for copying and resale to the public, and even the fullest texts were reduced to a form that could be given as presents: Martial includes among his dinner party favors for departing guests texts of Homer, Virgil, Lucan, Ovid, and others with no indication that these little books were abridged or excerpted.[35] Martial's own poetry and the occasional poems of his contemporary Statius almost certainly went through three phases: the first recitation, the preliminary private copies for individual patrons, and the subsequent multiplication of poems grouped in regular books for a wide reading public. This generation may have seen a short-lived climax in the book trade, in that Martial's first book of epigrams and his *Apophoreta*, or *Party Gifts*, both advertise the new format of the codex—our modern book with pages—sold by the bookseller Secundus, as well as the regular format in scrolls available at the shop of Atrectus in the Argiletum.[36] Despite the convenience of the codex as a traveling companion, it was not immediately successful, and we must imagine the writings of both prose authors and poets in the next century as disseminated in scrolls; only with the predominance of Christianity would the regular consultation of works of piety lead to the return of the codex as the reader's choice.

Although modern students pay little attention to the second century after the generation of Pliny and Tacitus, the few substantial writers of the period provide a rich account of their cultural world, a world in which oral performance is still as important as diffusion through reading. The surfeit of recitations at Rome attested by Pliny and Juvenal was not confined to poetry or to the Latin language,[37] and this century of the so-called Second Sophistic brought to Rom Greek celebrities from display orators like Aelius Aristides and Dio Chrysostom to the miracle-working and mythologized Apollonius of Tyana. These men performed before emperors and served as unofficial ambassadors for their cities, and their published writings were taken as models of elegant prose.

But there was another layer of literary performance, which straddles the thin line between actuality and fiction. The table talk of Plutarch, of Athenaeus, and the discussions in public places and private parties recorded by Aulus Gellius may be fictionalized, but the kind of miscellaneous dialogue that they represented must have been immensely popular, or it would not have been developed and published and survived into our times. These works carried the illusion of literary performance into the studies of remote readers for whom such learned dialogues represented the ideal culture of the distant city. Literary life has itself become the subject of a new metaliterature that depends on a readership educated in a fully developed national tradition. In this cosmopolitan century, primary literature, in the sense of creative poetry or prose, is represented only by the marvelous novel of Apuleius—an African transformation of the *Tales of a Donkey* (*Lucius, or the Ass*) attributed to the equally popular Syrian satirist Lucian. But this single work is a world in itself. This sophisticated and sensational narrative achieved for its age an escape from the limitations of genre, locality, class, or age group that had last been reached by Ovid's epic of transformation; but the changes from verse to prose, from myth to contemporary fantasy, reflect the new diffusion of Latin literature into a reader's world as diverse and far flung as the empire itself.

Generic Preoccupations

This brief survey has repeatedly used the term "genre," and done so legitimately, since the Romans from at least the time of Cicero thought in terms of different literary genres. The major categories of writing—poetry, oratory, history, and philosophy—knew further divisions, and Roman authors and poets thought in terms of each genre's development within the Greek tradition and later through

17

their own Roman literary history. From Greek theory they had inherited an organic conception of literary genres, as of other, non-literary arts, defined either in terms of formal properties (meter, the medium of narrative or mimesis, the social and moral level of those represented) or by the invention and exploration—the bending of the traditional form—of previous writers. The ancient conception of a literary genre as an organism considered its invention, growth, and maturity but also presupposed its eventual decline into decay and silence. But while some writers, such as Velleius, writing in the age of Tiberius, are content to explain the decline of oratory or tragedy in purely organic terms, Cicero two generations before him and Tacitus some seventy years after him looked for political and social causes. Cicero's biography of Roman oratory in the dialogue *Brutus* opens with the obituary of the orator Hortensius, but it is really an obituary for his art, tracing its rise and decline to shifting cultural and political circumstance—the establishment of public courts, which stimulated the power and fame of defensive oratory in the age of the Gracchi; the new summary court procedures in 52 B.C. that reduced the role of the orator; and the loss of political liberty under Caesar.

We should also include among the circumstances of literature the impact of a great poet like Virgil on those who fear to follow him, or the precedent of tragic poets condemned for treason, which contributed to the ultimate withdrawal of tragedy from the public and perhaps even the private stage. Romans steeped in their own literature measured themselves and their contemporaries against the Augustan achievement and passed their judgments, critical or sometimes more encouraging; yet for different reasons the orator Marcus Aper in Tacitus's *Dialogue on Great Orators*, the teacher Quintilian, and the younger Pliny as lawyer and magistrate speak more hopefully of their contemporaries and the future of Latin literature.

But they make assumptions that we would no longer accept, and they fail to ask questions that immediately occur to us. Seneca's tragedies and Petronius's novel are not mentioned by Quintilian in his survey of Roman achievement. Despite Petronius's extraordinary brilliance, and the background of Greek romantic stories and novels known to Romans of the late republic and recalled by Ovid,[38] the possibility of Latin prose fiction does not arise in critical discussion: after Petronius it will burst into a second flowering with Apuleius.

Although Roman critical discussions so often frustrate the modern student by their obsession with antiquarian detail or their approach to evaluation by moral or political, rather than genuinely literary, criteria, or their indifference to questions of structure and thematic coherence, ancient criticism is a significant part of the social history of literature, shaped by and shaping cultural assumptions. So it will be part of my undertaking to consider both the limitations of Roman approaches to what we would call literary history, and the effects of Roman self-representation as a culture on the literary culture of Roman society.

There is one more element. The idea of literature at Rome, at first defined for Romans by their experience of Greek literature, would come to be defined by their own highest achievements over the course of two centuries, but would never cease to be stimulated and fertilized by the Greek world around them. An important part of my theme will be to reflect the varying impact of Greeks and their fluency on stage and in text on Roman low and high culture through the successive stages of Roman society.

One

Rome at the End of the Republic

> I want you to know that since I returned to the city
> I have been reconciled with my old friends, that is,
> my books: not that I had broken off association with
> them out of discontent, but that they made me
> ashamed of myself for falling short of their precepts,
> when I threw myself into that distressing business
> with such untrustworthy associates.
> Cicero to Varro, *Letters to His Friends* 9.1

When Cicero wrote this letter to Varro in 46 B.C. it marked the end of one era and the (still unrecognized) beginning of another. Both men were prominent members of Rome's political elite; Cicero had held the consulship, and even been honored by the Senate with the title of father of the nation for suppressing the populist coup d'état of Catiline, and Varro had held the praetorship and commanded the republican forces for Pompey in southwest Spain during the civil war that had ended so violently with Caesar's victories at Pharsalus and Thapsus. But Cicero's hour of glory was seventeen years past: he was now sixty, an age that many Roman politicians did not reach. Most of those who lived so long would be ready to retire from politics. Varro was seven years his senior, and the fiasco of his province's eager surrender to Caesar must have left a bad memory. Both knew that while Caesar remained in power there would be no free political life. For Romans of the governing class, public service in politics or warfare was a man's prime duty and source of self-esteem, but they had learned from the Greek cultural tradition to give an almost equal value to the life of study, *theōrētikos bios*. For some this was the study of moral philosophy, *doctrina*, and the books that Cicero calls his old friends are clearly such books. Just as the ordinary Roman made his decisions on the basis of consulting his friends, so the educated man would take the writings of Greek philosophical schools as his friendly advisers. Although some works of ancient philosophy were theoretical or systematic analyses of principles such as we associate with the discipline, for the greater part men read, and composed, moral manuals to guide their lives, as the modern man is guided by self-help manuals, priests, or psychiatrists.

This was an extraordinary year: for one thing, it had almost 430 days. It was in 46 that Caesar implemented the corrections necessary to the Roman calendar in order to bring the months and festivals of the religious year into line with the seasons. January 46 B.C. enjoyed October weather; but an intercalary month of 22 days inserted before the traditional calendar year opened in March made one adjustment; two further months were inserted between November and December. The Long Year was also extraordinary because acknowledgment of the defeat of the republicans turned Roman political writers from looking forward to the backward commemorative genre of praise and blame. Cato, the ideological focus of republicanism, died by his own hand at Utica rather than expose himself to Caesar's clemency, and his fight was continued in a battle of the books. First Cicero began an encomium, but was hampered by the impossibility of doing justice to the dead man without condemning Caesar. Then Caesar's young officer Hirtius sent Cicero a pamphlet attack on Cato, followed by Caesar's *Anticato*, extending to two books. Cato's nephew Brutus contributed another encomium, and when Porcia, Cato's sister, also died, she provided another opportunity for political solidarity, and was eulogized by Cicero, Varro, and others.

The loss of these short works, both personal and propagandist, should not blind us to their consuming interest for the cultured political class of their day. Words were the chief political weapon, outside as inside the Senate house, in written as in spoken advocacy. Indeed, the Romans of all classes borrowed and even distorted literary quotations for political purposes. In the theater actors would point speeches in Latin adaptations of Greek tragedy to reproach Pompey ("to our misfortune art thou Great [*Magnus*]!") or a line from a Roman historical drama to praise the exiled Cicero.[1] After Caesar's murder, Brutus, as praetor superintending the dramatic performances of the Ludi Apollinares, intended to stage Accius's classic historical drama of his ancestor, Brutus the Liberator, to win popular support, but his enemies forestalled the too obvious design. In their private conversation, and letters too, men of this generation quoted Homer or Greek tragedy to convey their ideals or express their self-image: Cicero repeatedly saw himself as Hector, forcing himself to act well from shame before Polydamas and the Trojan wives; Pompey died quoting lines of Sophocles on the evils of submission to a foreign tyrant; and Cicero adapted the words of Eteocles from Euripides' *Phoenissae* to represent Caesar as sacrificing everything to the love of power.[2]

The allusive use of Greek literature may have increased when free comment was silenced with the return of Caesar. Certainly Cicero and his friends avoided overt political comment even in private letters. Cicero deliberately absented himself from the Senate and it took an extraordinary situation at the end of 46 to provoke his first public speech in five years. His republican friend, the ex-consul M. Marcellus, had not risked returning to Italy after Pompey's defeat but was living in Lesbos studying ethics with the philosopher Cratippus. Cicero, who saw his return as a potential symbol of renewed liberty, had to persuade both Caesar and Marcellus that this was desirable. Late in the year, with advance consent from Caesar, Cicero made a formal request in the Senate and Caesar graciously agreed to welcome his old enemy. This speech *For Marcellus* is thus a landmark in Roman rhetoric; not a defense speech, or a proposal, but a new and most unrepublican kind of oratory, expressing praise and thanks to Caesar in language that foreshadows the hollow encomia of the nobles of imperial Rome for its emperors.[3] Although exhortations to restore political and judicial normality are discreetly woven into the praise, the speech, brilliant and flattering, marks the end of real independent political eloquence, except for Cicero's epilogue of oratory against Mark Antony after Caesar's murder.

But the world of letters offered other values, and an escape from the contemporary political scene for both Cicero and Varro. These men were two of Rome's greatest writers, Cicero in power of eloquence and variety of genre, Varro at least in learning and the quantity of his interests. It was a strange irony that Caesar, who had imposed their political submission and sent them back full time to the literary culture that had always been their leisure occupation, was himself the only contemporary to match either of them in learning, taste, and literary talent. Cicero, Varro, and Caesar created the literary culture of this last immensely fertile period before Caesar's assassination. But there is much to explain about republican Rome and its cultural climate before we can appreciate the contribution of these three men to the nation's literature and cultural identity.

Roman Education, for Better or Worse

We must start with the education of the time. Inevitably, sometimes regrettably, education shapes the tastes and attitudes of the adult to his inherited culture. Roman education in Cicero's youth was not homogeneous, any more than American or British education is today. Just as modern education varies with the size and sophistication of a community, so it would vary between the metropolis of Rome and a provincial Italian town, and within each community would again differ according to the wealth and pretensions of a child's family. Children (probably only boys) of humble origin would be sent for a few years, from the age of seven to about twelve, to learn to read, write, and calculate from an ill-paid *litterator* or *ludi magister* in an upstairs room open to the street; however small his monthly fee, it is more than likely that boys would drop out when their parents could not pay. Prosperous tradesmen might be content

23

for their sons to learn arithmetic and basic bookkeeping before continuing to train in the family shop or workshop. When Horace's father the auctioneer decided not to let his son be taught along with the strapping sons of centurions in Flavius's local school at Venusia, he was definitely reaching above his class.[4]

So the elder Horatius took his son to Rome, "to be taught the subjects [*artes*] that any knight or senator would teach his offspring" (*Sat.* 1.6.76-78). Horace studied with a respected *grammaticus* called Orbilius, but although Orbilius earned his place not only in Horace's ungrateful memory but in Suetonius's *Lives of Distinguished Men,*[5] this education in the private school of a grammaticus was still second best to the options of those in the ruling class, who would own or patronize their own grammaticus and control access to his teaching.

The role played by education at home in these privileged families is one factor that makes it difficult for the modern student to grasp the early education of the young Roman; the other far more complex obstacle to our understanding is the dominance of bilingualism in Roman education. Thus Quintilian, who writes most fully and carefully about the education of small children, talks about education in Greek even before he discusses the prereading stage of the child under seven. Although he is writing about education more than a hundred years after Cicero's generation, the conservatism of all education and of Quintilian's own traditionalist approach allows us to use his evidence even for the previous century. He urges the parents to choose the child's attendant (*paedagogus*) carefully, as one who speaks well and can correct the child's—Greek. At least Quintilian recommends that the child should begin by learning to speak and memorize sayings in Greek, since he will pick up Latin incidentally from those around him. This is not just an ideal, for he warns against forcing the child to speak only in Greek for any extended time, as parents often do, and encourages the parents not to wait too long before the child is taught to speak in Latin, to prevent him from acquiring a Greek accent or adopting unidiomatic Greek turns of speech in his own language. Quintilian expects that instruction in the two languages will then be developed at the same pace. His goal is real bilingualism, in which "neither language obstructs the other."[6]

What happened, then, when the child who had learned to speak in Greek and Latin was taught to write? For the languages had different alphabets, and in some cases used the same letter for different sounds.[7] Quintilian's advice about introducing children to the individual letters and their shapes must surely have concerned Latin in the first instance. The child would need to complete the elaborate process of learning reading and writing by the imitation, first of individual letters, then of combinations and two-letter syllables (*ba, be, bi, bo, bu*). He would then gain confidence in his power to recognize, pronounce, and write in Latin, before he could turn his attention to Greek. It takes a modern student only a month of daily classes to become accustomed to the Greek alphabet. Probably the Roman child who had spent a year or more learning to read and write in one script would be able to acquire the other without confusion, but it must be pointed out that no Roman writer on education spells out the customary sequence or pace of learning, and even the careful Quintilian does not assign periods of months or years to the stages of early teaching that he describes.

Children who had been trained to read and write in this way had the potential for true bilingualism, but many factors outside the schoolroom would also affect their command of the two languages and their cultures. A modern comparison will bring out the factors favoring and obstructing bilingualism. In Canada, an officially bilingual country with a high standard of free public education conducted in either French or English, French, the language of the minority in most provinces but of the majority in Quebec, has a culture as rich as English, and there can be no question of cultural prejudice against the language. In addition, French is required in all provinces for public documents, and is a required subject in the predominantly English-speaking provinces for at least the five years of elementary school and some years of high school. In all provinces a degree of bilingualism is required in the civil service and rewarded by promotion. But the impact of bilingualism is completely different in the French and English communities.

Despite legal restrictions on English education and the use of English street signs in Quebec, the majority of native Quebeckers speak far better English than their English counterparts elsewhere speak French. Indeed, a bilingual civil servant is most often one whose mother language is French. Protests against the protection of French in Quebec come predominantly from immigrants whose mother tongue is neither French nor English, but who see English as the key to success in business, even to emigration to the Eldorado of the United States. The majority of residents are equally indifferent to the literary culture of the French- and of the English-language communities. In the English-speaking provinces the indifference of the general public has reduced the teaching of French to a lowest common denominator, which actually gives the high school graduate a poorer command of French after ten years than children in the schools of European countries would possess after four or five years of grammatically systematic instruction. The difference lies in the attitude. Outside Quebec command of French is not needed for commercial success, nor are there substantial French elements in most urban communities with whom there is an opportunity to converse in French; the requirement is essentially artificial for the majority of children. Since many of these come from allophone[8] immigrant families, they face the additional challenge of learning English as a second language when their parents speak Portuguese or Greek or Chinese.

Like Greek in Cicero's Rome, French is perceived as a cultural or elite language, and the closest approach to real bilingualism in English Canada is the selective education of middle-class English-speaking children in the few French-language schools or French "immersion" programs offered in large cities. Unfortunately this genuine attempt at bilingualism is not reinforced either by the needs of conversation in society at large or by strong public interest in literature, so the admirable educational programs available may have only a short-lived effect on the individual's culture. If the teaching of Spanish is ever required in the United States, this may well be its future.

The situation was quite different at Rome in the generation when Latin literature approached maturity. Not all classes may have shared the "wholehearted acceptance of Greek cultural values" described by Crawford,[9] but there was effectively no other culture in the time of Cicero's youth; any Roman with cultural pretensions would have a mind filled with Greek learning. As Kaimio has shown, Roman command of Greek was fostered by both social perceptions and cultural attitudes.[10] Greek was not only the language of learning. Because it was the language of the teachers themselves, it was essential to the pupil before he could embark on any kind of advanced education. The cultural primacy of Greek meant that Romans needed bilingualism more than their Greek teachers; the imperial power asserted its own language in public but accepted the language of its subjects in private life.

According to Quintilian, one reason for early facility in Greek was the student's need to be trained in Greek *disciplines*, since they were the source of their Roman equivalents. But Roman education took a much narrower view of what were proper school subjects. Where the Greek gentleman was educated in *mousikē*, the composition and performance of poetry or song set to the lyre, and *gymnastikē*, physical fitness, and even perhaps some geometry, astronomy, and medicine, the Roman subordinated everything except basic accounting to the primacy of language, first in reading, then in composition.

Once children had learned to read from their educated slave attendant or at a street school, the next stage took them to the grammaticus, for what would be their chief experience of education in literature. This period of literary education, sandwiched between elementary instruction in reading and the more advanced training in rhetoric that most boys began about the age of twelve, should be our main focus. This time formed the young Roman's attitude to literature, and for many it would not be enhanced by any further study at a more mature age. But the best of the teachers were men of some sophistication, perhaps better suited for critical discussions with their peers than for teaching young boys. The Greek term *grammatikos* originally denoted a learned man, a scholar engaged either in editing classical poetic texts, like the research scholars of the Mouseion at Alexandria, or in interpreting these texts to adults at leisure, or at least to young men already fully literate and skilled

27

at expressing themselves in speech or writing. These learned men, like the professional philosophers or sophists, were part of the lifelong concern with language to be found among the Greek urban leisured class.

Roman campaigns and conquest in Greece and Greek Asia Minor had brought such scholars to the city as refugees, dependents of Roman officials, or even as captives.[11] Thus the Roman wars against Mithridates brought Parthenius the poet as a captive to Rome in the 70s, and soon after Tyrannio the scholar grammarian, taken by Lucullus after the capture of Mithridates' capital, the city of Amisos. Such learned men were quickly restored to free status and treated with respect but were still dependent for a living on teaching what their Roman patrons required. If they were fortunate, they would be honored "houseguests," brought out to entertain guests after dinner or on public holidays, but wherever there was a Roman son to educate we can assume the learned *grammatikos* would teach at the level his pupil required. Quintilian speaks of Philip hiring Aristotle to teach the child Alexander to read[12]—an extreme case. But, in a lesser way, this seems to have been the origin of the relatively new Roman practice of using scholars of language and literature to train children in the years before their study with the rhetorician.[13]

Cicero in *De Oratore* assigns to the grammaticus "thorough treatment of the poets, the examination of histories, the interpretation of words, and the teaching of elocution,"[14] but this compact summary is too general to guide us; the evidence for how boys (and such girls as were present) were taught to approach poetry and historical narrative depends on Quintilian and on surviving school manuals from a much later period.[15] In Cicero's time, the texts, like the teachers, were predominantly Greek, but this period saw the emergence of learned Latin speakers from Rome and Italy who would teach through the medium of Latin and even profess to teach both Greek and Latin language and texts.

The main tool was the *praelectio* or *enarratio*, the teachers' commentary, combining—as modern commentaries do—grammatical analysis, explanation of rare or poetical vocabulary, mythological or factual information, and moral interpretation of the text for discussion. The process was elaborate and would cover only small units of the chosen text, predominantly Homer, which the pupils were then expected to read aloud and most often memorize before reciting back to their peers. The sheer detail of the reading means that only a small proportion of Homer could be studied (manuscripts would not be cheap or abundant, amd students might possess only the lines they had copied out). So detailed study would probably be complemented by familiarizing the students with synopses, like the summaries of the Homeric cycle provided by Proclus, or the mythological synopses of Apollodorus and Hyginus.[16] As a result students would know well, and consult as moral examples, some of the most famous passages of the *Iliad* or *Odyssey* and be equipped to understand Homeric Greek when they met it in later life.

The best may have exercised themselves by translating passages into Latin, but it is more likely that as boys they would confine their translation exercises to prose. Did they learn to write Greek? It is not certain, and several modern scholars have pointed to the case of Pompey, who quoted from Sophocles as he went to his death, but had to prepare the text of the Greek speech with which he would greet the Greek-born pharaoh Ptolemy. Horsfall, systematically pessimistic in his approach to Roman knowledge, rightly reminds us that "to read, to write, to comprehend and to speak a second language are four distinct, though related, talents."[17] After his education with the grammaticus, a boy might still find considerable difficulty in writing formal Greek, and his ability to read and comprehend Greek literature would probably be limited to Homer, to classical Attic prose, and to such poetry as he had been taught, stopping short of lyric, or of the more recent Hellenistic poets. To understand these would require continued study as an adult, pursued in company with a learned Greek, not least because there were no dictionaries; even the earnestly motivated would depend on a Greek companion or teacher to be their dictionary and commentator.

If we keep in mind that Romans had to learn without the abundance of texts we take for granted, but became at least passively bilingual as young boys, and so potentially bicultural, these factors will help us to assess the continued role of Greek in the next stage of education. This was the three or four years spent by the teenager with the *rhetor*, a teacher primarily of spoken oratory but also of exercises in written composition. Here too the teachers and the material were Greek. Cicero tells us in the *Brutus* that as an older boy he composed his practice speeches in Greek, because otherwise his Greek teachers would not have been able to correct him.[18] He admits at the same time that a large part of the training was concerned with enriching the students' expression and style, for which Greek, with its immense vocabulary and tradition of ornament, was more productive than Latin.

But this was not the only option. The great Crassus, who was Cicero's ideal orator from the previous generation, had trained by recasting either Greek oratory or Latin poetry, or even Latin oratory. And in Cicero's youth there had been an attempt to open a school of Latin rhetoric. The idea had greatly attracted him, but the same Crassus who was Cicero's model in oratory had used his power as censor to ban the new schools, claiming that they taught only ignorance and impudence.[19] Despite the censors, the situation changed. Two Latin manuals of rhetoric from the 80s, Cicero's *On Invention* and the *Rhetoric for Herennius*,[20] have survived, and the next generation must have been able to study through the medium of Latin. This is surely why Cicero feels it necessary in his survey of rhetoric at Rome to explain to Brutus, twenty years his junior, why he himself studied and exercised in Greek. The implication is that the medium of Greek had already given way to Latin in the teaching of rhetoric, as of language and literature (*grammatikē*). Even so, the manuals were constructed before the models. The boys of the next century would have Cicero's speeches and Livy's or Sallust's histories as models, but until Cicero published his *Verrine Orations* in 70 B.C., almost the only sophisticated texts of oratory or history would be Greek.

The Roman student's interest in rhetoric was caught up with his own ambition, and it is more than likely that the study of persuasive eloquence would displace any love of poetry he had acquired as a mere boy. The sequence of Roman education favored practical eloquence over imaginative literature, and this alone would not have given a Roman the love of poetry, philosophy, and history shown by a man like Cicero. For many this functional literacy and ability to speak would be enough—they would make their career in the courts or the Senate without further exposure to the culture of books. They would acquire some expertise in judging the speeches of advocates in major trials, or the public address of a magistrate, but their focus would be on evaluating content rather than appreciating form. They would attend the tragedies and comedies offered at the six main theatrical festivals of the year; they might hear a poet reciting topical epigrams or short verse in the baths; and in due course they would retire and write apologetic political or military memoirs.

But an increasing number of Romans from the wealthy and governing classes continued their education beyond the rhetor's school. Traditionally further education meant either private study of philosophy and rhetoric with Greek specialists at Rome, or travel to Athens, Rhodes, or the Greek cities of Roman Asia (the west coast of Turkey) to study in a philosophical school or with a famous rhetorician. Cicero had studied with a Stoic philosopher, Diodotus, and the Epicurean Phaedrus, at Rome, as he did with the Rhodian rhetorician Molo, but once the Sullan reign of terror was over, he was sent on a six-month visit to teachers of rhetoric in Asia Minor and again to Molo in Rhodes. When Cicero sent his son to Athens in 46, he secured for him both the teaching of Cratippus the Peripatetic philosopher and coaching by experts in Greek and Latin rhetoric. Caesar went to Molo to study rhetoric, and although Pompey had cut short this stage of education in his military youth, he studied *grammatikē* with Aristodemus of Nysa, and invited Aristodemus's cousin to teach his sons and probably his daughter too.[21]

Even in their later years, Roman magistrates passing through Athens or Alexandria would think it appropriate to listen to a philosopher's discussion or a display orator's performance; these were celebrities and it was smart to be familiar with them. Rhetoric and philosophy had a prestige altogether denied to the study of pure literature, which survived in the public ear only through its moral or patriotic message and had to be justified in those terms.[22]

It was not that Rome had no great poets. But for all his cultural loyalties, even Cicero could not claim that it had poets to match

Homer or the masters of Greek tragedy, still less the artistry of the archaic lyric poets or the learned poetry of Alexandria. Cicero himself had composed verse in translation or imitation of the learned Alexandrians when he was young; indeed, he was probably the first Roman to attempt a version of the astronomical poems of Aratus, the *Phaenomena*, describing the constellations and the *Prognostica* on weather signs. He had apparently written or translated two short mythological poems of a type fashionable in Hellenistic Alexandria, on Glaucus the marine god (entitled *Glaucus Pontios*) and on the Halcyon birds. Both must have been fantasy tales of metamorphosis, perhaps translations from Nicander's lost poem. The same tales were later adapted by Ovid in books 11 and 14 of the *Metamorphoses*: Ceyx and Alcyone were turned into the Halcyon birds, the young fisherman Glaucus was transformed into a sea-god.

The poetry selected by Cicero to enrich an original philosophical dialogue on a very Roman topic, his *On Divination* of 45 B.C., illustrates both the range and the limitations of the Roman poetic tradition. Following the practice of Plato and later philosophers, he sought out for this and other philosophical writings passages of verse as illustration and ornament. The subject of this dialogue lent itself to poetic illustration, since Homer and the myths of Greek tragedy were full of omens and prophecy. Cicero draws on Homer more than once and, since the rules of the genre excluded the use of Greek, provides his own verse translations, one of some thirty lines (*Div.* 2.63–64); for tragedy he is able to cite the poetic adaptations of Euripides and Sophocles by Ennius and Pacuvius, and we owe to this work the survival of magnificent and complex verse from Ennius's *Alexander* and *Andromache* (*Div.* 1.42, 66–67). In a lighter moment Cicero quotes a line of Plautine comedy (*Div.* 1.65), but all these Latin excerpts were composed by Romans as adaptations of Greek poetry. Cicero paraphrases Plato *Crito* 44a but translates the single line of Homer quoted by Plato; he even translates an extended excerpt from *Republic* 571b and d (*Div.* 1.60), and opens the main body of the dialogue with an extended sample of his own hexameter translation of Aratus on weather signs (*Div.* 1.13–15). What original Latin poetry does he have to quote? A massive didactic speech by the Muse Urania from his autobiographical poem *On*

His Consulship and a briefer narrative of a portent from his *Marius*. Of original Latin poetry besides his own, only a historical drama by Accius and Ennius's great historical poem, the *Annals*, find a place.[23]

If we add to Ennius's epic the early Roman drama adapted from Greek tragedy, this may not seem such a poor record for the first two hundred years of Roman poetry. But there are also significant omissions. Cicero's middle years had seen the work of the two greatest surviving republican poets. Lucretius, the follower of Epicurean philosophy and Democritean atomic physics, set out the scientific wonders of the world, not in prose like contemporary Greeks but in a great hexameter poem, *On the Nature of the World*. As an Epicurean, he had no belief in portents or divination and could hardly provide Cicero with examples for his treatise, but it is also true that Cicero, who had read Lucretius's poem and praises its artistry in a private letter to his brother,[24] never quotes from Lucretius, even to enliven the speeches of his Epicurean protagonists in other dialogues. It is less surprising that Cicero does not quote his younger contemporary, Valerius Catullus of Verona, who composed short poems in many styles, from Sapphic lyric to abusive iambus and hendecasyllable, and developed the extended form of epigram that became a new genre at Rome, the personal elegy.

Catullus admired and emulated Alexandrian Greek poetry, as Cicero had done as a young man. His most brilliant and beautiful poems were longer forms—wedding poems both lyric and hexameter, and the miniature mythological narrative in allusive Hellenistic style. Around him there had been a circle of sophisticated lovers of poetry, but Catullus seems to have died around 54 B.C. Many of his friends also died young, some violently in the bloodshed of the civil war, including Catullus's dearest friend, the orator Licinius Calvus, who showed equal talent in poetry and prose; and the poet Helvius Cinna, whose best known work, *Zmyrna*, a narrative of the incestuous passion of Myrrha for her father, took nine years and was so learned it immediately required a commentary for its appreciation.[25] These poems demanded almost as much learning to read as to compose, and Cicero, whose standards were shaped by his orator's desire to communicate with large audiences, may have had little patience with this self-consciously foreign school of poetry.

Literature and Nationalism

We have seen that Cicero as a cultural nationalist measured Roman literature against the wealth of Greek prose and poetry. He might be optimistic about the approach of his own national culture to maturity, but he would inevitably read, admire, and imitate the larger and more splendid Greek corpus.

Like the age of Dante in Italy or the Elizabethan renaissance in England, Cicero's last years saw longing for the literary culture of another more advanced society turn to a genuine hope of creating in his own language and for his own society a literature to mirror and foster its identity. If the image of literature reflected in these pages seems far from our own world of books and literary culture, it is only fair to recognize how the concept of what Erasmus called "good writings"[26] has varied from one century and nation to another, and how much was being created for the first time by Cicero and his associates.

We have briefly considered the influence of Roman republican schooling on the men of this generation and the variety of their national literature available to them. It is time now to reconstruct the world of books as Cicero's contemporaries experienced it and see how it would enter their daily life of reading and study.

When Horace said that "Captured Greece took captive its rough conqueror" (*Epist.* 2.1.156–57), he probably thought first of the conquest of mainland Greece, completed by 146 B.C., and Rome's increasing enthusiasm for Hellenic culture and works of art. But it is arguable that the conquest of the wider Greek world affected Rome even more powerfully, through the coming of Greek-speaking scholars to Rome, and through the confiscation by Roman commanders of the libraries of Greece and Asia Minor.

The major Greek libraries were assembled either by Hellenistic monarchs or by the philosophical schools. The first and greatest royal library was that endowed by Ptolemy Philadelphos at Alexandria, associated with a kind of institute for scholars, the Mouseion. It must in fact have been much closer to an Institute of Advanced Studies or an All Souls without the distraction of students than to modern museums, which have inherited its name. Among its successive fellows, the poet Callimachus composed both brilliantly allusive poetry and works of learning, including a now lost book catalog, the *Pinakes*. Later, Mark Antony was accused of giving the great royal library of Pergamum to Cleopatra, presumably to augment the collection of Alexandria and boost its role as an intellectual center at the expense of its rival.[27]

Rome still did not have any public library, 120 years after the otherwise abstemious Aemilius Paullus had absorbed by conquest the royal library of Perseus of Macedon, claiming it as his share of the booty in 167 B.C. and giving it to his sons for their education.[28] The more independent Cato chose a different method of educating his children; he had a Greek tutor for his son but taught the boy himself, composing an encyclopedic textbook *For His Son Marcus*. In the second century the alternatives were to read Greek books or write one's own text in Latin. Yet when the rebel Italian city of Asculum fell to Pompeius Strabo, he gave the books he received as booty to his son, the future Pompey the Great; it is not clear whether they were in Greek or Latin. Lucius Lucullus, conqueror of Armenia, amassed a fine collection of books, famed for the quality of the texts, and threw open his library in his country villa to all readers, making it accessible without restriction to the Greeks, who considered it a real home of the muses.[29] Cicero used the collection and describes in his third book *On Moral Ends* a visit to the library after Lucullus's death; there he found the younger Cato surrounded by volumes of Stoic philosophy, and the two studious men united in praising their deceased and generous friend (*Fin.* 3.2.7).

The great library of Aristotle's Lyceum contained many unique texts of his writings and lectures for his students. This was evacuated from Athens to Asia Minor in the war-troubled years after his death in 322, but had been brought back to Athens and was in the hands of the private collector Apellicon when Sulla captured the city in 86 B.C. Sulla in turn brought the collection to Rome. He had also co-opted the grammarian and bibliophile Tyrannio to restore, edit, and recopy the damaged texts, and thirty years later, at the time he composed *De Oratore*, Cicero writes of using Sulla's library at the villa of his son Faustus Sulla near Cumae. Some scholars have argued that Cicero would not have consulted the esoteric works of Aristotle in this library, but this is unnecessarily skeptical, when he was working on Aristotelian rhetoric and in daily contact with Tyrannio, the effective librarian and editor.[30]

Sometimes it seems that even Latin books had to come from Greece. In 60 B.C. Cicero wrote eagerly to his friend Atticus, who had lived at Athens for most of his youth, and asked him to arrange for the shipment of the book collection bequeathed to Cicero by Ser. Clodius, the Roman scholar and grammarian. Clodius, the son-in-law and heir of the scholar Aelius Stilo, is best known for his work on Roman comedy, and yet he lived and worked at Athens.[31] Athens had a healthy book trade, and public reading rooms of some kind, for in the same year Cicero had asked Atticus to make sure that copies of Cicero's own memoir on his consulship were made public around the city.

Booksellers had to produce each copy of a text individually, and must have done a lot of work to order; if they kept a master copy, they could always employ their scribes to copy new texts from it, whether by eye or dictation. But, of course, these scribes were Greeks, trained to copy Greek, and it is a mistake to assume that current Latin works were regularly copied for sale. Most writers of history or expository prose in Greece and Rome would think only of spreading a few copies to the people that mattered—whether to their philosophical pupils or political associates.

The burden was on an author to forward his own work to those he wanted to read it, and Cicero was exceptionally lucky that he could simply commission his friend Atticus to supply copies of his new compositions, for Atticus was one of the very few men at Rome who kept professional scribes and could produce multiple copies of a text for himself or his friends.[32] It seems that Crassus, a great man of business, also kept trained copyists, and Plutarch reports that he directed their education, even teaching them himself (Plut. *Crass.* 2.6), but Crassus's main interest will have been the production of accurate contracts and accounts. Any busy public man needed scribes to draft his contracts or legal agreements, but when at leisure they could be set to copying a Latin manuscript. Readers in the ancient world violated no copyright by borrowing a text and making their own copy before they returned it. This created a problem of literary etiquette for Cicero when his friend Caerellia borrowed from Atticus an early version of his *On Moral Ends*, which Cicero had not intended to reach the public. Caerellia had copied the text, and Cicero was afraid that this unsatisfactory draft might spread and displace his final "edition."[33] There must have been considerable blurring in this world of personal manuscripts between earlier and later, official and unofficial texts.

Thus Cicero would have various forms of access to Greek or Roman books: by reading in the libraries of his friends, by using his own growing library, which he seems to have kept at his villa in Tusculum, or by borrowing, copying, or arranging to have copied the texts owned by friends. At times Cicero seems to use Atticus as a personal interlibrary loan service, asking him to get a rare text for him or identify a current owner.

When the Roman had a book available to him, however, he would still have more difficulty in using it than we find in consulting a book. A *volumen*, or scroll, of papyrus contained a text of up to 60,000 words of poetry or perhaps 75,000 in continuous prose, written in columns from left to right along a composite sheet up to ten meters long. These had no page numbers or reference system, and longer works were often undivided by chapters. The text was essentially written entirely in capitals of even size so that proper names would not stand out to signpost a passage, nor were words separated or sentences punctuated. The lines of verse were respected, but otherwise the reader could not quickly find a place without reading from the beginning.[34]

Again books were more often labeled by descriptions of their contents than by their formal titles:[35] thus in lists of works by prolific authors, it is quite common to find real doubt in our sources about the identity of works. Did Theophrastus really write four different books *About Friendship*, or were the same two books circulating with different titles? It would be quite possible for a Roman to misunderstand a reference to one of these books in his Hellenistic authority and look in vain for the discussion in another related book.

Since there was no correction available for poor eyesight, the gentleman with a taste for literature regularly maintained one or more trained readers, educated Greek slaves who would find the volume identified by its label in its cylindrical container or book chest and read it to their master. At night there was only the weak light of an oil lamp, and many cultured Romans rose with the summer sun to read before the regular day's work overtook their privacy. And the regular day's work often began with the dawn. Men in public life had to greet crowds of friends and dependents before the official day began in the courts or the Senate, and one consequence of their position as benefactors and patrons was the loss of privacy. In the city they almost certainly had no private time for study. Certainly there was room in the great city houses for libraries,[36] but the libraries were usually established in the owner's country villa in the hills of Frascati near Rome or on the coastal strip of Latium and Campania. So we should imagine the cultured booklover listening to more often than perusing his texts, and cherishing the adjournments of the Senate for public holidays when he could escape to his villa and his books.

Elizabeth Rawson has shown in *Intellectual Life in the Late Roman Republic* the immense number and variety of educated Greeks living independently or as dependents in Cicero's Rome. Many of these were writers as well as teachers. The pattern of close relationship between Roman aristocrats and men of letters from the Greek world began in the second century. Greek cities often sent their intellectuals to Rome as ambassadors on public business. Two early instances are the learned linguist Crates of Mallos, sent by King Attalus to Rome in 161, and the triple embassy from Athens in 155, consisting not of lawyers expert in the boundary question under dispute, but of the heads of the three active philosophical schools: Critolaus, the Peripatetic; Diogenes, the Stoic; and Carneades, head of the Platonic Academy. Others came as hostages: Scipio Aemilianus, the inheritor of Perseus's library, grew up in the company of Polybius, who remained a hostage for more than twenty years, and composed his great universal history to demonstrate the reasons for Rome's rise to power. As an older man Scipio also traveled with Panaetius, the Stoic philosopher. In the next generation another Stoic, Posidonius, ambassador of his city Rhodes, was befriended by Pompey. Posidonius lived at Rome for long periods, and wrote learned works on history, geography, and science. These have not survived, but many Greek and Roman writers like Seneca drew their knowledge (or at times their errors) from him; his theories outlived the books that contained them. Sulla, Lucullus, and Pompey cherished poets and biographers to record their achievements, who might be actual freedmen, former slaves of the Roman magnate, or freeborn gentlemen from their Greek communities like Theophanes of Mitylene, Pompey's adviser and biographer,[37] or the poet Licinius Archias, given citizenship by the Luculli for composing poetic narratives of their campaigns.

Because Cicero composed a speech defending Archias's right to Roman citizenship, we know how Archias made his professional career as a Greek poet, first in the cultured Greek cities of Southern Italy like Naples (Neapolis) and Heraclea, then as a protégé and houseguest of Roman commanders. This man could versify and produce epigrams on the spot, and Cicero had hoped that Archias would celebrate Cicero's remarkable consulship in Greek verse, just as he tried to persuade Posidonius to compose a memoir in prose. We can still read the letter in which Cicero asked the Roman historian Lucceius to break off his continuous history, and produce an encomiastic monograph on Cicero's consulship.[38] The tradition of these monographs was to focus on a great man and dramatize his achievement, much as a tragedian would present the rise and downfall of his hero. Cicero was not unusual in wanting his political successes on record, but he was perhaps exceptional in hoping to be celebrated in both languages and in poetry as well as prose. Besides the autobiographical Latin epic in three books, he also composed a Greek prose memoir, which he sent in vain to Posidonius in the hope that the Greek would elaborate it into a full and formal historical monograph.[39]

These anecdotes represent the personal publicity that Romans sought through literature and fall short of the aesthetic standards by which modern critics value poetry; on the other hand, such topical and utilitarian poets with their well-directed praises were probably read with more interest than the modern public would show in the purely personal lyric. A scholar poet like Parthenius of Nicaea was far more influential through his contact with Helvius Cinna and the Neoteric poets around Catullus. Parthenius may have taught Cinna Greek; he surely influenced Cinna through his criticism, but he lived on to be the poetic mentor of the elegist Gallus and even of Virgil. It is a comment on the relationship between Greek scholars and their Roman patrons that Parthenius wrote a handbook for Gallus, the *Tales of Passion* consisting of some thirty love stories, each summarized in about two hundred words.[40] While we would much prefer to read Parthenius's literary judgments, these were probably never formalized, but confined to immediate reactions to specific texts. The Alexandrian tradition was more interested in exegesis of learned glosses and allusions than general aesthetic assessment of the poems that they expounded. And they must have needed great tact to advise Roman noblemen with little judgment of poetics or tolerance of criticism.

I have quoted these figures as a sample of the more striking personalities among the literary Greeks of Cicero's day. Around any individual, however, there might be a series of tutors and domestic philosophers, permanent or temporary companions on journeys or at the villa. Antiochus, head of the Academic school, traveled to Alexandria with Lucullus; Cicero, who when young had traveled to Athens, Asia, and Rhodes, gave a home to the Stoic Diodotus, who taught him as a young man, until Diodotus died in old age. In 46 B.C., the year of our opening letter, Cicero secured Roman citizenship for the Peripatetic Cratippus who was teaching his son at Athens, and Julius Caesar used his absolute power to legislate Roman citizenship for doctors and professors of rhetoric or philosophy who came to reside in the city.

In terms of pure literature the most interesting of the resident Greeks of this generation was Philodemus, the poet and philosopher. His books on the theory of poetry, rhetoric, and music were discovered as charred fragments in the ruined villa at Herculaneum of his patron Calpurnius Piso, after surviving for over a century in the family library until the villa was overwhelmed by Vesuvius in A.D. 79. Philodemus brought a new aesthetic value system into the criticism of poetry, rejecting the traditional emphasis on its moral value and power of edification, in favor of genuine craftsmanship of language and meter.[41] Cicero knew Philodemus and praised the elegance of his epigrams, but deprecated his philosophical theories, because Philodemus was an Epicurean. The Epicurean valued leisure for friendship and contemplation above public service; the Roman put public life first, whether as service or ambition, and had difficulties at times in feeling at ease with his own leisure.

Literature and the Amateur

Since leisure was a prerequisite for literary interests, whether active or passive, men like Cicero awaited the time and place when the Roman conscience could relax. It could be a national holiday, or springtime in Campania, or high summer in the Alban hills—when the Senate and courts are adjourned, and gentlemen have settled into their villas, bringing their secretaries and readers, and perhaps a visiting philosopher, to keep them company. Cicero often sets such a scene in his dialogues. After lunch and a midday rest they will walk in the formal gardens amid the statuary, and stop to sit in the semicircular exedra under a plane tree or by a fountain or fishpool. The discussion will not be directly of books, but of topics discussed nowadays by philosophers or historians, and probably a deferential Greek will be on hand to supply a topic for discussion or cite the opinion of Plato or a Greek historian.

Actual reading, even by a slave reader, was probably done in private, except in the period after dinner. Cicero's friend Atticus was probably unusual in allowing no other form of afterdinner entertainment for his guests than a reader, since his biographer Cornelius Nepos singles out this feature of his plain living and high thinking.[42] It would be natural for Atticus to select a text from his immense Greek library; others might favor a reading from their own latest work. But when Nepos declares that Atticus favored no other *acroama*, he suggests a wider choice. The fashionable Greek word means something to listen to, so we can perhaps rule out the acrobatics and lascivious dance drama of Xenophon's *Symposium*. The elder Cato declared that the good old Romans of the early centuries had listened to songs in praise of great men accompanied by the *tibia* (a sort of single or double recorder), but he may be trying to provide a Roman counterpart to the patriotic songs or *skolia* of the Greek symposium; at any rate, there is no evidence from this period that Roman guests at polite parties listened to songs or musical interludes. One alternative was recitation. It was not yet the practice to recite one's own poetry or declamations to guests, but tragedy or epic, whether Greek or Latin, could be given a semidramatic recitation by a trained actor. Strict etiquette probably excluded performance by a guest such as the famous Roscius with whom Cicero was on social terms, but if there was no skilled actor in the household, one could be easily hired. And apart from the collective experience of such readings followed by discussion, the host and his guests would have time for individual reading or listening to their slave reader in the early morning or during the afternoon rest. The normal practice of listening to, rather than looking at, texts helps to explain the extraordinary importance attached by Roman critics to the rhythmic and periodic qualities of a composition, while the lack of alternative entertainment will have increased both hunger for new compositions and tolerance for their lack of real intellectual novelty.

Literary Studies and the Recreation of Literary History

It may be because our sources for this world are themselves writers that there is so much stress on writing, rather than on reading, as the dominant literary activity. But even minor figures like Trebonius assemble collections of Cicero's witticisms, or compose biographical memoirs on the newly dead Cato. We do not need to go to the extreme and recall how Cicero's brother composed four tragedies in sixteen days.[43]

Others might compile abridgments of the longer historical works—for their own use? For others? To sharpen their memories, or as a record of a borrowed text for future use? It was an age of documentation and systematization: Varro, for example, continued the investigation begun by his teacher Aelius Stilo into the corpus of Roman drama, and his investigations have provided the only basis for our knowledge of early Roman theater history. The plays had survived as dramatic scripts in the possession of theatrical troupes and were subject to cuts and interpolations. If a famous name such as Plautus, the great comic dramatist, would recommend a play, then scripts by less popular or unknown authors would be attributed to him to increase public appeal. By the time of Varro, the more than 180 scripts attributed to Plautus had been reduced by Stilo to 25 authentic texts; undoubtedly Stilo proceeded mostly on grounds of style, but there was also the possibility of checking the records of the magistrates who conducted the theatrical games and bought the script for performance. If the title had not been changed and was not an overused one, like *The Heiress* or *The Twins*, the literary historian could track down the year of performance and original recorded author. So it was that, according to our later source, Aulus Gellius (*NA* 3.3.9–14), Varro was able to reduce the twenty-five authentic Plautine scripts to a corpus of twenty-one plays. His authoritative opinion gave them a guarantee of survival but effectively condemned any other possible scripts to neglect; the twenty plays that have survived to this day are generally assumed to be from Varro's authenticated group.[44] Varro must also have collected the performance records, called by the Greek name *didaskalia*, which have come down to us for the plays of Terence. A sample entry would read:

> The *Brothers* of Terentius presented at the funeral games of Aemilius Paullus held by Q. Fabius Maximus and P. Cornelius Africanus. The directors were L. Ambivius Turpio and L. Hatilius of Praeneste. Claudius's slave Flaccus composed the score for the Sarranian pipes. The entire script comes from the Greek play by Menander. It was [Terence's] sixth play, and performed in the consulship of L. Cornelius Cethegus and L. Anicius Gallus.

The Roman inquirer into literary history would thus have a firm year date for the first performance, the play's position in the sequence of Terence's compositions, and the name of the magistrates and occasion of this performance. The surviving examples of Varro's

Plautine collection were also equipped with this kind of information, including the titles and authors of the Greek plays, but most
of these are lost. Even so, some of the information is confused or
confusing; it is thought that only Ambivius Turpio, named in Terence's script, directed the first performance, and Hatilius has
slipped in from a revival. We know what kind of double pipes the
Romans used for theater (and ritual) accompaniment, but no one
knows what exactly were Sarranian pipes. Again the play is said to
be "complete from" (or "entirely by") Menander. Does this mean an
adaptation of the whole Menander script, or of nothing but the
Menander script? We know from Terence's own prologue to the play
that he added at least one scene from a different playwright, and this
would suggest omitting a corresponding scene from Menander's
text. In the end this documentation, which represents such careful
literary detective work, leaves open questions that still exercise
professional historians of Roman drama.

Another irony of the new concern to preserve and codify Rome's
literary history is the discrepancy that persists in Roman chronology despite the surge of archival work. A generation earlier the
learned tragic poet Accius had assigned biographical dates to the
early dramatists like Livius Andronicus. Varro's studies into the lives
of the poets and the dating of their verse texts seemed to show that
Accius had been about fifty years out in dating Livius not after the
First Punic War but the Second, in the better-documented second
century. The Romans of Cicero's circle thought they could prove
Accius wrong but, even after Varro's work, preferred to argue from
probability and relative dating.[45]

Dating, a major concern of the new scholarship, extended beyond matters of literary history into the whole problem of relating
Rome's own history to the chronologies of the Greek world established by Alexandrian scholars in the third and second centuries
before Christ. There was a choice of four or five foundation dates for
Rome itself, and king lists meant that a wrong start would set the
whole sequence of traditional history out of phase with the concur-
rent events of the Greek world. More a historical problem than a
literary one, it incorporated the dating of Greek poets and other
major writers and motivated a large proportion of the literary activ-

ity at this time. The political hazards of writing about the present during Caesar's last years as dictator reinforced the patriotic and historicizing urge to explore Rome's past so as to reconstruct a version that could stand comparison with that of Greek cities.

An early instance composed during the 50s was Cornelius Nepos's three books of *Chronica*, ironically praised by Catullus as "learned, by Jove, and the product of great labor." These seem to have taken Apollodorus's Greek chronology as a base, and synchronized with it major Roman events dated by Rome's independent and quite different system.[46] When not only Greeks and Romans but separate cities in mainland Greece used different calendar months and year dating systems, it really did take laborious research to match a Roman event with a definite consular dating against Athenian archon lists, or priestess lists of Argive Hera, or even the generally firm dating from year one of the First Olympiad in our 776 B.C. Thus Nepos and Varro argued for different foundation dates for Rome of 751 and 753, which must have affected any of their sequential records that could not be controlled by other evidence. Atticus had worked on genealogies for several of the noble families, and drew on this work to complete his *Liber Annalis*, or *Book of the Years*, which was ready for Cicero to use by our starting date of 46 B.C. With these works and Varro's investigation of the dramatic festival records, Cicero could now see Roman political and literary events in a trustworthy chronological sequence—and the new scholarly stimulus diverted his authorial energies from works of political self-justification and artistically ambitious belles lettres into literary history and criticism.

It was in 46 B.C. that Cicero composed and dedicated to his younger friend Brutus the first attempt to interpret Roman cultural history and match its evolution against the tradition of Greece and especially Athens. This work, usually called simply *Brutus*, is a dialogue between Cicero, Brutus, and Atticus set at Cicero's house at Tusculum and dated to the outbreak of the civil war. Hortensius, Cicero's predecessor as king of the lawcourts, and seemingly a vain and difficult man, had just died. The dialogue opens with an obituary and reflects the feeling that political oratory, like the orator and the free republic, has been silenced. The history of oratory, that most public and political literary form, is itself dangerously close to an obituary.

Cicero follows the courteous convention of complimenting the recent work of his friends—Brutus's moral essay *On Constancy* and Atticus's new chronology—before defining the theme of his discussion (*Brut.* 11–16). But he makes it clear that it is precisely the recent researches of Atticus and Varro that have enabled him to shape this account of the growth of literature at Rome. Thanks to them he can set the doomed art of political oratory against the panorama of all recorded Roman literature: first dramatic and epic poetry, then history, then expository treatises and dialogues. We, in turn, owe to this dialogue (whose literary merit preserved it despite the neglect of the Christian Middle Ages) our outline of the history of Roman drama and our knowledge of Varro's lost work, which Cicero used; but besides the public literary forms of drama and oratory, Cicero notes incidentally many other works written for private reading—the nonfiction of memoirs, manuals, and treatises. There are many detailed critical portraits of orators before Cicero's day, as both authors and actors. These may discuss their best-known speeches, their style and tactics, or their distinctive skills in self-presentation and performing their own texts.

On a larger scale, Cicero uses Greek literary history to project patterns on to Rome's less evolved tradition and identifies the external circumstances that foster or hinder literature. Here is a critic who recognizes the difference between reading and hearing a text, between composing in advance and extemporizing, and between the effect of the good speaker and the brilliant manipulator of his material on his audience. The *Brutus* is as near as surviving Roman texts will bring us to literary history. But it was written as part of a battle of critical standards. While Cicero had perfected the full periodic style of rich and varied speech, the new austere idealists who had followed the orator Calvus set themselves the goal of Attic plainness, aiming at a grace and simplicity like that of Lysias. No goal could be harder, as Cicero knew, but he also believed that simplicity of style had only a limited potential: the man who could only use a slender style would never be able to move his audience to anger or to tears. So he returned to the attack with a second work dedicated to Brutus, the one we know as *Orator*. The dialogue had recalled and assessed the past of oratory and led it up to its present frustration, but the new treatise, written in his own person, invoked the abstract Platonic idea of perfect style to describe the ultimately versatile artist in prose who could control every stylistic effect and had the aesthetic and moral judgment to do so. This work could be said to prescribe for the future and was the starting point for Augustine's even more influential treatise on the ideal Christian preacher in the fourth book of *De Doctrina Christiana*. The culture of Cicero was above all literary, in the sense of bellettristic; the culture of Brutus, being predominantly moralistic, was not satisfied.

Literature and Scholarship, Caesar and Varro

Let us leave the viewpoint of Cicero now to consider what literary culture meant for Caesar or Varro. When Caesar was young, he had composed and delivered effective speeches in the courts; he had also composed a tragedy, *Oedipus*, of which we know only that Augustus thought it did no credit to his adoptive father and suppressed the text. Caesar was alert to poetry and passed a shrewd judgment on the overrefined comedy of Terence—better as a model of diction than as drama. Suetonius tells us he was tolerant of the abusive epigrams and invective poems of Catullus and his coterie.[47] But although he enjoyed poetry and could quote aptly from Homer or Euripides, Caesar was Roman in turning away from poetry when he left his youth behind. Not that he was only interested to write the famous campaign narratives that so skillfully pretended to be straightforward factual reports, or the politically apologetic *Civil War*. This was a man who dictated a treatise on the principles of word formation and regularity in syntax to secretaries while he crossed the Alps on horseback, and who could dedicate it to Cicero with the claim that extending intellectual frontiers was a greater triumph than any military victory. One of his few critical precepts that has been reported advises to "steer away from an unfamiliar word as if it were a reef" (cf. Gell. *NA* 1.10.4). The implication is that when the listener or reader is shocked by a new word, it shipwrecks the text by breaking off his attention.

It is amazing that when Caesar was absolute ruler, and feared even by Cicero, the dictator could pass an otherwise intimidating evening as Cicero's guest in literary discussion—"no serious business, but plenty of literary talk," comments Cicero to Atticus in a relieved letter the next day.[48]

Concern with the native language was part of this declaration of cultural independence from the older Greek world. Varro shared with Caesar and Cicero an overwhelming interest in the nature of language in general and the development of their vernacular, recording Roman achievements as a parent would boast to his friends or address praise and encouragement to his son; he looks to Rome's orators and poets to set the Latin tongue on the right path. Where Caesar had argued for rationalizing the language and avoiding the eccentric, Varro seems to have studied both sides of the dispute between the normalizers and the lovers of usage in all its variety, and he argues from each side in turn in his massive and now largely lost work, *On the Latin Language*. But in discussing linguistic propriety he makes a fine distinction between the liberties of diction allowed the poet and the orator (he does not mention historians or philosophers, because their works are composed for private reading). If the public is to be educated in preferred word forms, it is the dramatic poets who must introduce them; they have the license to innovate and familiarize the public with new vocabulary. The orators (who are after all either lawyers with a case to win or politicians with an agenda) must conform to good standard usage to be understood and acceptable.[49]

Varro's work was on a large scale, and we have only six of its twenty-five books. Although he dedicated his first four books about etymology to a personal friend, Septimius, when it came to the theory of regularity versus usage he copied Caesar and dedicated those and subsequent books to Cicero, and thereby hangs a tale. Varro was older than Cicero and rather intimidating, and for months after Varro had announced his intention, Cicero worried himself and Atticus, almost daily, about responding to Varro's promised dedication. Indeed Cicero was already worrying about a dedication to Varro in 54 B.C., long before he had a literary debt to repay. What should he write for Varro? How should he do it? And at times he grows oddly impatient to see the literary tribute that Varro has promised him. In the end he found a solution that reflects the social complications of the literary scene.[50] He recast an existing treatise on the nature of perception, which he had set as a conversation between three deceased friends: Hortensius, his brother-in-law Catulus, and Lucullus.

This book was part of Cicero's conscious commitment to provide Rome with a corpus of philosophical texts answering those available in Greek. But he also wanted to arbitrate between the competing schools and propose his own synthesis of each issue of ethics or epistemology. His genre was the dialogue, following the model of Plato, and this entailed assigning theories that he had absorbed from extensive reading of Greek texts, to suitable Roman figures in a fictional context. Lucullus and his friends had seemed good candidates, since Lucullus patronized the Academic philosopher Antiochus, head of the "new" Academy, and traveled with him. Lucullus then could describe the philosophical debate that must have arisen when Antiochus first read the opposing treatise of his rival Philo of Larissa—some ten or twenty years before the setting of the dialogue. Cicero had studied the books of Philo and Antiochus and knew Lucullus well enough to invent a setting in Hortensius's villa at Bauli and an occasion when Cicero, Catulus, and Lucullus could visit Hortensius on their way to their own seaside villas at Pompeii or Naples. They stroll in the tree-shaded alley and Lucullus begins to recall his trip to Alexandria on public business in his first youth and the debate over Philo's book in which he took part. Like many of Plato's dialogues, this is a play within a play—but its contents are so learned and technical that all Cicero's careful introduction to Lucullus as a learned student of philosophy cannot make it seem plausible.

Cicero began to realize that it would be much easier to give the imaginary dialogue a more recent occasion, so that he himself could carry the argument for Antiochus's skepticism in discussion with Varro and the ever reliable Atticus. So the sixth of many anxious daily letters to Atticus triumphantly announces the solution to both problems. Varro will be honored and the dialogue will be less implausible. And the accident of textual history has preserved both the earlier *Lucullus* and the later version, labeled in our manuscripts *Academica Posteriora*, or *Academic Dialogues*, second edition.

Here is another fictional occasion in a real-life setting; Cicero is talking to Atticus in his villa at Cumae, when a messenger comes from Varro to say that he had just reached his villa from Rome and would have come to pay a visit if he were not so tired from the journey. Cicero and Atticus eagerly set out to visit him and meet him coming toward them as they approach his house; a nice solution to the demands of etiquette by which the younger or lesser man was expected to call on his senior. Atticus teases Varro on his recent literary inactivity—why are his muses silent?—and Varro replies that he is busily engaged on a major work, dedicated to Cicero himself.

This is the cue for a preliminary debate about the proper subjects for writing in Latin, which is far more relevant to our topic than to Cicero's own theme of epistemology. As the dialogue begins Varro is asked by Cicero why he has never written on philosophy, although it is so dear to him as a subject of study. His reply presents the dilemma of this generation of Romans. He argues that the Romans who are educated in Greek learning (the word is general but the reference is to philosophy) will choose to read their philosophy in Greek, and anyone who is indifferent to Greek culture will have no interest in this subject matter, which cannot be understood without a Greek education. Varro has two further, more literary, points, to make. He cannot bring himself to write clumsy artless prose like that of the Latin Epicurean manuals, which are equally defective in style and argumentation, and he hesitates to coin new technical terms in Latin to represent Greek concepts, when the educated reader will prefer the Greek technical terms and the uneducated will reject such language outright.[51]

Whether this argument was really Varro's opinion, or simply Cicero's interpretation, it represents the problems of any vernacular writer of a learned work. The readership of educated men is already small and many will understand the lingua franca better than the writer's native tongue. Should the theologian and educator Erasmus have written in Dutch? It never occurred to him to use anything but Latin. Should an Israeli scholar write in Hebrew, rather than English?

We recognize that creative writers—in our day the novelist, playwright, or poet—should use their own language both to be understood and to foster its development. It seems to me that Cicero and Varro would have agreed. Of course, Roman poets ought to write in Latin: they were the spearhead of the language as they were of innovation in its vocabulary. But Cicero, still on the defensive, returned to the problem in his introduction to the work *On Moral Ends* presented to Brutus in the same year, 45 B.C. Unfortunately, as he admits, Roman poets, in the predominant sense of dramatic poets, were not even original writers, but adapters of Greek tragedy and comedy. Hence, the educated Roman would surely prefer to read the original text, unless, as Cicero fondly hoped and argued, the Roman poet could offer real creativity of form: grace or wit of style, diction, and meter. Without this incentive the only argument for composing and reading Roman literary adaptations was patriotism, and Cicero was prepared to fall back on this.

> Sophocles wrote his *Electra* magnificently, and yet I believe we ought to read Atilius's bad adaptation—Licinius called him a harsh writer, but in my opinion he deserves to be read. To be ignorant of our poets is a mark either of utter laziness or affected arrogance. In my eyes no men are well educated if they don't know our own literature. (*Fin.* 1.5)

Varro did not claim to be a creative writer, and he argued—or at least Cicero's Varro argued in the second *Academica*—that he would refer educated friends to the Greeks for philosophy, because the Greeks were the originators of its theories. He himself would concentrate on making known to the Romans material no one had yet presented, and information for which there was no current source. The Greeks had not written on his Roman topics, nor had any Roman apart from his dead teacher Stilo.[52] Cicero's script for Varro allows him aesthetic modesty about his achievement but stresses the teaching or reference function of his work. But he also designed this introductory dialogue to include a separate encomium of Varro, which doubled the value of his complimentary dedication. "When we were like tourists lost in our own city, your books were our hosts and invited us home so that we could finally realize our identity and understand the world around us" (*Acad.* 1.9).

The encomium did not exaggerate. These research works fulfilled their function admirably, though they have not survived. Not only Cicero used the fruits of Varro's learning; historians, grammarians, biographers, and writers on Roman institutions and religion borrowed from his five hundred *volumina*, with or without acknowledgment. Starting with Horace's literary *Epistles*, Varro's debtors included Quintilian and Suetonius, then Donatus, Macrobius, Servius, and Augustine in the fourth and fifth centuries, and Isidore, bishop of Seville, in the seventh. Most of what we believe about early Roman history and culture comes from him. It is not surprising that Julius Caesar planned to make the seventy-year-old Varro director of his projected national library; Varro's own work was a reference library of *res Romanae*.

But it would be an injustice to see Varro only as an academic antiquarian documenting Roman literature and biography to provide a corpus of national reference texts. When he was not much younger, he had delighted himself and others with a whole range of mixed prose and verse fantasies known collectively as *Saturae Menippeae* after the Greek satiric texts of Menippus. We know from the conversation reported in the *Academica* that Varro had not been content to translate his Greek model, but preferred to use the Greek's free form as a vehicle for his own argument, seasoning it with wit and parody. Although neither Menippus's dialogues nor those of Varro have survived except as titles and fragments, it is easy to form some idea of this versatile genre from the surviving *Satires* or *Dialogues* of the Greek Lucian, who knew and borrowed from Menippus. If Christian antiquity had allowed these to survive, we would have an altogether different picture, not only of Varro but of his whole generation and the other, lighter side of its literary culture. The same man who wrote the *Antiquitates Rerum Divinarum* (untranslatable, but we might try *The Ancient Customs in Things Divine*) also wrote a *Fake Aeneas*, a *Ulysses and a Half*, a *Man with Three Cocks*, or mock epics like the *Battle of Goats*, and the *Battle of the*

Shades, or again pieces with facetious titles in two languages like *Chamber Pots Have Their Limits*, or *De l'ivresse*, or *One Mule Scratches Another*, or *De la séparation*.

The satires were mostly written before Caesar held absolute power and included a political attack on the Triumvirs, Crassus Pompey, and Caesar, called *The Three-headed Monster* (*Trikaranos*) and a satiric account of Rome called *Marcopolis* (a hybrid form like Yankville) with a proverbial allusion to big fish eating little fish and strange analogies between men's veins as the public water system and their intestines as the Great Drain.

Like the verse satires of the second-century poet Lucilius, these dialogues were openly partisan in politics; they also reflected the social context of literature and discussion. A piece on the theme of married men bears the title *The Saucer Has Found Its Drink* and describes an audience murmuring approval of a speech (on the evils of marriage?) "just as we used to do at the public baths in Rome." Varro's narrator, who calls himself "an old-fashioned type" threatens to answer arguments against marriage with a reversal of the usual Greek proverb: "the sensible man will get him a wife." The reader of Petronius's *Satyricon* may recognize some of the situations and topics of his picaresque narrative, but there was perhaps a touch of seriousness behind this satire if it countered the perennial Greek misogamy with solid Roman arguments for taking a wife.

These *Menippeae* were obviously full of proverbs, slang, cheerfully improper language, quotations serious and flippant, and Greek at all levels of allusion. The society that enjoyed this literature of entertainment was not the pompous establishment that outsiders often attribute to republican Rome. Jasper Griffin's *Latin Poets and Roman Life* has rescued Augustan society from the stigma of dullness and conformity by lavish examples from poetry and prose reflecting Roman indulgence in sophisticated Greek pleasures. To be fair to the last years of the republic, we should remember the role of humor and parody, and the high success of the "literary" mime in the theatrical shows of this very period. We would have a much more balanced image of the literary life of the 40s if Varro's *Menippeans* and Laberius's mimes had survived as fully as Cicero's philosophical works.

53

The generation that created and organized Rome's literary culture and sense of national identity may have been short on poetry and limited to a privileged few, but without its efforts, the full flowering of creative literature in the Augustan age could not have occurred. Although Cicero would probably have preferred a different development of Roman literature and culture than the dominantly poetic achievements of the next generation, he and Nepos, Atticus, and Varro had helped to form Roman interest in their own inheritance and train Roman taste, and Varro, the first and longest-lived of the group, survived to see much of the new blossoming take place.

Two

The Coming of the Principate:
"Augustan" Literary Culture

Julius Caesar was murdered on March 15, 44 B.C. Within eighteen months his great-nephew and heir, the nineteen year old Octavian, was consul and at the head of eight legions, which gave him the power to bargain with the ex-consul Mark Antony for his share in the military control of the empire.

Some of the paradoxical and confused allegiances of the intervening period can be conveyed by outlining the situation of spring 43. While Caesar's "assassins" Brutus and Cassius were in Greece and Syria raising forces to defend the republic, Mark Antony in turn was outlawed by the Senate at Cicero's instigation. He had been appointed governor of Transalpine Gaul, but was now trapped in northern Italy between the two consuls of the year, Caesar's nominees Hirtius and Pansa, and Octavian, newly appointed as praetorian commander against Antony. But the death of both consuls suddenly reversed the situation, clearing the way for Octavian to march on Rome and demand the consulship, to be followed in three months by his compact with Mark Antony and the insignificant Lepidus, to rule Rome and the provinces as a junta of three by virtue of their military power, reducing the Senate to acquiescence in their decrees.

Political life at Rome was now meaningless. But the three leaders could not stay reconciled with each other or with Pompey's son Sextus, who exercised a naval command based on Sicily that could cripple Roman trade and food supplies. For the next twelve years the rise of Octavian toward unchallenged control entailed major land and naval battles between Roman forces, severe hardships for Italy, and violent social shifts for individuals and groups alike. Most of the old noble families had lost their adult males to death or exile, but new elements surfaced in society, men from the Italian upper class or risen from the nonsenatorial class of Rome.

Two Survivors: The New Poets Gallus and Virgil

Several of the most talented young men of the 50s are lost from the record at the outbreak of the Caesarian civil war, and there is compelling evidence that not only Catullus but his friends Calvus and Cinna were dead.[1] Cicero's *Brutus*, written in part as a eulogy of the lost art of free speech, already contains a litany of other lost talents. But poetry itself returned to life with new poets, whose contemporary fame left a far fuller record of their lives than survives for Catullus and his circle. The careers and posthumous reputation of two of the senior poets of this period illustrate the response of society to their very different genres and self-presentation.

The elder, Cornelius Gallus, a Roman from the equestrian class, fought for both Caesar and Octavian, but also practiced the Alexandrian mode of poetry, combining learning with the intense personal feeling of Catullus. The younger, P. Vergilius Maro, from the former Roman province of Cisalpine Gaul,[2] was unfitted by health or fortune for military service; he would take up in turn what became the three canonical genres of serious hexameter poetry: Theocritean pastoral; didactic poetry, which combined the tradition of Hesiod with the new scope and richness of Lucretius; and a national version of heroic epic. Gallus won great acclaim as a poet, but the public success that raised him to be governor of the new territory of Egypt precipitated his downfall when his boastful inscriptions suggested a threat to Octavian's supremacy; he was recalled and took his own life when Octavian formally barred him from his friendship.[3] At this time Virgil had completed both *Eclogues* and *Georgics* and was known to be working on a national epic; he would live only seven years longer, but would be protected by his modest personality and lack of involvement in public life to become the honored poet of the new era and idol of the people.

Gallus is, in fact, an extreme case of the figure more significant as a link in literary history than for the quality or lasting fame of his poetry. It seems that Gallus wrote four books of *Amores* in elegiac meter to honor his mistress, the actress Cytheris, under a poetic name, Lycoris, which proclaimed her Apolline associations. But we know far more about how his contemporaries regarded him, than about his actual verse. He knew all the intelligentsia, including Valerius Cato, the much admired *grammaticus*, of whom it was said that he alone could make and single out real poets;[4] and Parthenius, who, as we saw in the preceding chapter, provided Gallus with material from Hellenistic myth and poetry to recast in Latin—either for miniature epic narratives, like Catullus's *Wedding of Peleus and Thetis*, or for learned etiological elegy in the mode of Callimachus.[5] Gallus even took in the learned freedman Caecilius Epirota, after Atticus had cast him out for abusing his privileged position as tutor to Atticus's daughter.

Virgil devoted two of his early poems, *Eclogues* 6 and 10, to Gallus and his poetry. The sixth is a poem of celebration, introduced by an initial compliment to their common friend Alfenus Varus.[6] In this poem about poetry making, Virgil puts into the mouth of the wild but inspired Silenus myths of cosmogony and illicit passion and celebration of the poetic tradition. This is seen as passing from demigods like Orpheus and Linus down to Gallus himself "wandering by the streams of Permessus" at the foot of Helicon: he is honored by Apollo and the muses, and presented with the pipes of the shepherd poet Hesiod, for his new enterprise—a learned adaptation of a Hellenistic poem on the origin of Apollo's grove at Gryneia in Asia Minor. Because *Eclogues* 6 clearly speaks of Gallus's new poetic theme, it is thought that many of the other themes may have been sung by Gallus himself.[7]

In contrast the final piece, *Eclogues* 10, is a poem of consolation, like the poems sent by Catullus to comfort his friends in distress.

Virgil declares he "must perform a brief song for Gallus, but one that Lycoris too will read." But he does not merely describe and praise his friend, as in *Eclogues* 6. He transports the heartbroken Gallus into Arcadia among his shepherds. In a rewriting of Theocritus's great first idyll describing the grief and death of the lovesick Daphnis, Apollo appears to reproach Gallus for his surrender to love, and his words provide Virgil's readers with the context of the poem: "Lycoris your beloved has followed another through the snows and brutal warfare" (*Ecl.*10. 22–23).

This is an extraordinary innovation, far beyond the boldness with which Theocritus figured himself and other poets into *Idylls* 7. Servius the commentator, writing four centuries later, hands down the tradition that some of Virgil's lines giving Gallus's reply "simply" adapt his own elegiac lament into hexameters.[8] But there is nothing simple about it. Here is a poet including his friend and older contemporary as a participant, even a star, in his fictional shepherd idyll, and combining the poet's published words with his own. Within a single speech, Virgil modulates from his bucolic tones to the more extravagant sentimentality of his friend Gallus, then converts the Gallan lament into a new resolve: the Roman soldier-poet announces to his Arcadian shepherd companions that he will now adapt his work set in Chalcidian verse to match the music of the Sicilian shepherds (*Ecl.* 10.50–51).

Here the modern reader faces the double challenge of allusive programmatic language and its ambiguous relationship to the hybrid world of Roman poets and Hellenistic shepherds. But this can scarcely have been less of a challenge to Virgil's first readers.

What does Virgil want them to understand? Not, surely, that Gallus will recast his etiological poem in pastoral form. This would be absurd. It could be purely a metrical statement: that Gallus has found elegy too constricting a metrical form for his undertaking and has decided to rewrite the poem in the freer and more extended form offered by the hexameter. But it is far more likely to reflect Virgil's pride than Gallus's poetic projects. It is a claim for pastoral, and Virgil is welcoming Gallus into the fold.

A less complex portrait of Gallus's work and personality is suggested by Propertius, who in *Elegies* 1.8 appropriates for his own situation Gallus's famous lament over the departure of his beloved, honors Gallus as his immediate predecessor in the writing of love elegy, and addresses to the poet an early mythological elegy (1.20) on the loss of Hylas, so different in tone and style from other elegies that it has long been thought a complimentary imitation of Gallus's own work.[9] Full of Alexandrian mythological allusion and rare names and word forms, loaded with sensual and visual impressions, and hints of erotic foreplay, the poem is a challenge even to readers familiar with the Hylas legend as reported by Apollonius, Theocritus, and Callimachus. Was Gallus's work like this?

Based on these reports about his teachers and intellectual associates, and these responses to Gallus of poets of great artistry and complexity—to Virgil and Propertius, we should add Ovid—scholars until very recently revered him as a key figure in Augustan poetry and devoted years of labor to reconstituting his poetry from the hints and echoes of those who outlived him.[10] But in the late 1970s this appraisal was shaken by one of the most startling finds of Roman literary history: a fragmentary papyrus found in the excavations of a Roman fort at Qasr Ibrim in Upper Egypt. The fort had been abandoned in 25 B.C., providing a firm terminal date for both the papyrus and the text it contained. This is the first known fragment of an Augustan poetry book, and an elegant product. Its beautiful capital letters and handsome layout suggest a presentation copy; only nine lines are preserved, marked off as two four-line poems, and the opening of a new text.[11]

In these few lines three clues appeared that made it inevitable that the author was Gallus: first, the address to "Caesar," anticipating the joy of watching his triumphal return from campaign; second, an address to Lycoris herself claiming that "at last the muses have made me poems I can utter as worthy of my mistress"; and, third, a boast that if he can continue to write so well he will not fear either Cato or Viscus as critics of his verse. Who could have written this but Gallus? Scholars have been more concerned to determine *when* the poems were written and to which Caesar than seriously to deny the attribution and father the poems on, say, Antony or Brutus (both lovers of Cytheris/Lycoris who supported Julius Caesar for a while) or dismiss it as a forgery or school exercise.

But the poetry is a disappointment. Let us assume that the Caesar is Julius, addressed by a relatively young Gallus in the months before Caesar planned to set out on his Parthian expedition. Let us agree that concern for Cato's approval suggests a Gallus just beginning his career, not the respected poet of the 30s. Even so, these lines are amateur in versification and unrefined in language: there is no trace of the famous allusiveness or learning. It is not enough to point to what Mrs. Malaprop called "a nice derangement of epitaphs."[12] It has been suggested that the poems form a final coda to a volume of longer units, approaching the end of the work with a brief recapitulation of its major themes.[13] This might explain the simplicity of the text, but for lack of a context we can only guess whether this was in some way atypical. Twenty years ago, when literary learning preserved only one line of Gallus, "two lands with but a single stream divides,"[14] its diction, assonance, and arrangement promised much; but Gallus's reputation now hangs on our willingness to discount the new evidence and trust the critical honesty of the poets who were his friends. Unless they were prepared to sacrifice their standards to their affection for the man, they must have known something better than these plodding verses.

Virgil shared at least one teacher with Gallus. Macrobius reports that he too used Parthenius as *grammaticus in Graecis*—not, surely, to teach him Greek, but to read with him and interpret the poets and learned commentaries on Homer of the Hellenistic age. Parthenius was after all a poet, and Aulus Gellius reports that Virgil actually adopted a line of Parthenius's Greek poetry into the Latin of his *Georgics* with minimal change; it is formed from three Greek names—almost pure sound. From *Glaucō kai Nērei kai einaliōi Melicertēi*, Virgil kept the first and last names but inserted the name *Panopeae* and punned on the Greek word *einaliōi* (seaborne) with another Greek name, *Inoo*, formed from Melicertes' human mother Ino.[15] If Virgil's work won fame and became the object of study in Roman schools within a generation, it was in part because Gallus's old protégé, Caecilius Epirota, introduced Virgil as the first Latin poet into the previously Greek curriculum of the grammaticus.

Virgil's works are perhaps the most frequently studied of all pagan Latin poetry, whether in the original or translation, and need no discussion here. But it is a measure of the development of Roman literary culture to see what layers of fictional biography and criticism rapidly formed around Virgil, and other admired poets. These myths reveal some of the ways Virgil's poems could be misread. To reconstruct his youth men sought clues from his earliest published work, the *Eclogues*; they brought him into association with teachers of the day; and they looked for light or small-scale poems to illustrate his thoughts and attitudes as a boy or young man. Some found unassigned poems and fathered them on Virgil, others may even have composed poems to pass off as his. Behind the biography to be found as preface to Servius's learned commentaries on Virgil's works, behind the longer Suetonian biography preserved by Donatus and the short one attributed to Probus, are generations of romantic fancy.[16]

It seems to be agreed that Virgil's father was a farmer of Andes near Mantua, that his mother was called Magia Polla, and that he was sent first to Milan and then to Rome for his advanced education after 55 B.C. But details were transferred to his life from his poetry: that his father lived by keeping bees; that like Corydon, in *Eclogues* 2, he was in love with a beautiful boy slave Alexander given to him by Asinius Pollio; that he was exempted by Pollio (or Varus or Gallus) from the local confiscations and was almost killed by a violent soldier who had claimed his land. Readers took the *Eclogues* as a roman à clef, trying to establish that Virgil "was" Menalcas, since lines composed by Virgil are attributed to Menalcas in *Eclogues* 9.[17] In the same poem we are told that Menalcas nearly died—so we are to suppose this happened to Virgil. The poet almost certainly was exempted from confiscation, and his *Eclogues* bear witness to his gratitude to both Pollio and Varus, who represented Octavian as his land commissioners in the crucial years after Philippi. But if the old slave Tityrus can describe in ecstasy how he was brought before a godlike young man who restored him to his pastureland (*Ecl.* 1.42–46), does this have to be Virgil's experience? The godlike young man evokes Octavian, but the poem is surely a blend of fact and imagination, which cannot guarantee biography.

The same scholars who were eager to provide Virgil with an early relationship with Octavian also brought him into the Epicurean circle of Philodemus and his friend Siro at Naples. However, chronology makes it unlikely that Virgil could have studied with Siro, as opposed to visiting him as an adult, spending cultured leisure in Campania to avoid the hot Roman summers.[18] Popular fancy even materialized an elementary teacher for him—the villainous Ballista, whose death by stoning the poet is made to celebrate in a two-line epigram—and others attributed to Virgil a poem dismissing the rhetorician's training and bidding regretful farewell to the muses, who are asked to return now he is grown up, but less frequently.[19]

There is material of value in these schoolroom introductions to the poet, and they reveal the kind of assumptions made and questions asked. It is assumed, for instance, that Virgil's poetry was commissioned. Suetonius says Virgil wrote the *Eclogues* to honor Pollio, Varus, and Gallus, the *Georgics* for Maecenas, and the *Aeneid* for Augustus; Servius has these great men propose the poetic enterprises to him. The *Lives of the Poets* agree on the years it took him to compose—three for the *Eclogues*, seven for the *Georgics*, and eleven for the *Aeneid*—and report occasions of performance. The first public performance of the *Eclogues* does not seem to be known; instead the grammarian reports that they were often sung *per cantores* on the stage, which would bring the poems to a wider audience; some of the *Eclogues* at least offer scope for acting as well as singing. For the *Georgics* and *Aeneid* Suetonius notes the first official recitation. Virgil read the *Georgics* to Augustus on four successive days when he rested in Campania on his return from the East (29 B.C.) and three books of the *Aeneid* (2, 4, and 6) on his return from Spain. This reading can be dated to 23 B.C. by the reference to the tragic death of Octavian's heir Marcellus. Augustus's sister and Marcellus's mother, Octavia, was present at the performance for the imperial family and fainted at the words of mourning that Virgil had added to his sixth book.

But most interesting are the details of how Virgil composed, details that must have been known to the friends who gave the written text of the *Aeneid* to the public after his death. This publication was against his express request, and perhaps they spread this account of his working methods to justify their version. According to Suetonius, Virgil first wrote a prose synopsis of the Aeneid divided into twelve books, and so was able to choose a narrative section in whatever order he pleased to work on; each day he would begin by dictating a number of verses, then devote the rest of the day to refining them, licking them into shape, in his own words, "as a she-bear licks her cubs." He might leave half lines at the end of a section, or fill the gap with a temporary prop (he called them *tibicines*). Indeed his slave secretary Eros spread the story of one occasion when Virgil was inspired to fill out one line and add another on the spot (*Aen.* 6.164–65). After composing he would recite passages with which he was not satisfied to a group of friends.

The fact that Virgil died without making the *Aeneid* public gave rise to more legends, such as the tale of Nisus the grammaticus that Virgil "changed the order of two books, and that book 3 once stood second in the poem."[20] A third of the Suetonian *Life* is devoted to Virgil's death, after the sea voyage from Greece on September 21, 19 B.C., to the actions of his executors Varius and Tucca, and to the posthumous criticisms of grammatici or rival poets. All these stories took shape to meet a popular need, since Virgil died famous, and according to Tacitus and the biographers he was both beloved and wealthy, to a degree no previous or subsequent poet would achieve at Rome.

The Roman Poetry Book, a New Literary Form

Wendell Clausen has rightly called the publication of Virgil's *Eclogues* "an epoch in Latin poetry," for with the *Eclogues* Rome received its first poetry book.[21] Poets before Virgil, notably Catullus and Gallus, had apparently published collections of their poems, but the *Eclogues* offers the first example of a closed artistic form.[22] As Clausen points out "the book of Eclogues differs esssentially from Catullus' book of occasional poems. In Virgil's book the design of individual poems has been adjusted to the design of the book as a whole." We must assume in both Virgil's case and that of later poetry books that the poet first recited individual poems and presented their written text to the friends whom they address or honor; then he went through a second phase of composition, editing and adjusting the text of each poem, to fit the position he wanted it to occupy in his book.[23] Although scholars have been overly ingenious in discovering details of symmetry achieved by the interrelation and sequence of the ten poems in the *Eclogues*, it is clear that Virgil arranged them in two balanced groups of five poems. The second is framed, as we saw, by *Eclogues* 6 and 10 to honor Gallus, the first group is framed by the first and last lines, calling upon Tityrus and Menalcas. Each set of five poems adds up to just over four hundred lines; within both sets the longest poems (*Eclogues* 3 and 8) are at the center.

Since the poetry book is in some sense the key to the new form and power of poetry in the Augustan age, it is important to pause and consider what this literary form implied about its public, and what it entailed, both for the poet sending it on its way and as experienced by the reader.[24] This is perhaps the first generation at Rome in which it is appropriate to talk confidently about the intended reader. Most Roman poetry up to this time had been presented orally, and the poets would expect their work to be known through their own and others' private recitations. In the first instance the written text will have been aimed to guarantee the correctness of subsequent recitations and impose the poet's control over his text. But the very composition of a poetry book implies awareness that there are expert readers and desire that these connoisseurs should have continued access to the poems and devote repeated attention to their form. The poet is not simply reaching out beyond the metropolitan elite, but wanting to change the nature of his contact with his audience, to submit his poems to deliberate scrutiny so that their formal qualities can be measured by the most demanding and considered standard. However few the hand-copied texts of Virgil's book of *Eclogues,* he wanted the poems to be savored in detail and in relation to each other (see p. 307).

The self-contained collection required special care in arrangement. Roman books had no table of contents, and the roll made it difficult to reach an inner unit without first surveying the opening poem. Hence the opening poem should be designed to announce the contents of the volume. This could be done either implicitly by its material (like the first elegy of Tibullus's ten-poem collection published in 25 B.C., or the first odes of Horace's first and fourth books) or explicitly by a programmatic statement or the use of programmatic allusions. The explicit type of opening might affirm the poet's choice of Greek model, his priority in adapting the genre, his source of inspiration (Apollo, one or all of the muses, even The Leader himself, as in Virgil's proem to *Georgics* 1) and usually his chosen matter and style (genre was understood to be defined by the meter, but also by the tradition of Greek poetry composed in that meter).

Dedication to a patron need not be formal: it was often implied simply by a parenthetic address during the opening poem. This pattern is common to Horace's *Satires* and the triad of books 1–3 of the *Odes*, and to Propertius's second book. But as in the *Eclogues*, the poet with more than one benefactor might have to exercise great skill in distributing the homage to his different addressees. Within their poetry books, the other Augustan poets, Horace, Tibullus, and Propertius, followed Virgil's example, controlling and varying both the content and length of poems; poems perceived as related to each other might be arranged chiastically or symmetrically. This feature will only emerge after the first reading, but then a reader, unlike the audience of early poetry, is able to repeat his reading and seek out design. With each new reading he finds new connections between individual poems separated from each other. He may even detect that a poem has been composed or included in order to create balance or symmetry by establishing connections across the book.

Within the book, especially collections of many short units, such as Horace's first book of *Odes* (thirty-eight poems) or his collection of *Epistles* (twenty letters), the poet may pair compositions on related themes (*Odes* 1.35 and 36 to Fortune; *Epistles* 1.17 and 18 on friendships with great men) or create short cycles such as the six great "Roman Odes" of Horace's third book, which include their own inner prefatory poem. There are infinite varieties of arrangement based on the pleasures of comparison and contrast, expectation and surprise. Because poems can be related in so many ways—

theme, meter, length, tone—it is as misguided for the modern reader to expect a single reason for a sequence as it is certain that there will be a fluid design unifying the whole.[25]

The poetry book also demanded special attention by both poet and reader to the final poem. Like a composer rounding off his symphony with a coda or his opera with a grand finale, the poet aimed to suggest closure by the form or perhaps by the recapitulatory content of the last poem. Tibullus, never overt in his principles of composition, uses the recapitulation of his themes in the tenth and last poem of book 1 to mark the completion of the book, and even achieves a kind of symmetry and sense of return—what the critics call ring composition. Virgil used the natural closure of evening and the ending of a rural task to recall his singing shepherds and bring the *Eclogues* to their completion; but there was an alternative known from Greek poetry, whereby the poet presented the overt closure of a signing off, or *sphragis*.[26]

Such a personal sealing of the poem would include the poet's name, his family or birthplace, and perhaps the circumstances in which he wrote. Thus the final book of Virgil's *Georgics* ends with a reference to his rustic and inglorious leisure, contrasted with the heroism of Caesar, engaged in victorious campaigning in the far East; Horace ends the third book of his three-book collection of *Odes* with his name, some beloved landmarks, and a hope for immortality; and Propertius writes a coda to his first book of elegies as if specifically answering a request from his patron Volcacius Tullus, to know about his family and home.

This short elegy (Prop. 1.21) presupposes the literary convention and deliberately frustrates it; neither Tullus, who knew the answer, nor the reader, who might not, is told Propertius's name, which first occurs in book 2. The poet who entitled his first book by its opening word *Cynthia*, the literary name of his beloved, has quite suppressed his own. But Propertius's second book achieves both ring composition and a lover's version of the *sphragis*. The poet's epitaph pronounced by his patron Maecenas at the end of 2.1, "a harsh girl was the doom of this poor fellow," is recalled and unriddled by the last couplet of the final poem: "Cynthia shall live, praised in Propertius's verse, if only Fame will count me among these poets."[27] The theme of literary fame common to this final poem of Propertius's second book, and the opening poems of his third book, to the opening ode of Horace's three-book collection, and to the closing ode, 3.30, shows to what extent first and last poems shared their special status and might share their material.

In this form the Augustan reader would meet all the finest short poetry of the period. But for every poetry book there was a privileged recipient, who would be first to know it, and would meet its individual poems as dedicatee and favored audience.

Private and Public Patronage

The word "patron" has been used more than once in the last few pages, and it is time to consider what role the patron played in the life and work of the poet and the enrichment of his society. Dr. Johnson's letter to the neglectful Lord Chesterfield has left lovers of English literature with a very negative conception of patronage. What form did it take at Rome? How did it benefit the poets, or coerce them? To take the extreme form of patronage, how do we understand the relationship of a Virgil or a Horace with the first citizen and commander in chief, Octavian turned Augustus,[28] whom Rome would remember as the first emperor?

Patronage was an intrinsic element in Roman society from its earliest times, and at all social levels. The landowner was patron to his tenants and other local peasants of free birth. The magnate in town was legally patron of all his emancipated slaves and might set them up in business and give them a wedding gift—but could claim their estate over the heads of their children if he wished. He would be patron to established men from his own tribe or district, to men who had served under him in the army, or been officials under him as a provincial governor. It would go ill with any man who defended a lawsuit or was candidate for a civil or military post, or needed business done at home or abroad if he did not have the right patron, and a Roman would have acknowledged, even if he used some milder word, that his future depended on the active goodwill of more powerful men.[29]

Even in modern academe there is a fine line between the undesirable situation in which a powerful figure can promote whom he chooses and the more evenly spread patronage that comes of seniors taking responsibility for helping talented pupils and other rising young people in the profession. So we should not think it corrupt for the Romans to have practiced benevolent patronage or a discredit to poets of ability if they associated with powerful men and received—or even asked—favors from them. This was the cement that bound republican society. Varro and Caesar and Cicero were patrons themselves and as elder statesmen may no longer have needed patrons, but only Augustus himself and the great nobles like C. Asinius Pollio or M. Valerius Messala Corvinus were in a comparable position during the following generation. Pollio, some fifteen years older than Augustus, had served as arbiter and reconciler during the triumvirate; Messala's noble blood gave him seniority beyond his years, and the consul of 31 B.C. would continue as acknowledged leader of the Senate until his death. Both these men loved and practiced literature and supported both the public world of letters and individual poets not so much with money as by giving them an audience and a social standing among the famous. The cultural life of Rome and Italy was shaped by the influence of Pollio, of Messala, and of the equestrian gentleman Maecenas, who would have called himself friend and adviser of both the powerful Octavian and the less privileged Horace, Virgil, and Propertius. Holding aloof from official administrative positions, these wealthy men could benefit younger men in public life and other professions, but were exceptional in their concern to create an environment of cultured leisure for the enjoyment of poetry.[30]

Despite the end of active republican government, such leisure was still a luxury for the younger men of senatorial rank, but condoned, even approved, for their elders and for those born outside the ruling class. Virgil and Horace came from this outer world and by the end of the civil wars had reached an age where their literary vocation was unchallenged; those born after them, even sons of equestrian families in Italian communities, would face imperial and parental pressure to join the senatorial class and give their youth to military or administrative service. For these younger poets the freedom to practice poetry was controversial, and their values and interests to some extent suspect to the princeps. Their choice of career and even more their choice of poetic genre and content can be seen as indifferent, if not hostile, to the official culture, and will be considered separately.

Patrons of poets could be writers themselves, and each of the three great patrons of this age is known to have written works in poetry or prose.[31] The poet would be well advised to acknowledge his friend's and patron's work, and give or imply praise. Thus both the shepherds in *Eclogues* 3 link Pollio with poetry; he loves their songs, and he in turn composes "new songs," an epithet that evokes the learned Alexandrian style without critical judgment (*Ecl.* 3.84–87). Horace too included honorable mention of Pollio's tragedies and his history of the civil war in the poem dedicated to him placed in the position of honor opening the second book of *Odes*. By stressing the difficulty and hazards of the civil war narrative, Horace diverts Pollio and the reader from the absence of actual critical enthusiasm for either work (*Odes* 2.1–12).

More commonly the noble patron would be honored in terms of his public achievements in war or government. The great *Eclogue* 4, prophetic of a savior child whose birth would inaugurate a golden age, addresses Pollio and dates the new era from his consulship and time as leader.[32]

But these poems, ostensibly the life and songs of shepherds from another place and time, are subtle and allusive in praising their patrons, and it is indicative of Virgil's delicate art in these totally new Italian pastorals that scholars still dispute the identity not only of the wonderful child to be—was it an expected child of Octavian? of Antony and his new wife, Octavian's sister? of Pollio himself?—but also of the protector addressed in *Eclogues* 8, 6–13:

> Whether you are now passing beyond the gorge of the Timavus, or following the shore of the Illyrian sea, will that time ever come when I can tell of your achievements? Will there be a time when I can make known across the earth your poems, the only verse worthy of Sophocles' tragic dress? My beginning comes from you, and my poem will end for you. Accept songs undertaken at your behest and let this ivy creep among the victorious laurels around your brow.

This seems to fit Pollio, who went from his consulship to Macedonia, where he won a triumph over the Parthini of Illyria, and returned in 39 B.C. to celebrate a triumph. More obviously it seems to refer to his tragic composition.

But could a poet have offered praise in such terms to any lesser general than Octavian himself? This doubt is surely the motivation for the recent debate among experts on the period, advancing arguments that require a modified chronology of the *Eclogues* to interpret the military and geographical references and the allusion to tragedy alike as designating Octavian.[33] During the 30s he would become the only recognized commander in the West, the only man automatically identified by references to laurels and achievements. How soon would such a "you" have to be Octavian and not some older but less charismatic general?[34]

Again we face the gradual conversion of Octavian's patronage into a monopoly. What room does a supreme commander leave for other patrons and their deeds as the theme of literature? Let me postpone this central problem of the age, to complete the portrait of Pollio as patron, and to illustrate from a lesser poet than Virgil the lengths of praise to which others might go—itself a partial answer to this problem.

Pollio was not just a practitioner and patron of disinterested literature. He had made quite a name as an orator during the last years of the free republic and, when he set up Rome's first public library in the Hall of Liberty (Atrium Libertatis), it was not only to contain poetry. The hall, built with the spoils of his victory, declared its traditionalism by honoring only one living figure with a bust: Varro, the polymath and lover of Roman antiquities, who was also an old republican and follower of Pompey in resistance to Caesar.[35] Pollio's library may have preceded the great Palatine libraries of Augustus by almost a decade; it no doubt provoked the completion by the new leader of his father Caesar's plan. The elder Seneca, who came from Cordova to Rome sometime before 30 B.C. and probably knew Pollio as governor of Spain under Caesar, reports that Pollio was also the first man at Rome to invite the public to recitations of his own work. Although Seneca's bare statement can be interpreted in several ways, it suggest that Pollio now changed the Roman practice from informal recitation to guests at home, to a public occasion announced in advance like a modern chamber concert: this is not to imply tickets or payment for attendance, but it does mean a wider publicity for the performer.[36]

Since Pollio was the donor of the library in the Hall of Liberty, it is tempting to assume he held his readings there; it is not so clear that he also invited guests to hear the work of other poets. If he only invited audiences to hear his own work, this would set a literary precedent, but hardly one of patronage. But there is support for assuming more generous practice from the parallel case of Messala Corvinus, at whose home, according to Seneca, Sextilius Ena read from his poem on the civil war. Ena himself had invited Pollio, but when he reached the words "I must lament Cicero and the silence of the Latin tongue," Pollio, strongly critical of Cicero and proud of his own eloquence, stalked out in disgust, declaring "I don't intend to listen to someone who thinks I am incapable of speech."[37] On this model a patron who offered his house for a reading would allow the poet himself to invite an audience.

The incident is undated but attests both the recitation of poetry and the continued interest in the theme of civil war. Messala Corvinus was an acknowledged patron of Tibullus and Ovid. His own writings were not poetry, as far as we know, but public speeches recorded after the event and learned treatises on linguistic purity and other aspects of grammar.[38] Certainly he gave his encouragement even to lesser poets than Tibullus, or Ovid, such as the poets of the Sulpicia cycle and the unknown author of the *Panegyricus Messalae*, all preserved in a kind of family sponsored anthology. Tibullus addresses Messala and acknowledges him both incidentally and in explicit poems of celebration—the great tour de force associating Messala with Osiris (1.7) and the hymn to Apollo (2.5), which simultaneously honors the inauguration of Messala's son Messalinus as one of the fifteen priests of Apollo and curators of the Sibylline prophecies. With its vast panorama over early Rome and Troy, the ancient prophecies to Aeneas and recent omens of divine anger at civil war, Tibullus's longest poem is far from a standard encomium, and its personal references combine evocation of future triumphs for Messalinus with regret at Tibullus's own distress in love. This is a poet who can honor his patron on his own terms, with the discretion to make his praises subtle and associative.

But the implications of patronage are more blatant in the work of a less gifted poet. The *Panegyricus Messalae* is not technically incompetent, but it lacks the originality to charm the reader or hold his attention, and it cannot disguise the employment of standard techniques to ingratiate the author with his patron and expand .on the limited material. The poem may be early, before anything by Tibullus or Propertius. With one exception, even its resemblances to Virgil or Horace are better explained as products of a growing Greco-Roman tradition than specific borrowings from older poets.

> Let me sing of you, Messala, though your acknowledged valor holds me in awe: even if my weak powers may not be able to sustain it, I shall begin. If you should praise my poems by their own merits they would fail: let me be merely a recorder of your mighty feats. Nor could any man but you weave your deeds onto the pages so skillfully that they would not outshine his words. For us it is enough to have wished the attempt, nor should you spurn these puny offerings.(1–8)

Here are many of the motifs more subtly handled by a Horace or a Propertius—the plea of inadequacy, countered by the will to serve, which will be followed by the imagery of praise as sacrifice to the gods, and the claim that many poets compete already to sing the hero's praises.[39] The poet sets himself to praise Messala according to the rules of rhetoric: his noble birth (28–33), his eloquence, matched by his military genius (39–44), followed by a full elaboration on each topic. Thus the theme of eloquence enables him to compare Messala with Nestor and Ulysses—since Homer, the exemplars of eloquence and wisdom—amplified by a twenty-line recapitulation of the contents of *Odyssey* books 5–12.[40] Military skill is indicated first by an enumeration of its parts (choosing a camp, directing cavalry and infantry, etc., 82–105), then a listing of Messala's past campaigns, calling to witness each in turn of the tribes he has defeated (106–17);[41] then, as if conscious that Messala's civic talents have not been given their due, the poet honors his role as Augur, securing Jupiter's blessing and public prosperity for the recurring year (118–35).

At this point praise for past achievements should yield to prophecy, and a further fifteen lines exhorts his patron to win triumphs over Gaul and Spain, Libya, Armenia and the far East, the ultimate Britons, and, as if this were not enough, the southern hemisphere (136–51). The advantage to the poet of this preposterous exhortation is that he can work in a learned account of the Eratosthenic five zones of the earth and draw on the *Georgics* for amplification (135–75).

To satisfy Messala's taste for Alexandrian learning, the poet lavishes Hellenistic allusions. Thus his poor offerings to his patron are compared with the humble hospitality of Icarius to the god Bacchus (subject of Callimachus's *Erigone*) and of Molorchus to the hero Hercules (theme of an elegy included by Callimachus in his third book of *Aitia*). His would-be prophecies are compared with those of "Amythaonian Melampus" (120)[42] and he incorporates mythical tales into the geographical survey—the legend of Cyrus and the river Gyndes, and the foundation myth of Cyrene, Callimachus's home (139).

Once the poetic petitioner has done everything possible to amplify his subject matter, what else is required? First, an excuse to end the praises: another poet, Valgius, can more worthily celebrate Messala in Homeric hexameters. Next a hint at personal need: he lacks the repose to write further, because fortune has taken away his former estate, and his growing years make him anxious for the future. This leads into protestations of loyalty. However the poet is impoverished, his muses (already invoked at 24) will not fail to celebrate Messala and he will accompany Messala through the dangers of sea travel or warfare or even cast his puny body into the fire of Aetna (193–97). Such a *felo de se* could hardly be of service to Messala and ineptitude has clearly gone too far; but it will go further.

> No fates will end my work of praising you
> nay, even when my bones are in the tomb
> whether an early day brings on my death
> or long life still remains, though I be changed
> into a steed that canters o'er the plain
> or bull, the glory of the dawdling herd

or bird born on swift wings through flowing air
when long age shall restore me to a man
I'll weave new praise of you upon my page.

Was Messala perhaps a follower of Empedocles? This would explain the surprising references both to suicide in the crater of Aetna and to future transmigration. This must have represented a first approach to the great man. Did Messala pay him to go away? Hardly, for the poem has survived within the corpus of poems composed by his protégés. Did Messala not notice its naiveté? Probably this was the normal level of poems composed in quest of patronage. Apparently both Messala and his heirs thought the tribute worth preserving with the rest of their domestic anthology. For the modern reader, routinely hostile to *all* courtly or encomiastic poetry, this sample of routine client poetics may increase his or her appreciation of the originality, taste, and verbal artistry shown by real poets.

It is interesting that neither client nor patron felt any tactlessness in contemplating Messala as conqueror of Spain and Gaul, Libya, Egypt, and Armenia. Surely this grand parade of triumphal titles might seem a threat or insult to the great leader Octavian, now Caesar Augustus. We can only assume that the poem was for in-house use and remained unknown beyond the household.

The Emperor as Theme and Patron

Praise poetry whether of Messala or of Octavian/Augustus was a less straightforward task than the demands on English poets heralding the accession of young Elizabeth I, or French poets when the aging Louis XIII was succeeded by his grandson Louis XIV. These were successors to a recognized monarchy. But Octavian had been first a triumvir, one of three men nominally sharing a transitional power to reorganize the state, then the repeated holder of annual consulships and military commands, to become in 27 B.C. Augustus, the first citizen (*princeps*), differing from the senior members of the Senate in the old republic only in his combination of civil authority and military power. The justification of this power was the dreadful horror of civil war to which his victory had put an end.

Just as his military success had conferred the greatest blessings on his country, so it was necessary that men thereafter should believe he was greater than other military commanders.

Since Rome first adapted Greek epic poetry, its ruling class had seen poets as publicists for the glories of war, whether the national victory over Carthage in the Punic Wars or the successes of individuals, campaigning like Lucullus or Caesar in remote provinces. There were Latin poets, as well as Greek professionals like Licinius Archias, who composed epic or epigram for republican generals, and the Augustan age had its resident Greeks—Crinagoras, or Antipater of Thessalonica—who used verse to honor the princeps.

For the poets of this generation the problem of imperial expectations affected both aesthetic liberty—the right to choose their own genre and poetic content—and material success. The genre of epic could only be used, it would seem, to celebrate the princeps. Epic had been belittled by Callimachus, the arbiter of Alexandrian taste, who condemned it as overblown and artistically limited. (It was not Homer he had in mind but the recent epics of men like Choerilus, who versified Alexander's campaigns).[43] Thus sophisticated Roman poets were prompted by their cultural models to avoid the large and public poem in favor of shorter, more private forms, artistically self-contained and highly wrought. But the tradition set by Naevius and Ennius and their own patriotic pride urged them toward national epic and homage to the new leader.

It is not necessary to imagine that Octavian actually urged Virgil to compose an epic *Augusteis* or pressured Horace to compose Pindaric odes on his victories: the tradition for celebratory epic had always been there. Indeed, it was not for Octavian but for an inferior commander, Alfenus Varus, that the young Virgil of the *Eclogues* adapted the Alexandrian poetic device of the divine veto to explain his poetic choice of smaller themes:

> I was composing a poem about kings and battles, when Cynthian Apollo plucked my ear: "Tityrus, a shepherd should feed fat sheep, but produce a slender song." So now I will practice a rural muse on my thin reed-pipe—for there will be others in plenty eager to sing your praises, Varus, and record grim wars. I sing as I am bidden.[44] (*Ecl.* 6.3–9)

The god was a worthy symbol of the poet's artistic conscience, and gave him the justification of higher orders. Whether the poem was an answer to Varus's direct request, or served as indirect notice of artistic integrity to forestall such requests, it is the first of a series of poems in which Augustans vindicated the right to choose their theme.

These *recusationes* (poems of excuse) honored their great addressees instead by the dedication itself and by the opening acknowledgment that Varus, or Agrippa, or above all Augustus had won heroic victories too great to be expressed in the modest verse of the poet's minor genre. The composition of small-scale elegy or lyric both spared the poet from recycling the hackneyed words of praise, and offered the chance to satisfy the great by a few brilliant words evoking their unprecedented achievement. But some at least felt genuine admiration and gratitude to Augustus for restoring and maintaining peace, and the greatest of these came to honor Augustus through the generous friendship of the patron and poet Maecenas.

The Best of Patrons, and the Patron's Greater Friend

If readers of Augustan literature forget that Virgil once enjoyed the favor of Pollio, it is because this early association was entirely eclipsed by his subsequent friendship with Maecenas, whose name has come to symbolize the role. "Grant us leisure, but leisure such as Maecenas once created for his Flaccus and his Virgil," and "Let there be men like Maecenas, my friend, and there will no shortage of Virgils," were Martial's comments a century later.[45]

Cilnius Maecenas may have inherited from his Marian family the connection with Julius Caesar that made him a friend of Octavian; our earliest evidence for his role as patron of poets comes not from Virgil but from Horace. Virgil's poetry was not in the personal genres that would allow him to include overt autobiographical detail, and the accounts of his life by Donatus and Servius do not explain how Maecenas came to know him. But Horace opens his first poetry book, the *Satires*, with Maecenas's name, and speaks with both gratitude and intimacy. *Satires* 5 shows him with Virgil and Varius the tragedian accompanying Maecenas on the diplomatic mission to Antony at Brundisium in 38 B.C., and in the autobiographical *Satires* 6 Horace describes how his dear Virgil, *optimus . . . Vergilius*, and Varius recommended him: he had his first shy interview, and after nine months Maecenas called him back and asked him to be one of his friends.[46] Horace may have lived with Maecenas at intervals, for he describes himself as foolishly disturbing Maecenas when he was reading or silent (1.3.64–65) but he is equally proud in these early poems of his own small apartment and of his association with the great.

Recent scholarship has shown that Horace was never "poor" and that the official position he received as a quaestor's accountant would be a comfortable living; we should never have believed his modest disclaimer that "shameless poverty drove me to make up verses."[47] In the first years of acquaintance (probably 33 B.C.), Maecenas gave the poet a Sabine estate large enough to hold five tenant farmers and their families as well as the master's house. More than wealth, this meant freedom from material care, and a beautiful refuge from "the smoke and wealth and din of the city" (*Odes* 3.29, to Maecenas) in which he could give his heart to poetry. Martial, again, would envy the "leisure that Maecenas gave to his dear Flaccus and his Virgil" (1.107). In *Satires* 1.9, Horace expresses his gratitude through the figure of a pretentious social climber, who attaches himself to Horace (the verb *adsectari*, "to escort," describes one service of the humble client toward his betters) in order to worm his way into Maecenas's circle. The fellow presents his credentials: no one can write more lines of verse or compose them faster, no one can dance more seductively, and, what's more, he can sing well enough to make Hermogenes jealous. Not only does he show that he thinks of friendship in terms of competing to displace others; but he treats poetry as a social entertainment on a par with dancing and singing—both of which the Romans thought undignified. Horace uses the real or imagined situation to express in his verse the value he puts on Maecenas's society: "We don't live like that—the way you imagine: no home is more honest and foreign to that kind of dirty trick. I tell you, it is no obstacle to me that one

man is richer or another more learned: each man has his own place"
(*Sat.* 1.9).

Here as in many other poems, Horace is simultaneously vin-
dicating the two things that are most dear to him: his friendship and
his work. Both his art and Maecenas stood above the everyday norm
of poetry and patronage. This is the problem that students of the
Augustan age sometimes fail to recognize: that the poet and patron
about whom we know most are not typical of anything but themselves. The relationship once made was exceptionally dear and
close. It is quite probable that Maecenas's relationships with Virgil
and with Propertius were more conventional, but from Horace's
account there must have been a warmth and generosity about Maecenas that had nothing to do with patronage. His worst offense
against Horace seems to have sprung from emotional dependence,
seeking comfort in ill health, or pressing too urgently to have his
company in Rome at a time when the poet's weariness of mind
drove him to be alone in the country.[48] Certainly patrons in general
expected poets, like house philosophers, to keep them company
and provide distraction, but Horace's protests to Maecenas in *Epistles* 1.7 read more like the remonstrances of a brother or lover than
of a social dependent to a demanding patron. They had by this time
been friends for over fifteen years, and Horace was forty-five years
old. It is not surprising that Horace asserted his own needs, but it
does surprise that he should have wanted to publish this picture of
their relationship. This is a problem with all personal poetry, when
it acknowledges disagreements, and perhaps the epistle corrects a
public misapprehension by making clear that Horace's independence was accepted by his old friend.

Maecenas was himself a writer of prose and poetry, but the short
excerpts quoted by Seneca and Quintilian show that he wrote as he
lived, with almost decadent affectation.[49] This should not detract
from the respect he had earned; he was trusted by Augustus with
state secrets and even authorized to act as prefect of the city of Rome
in the princeps's absence. Again, despite his own taste in composition he had the trust of fastidious poets. It is a commonplace of
Horace and the satirical tradition that the poet may have to sooth
the vanity of a patron who composes bad verse.[50] If Virgil, Horace,

and the temperamental Propertius kept his friendship and heeded his suggestions, Maecenas must have won them by extraordinary personal qualities.

Was Maecenas a medium for Augustus's indirect demands from the world of poetry, a master in public relations? Sir Ronald Syme's *The Roman Revolution*, a product of the age of dictators, the disillusioned 1930s, treats Maecenas, Virgil, and Horace in a chapter entitled "The Organization of Opinion." But there is only one reference by these poets to Maecenas's commissioning a work; it is in Virgil's introduction to the third of his *Georgics*, the descriptive poem about the art of farming in Italy dedicated to Octavian, as a deity who has shown compassion for the peasants victimized by war. There the poem is called Maecenas's "difficult orders," *haud mollia iussa*. But the words reflect two conventions: first, that any substantial work was presented by the author as responding to another man's demand (*iubere* and *iussa* are ethically neutral words), and, second, distinguishing between "hard" and "soft" poetry. The poetry of war was hard, and farming is characterized throughout the *Georgics* as backbreaking labor, a sort of civilian heroism comparable with that of warfare. Thus the difficult orders become little more than the suggestion of a poem about a hard world.[51] If Maecenas did propose the theme of this poetry, it was a wonderful choice for Virgil, who had ultimately higher values than the mere refinement of Alexandrian allusion in the dream world of the *Eclogues*.

Other poems, one by Horace, two by Propertius, address Maecenas and seem to decline his pressure to compose epic sagas of Augustus's great victories, but they reflect the convention of *recusatio*, and the humorous retaliation of both Horace *Odes* 2.12 and Propertius 3.9 suggests that Maecenas understood the principles of both the poets. Horace declares that Maecenas himself should write Augustus's praises; he will handle the campaigns better in prose than Horace in verse. As for Propertius, he presents himself as a miniaturist: in staying within his limitations, he is copying Maecenas's own attitude of self-effacement and withdrawal from public activity. Why, if Maecenas leads, he will even sing of Jupiter and the Olympian triumph over the giants and the course of Roman history from Romulus to the suicide of Mark Antony. This is as much a threat as a promise (3.9.49–56), and not without malice; in his only previous poem to Maecenas, Propertius had raised the possibility that he would record some of Augustus's more embarrassing victories from the decade of civil war (2.1.23–36).

The years of the greatest Augustan poetry were so dominated by attention to the leader and his program of national recovery that we must consider the evidence for Augustus's changing personal relationship with the poets as a major factor in the wider transformation of culture. It is not that he was intellectually dominant; indeed, his education with the Greek rhetorician Apollodorus was abruptly terminated by Caesar's death, so that the poets were not only older than he, but better educated.

We know from Suetonius that Augustus used colloquial Greek, but it is unlikely that he had studied Greek poetry or read the Alexandrian models of contemporary Roman poets. His only attested personal taste in Greek poetry is a love of Aristophanic Old Comedy, which he even staged at public games.[52] But he listened to living Roman poets: already in the early *Satires* Horace speaks as though he has recited for Caesar; he may not yet be ready to write of the invincible commander's deeds, but he has written good poems and been praised by Caesar for them (*Sat.* 2.1.83–84). Virgil invokes Caesar among the rural gods at the opening and close of *Georgics* 1, and honors him in the preface to the third book, and the epilogue to the whole poem. If there is no reason to believe the princeps had "suggested" the poem, he was eager to hear the completed work. When he returned from the Actium campaign, he listened to the *Georgics* on four successive days. According to Suetonius[53] he was even more eager to know the *Aeneid*, and wrote from Spain begging the poet with mock threats to send him a copy of the first book, or any portion of it.

Virgil had promised in the *Georgics* to raise a poetic temple and offer Italian games in honor of Octavian's triumph, and he would offer in the eighth book of the *Aeneid* a brilliant description of the naval victory at Actium, and of the triple triumph; in this he portrays the princeps seated in front of his great Palatine Temple of Apollo to review the endless parade of captive nations (*Aen.* 8.720–

28). But this book was not yet written when Virgil recited to Augustus. If he ended his recitation with book 6, this would honor the ruler through Anchises's great enumeration of the Roman heroes still unborn, a parade that includes Augustus without the crudity of making him the final climax of the list. And he is presented, not as a conqueror, but as an heir to Julius Caesar and descended from gods, the founder of a second golden age of peace equal to the legendary prehistory of the land:

> Here is Caesar and the descent of Iulus destined to come beneath the mighty pole of heaven. Here, here is the man whom you have so often heard promised to you, Augustus Caesar, born of the gods, who will again found the golden ages that were once enjoyed through the farmlands of Latium when Saturn was King. (6.789–94)

Virgilian scholars have sometimes suggested that Augustus would be disappointed by the poet's oblique refraction of his achievements through the life of his ancestor. But surely this modern commander, who relied heavily on his subordinates and was not distinguished for tactics or gallantry in the field, recognized that the campaign epic was not the medium to immortalize his services to Rome.

Peter White has recently shown very persuasively that Augustus's behavior as patron was simply a continuation of the pattern established by nobles during the republic. But the fact of his power overshadowed the civility of his behavior, and relationships cannot have kept the parity he wished. Only after 20 B.C. is there evidence for direct literary intervention by Augustus. This first known intervention was unquestionably right. When Virgil died in 19, the *Aeneid* still lacked the last touches to satisfy his own perfectionist standards. It is said that Augustus intervened with Varius, the poet's friend and executor, to have the work "published" as the poet had left it. For the first time in Roman literary history a poem was produced and sold in many copies. Pliny's claim that Augustus put his authority behind the work honoring himself and Rome's foundation by his ancestor[54] explains to some extent how the *Aeneid* became immediately famous. Some of the petty criticisms of Virgil documented by his biographer can be ascribed to jealousy at its unique official status. Augustus had acted once before on behalf of a favored artist, when he rewarded Varius with an unprecedented sum for the tragedy *Thyestes*, staged at the games in honor of his triumph in 29 B.C.—but it was Roman practice for a magistrate to commission stage plays and reward the poets.

A far more splendid opportunity for imperial patronage arose in 17 B.C. Augustus had held his honorific title for ten years, and was approaching the forty-sixth year, which marked the Roman's transition from youth to being *senior*—originally the age limit for the reserve forces as opposed to active warfare. He offset this mark of aging with the great Secular Games, having found astronomers to declare that this would be the first year of a new Etruscan *saeculum* or era.

The games must have been prepared long ahead and dominated national interest. There was to be a new version of the ritual procession incorporating offerings to Augustus's Palatine triad of Apollo, Diana, and Latona with the traditional rites to Jupiter, Juno, and Minerva on the Capitoline. Tradition had it that Livius Andronicus, Rome's first poet, had composed the Secular Hymn in 207 B.C. Now Augustus asked Horace to compose for him the festival hymn to be sung by a choir of boys and girls. Horace had included several lyric hymns, including a fine address to Apollo and Diana, among his three books of *Odes* published in 23. But those were poems, not public performances, and the *Secular Hymn*, a poem of some sixty-four lines, was to be truly sung, and by a choir of twenty-seven adolescent boys and twenty-seven girls. It must have been severely limited by the demands of ritual, musical accompaniment, and the talents of the young performers. It was appropriate to both the choral performers and the needs of the audience[55] that the text should be straightforward, dealing with simple values in unallusive, almost prosaic order. This could not match the allusive brevity of Horace's greatest odes, but he remained immensely proud to have composed this national hymn, whose words were officially inscribed among the records of the games.[56]

Perhaps Augustus did not understand the poet's personality as well as Maecenas. A letter preserved in the archives and quoted by Suetonius[57] seems to suggest that he was jealous of the closeness between Maecenas and Horace; he wanted the poet to leave Maecenas and become his own private secretary, something quite alien to Horace's independent nature.[58] But Augustus took no for an answer; only after he had known Horace for more than twenty years did he directly ask the poet to write for him. Suetonius represents it more crudely: he "compelled" Horace to write the fourth book of *Odes* by commissioning the victory odes for his stepsons Tiberius and Drusus, and "extorted" the poem that we know as the *Letter to Augustus*. But this forceful language can be corrected from Suetonius's own evidence—the humorous excerpt from Augustus's letter: "I want you to know that I am cross with you because you don't choose to talk to me in most of those writings; are you afraid it will shame you before posterity if you are seen to have been my friend?"[59]

I have already referred more than once to Horace's *Letter to Augustus*. This public reply is both diplomatic and realistic, a respectful letter beginning with honest praise and sympathy for the ruler's responsibilities. The central, literary theme of the letter deserves separate treatment; but Horace begins and ends with Augustus, and the reciprocal services to each other of princeps and poet. Augustus is praised for his restoration of law and good morals, and reminded that previous heroes and benefactors met adversity in their lifetime; in contrast Rome already offers him cult as an unprecedented hero. Toward the end Horace deals tactfully with the ruler's implicit request for public celebration through his poetry. He gently reminds Augustus that his great achievements were best honored by poets with the gift for epic, like Virgil and Varius; he, Horace, could not rise to songs of battle and would not wish to harm his leader by unworthy praise. Bad poems, like bad portraits, dishonor and bring ridicule upon their subject.

But in his last book of *Odes*, perhaps contemporary with this "letter," Horace gives direct praise to Augustus through the victory odes that credit to him the character and achievements of his stepsons. He even offers something close to veneration in the two poems directly addressed to Augustus. These odes (4.5 and 4.15) set the services of the princeps to Rome in the context of national and individual peace. Expressing a spirit that harmonized with the increasing age of both poet and emperor, the poems end in serene enjoyment of mature leisure, as the grateful Italian farmer includes the good leader of his people in his family prayers at the evening meal.

Both leader and poet had mellowed, and their close age and shared experience gave Horace something he could genuinely celebrate. In these poems of his last years Augustus is simply *dux bone*, "good leader"—not words that anyone could truly have used of the warring commanders of the late republic. In 8 B.C., when the dying Maecenas asked Augustus to look after Horace as he had cared for Maecenas himself, this must have been welcome to both poet and leader.[60] On the basis of the ancient evidence for the private relationships of the princeps and the poets, I cannot accept that either Virgil or Horace could have composed his works if he had not genuinely known and admired the Octavian who became Augustus, and shared most of his ideals and aims.[61]

Performance and Readership

The urgent theme that Horace had made the heart of his *Letter to Augustus* was the indifference or hostility that the new poets experienced with a conservative and aesthetically uneducated public.[62] The mass of Romans had been taught to be proud of the old Roman writers of epic and drama, and continued to praise what they knew because they knew it. The familiar narrative material made no demands on their powers of understanding and carried their interest by obvious emotional and verbal devices. But the new poets were not popular. More than one of the *Epistles* reflects Horace's discouragement, and in so doing gives us important evidence on public taste and the occasions and places when poetry would be heard and criticized in the city. In the beginning his *Satires* mention enemies as often as the friends who are so much better known from his accounts. The amateur poets Fannius and Crispinus are quoted for their improvisations and too facile composition.[63] Even around the princeps there were associates like the singer Tigellius Hermogenes who belittled Horace's work. Like many Romans, Augustus enjoyed entertainment by singers and dancers at his dinner parties, and it is not surprising if his popular entertainers were both hostile and jealous of Maecenas's protégés. Even Maecenas could carry his enthusiasm for popular pantomime to the point of falling in love with his own freedman, the dancer Bathyllus. Horace might tease him in an early poem,[64] but this shows the competition faced by pure literature.

Although Maecenas's literary circle was not typical of Augustan social life, it was a wide one. If Horace only performed for his friends, and that on demand (*Sat.* 1.4.73), he still can cite a long list of them: Plotius Tucca; Varius, the tragedian; Valgius, the elegist (to whom he addresses a gently mocking poem, *Odes* 2.9); Aristius Fuscus; and the Visci brothers, Pollio, Messala Corvinus, and Bibulus and Servius, all scions of republican families. Although most of these friends are addressed in *Odes* or *Epistles* and more than one poem shows him on intimate terms with the aristocrat Manlius Torquatus and with younger men like Septimius, Iulius Florus, and Lollius Maximus, we should not assume personal friendship with his more prominent addressees like Sestius or Augustus's private secretary Sallustius Crispus.

Worse than jealousy was crude and superficial imitation. It seems that the success of Virgil and Horace himself had led to a fashion for versifying, and Horace writes with horror of dinners where young men and old put on wreathes and improvise poems: "Skilled and unskilled alike we churn out verse" (*Epist.* 2.1.117).[65] Poetry had always been part of a young man's training: even the young Octavian had once attempted a descriptive poem on Sicily, and a tragedy on the death of Ajax.[66]

Apparently Horace's friend Calpurnius Piso had two sons, who thought of writing tragedies; their ambition is the ostensible origin of the *Letter to the Pisos*, known to most of us as the *Art of Poetry*. In fact Horace had not intended his verse letter as a manual of poetry, but it was used as such by the time of Quintilian, who gives it this name.[67] In the last part of this letter, Horace makes it clear that amateur poets were a real hazard, especially if the amateur was not young and teachable, but old and rich, open to flatterers who praised his bad verse, and intolerant of men who offered genuine criticism—or poetry.[68] The comparison between men's standards in criticizing music and poetry recurs more than once, since poetry was seen as an alternative afterdinner entertainment. At 373–76 Horace notes that no host would tolerate a dissonant choir (*symphonia*, 374) any more than he would put up with bad perfume; but clearly men had not learned criteria for judging poetry. People who would require practice of an athlete or piper still believed they were marvelous poets, despite their clumsy composition (416–18).

With hungry dependents the wealthy man could be sure of a favorable audience. But even among peers he would not find real criticism. Romans used to poetry as a narrative vehicle for patriotic memories would not understand the need to refine the individual line, to eliminate harsh metrical effects, to prune excessive ornament or work for clarity. The problem was that Romans did not take poetry seriously; they saw poetry as a light entertainment, *nugae*, and even those who felt the awkwardness or vacuity of a friend's verse would put courtesy ahead of criticism (450–51).

It is not surprising then that Horace shunned both casual social readings of his work and public recitations. These could take place in the schoolrooms of the grammatici or, more conspicuously, in temples and public spaces. In his first collection of *Epistles* he claimed that his indifference to the grammatici had cost him goodwill; the disappointing reception of the first three books of *Odes* is another reflection of the conservative cultural life at Rome. The *Odes* were in the lyric meters of the great poets of archaic Greece, an unfamiliar form of poetry to Roman readers. Even the new poets around Catullus who took their standards from Alexandria would have been more accustomed to other meters and other genres of poetry. Probably many of the more private odes were not appreciated at Rome, even in the next generation when other works of Horace were quoted and admired. To this day the most famous are the few proudly national poems like the Roman Odes (3.1–6) and some of the explicit moralizing pieces, rather than those playing on Greek taste and private pleasures. Horace argues that his readers loved his poems in private but denied them public esteem because he had not courted the public with dinners and gifts, or made himself known by reciting in the halls of the professional exponents.[69] Certainly these grammatici, like modern critics, could make a man's reputation. Caecilius Epirota, trained by Atticus, had popularized Virgil's *Eclogues* by giving them formal reading and criticism in his classes. But according to Horace, men were so untrained and public opinion so submissive to authority that critics could prejudice a reader against a poem he had enjoyed. Has anything changed?

There may have been different factors at work with different generations here. The older men would seek out political memoirs, histories, or philosophical prose; if they turned to poetry it was not for aesthetic satisfaction, but as a source of morality or patriotic pride, so they would not read lyrics. The younger men and women in contrast probably opted for the easier appeal and emotional sublimation of love elegy. Jasper Griffin has recently brought out the extent to which Greek fashions in clothes, entertainment, and sexual interests had spread among the younger set from which came, for example, the love elegists Propertius and Tibullus.[70] Both books of Tibullus and the first three books of Propertius were known by 20 B.C., when Horace published his first collection of *Epistles* and, although he says so little about the genre, their success may have sharpened his disappointment.[71]

Besides the halls of the grammatici, Horace more than once mentions a temple as the site of readings: in his *Satires* for example he refuses to write the sort of poems "that echo through the temple in competition with Tarpa as judge" (*Sat.* 1.10.38). Tarpa was Maecius Tarpa, a critic mentioned by Cicero in 55 B.C. as helping to determine the choice of plays for Pompey's games. Is this merely a reference to dramatic tryouts for the games? The other allusion is in conflict. In the relatively late letter to Florus, Horace complains of the disturbances offered by the city that prevent him composing lyric poetry. Then he sets up an imaginary match between himself and a composer of elegy:

> See how pretentiously and with what striving we gaze around at the temple, open to welcome Roman poets. If you are free, follow and listen from a distance to each man's offering and how he weaves himself a garland: we take a beating and exhaust the enemy with a fair exchange of blows like Samnite gladiators in a slow combat at the first light of evening. I come off Alcaeus on his rating. How do I rate him? As

Callimachus, who else? If he seems to raise his claim, he is hailed as Mimnermus, and swells with the self-styled title. (*Epist.* 2.2.92–101)

Scholars have usually taken this unnamed rival as Propertius, who emulated Callimachus, and whose poems borrow programmatic themes from Horace. What is more important is the occasion described. Were there regular contests, or successive readings, by the poets? We can no longer believe the nineteenth-century idea that a college of poets existed at this time, as either a group or an institution,[72] but the precedent of Asinius's recitations makes it probable that other public recitals followed.

One temple had a special claim to be the recital hall. When Augustus erected the marble Temple of Apollo of Actium beside his own residence on the Palatine, he set a statue of Apollo Citharoedus, the god as patron of lyric and poetry in general, in front of the shrine. The next year (28 B.C.) saw completion of the porticoes in yellow Numidian marble linking the temple to twin libraries, one Greek and one Latin, on either side. Propertius went to see the opening of the new porticoes and commemorated it with an elegy (2.31) describing the dazzling Parian marble, the rooftop quadriga, the statue of the god (said by a later source to have been modeled with Augustus's face), the ivory doors that depicted Apollo's destruction of the Niobids and the Gauls who attacked Delphi. Inside the shrine he notes another statue of Apollo as poet, singing in the long robes familiar from the Greek poetic contests. These contests were familiar to Romans from the Greek games of Naples (a favorite pleasure of Augustus at least in his old age)[73] and the Roman versions presented from time to time by Augustus himself.

Surely it follows that the temple in which Horace sets this imaginary contest is the Palatine temple, the scene of actual recitals or contests. Its open welcome would then carry a double meaning: Augustus's new library may have been full of Greek texts, but there was room in its Roman half for Latin poets. It would still be empty to welcome the poetic texts as the temple would welcome successful poets. Admittedly there is little evidence for the texts admitted to the Roman collection. Suetonius in his *Life of Caesar* reports that Augustus ordered the librarian Melissus not to include his father

Caesar's juvenilia. The collection grew to include new poetry such as Ovid's works, for Ovid's lament over the expulsion of his *Art of Love* implies the inclusion of his previous work and guarantees the presence of the earlier generation of Augustan poets.[74]

The temple itself should be seen as a demonstration of the princeps's artistic and cultural policies; if his choice of Apollo was influenced by the presence of Apollo's shrine at Actium, it need not have led to the representation of the god as a poet-composer. Rome had reached its material supremacy in the Mediterranean; now it was time to match the Greeks in literature and art. In the *Letter to Augustus* and again writing to the Pisos, Horace argued that Rome must now compose and criticize poetry by Greek standards; Augustus himself must pay as much heed to the refined poets who compose for the reader as to the playwrights, if he really wants to fill his worthy monument to Apollo with books. Continuing the image, he will call the new poets the temple wardens of their leader's *virtus*, his excellence in war and peace (*Epist.* 2.1.214–17, 230).

This contrasts with the more conventional Roman attitude to poetry exploited by Horace for his mock defense of the poet in the same letter. As he claims, the poet is innocent and harmless, even mildly useful to society: he may be a poor soldier but he serves the city by shaping the child's unformed speech (poetic texts were used to teach reading) and providing friendly instruction; he describes noble deeds and offers edifying examples; he even teaches girls to pray; and poetic hymns obtain divine aid, bring on the rain, and turn away disease and danger (*Epist.* 2.1.118–36).

This explicitly religious function confirmed Horace in his more unofficial role as spokesman for national ideals; both justify the proud name of *vates*, which Horace revived to express the poet's recognized status as a public figure and vehicle of inspired authority.

Vates was the old Roman word for poet-seer, displaced two centuries earlier by the fashionable Greek loan word *poeta*. The ideal had come early to Horace, who first called himself Rome's spokesman in the visionary *Epodes* 16 summoning his fellow citizens to take flight from civil war; but that was in the years of trouble before Octavian earned the name of Augustus. Horace will reaffirm the poet's power to serve the gods and immortalize men in the last book of *Odes*. Heroes before Agamemnon died forgotten because they lacked a "holy poet" (*vate sacro, Odes* 4.9.28), and when the grown choirgirl looks back to her moment of glory singing his *Secular Hymn*, she thinks of "Horace the poet" (*vatis Horati*, 4.6.44). Thus Augustan policy gradually embraced the new poets, and used imperial monuments to give a new importance to the art and rescue it from the utilitarianism of their society.

Yet the success of lyric poetry was short-lived. Horace in his old age could boast that he was pointed out by passersby, and his name was known in remote parts of Italy. A century later, however, our sources on the Augustan age of poetry barely mention him, in comparison with the fame that accrued to Virgil. Indeed, both Suetonius and Tacitus report Virgil's great wealth, apparently from the gifts and legacies of friends, and his fame in his own lifetime. This may have begun as early as the 30s when his *Eclogues* were dramatized and performed: according to Tacitus, on one occasion after a recital of his verses, the whole theater crowd rose and saluted the poet with as much veneration as if he were Augustus himself. The bashful poet[75] was a classic before he died. By composing works that could be seen as a match for Homer and Hesiod, he gave Rome a classical literature, with both the pride and the potential hazards that are produced by an unchallenged poetic canon. Later chapters will show how his success both fostered and hampered the serious poetry of subsequent generations.

Spoken and Written Prose in Augustan Society:
Rhetoric as Training and Display

The poets dominate the modern perception of Augustan literature because rare talents coincided with the enlightened policy of an absolute but idealistic ruler. Yet in bulk the literary output of Augustan Rome was predominantly in the genres of prose: not perhaps philosophy, which was studied either privately, or abroad in Athens or Asia Minor, but history and scholarship and the new forms of rhetoric, which were practiced by Romans and resident or visiting Greeks alongside each other. Grammarians and rhetoricians were on hand to advise the adult author and teach his growing sons, and, in the performance as well as teaching of rhetoric, Greek speakers associated on a par with Latin orators from Rome and the provinces. As a social activity and a literature of performance, the declamatory rhetoric of this period should be considered first. This activity was essentially ephemeral and improvisational, something between the extemporization of jazz and the adaptable script of a drama workshop or television documentary. It is only the coincidence of the elder Seneca's longevity and nostalgic total recall that has preserved this oral art in and as a literary form. But old Seneca's interest in the rhetorical displays of his youth hardly exaggerates the significance of declamation in the culture of Augustan society: Suetonius, Tacitus, and Quintilian confirm the craze for public declamation as an alternative vehicle for rhetoric in the changing political circumstances of the new principate.

The activity itself was not new: producing model speeches—exercises on a set theme—had always been part of the young speaker's training. Cicero, for example, composed such pieces in Greek, and outlines a *thesis* or moral issue in Greek in a letter to Atticus: "should the patriot stay in his country under tyranny?"[76] The speeches he rehearsed with Hirtius and Dolabella in his Tusculan villa may have been equally generalized, or they may have been in the new style of declamation. This might take a precise historical situation and compose advice to the great man facing a decision—this so-called *suasoria* was good practice for political advocacy. Alternatively it might imitate a court case by constructing a complex fictional scenario of private wrongdoing and composing a speech of defense or accusation for the individual. Such *controversiae* usually involved family crimes and quarrels so as to deal with inheritance law and problems that boys in the rhetorician's school could understand, but they would leave room for details supplied by the speaker to color the pleading with pity or indignation.

What was new was the importance attached to this activity. Its impact was now redoubled. First, the teenaged boys in the rhetorician's school would take their turn to compose such briefs; they were not required to know details of the law, but rather to evolve arguments from probability and use paradox and striking aphorisms and dramatic characterization. This forced each boy to be more ingenious than the one before him and led to increasingly clever and artificial speeches.

Later too, as adults, men continued to practice declamation for public display, and well-known orators competed to demonstrate their skill. These competitions seem sterile to us, but they were attended by the leaders of Roman public and literary life. In some respects Seneca's reminiscences misrepresent the regular training: for example, the schools certainly offered basic instruction in organizing argument, as is clear from the complete or outlined *Declamations* attributed to Quintilian, but Seneca's memory pulls out the memorable one-liners from these sessions like currants from the cake.

Seneca is interested in personalities. His prefaces to each book of reminiscences are like the work of a modern theater critic: they single out and portray individuals like his friend Porcius Latro, a workaholic with a zeal for writing and an amazing memory, or Arellius Fuscus, a teacher with a taste for fine and poetic phrasing, or the statesman Asinius Pollio. Seneca heard the young Ovid declaim and criticizes his weakness in argument and unwillingness to discipline his gift for epigram; he seems to have conversed with Livy, whom he quotes several times,[77] and knows prose writings (surely not declamations!) of Virgil.[78]

No man was too busy or too great to attend these strange performances. On one occasion Latro spoke in the presence of Augustus, Maecenas, and Agrippa, the great general who was Augustus's close friend and son-in-law. Maecenas himself was a regular, although his interest was primarily in poetry; three times Seneca cites him for his support of Virgil and defense of his language against critics (*Suas.* 1.12, 2.20, 3.5). And Seneca treats even Augustus's presence as a regular event, which nonetheless had its effect, illustrating how Rome was becoming a city of courtiers who carelessly abandoned freedom of speech for flattery. He cites a witty antithesis coined by Varius Geminus when the princeps was present: "Caesar, those who dare to speak in your presence do not realize your greatness; those who do not dare do not realize your tolerance" (*Controv.* 6.8). This was the period when men began to praise their leader for behaving like a citizen, *civiliter*; soon he would expect to be treated like a god.

Participation was in both languages, and Seneca lists a dozen regular Greek participants; but he sees the Greek character and the Greek language in different terms. He praises a declaimer Agroetas from Greek Massilia, noting that his undeveloped skill showed he had not lived among Greeks, but his strong sentiments showed he had lived among Romans (*Controv.* 2.6.12). He alleges that Greek declaimers would allow themselves any license whatever (*Controv.* 1.2.23) and tells his sons that he has repeated Greek aphorisms to show that the transition from Greek to Latin eloquence is easy: everything that can be said well is common to both nations, and matching their different talents showed that Latin has as much resource in expression, though less license (*Controv.* 10.4.23).

The rhetorician's society is truly hybrid. The Greek-born Argentarius never declaimed in Greek and marveled at anyone not content to be eloquent in one language; he saw men declaim in Latin, then cast off their toga, put on their Greek pallium, and take on a new personality to declaim in Greek, like Clodius Sabinus, who performed in both languages on the same day. We can gain some measure of the bilingualism from Seneca's own incorporation of Greek technical terms (like (h)*ermeneuma* or *hexis*, or *cacozelia* or a Greco-Latin compound such as *locus philosophoumenos*) into his text without hesitation or apology.[79]

Another form of hybridization was the interaction of rhetoric and poetry. A stock theme of declamation was the dispute between Ajax (symbolizing brawn) and Odysseus (symbolizing brain) for the arms of the dead Achilles. The young Ovid heard Latro's epigram "let us hurl the arms into the enemy and then recover them" and later incorporated it into the same scene of his *Metamorphoses* (*Controv.* 2.28) citing *Met.*13.121. Elsewhere (*Suas.* 3.7) Seneca shows how both declaimers like Gallio and Montanus and younger poets like Ovid would borrow poetic descriptions or striking phrases from Virgil for their own work. Virgil's fame meant that the borrower could gain both depth of meaning and personal credit by open allusion to the well-known texts.

Gradually the barriers between the decorum of prose and poetry were being forced by the jaded taste of participants and audience, who spent too much time in handling material without moral or intellectual significance. Later generations continued the transfusion of genres. Readers of Seneca's son, the writer of philosophy and tragedy, have found in his plays sayings quoted by his father from the declamations. But these problems were yet to come. If declamation competed with poetic recitation for the ears of the educated public, it was still the case that neither the poets nor the historians of the early Augustan age were themselves the products of training in declamation.

The First Real Histories

Of all the forms of literature practiced at this time, history and antiquarianism were the most bookish and least concerned with performance. It would probably be fair to say that history was still the preserve of statesmen and gentlemen and that neither the writing of history nor the reading of it was fashionable. There was a book trade to spread the works of Horace and Virgil and carry their works to Italian towns and the more settled provinces, but histories do not seem to have been produced for a large market, and if Pollio recited his *Histories* he may have been the only historian to do so.

It will be useful to draw a distinction between historical works aimed at bare record or scholarly research and formal histories with imaginative literary qualities that were read by a wider public. These I will keep to last because of their greater significance to Roman culture in their time and after.

Roman historical writing had originated in a desire to put national history on record, and expanded to include the apologetic function of presenting Rome to the Greeks. But during the republic the Latin historians were not sophisticated either in style or in the dramatization of their narratives: Cicero knew their limitations and recognized that Rome had not yet acquired the art of writing great history to match that of Herodotus or Thucydides. There was a time when he hoped to compose histories himself,[80] but he did not have the continuous leisure from politics until he had been deprived of the freedom to express his historical judgments on his own age. Philosophy had proved a safer genre.

My first chapter illustrated how the researches of Cicero's generation gave the Romans a firm sense of their past by establishing a chronology and synchronizing it with events in the Greek world, and by systematic documentation of institutions and personal careers. A typical scholarly historian of the early Augustan period was the senator Aelius Tubero, who had a family tradition of learning, and who acted as patron for one of the most important Greek figures of this time, Dionysius of Halicarnassus. Tubero's work in at least fourteen books stretched from the Trojan War to the beginning of the civil war between Caesar and Pompey, and seems to have been archaizing in style but rationalizing in interpretation: he apparently explained the Trojan horse as a weapon akin to a battering ram, so that Troy would have been taken by storm and not by either human guile or misplaced reverence. But his Greek protégé Dionysius based his *Roman Antiquities* on the learning of Varro and the study of every surviving Roman historian from Fabius Pictor and Cato to the recent romanticizing annalists.

The *Antiquities* opens scientifically with a survey of sources and examines the traditions of the colonization of Italy in close geographical detail. When he came as an immigrant to Rome in 30 B.C., Dionysius was a trained rhetorician and literary critic and he expands his twenty books with lengthy speeches designed to include all the political and moral considerations relevant to each successive occasion or crisis. The work took him at least seventeen years, and was preserved and quoted for its learning rather than any genuine literary appeal.

Dionysius is primarily interesting to us because he was clearly aware in both his historical and his critical writings of the new atmosphere under Augustus and the opportunities it offered to the man of letters. The mixture of antiquarian explanation and plausible fictional detail in his narrative makes a poor work of art but a valuable source for the lost authors he consulted; to the extent that he represents Varro's *History of the Roman Nation*, for example, he illustrates the kind of information available to Virgil for composing the Italian books of the *Aeneid* or to Ovid for recreating a Roman legendary corpus in the *Fasti*. We do not know whether educated Romans read Dionysius's criticism of the classic Greek orators[81] or his essays on the arts of composition and imitation in rhetoric, but his *Roman Antiquities* must be reckoned with as a source for the culture of his day.

This was a time of quasi-scientific encyclopedias; thus Varro had turned in the 30s to his manual of Roman agriculture, and the professional military engineer Vitruvius would compose his ten books *On Architecture* and dedicate them to Augustus. One other figure, the geographer Strabo, deserves mention for two reasons. The first is his contribution to contemporary knowledge of both geography and history—his survey of the Mediterranean world combined the precise geographical learning of Alexandria with historical and social information about the origin and government of Mediterranean communities. The second is the light that his introduction casts on contemporary literary theory. Strabo condenses into a long chapter some of the main issues of literary criticism that would preoccupy laymen and writers, both Greek and Roman.[82] What was literary criticism doing in the work of a geographer? It arose from Homer. Strabo and his Alexandrian source, like centuries of Greeks before them, looked on Homer as the first teacher— in this case, the source of geographical instruction. But Eratosthenes had argued that the purpose of poetry was to charm or entertain, not to instruct.

In this continuing Hellenistic battle over the function of poetry between Stoic theorists who justified it by its role as education and Epicureans like Philodemus who saw it as aiming to give pleasure, Strabo wanted to stress the utility of poetry in order to justify reliance on his Homeric material. Even Horace, as we noted in his defense of the poet (*Epist.* 2.1.118–38), had endorsed the criterion of usefulness long common at Rome. In his *Letter to the Pisos* he solved the false dilemma by requiring that the best poetry should satisfy both criteria, and "mix the useful with the sweet" (*Ars* 343). When Roman poets and Greek geographers both argue the debate at length, it is fair evidence that the pragmatic city was still hesitating to accept aesthetic values. But there was a genuine disinterested culture in a significant elite, which would be sufficient to guarantee the continued growth of literature in the Roman world.

We pass from historical and related scholarship to Roman history as literature. The Roman reverence for the past had led increasingly with the growing power and wealth of the nation to a feeling of degeneration and moral decline. This had been a keynote in lesser historians since Rome destroyed its last major rivals, Carthage and then Corinth, the economic capital of Greece. Thus the aspiring historical writer, who faced the traditional choice between a long-term history of Rome from its beginnings and a recent history of his times, would also be facing a choice between negative and positive coloring—or, put more crudely, an optimistic or pessimistic presentation of human affairs.

Rome's two major historians of this period can be contrasted in just these terms. Sallust (C. Sallustius Crispus) was a Caesarian who had disappointed his leader; after misgoverning the province of Africa, he retired to become a historian when politics offered him no further fame or profit. His shady political record does not perhaps justify doubting the sincerity of his highly moralized histories, but each of his first two monographs, complete narratives of a foreign and a domestic crisis from the late republic, focused on the response of Roman government to the challenge of a single figure, more villain than hero, but above all dramatic in his extraordinary career. These works, the *Catiline* (*Bellum Catilinae*) and *Jugurtha*, applied the standards of Hellenistic tragic history, stressing the sudden reversals of fortune and evoking pity, or anger, by the pathetic descriptions of cruelty or suffering.

In modern times this man would be a brilliant journalist, for he is marked by three qualities that distinguish the journalist from the serious political or military analyst. The first is his easy adaptation of the ideas of better thinkers; there are echoes of famous judgments and ideas from Plato and Thucydides, and less obvious echoes from Xenophon and the histories of the elder Cato. The second is his preference for emotional effect over accuracy of detail or fairness of assessment; this is less the political bias of the radical supporter of Caesar against the conservatives than an apolitical indifference to truth if it might reduce drama and excitement. Last but not least, he is memorable for his violation of established prose style to demand attention by a personal idiom based on archaism and abrupt asymmetry. Any of these features would guarantee the success of a work of fiction: Sallust has more merit as literature than history. Thus although his immediate successor, Pollio, disliked and criticized him for his mannerisms, Sallust's arresting style and the pace and power of his invective inspired imitation by Tacitus, a far greater historian, and kept him a continuing place in the schools of pagan Rome and Christian medieval Europe.

As Octavian's power grew, it affected the position of those attempting to compose recent history. He had an official secretary and biographer, in the Syrian Nicolaus of Damascus, much of whose work survives; he also put forth an official version of his career, which we can reconstitute from the epigraphic record of his *Res Gestae* (the achievements of the deified Augustus), set up on stone outside his mausoleum at Rome and in provincial capitals after his death. In this version Brutus and Cassius were parricides and public enemies, Sextus Pompey a pirate heading a fleet manned by slaves and runaways, and Mark Antony the corrupted consort of a foreign woman and Oriental tyrant.[83]

In the circumstances only a Pollio could risk the minefield of a history of the civil war: like Sallust he had been a partisan of Caesar, and he seems to have been equally negative in his interpretation of his times, but the surviving excerpt on the death of Cicero[84] shows that it was carefully composed, if quirky and eccentric in style. One cannot assume that it was forgotten because it had less literary merit, since it is unlikely that the early emperors would have encouraged its popularity. But he seems to have been read only by historians and biographers—his friend the elder Seneca, Plutarch, Suetonius, and Appian. For a historian to contribute to literary culture, he must appeal to a wider audience.

The main reason for the loss of interest in Pollio's work will surely have been his eclipse by a greater literary talent, a historian without real precedent at Rome. Soon after Octavian's return from the Actium campaign, Livy (Titus Livius) began researching for his history of Rome from its foundation. He was not a retired senator or general from Rome itself but the son of a wealthy family from Padua in northern Italy. We know very little about his personal life, but he clearly frequented the same declamatory schools and displays as Seneca the Elder. Seneca quotes approvingly Livy's criticism of archaizers: "They are mad, but on the right side of madness." But on another occasion he sees Livy's preference of a Thucydidean aphorism to Sallust's shorter Roman version as mere professional jealousy. Livy is heard quoting a Greek rhetorician, and he married his daughter to a Roman declaimer, Lucius Magius.[85] Was he closer in social terms to the declaimers and rhetors, or to gentlemen like Pollio, who made their houses available for literary performances? To Pollio, himself from the Po Valley, Livy seemed an outsider. Pollio made fun of the younger writer for his Paduan provincialism, perhaps less a matter of Livy's style, as used to be thought, than of his attitude to Rome itself. Certainly Livy had an outsider's respectful conception of the old *res publica* of senatorial government: this and his prolonged attention to the more legendary period of early history may explain the old-fashioned idealism of the books that still survive.

Early on Augustus took a kindly interest in the author's work: he smiled on him indulgently as a Pompeian and displayed his goodwill toward Livy, like his affection for Horace, as evidence of his political tolerance. It is interesting that Livy specifically notes in an early book (4.20, written around 25 B.C.) an adjustment to the historical record provided to him by Augustus himself. Livy had read in his sources that Cornelius Cossus was military tribune when he killed an enemy chieftain in single combat and dedicated the spoils, called *spolia opima*, to Jupiter Feretrius. But in a unique contemporary allusion, Livy notes that Augustus, "the restorer and founder of all temples," had paid a personal visit to the temple of Jupiter Feretrius, and read on the corselet dedicated by Cossus that he was consul at the time of the dedication.

The principles controlling the award of this highest honor were a recent political issue. A young commander, Licinius Crassus, had killed the chief of the Bastarnae in battle and wanted the personal glory of dedicating the spoils to Jupiter. Augustus refused the privilege, claiming that only a commander under his own auspices such as Romulus, or a consul, was eligible for this distinction: hence the revision of Cossus's career. Apparently even early history was a delicate business: on this occasion the historian states the inconvenient evidence but is not about to lose imperial goodwill. Like Virgil's *Aeneid*, this history originated as an authorized work, owing its first success both to its merits and to official approval.

Livy expresses his attitude to the history of Rome and Italy in a deeply personal preface to the entire work. Recognizing the horror of civil war and the difficulty of disciplining his fellow citizens to work for moral and economic recovery, he turns in near despair from the present to the past: the historian speaks nostalgically of the spirit of antiquity that pervades him as he contemplates Rome's ancient heroic origins and the virtues of its forefathers that secured its rise to greatness. The preface clearly conveys the urgent need for the reforms of the Augustan program, and Livy's fears that it may meet resistance. In the same way Livy's narrative reconstructs in the first Romans the ideals that Augustus wanted to set before his people.

The monumental work would reach over 140 books, but Livy can never have imagined at its outset that he would write—or live to write—so many. For later writers like Valerius Maximus and Pliny the Elder, Livy's account of the monarchy and republic became definitive, superseded only by successive abridgments in less literate ages.[86]

Livy organized the material in groups of five and ten books, but where the first book carried Rome to the end of the kingship, almost 250 years, as known history expanded the period covered by each book decreased. The ten books that cover sixty years from 287 to 218 B.C. are lost, but the next ten books (21–30) cover only the seventeen terrible years of the Hannibalic war, and his narrative has only traveled another forty years when the surviving text breaks off in book 45. Did Livy's contemporaries, like modern readers, prefer the vivid characters and tragic coloring of his first book and the heroism of Rome's desperate defensive war against Hannibal's invasion? These are the books whose stories recur in Augustan poetry. The closeness of detail between the legends used by Virgil or Ovid and their telling in Livy's first book comes both from direct imitation and their common reliance on Varro.

I suggested that Livy's history was in some sense an authorized undertaking, but its early books may have been the best known. There are signs that its status may have suffered as the principate became entrenched and met with setbacks such as the withdrawal of the future emperor Tiberius in 6 B.C. Certainly T. J. Luce has recently shown[87] that by the climactic year of 2 B.C. when Augustus was hailed as father of his country and inaugurated his monumental forum complex and Temple of Mars the Avenger, the princeps had turned to another source for the public version of the past that he would inscribe beneath each of the Roman heroes in his ceremonial porticoes.[88] Some of the miniature biographies of the Forum Augustum survive on their stones and in most of them the Livian account has been pointedly corrected by a more positive version of the hero's role in Roman history. Although the forum is damaged and its gallery of commanders lost, it must have contributed more than any literary document to this generation's view of its history and its country's values.

Like the Forum Augustum, Augustus's other monuments, the Altar of Peace, with its solemn procession of the imperial family and its parade of priests and senators, the great linear Horologium or sundial whose shadow stretched across the campus to point toward the altar, and the emperor's mausoleum itself associated the Julian dynasty with every source of national glory—history, religion, and present affluence.[89] Thirty years after Actium, Augustus may well have wanted the past civil war to be forgotten, and Livy as he approached the age of Sulla, and Pompey and Caesar, will have sought ways to postpone publication of the work that had become his life.

What do we know of this life? Nothing except the record of his work, which suggests to experts that Livy will have been approaching book 75 and the Social War by 5 B.C. He and Augustus both lived on to a time when Livy's history reached the civil war and Augustus's own rise to power. While the poets from Virgil to Ovid knew and used Livy's early history, we can understand Livy's reasons for deciding to withhold his later books from publication.

Thus readers of the Augustan age will not have known Livy's treatment of more recent history. It will have been the "upbeat" early history that shaped the Augustan perception of their country and its heritage. When we come to consider the changing mood of the last decade of Augustus's principate, it will be clear that Livy was well advised to postpone publishing the history of this period until after his own death.

Three

Un-Augustan Activities

The Literature of Youth

Some people might retort to this heading that the young are too busy living to give much thought to literature or to celebrating other persons' lives, real, mythical, or fictitious. But young people do adopt for themselves new forms of music and verse, most often in opposition to the tastes and traditions of their parents, or to what they see as orthodoxy. This has been so obvious in the counterculture of the 1960s and 1970s, with its enthusiasm for assertive music and for its performers as heroes and role models, that it may seem dangerously facile to retroject this kind of behavior into Rome's more disciplined society. Yet within the limits of Roman decorum and the license allowed to youth before it "settles down," we can trace the same kind of resistance to parental and societal pressures and the same endorsement of alternative value systems.

Roman fathers of the privileged classes would usually direct their sons toward three approved patterns of behavior.[1] First, they should put in a successful period of military service as cavalry or infantry officer. If they did not choose to become career soldiers, this service would qualify them to begin the career track for membership of the Senate through elective magistracies. Alternatively, they could earn respect in public life as advocates at Rome, or as magistrates in Italian communities where their families had estates; they could even add wealth to family prestige as partners in companies operating government contracts or in private enterprise. In any case, they would marry within an approved circle, so as to increase the network of inherited alliances and produce the next generation to perpetuate the family.

Traditionally a period in early youth was allowed for the satisfaction of wilder energies. If hunting and warfare were no longer the heroic activities depicted in Homer or Xenophon,[2] military service at least had the double attraction of foreign travel and wealth from booty and prize money, while the existence of domestic slave women and independent courtesans offered both sexual release and sexual experience. But already in the age of Catullus—the first period when our sources permit us to know something of the life and taste of educated young Romans—changes in society were destabilizing traditional expectations. Catullus expressed in his poetry the idealization of a love affair such as many young men must have kept quiet, and treated with hostility the established world of provincial administration and military careerism he had been expected to follow.

Catullus made personal poetry of both his loves and his hates, but only one side of his art will continue in the more authoritarian age of the Augustan poets. No counterpart survives, and perhaps none was written, to the insulting epigrams Catullus launched against his father's powerful friend Julius Caesar and Caesar's military associates,[3] or his abuse of the provincial governors Memmius and Piso, denouncing the wealth they had stripped from their provinces but refused to share with their young aides-de-camp.[4] Horace wrote similar abusive poetry in his early *Epodes*, but picked on anonymous profiteers and poetasters; in his sexual abuse too, he replaced Catullus's named male and female victims with anonymous old women. This was not a poetry of political or social protest in any sense, but a satirizing of those who were already social butts.

There was no prudery about sex itself: it was a male pastime to compose boastful epigrams or hendacasyllables[5] about virility such as Catullus's poem 56: "what an absurd and amusing thing, Cato! worthy of your ears and laughter: laugh, Cato, as you love Catullus, for it is absurd and just too amusing. I just found an adolescent ramming a girl; so, if it please Venus, I flogged him with my own stiff tool." Indeed there was a whole genre of poetry offered to and about Priapus, the well-hung god of pederasty, dealing wittily with lust and active feats of sexuality. This was manly, just as it was a good male joke for the young Octavian to mock Antony's wife Fulvia, who was said to be in personal command of the rebel army at Perugia in 41 B.C. Antony was away in the East and had taken up a Greek mistress, Glaphyra, so Octavian makes a neat epigram out of Fulvia's frustration, ending with the alliterative sally that "he would rather fight Fulvia than f—— her."[6] Sexuality was a weapon to be used to enhance one's own image or diminish that of another. Thus, in the years when Octavian had broken with Antony, he fostered scandal in Italy about Antony's subservience to the Egyptian queen Cleopatra and their drunken orgies, which is still reflected in the myth of Antony after his death. But the "harlot queen of perverted Canopus" (Prop. 3.11.39) proved an easier butt than the great general, popular for his very indulgence in life's pleasures. In typical youthful protest Propertius argued for this life of pleasure as if it were the cure or at least alternative to civil war: "if all men wished to spend their lives like this, and lie with limbs heavy with drink, there would be no cruel steel nor warships, nor would the sea of Actium toss our bones."[7]

This form of dissent—the glamorizing of love affairs with boys or women—will persist as a symbol, sometimes indirect, and sometimes overt, of resistance to society's demands. Catullus set the style that would dominate the love elegy of the Augustan age, and he did so by both loving and writing in a new way. Love had always been a theme of Hellenistic poetry, whether as center of a comic plot (which was brought to a socially acceptable outcome in marriage) or as theme of light epigrams. These were composed as an accepted social game to herald the shifting infatuations of the poet and his friends. Like the Alexandrian epigrammatists, Catullus's friends had romantic attachments to young women from the entertainment world, who made a profession of being loved. Catullus writes about such women, but also about young men or boys: in more than one poem he expresses passionate desire for the young Juventius.[8]

The difference arose when Catullus fell deeply in love with a quite different kind of woman—the aristocratic widow (if she was already a widow) Clodia, an "older woman" in experience if not in years.[9] By Roman standards intercourse with such a woman, whether married or widowed, was a social offense, fornication[10] if not adultery, but many wealthy women married to elderly, absent, or indifferent husbands had ceased to care.

The poems that Catullus wrote to express the pain of his unrequited and betrayed love did not copy an existing genre, but grew out of circumstance: these included short poems in several meters, and several longer poems in elegiacs, one of them (68) an extraordinarily beautiful and complex elegy expressing his emotions through mythological comparison with the prematurely widowed heroine Laodamia. Thus he created personal love elegy, a genre that developed its own practitioners and public. He had treated his Lesbia (the poetic name he used for Clodia) as a unique, dominant mistress to whom he was subordinated like a slave. This new emotional approach determined the tone in which later elegists would compose their real or fictitious loves around a single woman—as it were, "the book of the affair."

From this time on love poets wrote not just for the immediate occasion, to offer a poem to their woman, or read it to their friends at parties, but with an expectation that others would want to buy and read the poems. Propertius speaks of the girl who drops her copy of his poems on the bench as she awaits a rendezvous with her young man; he claims that a crowd of girls loves his every word, and that his *Cynthia* (the name of both his beloved and the first book of poems) was read all over the Forum, and had made him notorious. If he wanted revenge on his beloved, he had only to compose an epigram against her, "Cynthia, strong in beauty, weak in faith."[11] Lovers are his public, but not simply those who hear him recite. Unrequited lovers will read him to learn from the poet's misfortunes, and his text (*pagina*, the word for a column of verse) will be an instructor to those in love.[12] Ultimately, as we will see, the very popularity of this kind of poetry would rebound against its poets.

Love and Elegy

The genre of elegy, as we noted in the preceding chapter, had not previously been concerned with love, whether passing or passionate. The early Greek elegists had used the meter for marching songs, or to offer their friends comments and advice in a man's world of friends and enemies. Theognis included some love poetry among his elegies, but most of the erotic material is thought to have been added to his work in later generations. Solon used elegy to address the Athenian people about his political reforms, Phocylides to circulate proverbial wisdom. Hellenistic writers took over the epigram, the short inscribed poem in elegiac meter, and adapted it from real dedications and funeral epitaphs to fictitious or historical contexts, then turned it into a medium for brief and witty social vignettes or literary criticism. In its most developed form it was used by Callimachus as a less solemn vehicle for narrative poetry recalling myths and the origins of cult practices or monuments. In his hands, even hymns could be set in elegiac meter,[13] but the meter itself, clipped by the limits of the self-contained couplet,[14] entailed a certain detachment of tone and a quirky variability of diction and narrative tempo. On the other hand Romans of the late republic could read an abundance of elegant, even beautiful, love epigrams by Callimachus himself, Asclepiades, Meleager, and others, including the philosopher and critic Philodemus, who visited Rome in Catullus's own time. They probably knew no more than we do about the lost collections of love poetry by the earlier Greek elegists, Mimnermus and Antimachus. Still, it is fair to say that, even after Catullus, love elegies were only a subcategory of a much wider genre of personal poetry, determined not by content but by metrical form.

It would be misleading to call Catullus a love elegist, since many of his love poems are not in elegiac meter, and those composed in elegiac meter are either shorter or far longer than would become the norm in Roman love elegy. It seems likely too that Gallus, like the Roman elegiac poets Tibullus, Propertius, and Ovid, whose work survives, used the meter to write of other topics, some literary, some learned and antiquarian. But although Gallus had other poetic ambitions, planning a learned poem on the origin of Apollo's shrine at Gryneia, his fellow Romans thought of him as the writer of *Love Poems* (*Amores*) and associated him forever with the pen name Lycoris that he gave to his mistress Cytheris. So when Virgil addresses Gallus in *Eclogues* 10, he represents him, as we saw, as a deserted lover and quotes from the poet's laments, adapting the elegiac meter to his own hexameters.

From these quotations it is clear that Gallus stressed the conflict between his duty as a soldier and his yearning to follow Lycoris: the life of the soldier "bearing the arms of rough Mars" is opposed to the life of love. In other elegiac poets, who did not have Gallus's success as an officer, the soldier features as a rival and military service as a threat, to be rejected for love's sake.

The young Propertius tells his patron, the nobleman Tullus "I was not born for glory or for warfare." He even supports his refusal to marry by the claim that "no child of my blood will be a soldier."[15] Indeed, he reserves the adjective *durus*—rough, harsh, almost ugly—for war, for the soldier, and for epic, the poetry of war: it becomes a code word for what is rejected in life and poetry, and is opposed to the ostensibly negative word *mollis*—soft, delicate. Such a word would have been used by a Roman father to shame his son; in the elegist's vocabulary it becomes an ideal, along with the more literary label *tenuis*—refined.[16] In conformist moods Propertius will call war and its poetry heroic (2.1.28, 2.10.1–4); at the extreme of resistance he will oppose *arma* to *amor*, and set in successive poems the armed campaign of the god (Augustus) Caesar and the peace patronized by the god Amor. The opening phrase of 3.4.1, *arma deus Caesar*, is answered by 3.5.1: *pacis amor deus est.*

Tibullus opens his first book of elegies with a negative picture of the soldier's life, and the last poem of the book curses the inventor of swords as an iron savage.[17] Like Propertius he contrasts himself with his noble patron: "it is right for you, Messala, to wage war on land and sea, so that your mansion can display the enemy spoils. But the chains of a fair girl hold me captive and I sit like a doorman before harsh doors."[18] The love elegist presents himself as conquered by his beloved in the war of love. The antithesis of *arma* and *amor* will provide Ovid with much of the wit of his less than serious elegy; it is probable that the first words of the *Amores* are the first words he published, and they deliberately mislead with the heroic statement "Arms and fierce wars in mighty meter I prepared / to utter" before he converts his second line into the elegiac couplet that unfits his verse for epic and declares his allegiance to Love. Love is both an enemy and a rival to warfare as a way of life, and one of Ovid's neatest elegies is constructed on the paradox that every lover is a soldier—in his mistress's service (*Amores* 1.9).

The code of love elegy, glorifying subjection to the mistress, also depended on rejection, jealousy, and frustration for its subject matter. Alongside appropriation of the language of military service was the less Roman admission of being the slave of love: both the army and slavery imposed absolute obedience, and the mistress took on the status of a commander (Propertius at least uses the technical words for giving commands, laying down the law, imposing treaties, and other marks of authority) or of a master.

These poets were disengaged, at their strongest dissenting, rather than in open rebellion against society, and there is a risk of exaggerating the significance of the protests against duty that recur in each of the surviving elegists. They are not anti-Augustan in some political or ideological sense, nor do they show any hankering for the old republican system. It is true that Augustus systematically encouraged young men of good family to take up serious political and military careers, and passed legislation to foster marriage and parenthood, as well as severe legislation penalizing the adultery of Roman wives.[19] But individuals, particularly those not from established families, were not monitored or penalized for writing about their way of life.

When the love poet Tibullus respectfully distinguishes between the achievements of his patron Messala, for whom warfare is right and proper, and his own humiliated dependence on Delia (another pseudonym—there is no hint of her status), even when he rejects the brutality of war and discomfort of campaigning, it can be read as a young man's license, like his cycle of homosexual elegies for the boy Marathus. If this had been fact, and Marathus a senator's son or a young legionary, Tibullus would have been committing a criminal offense,[20] but Augustan Rome was tolerant of sexuality with licensed playmates.

Propertius is at times more defiant but there is still no evidence that he met official disapproval. Augustus might have been offended, not so much by the poet's refusal to marry (2.7) or join a military governor's staff (1.6), as by the two signature epigrams at the end of his first book. The first evoked a kinsman who had fought against the young Octavian at Perugia and been killed by bandits as he tried to escape from the siege; the second, in which the poet gives his name, identifies him by the pyres of citizen dead—that is, citizens killed by their fellows, a shocking image—from the time of civil war. The two poems must be read together; thus Octavianus Caesar is named as the opponent in the first, but the discord of civil war is reserved for the second. But together they do nothing to justify Octavian or give him apology.

Yet this book attracted the attention of Maecenas, who apparently hoped Propertius would turn his talent to celebrating the new leader. The opening poem of the second book, which proclaims Cynthia as the poet's inspiration, answers Maecenas's imagined request to write heroic epic with words that sound like the conventional courteous poem of excuse, but quickly return to the litany of civil wars—Mutina, Philippi, and "the cast down altars of the ancient Etruscan race." This is not just Propertius's own grievance: it reminds Maecenas, "born of the blood of Etruscan kings"[21] of an offense against his own people. The poet writes with angry loyalty, and it is amazing that he should have published this reminder along with poems that expressed a conventional desire to serve and honor the princeps and his future triumphs. Was this a warning that it was better to let him write on the neutral topic of love? Augustus respected old loyalties in Livy and Horace, and probably accepted their persistence in others.

Love elegists were not limited to lamenting failure in love, and it is important to recognize that all the known elegists had high standards of poetic artistry and absolutely distinctive personal styles. These are poets, not just advocates of a particular and unorthodox way of life. Tibullus, the gentlest figure, does not step outside his poetic context to speak of his artistic inheritance or models but, within the range of his nostalgic and almost pastoral personal poems, maintains a harmony that is achieved by extremely fastidious diction and composition. If these texts shape an external identity for the poet, it is not a literary identity based on models or principles, but his identity as a country dweller. In contrast Propertius, and to a lesser extent Ovid, assert their literary affiliations and identities, parading their models in poetic manifestos, and enriching their personal material with mythical analogies and complex wordplay. From his third book onward Propertius in particular offers the full panoply of programmatic claims to inspiration by Apollo, Bacchus, or the Muses, and many variations on the symbolism of triumph and sacrifice and ivy wreaths earned by treading untrodden paths and drinking drafts from unsullied springs.[22]

For Propertius love becomes as important as a generic literary banner in representing his own experience. Apparent erotic rivalries can disguise literary battles, as he defends the genre he has adopted against all comers. Life and art are mixed in 2.34, the extended address to Lynceus (an allusive pseudonym) who is both poet and lover; he has supposedly tried to steal Cynthia, Propertius's mistress, but his real offense is to pursue the wrong type of poetry. Here as in the earlier poems to Ponticus (1.7 and 9) love elegy is vindicated not by any aesthetic principles but by two arguments: it wins the poet his girl, and it wins immense popularity and approval from the young who need help with their own loves. This genre has its own system of valuation, and even Virgil is honored at greater length in this last poem of the second book for the love content of his *Eclogues*, than for the *Georgics* or the forthcoming *Aeneid*—although Propertius salutes it reverently as a second *Iliad*. Propertius rounds off the second book with a proud apostolic succession of love poets from Catullus and his Lesbia, to identify himself through Cynthia, the name of both his mistress and his first book. Elegy sets up its own self-contained world in competition with the society of nonlovers, the old, the married, and those pursuing orthodox public lives.

Propertius grew older and more orthodox, and duly wrote not only poems to celebrate the legends of Rome's famous sites but a full-scale elegy to commemorate the anniversary of Actium. And Propertius was first respectable, then dead, long before Augustus passed from his confident prime into an anxious and almost paranoiac old age. Another elegist was born too late, and matched his wit and irreverence against a more violent adversary. But to understand the career and downfall of the last of the elegists, we must review separately the years when Maecenas and Horace were dead and Augustus's family life and national role were threatened by disgrace and disasters.

Ovid the Scapegoat, and the Sorrows of Augustus

Ovid was born in 43 B.C., the year "when both consuls fell by a matching doom," as he would describe it in his poetic autobiography.[23] It had been the year when Octavian made himself consul after Hirtius and Pansa both died on campaign in northern Italy, one of wounds, the other, it was sometimes alleged, poisoned by Octavian's doctor. Ovid could certainly have found a more flattering way to describe the year of Octavian's first consulship, if he had not composed this autobiography in exile and disgrace. This poem tells us all we know of his early life. As the younger son of a wealthy landowner from Sulmona, he was honored like his brother with Augustus's mark of encouragement, the broad purple band on the toga that identified young men destined for senatorial careers. Perhaps his father pinned his hopes on the eldest, and let Ovid play with his verse. Instead the brother died when Ovid was already a young man; he grieved, but resisted the pressure to embark on a public career as a lawyer. (You will remember that Seneca admired Ovid's display speeches in the declamation schools, but thought he was weak on argumentation.) So early on the young man discarded the princeps's honor and started to compose elegy (*Tr.* 4.10.35f.).

For the period before 2 B.C. the actual order and date of Ovid's poetry is unverifiable. He tells his readers that he listened often to Propertius and other young poets named by Propertius—Ponticus, with his epic on Thebes; Bassus, who wrote iambic invective; and Aemilius Macer, author of poems about birds and serpents. He heard Horace and admired his metrical versatility but was too young to do more than see Virgil and Tibullus on public occasions. His admiration for Propertius shows through his work, which seems to have begun with first-person love poetry ostensibly centered on a special lover, Corinna, but stooped, as Propertius would never have done, to invent entanglements with Corinna's maid and other unknown women. Propertius may also have provided the inspiration, with his imagined love letter of a Roman wife to her husband away on campaign (4.3), and his developed monologue of the passionate Tarpeia (4.4), for Ovid's *Letters of Heroines*, a series of poetic speeches in character by deserted or separated mythical women.

These show his ability to adapt elegy to a different, essentially dramatic, genre and, within the range of female speakers, to widely different personae. The presupposition of loneliness or betrayal imposes a certain monotony on these letters, but we can see that Ovid began and ended his original volume[24] with the most virtuous of his female caste: Penelope at the beginning, the tragic wives Laodamia and loyal Hypermestra at the end. At the beginning too, come the loving captive Briseis, and innocent but seduced girls Phyllis and Oenone (*Her.* 2, 3, 5). He reserves the passionate and wicked women of Euripides—Phaedra, Medea, and the incestuous Canace, pregnant with her brother's child—for the inner positions, so that the reader would have adjusted his or her moral sights before reaching them.

These letters must surely have disturbed members of the older or parent audience, if they heard or read them; but, as in modern society, it is likely that the generations enjoyed their entertainment apart. It would be difficult for a husband or father not to feel some offense at one particular pair of elegies that occur late in the second, revised version of the *Amores*. The first (2.19) protests to a fool of a man who is spoiling Ovid's fun by not guarding his wife. In this and the companion piece, 3.4, Ovid trades on the popular adultery mime in which the deceived husband or *stupidus* was the butt, and adopts its morality only to cap its cynicism by disdaining an adulterous relationship that was too easy.[25] "The man who makes love to a fool's wife would steal sand from a public beach . . . you are easygoing and suffer what no husband should, but I am finished with a licensed love . . . what use have I for an easy, a pandering husband?" (45–46, 51–52, 57–58). Augustus too had no use for a pandering husband, but his legislation authorized outsiders to prosecute an adulterer if the husband failed to do so, and rendered the husband liable to the penalties for pandering. Yet Ovid can turn his fancy against the watchful husband: "a watched wife will still be adulterous at heart and when every door is closed the adulterer will be inside . . . I like a forbidden pleasure. The man offended by an adulterous wife is too boorish and old-fashioned, and does not know the ways of the city as he should" (3.4. 5–6, 29–31, 37–38). Surely these poems would have offended the emperor in his role as moral leader. What no one can establish is whether the second, three-book edition of Ovid's *Amores* represents a selection made on aesthetic principles from the original five books or an actual change (for better or worse) in moral tone.

The cynicism of the poems I have quoted matches the more overt encouragement to seduction of the notorious *Art of Love*, two books of which were published in 1 B.C., with an unconvincing warning to virtuous women not to read beyond the introduction: "I tell only of safe love and permitted affairs: there will be no grounds for prosecution in my poem." Here was a poem pretending to teach a serious skill, but instructing young men how to seduce, and worse, it was followed within a year or two by a book instructing young women, and a so-called *Cures for Love* that recommended expelling the old love by taking on a new one. The extension and revision of this parody could not have been worse timed, for it coincided with a series of blows to the house of Augustus.

Augustus had only one child, his daughter Julia, born to his previous wife Scribonia in 39 B.C. He had married Julia quite young to his own friend Agrippa, by whom she had produced two sons, Gaius and Lucius, two daughters, and a son, Agrippa Postumus, born after his father's death. In 17 B.C. the leader had made the infants Gaius and Lucius his own sons by adoption: as the boys approached manhood he personally introduced them to the Senate, in 5 and 2 B.C. respectively, and had them marked out for consulships as soon as they should reach twenty. But after their father died in 12 B.C. Augustus had made Julia marry his stepson Tiberius. The marriage was against the choice of both partners, and after their only child, a boy, was born dead, they separated. Tiberius, who had already proved his excellence as a military commander, was offended by the promotion of the young Gaius and asked to retire to Rhodes. Thus Julia was left alone soon after the age of thirty, but not free to marry again.

In the same year, 2 B.C., that Augustus himself was honored as father of his country, and introduced Julia's second son into the Senate as a future consul, he learned for the first time that she was involved in adultery. He had seduced married women himself in his youth, including the respectable Livia, but that was before his rigorous legislation against adultery, which even authorized a father such as himself to kill his daughter if he found her in an adulterous act. Only extraordinary emotional imbalance could explain why Augustus denounced his only child to the Senate, making a public scandal of her private if indiscreet immorality. Fathers tend to be unrealistic about their own daughters, and Augustus's rage and shock are clear from the fact that he disowned her and expelled her to a barren island, forbidding her ever to be buried in the family vault.

And it was at this time that Ovid began to recite his *Art of Love*. For several years nothing happened. The nineteen-year-old Gaius was sent out on an expedition to Armenia to settle the sovereignty of that buffer state with the ruling house of Parthia by diplomacy or arms. The first book of the *Art of Love* includes a grand send-off, praising the young prince and anticipating his triumphant return, but advising the apprentice lover to exploit the crowds to pick up a new girl. The praise of young Gaius is the first dynastic encomium of many to come; where Horace had been content to praise the princeps and honor the actual victories of his stepsons, Ovid was prepared to spin compliments and extravagant hopes for any member of the imperial house. But two years later the prince died in Armenia, and his younger brother too would die in A.D. 4. Tiberius returned from Rhodes and was duly adopted as Augustus's heir (and, by implication, the successor to the ill-defined monarchic power of his father).

Public affairs went from bad to worse; there was a revolt in

Pannonia and a failure in the corn supply, which normally kept the citizens of Rome fed and content with their ruler. Pliny tells us that at one point Augustus contemplated suicide: he was seventy and had never been strong. The worst external disaster was yet to come, when three Roman legions were massacred in an ambush in the forests of Westphalia, leaving their whitened bones to tell the tale to a later generation. But in A.D. 8 a second domestic scandal echoed the first. The younger Julia, daughter of the disgraced Julia, had been married for some years to Aemilius Paullus. She was now alleged to have been adulterously involved with five noblemen, among them Iullus Antonius, son of Mark Antony and Augustus's late sister Octavia—an obvious candidate for the succession. Most students of this period treat the "adulteries" with skepticism: were they a political conspiracy? Were the accusations part of a plot by Livia to get rid of the Julian descendants that threatened the succession of her son Tiberius?[26]

No one knows how Ovid was involved in the scandal, but he seems to have been summoned to the palace and banished: not put on trial before the Senate or any standing court for treason, but simply relegated by Augustus's personal command. He had a day to leave Rome and was not allowed to choose his place of exile. The denial of a public hearing and his unwillingness ever to explain what it was that he had not done show that he was privy to some dynastic crisis, as does his removal from civilized urban society. An educated Roman could easily have settled in Athens, like Cicero's friend Atticus, or Mytilene, like M. Brutus, or Rhodes, as Tiberius had done. These were cultural centers for both Greek and Latin speakers, with a book trade, with rhetoricians and scholars to talk to and social occasions for recitation. Augustus allowed Ovid to keep the income from his property but sent him to the edge of barbarism, the small settlement of Tomis (now a Romanian seaside resort) on the north western coast of the Black Sea. Ovid would remain there until Augustus became a god and his "son" Tiberius succeeded as emperor (the position was now defined and acknowledged) and live on for three more years.

In the circumstances it suited both the poet and the emperor to act as though the *Art of Love* was the real offender. And yet it had been in the public domain and read for at least six years by A.D. 8, and Ovid was already busy with two irreproachable works: he had gone some way with his elegiac retelling of the Roman calendar and its legends, and had virtually finished the *Metamorphoses*. The brilliance and complexity of this work, covering myth and history from the Creation to the apotheosis of Julius Caesar and impending glory of Augustus, fully compensates for the feeling of anticlimax which one would otherwise feel, contemplating the last decade of Augustus's principate. As it was, the exiled Ovid claimed the *Metamorphoses* was unfinished, and he had tried to burn it, but that other copies were in circulation and still survived (*Tristia* 1.7.13–34). He even composed a prefatory epigram of six lines for the unauthorized text, protesting that he would have corrected its flaws, if he had been allowed. The story of the bonfire emulates the now established legend of Virgil's *Aeneid*, but Ovid probably took both poems into exile with him: he was working on revision of the *Fasti* when he died. He had planned a calendar of the whole year; instead, he completed only the first six months, either because he lacked the learned books to help him complete the year or from loss of faith in the enterprise.

For the student of poetry one fascinating aspect of these two major works is their interplay and mutual influence, most apparent whenever the poet tells the same myth in the different contexts and meters of the two poems. Each genre, elegy and epic, had its own tone and narrative characteristics as well as its meter, and Ovid displayed his versatility by telling the same tale in quite different styles.

Innocence and Power of the Book

Now the most pampered favorite of Rome's literary culture was forced to live without any access to that culture—to live on memories and hope. Exile did not silence Ovid, but it remains a mystery how his poems of exile survived and circulated. Writers of the Neronian age knew and learned from his poems written in exile, but they could not have depended on the isolated private copy, and the books were banned from the official libraries. This corpus, with its elegiac characteristics of meter, addressee,[27] and prevailing tone of lament or protest, is nonetheless an entirely new genre, a collection of personal letters describing Ovid's frontier setting, his limited activities, his emotions and his attempts at composition.[28]

Great poetry and famous books have been written in exile: one thinks of Heinrich Heine or Thomas Mann or Nabokov. But these were exiles in an alien but rich and complex civilization, which fed their imaginations and gave them other educated men with whom to communicate. It would be perhaps more accurate to compare Ovid's poetry from Tomis with books written in jail. Religious martyrs like Boethius or John Bunyan, or jailed or exiled political leaders, could write great books because of their faith or mission to reform a nation. But Ovid, like poor Oscar Wilde, had no ideals outside his own art. And his most extended personal poem, the second book of *Tristia*, written early in the exile years, is an entirely new kind of poem, a defense of his life and his art addressed to the emperor himself.

This appeal shows a shrewd understanding of both the formal rhetoric in which Ovid was trained and the psychology of implication, which cannot be taught.[29] Formally his plea for a mitigation of his exile was a *deprecatio*, a plea without any extenuating circumstance or procedural justification. He begins, then, with protestations of loyalty and arguments from the propriety of his personal life that show the inconsistency of Augustus's severity to the poet. But for the student of literature and its role in Augustan society, the second half of Ovid's defense—the defense of his book—provides the most interesting material. Here Ovid opens his rebuttal of the charge of corrupting the innocent (woman) reader with a marvelous picture of the young Roman wife beset by threats to her purity in the lurid world of Roman books and public space: why, in the judgment of prudes even reading Ennius and Lucretius endangers her by introducing the extramarital parentage of Aeneas and Romulus (255–62)! Everywhere in Rome offers opportunities for seduction, every temple reminders of divine misbehavior.

Like Catullus[30] and other poets of love, Ovid insists that his life is chaste and his poetry fictitious, designed only to please an audience (353–58). His defense is that many other writers have written of illicit love affairs before him; so he provides in his own support a tendentious survey of the Greek and Roman literary canon. This list may not tell us what Greek works the educated Roman actually read, but it indicates what they were supposed to read. Giving himself an easy start Ovid begins with Greek lyric poetry, moving from Anacreon and Sappho to Hellenistic epigram and comedy (Callimachus and Menander), before returning to Homer, the great teacher. He has trouble finding support in the *Iliad* but points to the abduction of Helen that caused the Trojan War; from the *Odyssey* he cites the suitors and Demodocus's song of Ares and Aphrodite. The incestuous and murderous plots of a string of surviving or lost Euripidean tragedies (which Ovid himself had mined for the *Letters of Heroines*) provide him with much stronger precedents, as do the Milesian tales and novels (now lost, 361–419).

Roman literature offered less scope, but Ovid can cite from Catullus and the Roman neoterics various senatorial writers of epigram and the elegy of his predecessors (427–66).[31] Ovid is shaping a twofold defense of his *Art of Love*, first of its theme, then of its genre. If Catullus and the elegists can write of their love affairs without penalty, then his own poems of love should not be treated differently. If, on the other hand, he is blamed for writing didactic poetry, a manual of instruction in a trivial and time-wasting activity, he can list such manuals in verse by many of his peers, even manuals of dicing, which was traditionally illegal—and a favorite pastime of the emperor.

The theme of illicit love also gave Ovid precedents from the contemporary popular theater. He at least did not compose those mimes about adultery performed at public expense in the theater in front of the emperor's own eyes; there were many such salacious mimes on show, and Augustus had seen them without alarm.[32]

Each time Ovid's argument touches too closely on Augustus's own tastes and habits he leads away, only to return. The next theme is the visual arts, first, paintings of erotic encounters in private homes and establishments, then back again to the Julian monuments. Venus Genetrix, the Julian ancestress, had always been a source of fun for the poet, and she has already been exploited by Ovid three times (261, 295, 299) before he recalls the naked Venus in the temple consecrated by Augustus to his father Julius. This forms the transition to Ovid's last precedent: the revered Virgil. Why, even "the author of your *Aeneid*" as he calls him, brought his hero and his weapons (*arma virumque*)[33] into Dido's bed in an unsanctioned union—and this book was the most read and loved part of the whole *Aeneid*. This was Ovid's strongest counterargument: no writer was more immune to criticism than Virgil, and the popularity of the "book of Dido" would persist until the age of Augustine and beyond.

It is clear that poets normally justified their profession by patriotic works, encomia (*laudes*) of generals or noble ancestors, and Ovid knows that he could be reproached with sins of omission as well as with his published work. This is why his poem moves to its end with the positive record of the orthodox poetic genres in which he had composed—epic (even if unmilitary), tragedy, and his *Fasti*, the new-style learned patriotic elegy dedicated to Augustus, and only prevented from completion by his exile (549–56).

The poem has brought the *Metamorphoses* into play within twenty lines of Dido and the fourth book of the *Aeneid*. There was a natural connection between the two great works. Little is known about the composition of the *Metamorphoses*, but one thing is clear: that Ovid's very different poem was composed in a spirit of emulation toward Virgil and the now sacrosanct *Aeneid*.[34] Politically too he had aimed to satisfy the emperor while weaving his many-threaded poem from the romantic themes of his choice. Thus Ovid brought the final, Roman, section of his poem to a grand patriotic finale with an unblinking account of the martyrdom of Julius Caesar and his deification by Venus, ancestress of the Julian clan, and a comparison between Julius and Augustus that privileged the emperor and hailed his not too distant immortality. But if Augustus had turned to the beginning of the poem, he might have questioned the reverence of a comparison between himself and great Jupiter, at the moment when Jupiter has discovered a conspiracy against his life and reveals to a loyal Senate of gods that he has already judged and punished the offender, but wants further reprisals against the human race for its disrespect. It is all done obliquely, through a description of Olympus in terms of the Roman Palatine, but the implications shine through the text. And as the poem draws to a close the glorious finale of the emperor's apotheosis is not in fact the end: Ovid claims the last seven lines for himself and his art, borrowing the symbolism of Horace to proclaim that neither wind nor weather nor the anger of Jove shall destroy the work he has brought to an end.[35] The anger of Jove? Horace never made such a claim; but this is the regular encoding in Ovid's exile poetry of the punishment imposed on him by Augustus. And, in retrospect, it seems most likely that these seven lines were only added as a coda when the poet in exile had nothing more to lose and Augustus had gone to his immortal destiny.

Did Ovid still hope for an improvement in his lot when the great appeal was completed and sent to Rome? He is only asking for a less dreary place of exile—but he must surely have realized that he would not get it: for the book he is defending was not his real offense. All the poem can achieve, and continues to achieve with posterity, is to expose the injustice of his emperor. Each time that Ovid acknowledges Augustus's right to condemn him and compares his anger to the thunderbolt of Jove, the hyperbole of the now conventional image underlines the emperor's human limitations. Ovid's defense, though disingenuous, gives a vivid picture of the social and literary world of late Augustan Rome, which holds the reader by its very variety. It is a unique blend of poetry and forensic apology, flexible in tone, urgent in argument, and rich in content.

The private letters of the *Tristia* (poems of lament) are more modest in theme and scope. This new, autobiographical poetry has something in common with the *Epistles* of Horace but is contrasted by the otherness of Ovid's new and barren world and the unknown future: any letter might go unanswered, and he might never see any of his friends again. In one letter Ovid compares writing when there is no one to hear your verse to dancing in the dark:[36] a listener stimulates enthusiasm, and talent thrives on praise.

Besides the isolation from his public and his living colleagues, there was another obstacle to Ovid's old style of learned and allusive composition. Catullus had complained during a short visit to Verona that he could not write without his library; he had only a single

book box to give him ideas. Ovid was even more widely read than
Catullus. It is doubtful whether he could remember the immense
range of his previous reading with the precision necessary for the
allusive art he had practiced. This may be one reason for the concentration of his exile poetry, not on traditional literary themes, but
on his own experience. The few mythological poems (*Tristia* 3.9,
4.4; *Ex Ponto* 3.2) show that Ovid could have retold the tale of
Medea or Iphigenia as many times as he chose. But he needed to
describe his experiences in order to define his own existence, and
this element would increase in importance as the practical effects of
letters of appeal diminished. The man became a voice: I write,
therefore I am (*cano, ergo sum*).

But what happened to the poems, or the books into which he
grouped them? In the opening poem of the third book of *Tristia*,
Ovid's new poetry book is turned away first from the Palatine
library, then from the libraries in the Portico of Octavia and Pollio's
Hall of Liberty. It has no public resting place, and must take refuge
with the common reader. Did Ovid's friends circulate his work
among each other? In fact, both Pompeius Macer, director of the
Palatine library, and Maecenas' freedman Melissus, in charge of the
Porticus Octavia collections, were friends, whom he addresses or
mentions in even his latest poems.[37] If the librarians had taken the
Art of Love off the shelves, were they also bound to refuse these later
books? It is difficult to see how the books from exile could have
been acceptable, when so much of their content argued against the
imperial verdict.

The opening letter from Pontus (*Ex Ponto* 1.1.) is bolder; openly
addressed to Ovid's friend Brutus, it asks him to give the new books
a private home: he will be able to keep them in the place once
occupied by the *Art of Love*, without risking offense. Unlike the
Tristia their title does not seek pity, but their content is unchanged
except that Ovid now dares to name his correspondents. It cannot
harm Brutus; after all people still read the words of Antony and
Marcus Brutus, who actually fought "against the gods"—gods,
since in these later poems Augustus and his family are given divine
status (*Ex Ponto* 1.1.23–24). Were these works still in the libraries?
Perhaps Ovid means only that they had not been explicitly banned

like his own. Ovid argues that since his book is full of honor to Caesar, Brutus can always suppress his name and keep the book as an anonymous encomium.

It may have been part of Ovid's policy to exaggerate the omnipotence of imperial displeasure. Since all the exile poetry has survived to this day, it would seem that unauthorized poetry could make itself known by private circulation at Rome. But it is an extraordinary fact that no other voice is extant from this last decade to comment on the state of intellectual freedom or suppression. Those who were writing at this time, like Livy, kept to the neutrality of their subject matter. This silence, after the unbuttoned social and literary reflections of Horace's *Satires*, is almost shocking.

Besides poems of real originality and descriptive and critical interest, Ovid's last books include quite a few elegies that conform to the expectations of the dynasty and the courtier's obligations to the consolidated institution of the principate. The poems of petition are nicely adjusted to the social status of the recipients, and their differing relationship both with Ovid and with the princeps as source of power. One of Augustus's friends, Fabius Maximus, was particularly close to Ovid, who will later blame himself for Maximus's suicide under a cloud shortly before the death of Augustus. For the nobles there are poems celebrating their consulships, for the princes of the imperial family poems honoring actual and future triumphs. In the final years of Augustus's life authors might have to take sides between his direct heir, Tiberius, and his secondary heir, the young prince Germanicus. Already in 20 B.C. Horace could direct his *Epistles* systematically to members of the suite of Tiberius, such as Julius Florus, Septimius, and Celsus (*Epist.* 1.3, 8, 9). So Ovid attached his star to that of Augustus' grandson and Tiberius's nephew Germanicus, addressing *Letters from Pontus* to the circle around him, Salanus (*Ex Ponto* 2.5), Suillius, Albinovanus Pedo, Tuticanus (*Ex Ponto* 4.8, 10, 12, 14).

When Augustus died, Ovid rewrote the proemium to his *Fasti* after the model of Virgil's *Georgics*, hailing the prince as his inspiration and proclaiming his love of the imperial family and desire to celebrate its praises. His last two poems (*Ex Ponto* 4.8, 9) mark a stifling loss of political independence. Tiberius is now emperor. The letter to Ovid's son-in-law Suillius speaks with reverence of his patron, or rather his god Germanicus; Ovid is proud that his poetry has contributed to the immortality of Augustus by his words of praise, and offers a similar service, through Suillius, to Germanicus himself. The key passage moves from the new divinity of Augustus to the emperor's *maiestas*.

> Gods too, if I may rightly say it, can be created by poetry and such majesty has need of the singer's voice. . . . thus Bacchus victorious drew his glory from conquering the Indians and Hercules from captured Oechalia. And just now, Caesar, the hymns of poets have had their share in consecrating your grandfather, whose virtue has included him among the stars. (*Ex Ponto* 4. 8.55–56, 61–64)

Horace, again, had been first to apply the term "Your Majesty," *maiestas tua*, in his *Letter to Augustus*, when he explained his inadequacy to do justice to Augustus's greatness (*Epist.* 2.1.257–58):[38] the concept would soon become a vehicle to convert allegations of disrespect toward the emperor into accusations of high treason.

In the longest poem (*Ex Ponto* 4.9, in honor of the new consul Sextus Pompeius), Ovid demonstrates his piety toward the dynasty. This letter shows the extent to which imperial cult had now been carried. Like a photo of Lenin or Saddam Hussein, Ovid has a shrine to Augustus in his home, in which the god is flanked by his wife and son (the emperor Tiberius) and the two new heirs, Tiberius's own son, Drusus, and Germanicus. In case this is not enough, he ends the elegy with prayers to the dead emperor and a report of the hymm he has composed: now that Augustus is a god, he can survey the whole earth and will both see and hear Ovid's homage. The poet may never have composed either this hymn or the even less plausible hymn in the Getic tongue.[39] But new circumstances required a new kind of poetry, and Ovid pioneered the language of the imperial court, shaping its ritual compliments with an imagination and dexterity that later poets would not be able to achieve. Was there irony in the prayers to the new god? Surely. Ovid must have taken a grim satisfaction in outbidding lesser poets. But we should not assume that he was writing in open mockery, so that Roman readers might privately sneer at the ruler whose spirit they publicly worshiped.

The scattered comments of later historians reflect a drying up of prose writing as well as poetry in this last phase of Augustus's principate. The elder Seneca saves for the preface to his last book of the rhetorical *Controversiae* his most telling evidence for the loss of freedom of speech. There are stories about the disgrace of obscure men, such as a Greek historian Timagenes whom Augustus patronized and then rejected in disgust at his malice. When Pollio (still alive as late as A.D. 5) took in Timagenes, Augustus asked him if he was now planning to keep a zoo. Timagenes publicly burned his own histories of Augustus's achievements (Sen. *Controv.* 10.5.22). But this gesture worked both ways. Spiteful enemies ensured that the books of Titus Labienus, an orator and declaimer who earned the name Rabienus (Mad Dog) for his savage invective, were officially burned. He had courted notoriety by ostentatiously passing over certain sections of his work when he recited it in public, and claiming that they would be read after his death. But this was only a beginning of official persecution. Labienus's enemy, Cassius Severus, met a similar fate. He was accused in A.D. 12 under the newly defined offense of publishing anonymous pamphlets.[40] Tacitus's account of his writings leaves their genre and medium unclear (were they slanderous letters spread around court circles, or formal histories of his own times?) but their content was apparently the usual random charges of adultery and conspiracy. Cassius Severus was not a nobleman or politically important, so he was merely condemned to exile.

Seneca, who brings the fate of Labienus and Severus together in his protests against the suppression of freedom of writing at this time, has both a literary and a political comment. Looking back he believes that oratory and prose literature were already degenerating, and he is glad that such repression began only when real talent was in decline; but he expresses his admiration for Labienus who had the spirit to write freely "amid the depths of the prevailing peace."[41] The ominous phrase "prevailing peace" foreshadows the explanation that will be given by Tacitus at the end of this first imperial century for the disappearance of worthwhile oratory from Rome. The peace in the last years of Augustus's principate was that of absolute power and diminishing tolerance. This alone was sufficient to explain the disappearance or abortion of any real talent. In such times men cease to speak or write on public themes. But there would be worse times ahead before both spirit and talent revived under Nero.

Four

An Inhibited Generation:
Suppression and Survival

The first examples at Rome of the suppression of overtly political writing contained hints of worse to come. The intimidation of the old governing class made famous by Tacitus's account of the reign of Tiberius had begun in Augustus's lifetime and should probably be dated to A.D. 4, the year Augustus lost his second grandson and heir, Lucius, and reluctantly transferred the role of successor designate to Tiberius.[1] To understand Tiberius's position and his effect as princeps on political life and literature, one must put together some of the paradoxes of his biography. He was born only a year after Ovid, but reared by parents in flight and exposed to the shifting loyalties of the triumviral wars. Brought up in his stepfather's house, he achieved major successes as a military commander but was passed over for the succession. He marked his resentment by self-exile to a life of secluded study on the Greek island of Rhodes, but was called back and promoted to the role of co-Caesar with Augustus when he was already over forty-five, a *senior* by Roman reckoning. Augustus lived on beyond all expectations and Tiberius was finally expected to take on the principate as a middle-aged man of fifty-six.

Remembering the old senatorial government and aware of the

unpopularity of the last years of Augustus, he was genuinely reluctant to take power, and eager to revive senatorial responsibility for decision making. But it was too late. The insecure and suspicious ruler was a victim of the longevity of both his adoptive father Augustus and his mother Livia, who survived and asserted herself in public life until her son Tiberius was seventy-one years old. Tacitus's highly colored historical narrative highlights the continuing climate of suspicion in the society of court and Senate by inserting notices into the Tiberian narrative designed to recall the victims of the previous reign. First the women: notices appear in his *Annals* on the death of the exiled elder Julia (1.53) and on Julia her daughter, brought into the narrative both at the return of her alleged lover and on her death (3.24, 4.71). The reiteration of charges of adultery against princesses of the dynasty or other noble women reflects political convenience rather than the women's behavior. Charges of adultery against women corresponded to more political accusations against men of the same class. Tacitus also brings twice into his Tiberian narrative the fate of Cassius Severus, who had been exiled for pamphlets containing slanderous accusations of this type; his case is adduced at 1.72, to explain the terrible growth in the exploitation of the law of *maiestas*, "high treason." This would be extended to cover even private comments against the imperial dignity, or writings ostensibly harmless that could be distorted and construed as subversive. Severus is mentioned for the last time ten years later at 4.21, not because he had died, but because he had maintained his slanderous writings, even on Crete, forcing the Senate to relegate him to the barren island of Seriphos. Were these texts actually disseminated from Crete to the capital? It is hard to imagine them as a real threat to the imperial reputation.

Severus's removal precedes by only a few chapters the most famous passage in Tacitus's account of the growing intimidation, the prosecution of the old senator Cremutius Cordus, for political judgments that had been recorded in the text of his histories and read before Augustus at least twelve years earlier. Tacitus himself had lived through fifteen years under a similar loss of freedom of speech, but this episode provokes him to abandon his narrative for a personal expression of disgust at the oppression, the malice, and the mutual destructiveness of his own class that he was bound to record in this period.

What was Cremutius's offense? That he had in his *Annales* praised M. Brutus and called Cassius the last real Roman. The charge had been cooked up by clients of the rising menace, Sejanus, but provoked the fury of the emperor himself. Tacitus uses Cremutius's self-justification to recapitulate the loss of freedom of speech since the days of Livy (a notorious admirer of Pompey) and of Pollio and of Messala Corvinus, who had proudly called Cassius his commander. Leaving history behind, he adduces writing in other genres—the eulogy of the dead Cato by Cicero, the letters of Mark Antony,[2] the abusive lampoons of Catullus and Bibaculus against Julius and Augustus. Cremutius ends by protesting the right to honor the dead, and predicting that his own condemnation will preserve the memory not only of Brutus and Cassius but of his own life. Both Tacitus and Dio (57.24) reports the official burning of his books by the aediles at Rome and by relevant magistrates elsewhere. But secret copies were preserved, and republished, along with the banned works of Labienus and Cassius Severus, by the express edict of Caligula—though we may suspect the new emperor of acting in malice against his predecessor rather than love of liberty or respect for literature.[3]

Permissible Literature: Prose

In this climate one might have expected the complete cessation of prose writing, the medium of literature composed by and for the senatorial class. But the fifty years after the death of Augustus are represented by three surviving prose works, two of them Tiberian.

The universal history of Velleius Paterculus was composed under Tiberius and finished just before A.D. 30. Because the beginning of the work and a great deal of the first book is lost, we do not have his dedication or his professed reasons for attempting this work, but the books were dedicated to M. Vinicius, the consul of 30, and culminate in an extended and honorific account of Tiberius's military achievements, his rise to become Augustus's successor, and his principate up to that time. Velleius was a career officer who had served with Tiberius; thus he had genuine motives for loyalty and genuine knowledge of the campaigns that occupy the last third of his second and final book. In recent years the articles and editions of A. J. Woodman have caused a reconsideration of Velleius, both as a historian and in terms of his political purpose. Because the Roman histories that survived from the classical period consist either of short monographs on limited episodes or of large-scale multi-volume histories such as those of Livy, Tacitus, or the late Ammianus Marcellinus, scholars have misinterpreted the short "summary universal history" of Velleius as a derivative and hasty synopsis. They have tended to treat the account of Tiberius's military career, often dismissed as mere panegyric, as the purpose of the whole work, writing it off as tendentious rhetoric rather than historical record. Woodman has shown that Velleius's praises of the emperor are combined with a recognition that Tiberius's rule was deteriorating under the influence of Sejanus, and that Velleius praises his best of emperors (*princeps optimus*) in traditional but cautious language. This is a loyal history but not an official or a hollow one.[4] And it is in some sense an innovation, for it is the first known brief history since the *Chronica* of Nepos and *Annales* of Atticus eighty years previously.

Velleius has a special importance for those interested in Roman conceptions of literary history. In a separate excursus toward the end of the first book he surveys the achievements of Greece and Rome in literature and the arts, to argue that any genre of writing or painting or sculpture has a natural maturity, a period of one to two generations when it will blossom, then gradually fade, to be replaced by the flourishing of another art form. His survey, however brief, can serve as an index of cultural literacy (to borrow the term from E. D. Hirsch) in the age of Tiberius. Like Cornelius Nepos's *Chronica*, Velleius's earliest section uses Homer (dated to 920 B.C.), Hesiod (dated approximately to 800 B.C.), and Archilochus as significant representatives of the archaic period, and takes time to praise and rank Hesiod as second only to Homer in the authority of his work.

The word "authority" deserves a brief digression; it somewhat undertranslates what will become a key term in the reception of poets and prose writers during this age. *Auctoritas* had once meant the status that guaranteed the validity of a command; in the age of secondary writing and stylistic imitation, it came to cover the status of a writer conferring validity on facts and correctness on language found in his text. Canonical writers became *auctores*, and the modern popular usage of "author" derives from this time. What Velleius provides, here and in the longer passage we are about to examine, is a canon of the authors one was supposed to have read—or at least to take seriously.

A further question suggests itself. Canons can continue to receive lip service from a society that does not actually know the admired texts. How many of us actually read Nathaniel Hawthorne or Laurence Sterne? How many educated Romans actually read Greek poets, once they had read their quota of Homer at school?

It is quite possible, then, that Velleius borrowed his canon of Greek authors along with the whole theory of the rise and fall of the arts, and contributed only paraphrase to his presentation. Recent scholarship has tested his analogies between the Greek and Roman literary canons and observed that he seems to be adapting a Greek theorist who wrote from the point of view of third-century Athens: Velleius is fitting his Roman canon willy-nilly to a Greek model, which itself could usefully have been brought up to date.[5] His argument is that the most distinguished minds in each kind of art have lived and adopted the same genres within the same space of time: his examples are Greek tragedy, with its three great poets, and the canonical three poets of Greek Old Comedy, and three of New Comedy. Three is a fine number: did Velleius or his contemporaries know any plays by Eupolis and Cratinus, or Diphilus and Philemon? He adds that philosophy, which arose with Socrates, did not flourish after the deaths of Plato and Aristotle and that Greek oratory was concentrated around Isocrates and the generations of his pupils and those they taught.

But Velleius's Roman counterparts do not quite match: tragedy is centered on Accius (in fact the last successful tragedian of the republic), comedy on Caecilius, Terence, and Afranius in the same period. What has happened to Plautus and Ennius from the end of the third and turn of the second century? Is this a conscious exclusion, resulting from the criticism of archaic Latin voiced by Horace?

Velleius introduces the historians—not part of his Greek canon—and sees them as limited to a period of eighty years, ending with Livy. But Livy had been dead only fifteen years. Was Velleius sure historical writing was played out? Oratory, his last instance, is seen as only successful in the age of Cicero and of those who knew him. He attributes this pattern to the relationship between artistic success and imitation. When an art is rising, the younger generation imitates the old and advances beyond it; but once perfection has been reached, the successor generation in despair abandons imitation to find a new field for achievement. The borrowed theory found acceptance because it fitted the mood of the times. The elder Seneca too, whose retrospective account of declamatory rhetoric casts so much light on the social history of oratory in the age of Augustus,[6] writes in the same decade about the decline of oratory. It is less surprising that this old man, who knew Virgil, Livy, and Ovid, should be acutely aware of cultural decline. He assigns it partly to moral causes (the young are degenerate: you can tell by their dreadful clothes and hairstyles) and partly to the principle assumed by Velleius that the arts are organisms whose prime will inevitably be followed by decay.

Velleius's model did not include epic or lyric in his canon, since they were not an Athenian achievement (and could not be squeezed into a neat generation or two), so Velleius does not mention Virgil or Horace here. But a second installment of cultural history lists the great talents that flourished in the years since the birth of Augustus—the many orators, Sallust, imitator of Thucydides, and poets such as Lucretius, Varro of Atax, who adapted the *Argonautica*, and Catullus. In last place "the great men of our own age" comprise Virgil, the princeps of poets (remember what the word now meant to Romans) Rabirius (!), Livy, Tibullus, and Naso, "each of whom achieved perfection in his own genre." The inclusion of Rabirius, author of a now lost epic on the Actium campaign, and omission of Propertius and Horace show the Roman bias of Velleius's literary judgment. Epic was serious, and Rabirius wrote on the Roman theme of the civil war; even Tibullus had written poems honoring the general Messala, and the cult of Palatine Apollo. Lyric poetry and Alexandrianizing elegy required learning, concentration, and imaginative interpretation, and were usually on private rather than public themes. They were not "major" or serious genres, nor was satire, or better *sermo*: hence, even Horace goes unmentioned.[7]

One work of prose in this generation is dedicated to Tiberius himself: the collection of *Memorable Deeds and Sayings* of Valerius Maximus. Let his words stand as a sample of imperial "newspeak" little known to classicists who read literature for its merit, not its significance as a cultural document.

> So I invoke you, Caesar, to aid my undertaking; you, in whose hands the unanimous approval of gods and men has chosen to place the control of earth and sea, you the surest salvation of our country. By your heavenly foresight the virtues of which I will write are most kindly fostered and the vices more severely punished. For if the orators of old did well to start with Jupiter Optimus Maximus, if the most distinguished poets made their beginning with some deity, it is all the more proper that my puny talent [*parvitas* (!)] has taken refuge in your favor, in which as men believe all other divinity is subsumed, and which equals through your ready protection your father's and grandfather's divine stars, whose brilliance has conferred much noble distinction upon our ceremonies. For we inherited the other gods but have given the Caesars as our legacy. (Prologus 1)

What Valerius has composed, or rather assembled, chiefly from Cicero and Livy, is a collection of edifying anecdotes under appropriate headings, each first narrated, then rounded off with a moral. A sample is the chapter on Chastity, which begins by addressing the deity, then records celebrated examples of chastity, including Lucretia and Verginia, then instances of unchastity properly punished by Roman fathers or public condemnation. Here, and in other chapters, he follows Roman examples with a few stories of foreign vice or virtue. These are a Greek matron who jumped into the Red Sea to escape capture by the enemy, a captive Gaulish queen who killed the centurion who had raped her and presented his head to her husband (the story comes from Livy), and some captive Teuton wives who killed themselves when Marius would not allow them to become Vestal Virgins. The book is not literature and cannot be read continuously: rather it is a reference work for orators, or more likely declaimers, needing precedents for the subjects of their speeches. But it is also an index for students of the conventional images left by past Roman history, and his anecdotes reappear with the same moral coloring or conclusions in subsequent prose and poetry. The citation of Greek and other foreign examples formalizes a practice observable in earlier oratory and poetry; the Roman traditionally would support his arguments with both Greek and Roman parallels. Both the matching of Greek and Roman and the use of comparison as a medium of moral or literary criticism were Roman ways of thinking, features taught in the composition of encomium and to be found in earlier rhetoric and history. Thus Cicero's impersonation of Cato the Elder in *De Senectute* follows each instance of exemplary behavior by a Greek with a corresponding and, if possible, more impressive deed or saying by a Roman worthy. Explicit paralleling of Greek and Roman deeds and lives goes back to Cicero's contemporary Cornelius Nepos, whose collection of exempla in three volumes is lost, but who followed the alternating pattern of Greek and Roman lives in his eighteen volumes of brief lives of *viri illustres*—"famous men," including historians, poets, orators, philosophers, and generals. It has been convincingly argued by Joseph Geiger that the extant book of foreign generals is an addendum to the sequence of Greek and Roman figures in all preceding books.[8] Valerius seems to use the same categories as Cornelius Nepos, but reverses from the chronological order of setting Greek before Roman, to the Romanocentric arrangement, which follows the main Roman model anecdotes with shorter *externa*, both Greek and barbarian (Persian or Carthaginian) material, drawn from Greek or Roman texts. The Roman habit of implicit or explicit consideration of domestic and Greek material and the construction of parallel biographies become explicit in Plutarch's *Parallel Lives*, many of which even follow the independent biographies of his paired Greek and Roman heroes—say, Alexander and Caesar, or Dion and Marcus Brutus—with a short comparison of the virtues and vices of the two subjects.

But competitive comparison with Greece was endemic in Roman historical writing. Even Livy interrupts his national history after

Rome's defeat by the Samnites in book 9 to argue that if Alexander had turned his armies west toward Italy, the Romans would have beaten his expeditionary force because of their moral and professional superiority.

The Romans had long been obsessed with Alexander. Both Caesar and Pompey had imitated the world conqueror and been compared with him by their admirers. Alexander was a favorite hero of the declamations, and his history was adapted and elaborated at some time during the early principate in a romanticized narrative of ten books by Quintus Curtius Rufus. Its date is disputed, but both Pliny and Tacitus know of a Curtius Rufus, governor of Africa in the reign of Claudius (A.D. 41–54) and both its theme and its style— similar to Velleius and Valerius—lead me to treat the history of Alexander as a work of this period. The safe antiquity of fourth-century Greece was another outlet for the aspiring historian, its material free of dangerous political reference and with a geographical appeal to the increased Roman knowledge of the remote Asian hinterland. This is history as entertainment, based on the Hellenistic recipe of exotic marvels, gallant deeds, and the human interest of swiftly changing fortune and a tragic end.

Moral Treatises and Letters

Velleius, Valerius, and Curtius all came from outside the senatorial class and, in different ways, escaped the risk attached to contemporary history. It was also still fairly safe to compose treatises on personal morality. Besides the Greek writings of Roman moralists like Q. Sextius, Papirius Fabianus, or the later Musonius Rufus, there still survive the philosophical "dialogues"9 of the younger Seneca. Several of these were written during the exile imposed on him in the first eight years of Claudius's principate, others after his return, perhaps even during the rule of Nero. Seneca's three works of consolation for bereavement, to his mother, to Marcia (daughter of Cremutius Cordus), and to Polybius, the powerful freedman secretary of Claudius, all belong to the Claudian principate, as may his dialogue *On Anger* in three books. But some later dialogues, the extended study of social obligations known as *De Beneficiis*, and the multivolume philosophical correspondence (*Epistulae Morales*) with Lucilius, reflect Seneca's concern with private ethics in the time of Nero, during his years as an active imperial adviser, and then in retirement after A.D. 62.

The body of letters, dated to his last years in retirement, raises the issue of the role of the letter in Roman society. How did this essentially private act become a literary genre, adopted by writers of both prose and verse? We must assume some Roman familiarity with formalized "letters"—better perhaps called epistles—to generate anything as artificial as Seneca's thematically unified series of protreptic letters to his real-life friend.

Despite hints of the letter form in the early satirist Lucilius, and the versified letters of Spurius Mummius from the same period of the second century,[10] Cicero himself is the first author to leave a body of real-life correspondence. His eight hundred and more extant letters included practical business letters of recommendation and solicitation as well as intimate, sometimes daily letters to Atticus, Quintus, Terentia, and Tiro, more social letters to acquaintances, and political or quasi-diplomatic communications to Pompey, Cato, and various leading senators.

While it was normal to keep copies of important letters, and even to circulate them deliberately,[11] Cicero does not speak of publishing any collection until the last years of his life, when the selection of seventy letters mentioned to Tiro probably consisted of formal letters of recommendation—intended to serve as a model for others to imitate.[12] After Cicero's contemporary Nepos, Seneca will be the first writer to cite Cicero's letters,[13] and it is possible that recognition of the great statesman's correspondence influenced Seneca's choice of this paraliterary form to frame his personal exhortations to Lucilius in circumstantial contexts. Most of Seneca's early letters are grounded in place and occasion; only the last sequence of much longer and doctrinally more complex letters abandons the sense of occasion for more systematic ethical argument.

But what had intervened in the century from 43 B.C. to the 60s? We hear from Nepos of a constant exchange of letters between Atticus and Octavian, but only for purely day-to-day personal enjoyment. Later, indeed, as Augustus, Octavian would even ask Maecenas to let Horace serve as his secretary, but this can hardly imply that Horace would have ghost-written standard letters as modern speech writers compose presidential speeches. There were experienced imperial secretaries, slaves or freedmen, for such work. Better, I think, to imagine the position in part as pretext for sharing his working day with Horace and enriching his distracted mind with Horace's thought and language for correspondence with peers and men of letters. Horace might have helped to compose particularly delicate or important communications: it is perhaps significant that Augustus's intimate letters to his family have an easy tone that would be congenial to Horace. It was about this time (20 B.C.) that Horace published his first collections of *Epistles*, letters addressed to friends young and old in the relaxed hexameter verse developed by Roman satire. But their meter and relative unity of theme distinguished them from the "real" letters for private sharing of news and views. The affably presented moral themes of several of Horace's letters might well have provided Seneca with a stimulus for adopting the letter form, but it is more likely to have originated with Greek letters of Epicurus on moral themes, from which Seneca cites in the first books of his letters.

One other form of letter, the elegiac letters of Ovid written from exile, is important for its role in broadening the personal reference of Roman elegy to the sorrows of exile. But, despite the epistolary form and real addressees and requests of Ovid's *Letters from Pontus*, Ovid shapes most of them as vehicles for narrative, descriptive and programmatic "poetic" themes. It would be legitimate to doubt the influence of these collections on either Seneca's systematic ethical letters or the autobiographically focused letters of Pliny.

It is more remarkable that so few authors are known to have crafted literary letters in these years when political duress might have recommended the composition of polished vignettes from strictly neutral private life. The answer perhaps comes from the sheer abundance of minor poetic forms available to convey personal experience, all attested by Pliny's correspondence as practiced among educated men. We shall return to these personal forms in Chapter 6.

Didactic and Descriptive Poetry

Despite the emerging tradition of ethical prose writing on personal themes, prose at Rome was primarily a vehicle for comment on public life, and the preferred vehicle during the republic. The age of Augustus, from the confident poetry of his first decade to the elegiac celebrations included among Ovid's poetry of exile, found in poetry a more flexible medium for panegyric, since its command of mythology and tropes such as hyperbole lent itself more easily to praises not warranted by achievement. But neither Tiberius nor his two successors, Gaius (Caligula) and Claudius, seem to have invited panegyric. The evidence we have already considered warrants Ahl's assessment, that "Tiberius, Gaius and Claudius seem to have been more interested in stifling dissent than encouraging poetic panegyric or poetry at all."[14]

Many writers of this period chose to practice poetry, less from inspiration than because its subject matter was safe, offering a better prospect of writing without fear or dissimulation. In the period from the end of Augustus's rule to around A.D. 60, the gentleman in retirement or at leisure might indulge in the scholarly study of poetry like the professional grammaticus, or pursue its composition. This took two very different forms: the didactic poem and the mythological drama. However, the complex relationship between the drama and the theater makes it advisable to postpone consideration of dramatic writing, treating it after we have considered the composition of learned poetry and the evidence for the practice and prestige of literary learning in this period.

Much ancient didactic poetry was really scientific, or concerned with the workings or the marvels of nature. Two poetic works on the movement of the stars date from the principate of Tiberius and were at least partly dedicated to him. This was very fitting, since his interest in astrology was intense and fostered by his personal astronomer-astrologer Thrasyllus. The prince Germanicus, Tiberius's adoptive son, probably began his version of Aratus's astronomical and meteorological poems in the lifetime of Augustus; he would die in A.D. 19, leaving a fairly complete version of both poems. The proem to the emperor may well have been added late in composition, like the few lines alluding to the death of Augustus.[15] It followed the tradition established by Virgil's *Georgics* of appealing to the emperor for inspiration:

> Aratus began with great Jupiter; my poem, however, Father, claims you, greatest of all, as its inspirer. It is you that I reverence; it is to you that I am offering sacred gifts, the firstfruits of my literary efforts. The ruler and begetter of the gods himself approves. . . . May your presence and the peace you have won aid your son; grant your divine power to favor me as I attempt to tell of this in Latin verse. (1–5, 15–16, trans. Gain)

The poem is something more than a translation, making some correction of astronomical errors and including one powerful new excursus on the flight of personified Justice from the earth. But it is essentially an educated man's exercise in adaptation, not the work of an independent poet.

The other work partly dedicated to Tiberius is the *Astronomica*, a poem in five books by the Stoic Manilius. Although Manilius's work is difficult for modern readers because of their ignorance of astronomy, it can be both powerful and moving. Not simply an astronomical handbook, it is concerned to explain astrology and the control of human destiny by the stars. This was a serious component of Stoic philosophy, to which Manilius adhered, and the poet more than once combines pride in the importance of his theme with protests at the staleness and triviality of traditional poetic material.[16] But the power of the stars was a preoccupation of both Augustus, who propagated stories about his conception under Capricorn and used it as his device on coins and cameos, and of Tiberius, his heir. The first book is explicitly dedicated to Augustus and followed by further loyal allusions, but by book 4, Augustus is apparently dead and Manilius turns his compliments to Tiberius:[17]

> Beneath the chaste maid [Virgo] Rhodes prospers on land and sea, the erstwhile abode of him who was to rule the world as emperor; the whole island is consecrated to the Sun, and Rhodes was in very truth its house at the time, when it received into its care the light of the mighty universe in the person of Caesar. (4.763–66)

Two lines below, Libra, the sign of Tiberius's birth, is praised for its beneficence: "what sign could better have the care of Italy, if Italy could choose, than that which controls all?"

Didactic poetry was safe, it was moral, it was learned: was it also read? We should add in passing the poem of Grattius on hunting—already known to Ovid in his last years[18]—and a poem of over six hundred lines speculating on the physical causes of the Sicilian volcano, the *Aetna*, a learned poem full of mythology. The latter must have been written well before A.D. 64, for Seneca will tell his correspondent Lucilius in that year that the subject of Aetna has been treated *more than once*; again, the poet's reference to the coastal region of Naples as safe and Vesuvius as long inactive (432) must have preceded the earthquake of A.D. 62. Propertius and Ovid had both toyed with the notion of writing poetry about nature, and the early first century saw continued speculation in prose. Seneca's *Natural Questions* and Pliny's *Natural History* give special attention to earthquakes and volcanic action.[19] These poems are surely more a product of the cultural climate than an influence upon it.

My last example of didactic poetry combines the old Roman function of utility with the new emulation of Virgil. Columella, who ends the preface to his *De Re Rustica* (*On Agriculture*) with an optimistic version of the arguments in Velleius and Seneca about the problems of postclassicism, wrote eleven books on farming and stock breeding in literary prose. I have included this author among the would-be poets because he turned to poetry for his tenth book, adopting Virgilian hexameters to describe the garden. Columella justifies this (quite competent) poetic account of the flower garden as composed out of piety toward Virgil, who in *Georgics* 4 had regretted that for lack of space he must leave the art of flower growing for other poets to record.[20] But Columella surely adopted verse because he wanted to try his skill, although he presents this in the preface to book 10 as compliance with the *vates venerandus* (the revered poet). With imitative reverence his survey concludes with a closure recalling *Eclogues* 3 and a four-line coda adapting key phrases from the *Georgics*; in final place he sets his own version of Virgil's famous claim in the "Praises of Italy"[21] that he "dared to open up the springs and sing a Hesiodic song through Roman cities." Columella's literary piety is representative of the times.

The Scholar, the Gentleman, and the Pretender

We know that from his own lifetime Virgil's work was taught by the grammatici and quoted in the schools of declamation. Some examples of Virgilian scholarship from this period are the lost defense of Virgil against his detractors (*Contra Obtrectatores Vergilii*) by Asconius Pedianus, whose learned commentary on Cicero's speeches survives in part as evidence of his high standards as a scholar;[22] the critical notebooks of Annaeus Cornutus reported by Aulus Gellius;[23] and the boastful Remmius Palaemon, who claimed that Virgil had foretold his own coming with the name of his shepherd judge Palaemon in the *Eclogues*. If we move ahead some twenty years we come to Suetonius's last grammaticus, Valerius Probus of Beirut who devoted his life to editorial and critical work on the texts of Virgil and other authors.[24]

But new knowledge drives out old. When Romans began to make their own literature a large part of their schooling, what happened to the Greek literature that had previously been the substance of their poetic and rhetorical education? There are no signs of a reduced knowledge of Greek literature until perhaps the generation born under Tiberius. Because the emperors' literary culture and knowledge of Greek is given special attention in Suetonius's *Lives of the Caesars*, we can use them as individuals to illustrate the scope of contemporary Greek studies and compare each one with his successor.

Tastes and Prejudices of Augustus's Imperial Successors

Tiberius himself was exceptionally well educated, as was the emperor Claudius, born in 22 B.C., in contrast with Caligula, born a generation later than his uncle Claudius, although he preceded him in imperial power. Tiberius was a purist in Latin, a follower of Messala Corvinus, and fastidious in his use of language.[25] In Greek he must have received a similar education to his contemporary Ovid, and he studied rhetoric with the Greek rhetorician Theodorus of Gadara; he would spend a further seven years in informal adult education with Greek academic companions as a resident in Greek Rhodes. But more to the point was his consuming interest in Greek poetry and in *grammatikē*, which dealt with the form and content of poetry. His favorite poets were the immensely learned and allusive Alexandrians Euphorion, Rhianus, and Parthenius, although he was surely too young to have known Parthenius in person. He also composed poetry in both Latin and Greek: a Latin elegy for Lucius Caesar (in A.D. 4) and Greek poems in imitation of his Alexandrian models. Suetonius reports that he insisted on introducing the works and busts of these Greek poets into the public libraries with the great authors of the day.[26]

Apparently Tiberius was as much a pedant as a lover of poetry; he spent his leisure and provided his dinner party entertainment by interrogating Greek grammatici about mythological trivia such as "what name Achilles took among the maidens" and "what songs the sirens sang."[27] When one grammarian, nervous of failure, tried to sneak advance information from the domestics about the *auctores* (not just writers, but the right writers) that Tiberius was reading at the time, he was detected and dismissed, to commit suicide soon after.

Despite his fluency in Greek, Tiberius observed etiquette and did not use Greek in the Senate; he even tried to avoid the use of Greek technical terms like *monopolium* and *emblema* in Latin. Here certainly is a man whose practice, however tiresome, would encourage the continued study of Greek as a working language and a cultural medium. Caligula, in contrast, expressed open contempt for Greek and Roman writers, both living and dead,[28] and was chiefly an innovator in setting up contests in Greek and Roman oratory at Syracuse (a Greek-speaking city) and Lyons. This is the first instance of a pattern that will be repeated with Nero—a capricious emperor sponsoring public displays in the literary arts[29]— but Caligula merely embarrassed the contestants, making the losers compose speeches praising the winners or, in extreme cases, delete their own words with a sponge or their tongue.

Claudius, always represented as a figure of fun, seems to have been seen as only fit for scholarship, and was deliberately kept occupied in research and writing by his concerned parents. Livy had suggested he apply himself to history, and he was helped in his *History of Rome from the Death of Caesar* by Sulpicius Flavus. But his honesty incurred constant reproaches from Livia, so that he skipped the years from 44 B.C. to Actium and started again— leaving forty-three books. He spoke Greek easily[30] and chose to write his long eight-volume history of Carthage and his twenty volumes on the Etruscan nation in Greek, not Latin. Was this to reach a wider public, or because he saw these books as ethnographies in the tradition of Posidonius? Or was he simply excerpting, lifting his learning from Posidonius and earlier Greeks? Claudius seems also to have been interested in poetry and *grammatikē*. It is perhaps unfair to draw inferences from a parody, but in Seneca's brilliant satire, the *Apocolocuntosis*, or *Pumpkinification*, of Claudius, composed after his death, the emperor quotes Homer at the drop of a hat, and when Heracles accosts him in Homeric language he is delighted to find *philologos homines* (scholarly types) among the gods.

Perhaps the phrase *philologi homines*, like *auctores*, is another clue to the changing role of Greek literature from being the educated man's pleasure and inspiration to serving as a hobby for the pedantic. The ordinary Roman would know the Greek of the theater and snack bar (the *thermipolium* was the Roman ancestor of the *bar* and *tavola calda* in Italian towns). Most of the wealthier classes and all the imperial slaves and freedmen would command the working Greek of the accountant and administrator. They would still expect their client philosophers and teachers of rhetoric to be Greek; though Seneca the Elder can quote Roman philosophers from the time of Augustus, many of these adopted the Greek language for their writings. The same men of leisure who declaimed and composed poetry and memoirs would include Greek authors with Roman among the readings offered to their guests, and quite a few might have a Greek book collection to match their Latin library.

The body of philosophical letters addressed by Seneca to his friend Lucilius and composed in 64–65, the last two years of his life, show both the range of current learning and the educated man's regard for Virgil, which we have already seen attested in so many ways. As a moralist Seneca turns to Virgil for illustrations of human struggle and inspiration. Naturally he uses Virgil's Aeneas, anxiously fleeing from Troy with his father, son, and wife, as his example of the fears caused by responsibility for others;[31] in another letter he quotes Virgil's description in *Georgics* 3 of the thoroughbred war horse as a model for the man of real courage, and a parallel for his own Stoic hero, Cato of Utica.[32] Most interesting for our purposes, is a late letter (108.23–30) in which Seneca describes how his educated contemporaries read literature. His own ideal was, of course, the moral reading, but he found that students eager to please their teachers were missing the moral focus, and substituting cultivation of the intellect for that of the character.

This particularly significant letter distinguishes between the uses to which different types of instructor would put great literature: Seneca illustrates from Virgil and from Cicero how three kinds of scholar, the grammaticus, the *philologus*, and the philosopher would read a text. Taking Virgil's famous half line on the irreversible flight of time (*Georg.* 3.284), he shows that the future grammaticus would pass over the moral of making good use of one's life. Instead he would be interested in the frequency with which Virgil used the verb *fugere* (to flee) in this context, and would cite a parallel passage to illustrate his literary argument.[33] Seneca's second illustration cites from a prose classic of political theory, Cicero's *On the Republic*, a section now lost, in which Cicero reported the Greek Carneades' case against the utility of justice. Once again the academics would be diverted from the moral challenge of this passage; a grammaticus would make comments on changes in word form and usage (our morphology and semantics), and he would proudly quote from the early poet Ennius models for both the Ciceronian and Virgilian passages. (Here Seneca is surely showing off his own literary education, not so very different from education in the classics a generation ago.) The *philologus*, a relatively uncommon term,[34] would seek antiquarian learning about the history of Roman institutions and religious practice. This was the education and culture typical of Seneca's age.

The social pressure to display literary culture seems to have been so great that even uneducated men tried to conform. According to Seneca, Calvisius Sabinus, who wanted to seem an educated man, had a terrible memory, especially for names, so he bought slaves who knew Greek poetry by heart. (Seneca adds that they had to be commissioned and trained, so it cost him a great deal.) One slave "knew" Homer, another Hesiod, and nine others knew each of the nine lyric poets (more canons! And Seneca is clearly improving on the original story). At dinners Sabinus would start to quote verse with a slave at his side to prompt him, and still dry up in midverse. Finally a friend urged him to have grammatici as readers instead. These would be able to interpret and comment on the poetry as well as reading it, whereas Calvisius's slaves were simply native Greek speakers who had memorized the poetry parrot fashion; Calvisius claimed that they cost him a hundred thousand sesterces[35] a head. He would have no use for the books that his friend said he could have bought far more cheaply than the slaves, since he did not want to enjoy the texts, but to display them to his dinner guests.

Does the Calvisius story—whether fact or plausible fiction—tell us anything about the relationship between literature and entertainment? It shows that literary recitation was expected as part of a social evening. If one hired readers trained in literature—grammatici in this sense—they would surely bring their own books. Could Calvisius not have invited freeborn grammatici in return for a meal or a standard client's gift?

Perhaps it is foolish to try to deduce social customs from an obvious deviant like Calvisius, but there must have been many like him, who rose to wealth without education and needed to keep up with the Annaei. Many detailed pictorial representations of the *Iliad* and other poems of the Homeric cycle on miniature stone reliefs have been found in Italy; these identify each book of the epic with summary titles and individual scenes in which the characters too are labeled. It has been suggested that these intricate and expensive pieces of work served as cultural aids or display for such householders.[36] They would simultaneously remind the owner of the action of the *Iliad* and declare to his guests that he was a man of culture.

The most famous example of this kind of ignorance is the freedman Trimalchio in Petronius's picaresque novel, *The Satyricon*. He went as far as to buy his own libraries in bulk, but clearly did not consult them. It is Trimalchio who tells his guest that a piece of silver plate represents "Daedalus locking up Niobe in the Trojan horse." Even the works of art of this period usually required a minimal knowledge of Homer and other sources of Greek mythology. The ordinary man could absorb this from his school years with the grammaticus and then get on with the business of making money. The educated man may have had as much boredom as pleasure from the social role of such literary lore, but he would continue as an adult to hear, if not to read, the major Greek and Roman poets and to use literary quotation as a social grace, in the way that we allude to best-selling novels or plays from the New York and London theaters.

The Divergence of Theater and Drama

So far we have said nothing of drama or the theater, categories that usually overlap, but which ceased to be coextensive during this period. Despite Horace's careful instructions to the Pisos, father and sons, in the epistolary poem usually called the *Ars Poetica*, serious tragedy was becoming less frequent at Rome, and it is unlikely that any satyr plays were composed or performed.[37] The record of known tragedies is significant. Q. Varius was commissioned by Augustus for an immense sum to write his tragedy *Thyestes* for the games celebrating Augustus's triumph in 29 B.C. Quintilian a century later declares that it can compete with any Greek tragedy, but it has not survived.[38] Ovid also wrote a tragedy, the *Medea*, from which one line survives, quoted by Quintilian: "I was able to save [you]: do you ask whether I can destroy [you]?" (Quint. 8.5.6). In his critical survey Quintilian is more restrained about Ovid's *Medea* than in his enthusiasm for Varius's play, commenting that this shows how much Ovid could have achieved, if he had preferred to control his talent rather than indulge it.[39] It seems clear that Ovid's play was never staged, and likely that he intended it only for a concert performance.

So what was happening in those three magnificent stone the-

145

aters, the theater of Pompey opened in 55 B.C., that of Marcellus, finished by Augustus, and that of Balbus from the same period? The spectators of tragedy in Horace's letter to the emperor Augustus (*Epist.* 2.1.199–207) roar so loud that the playwright's script cannot be heard, and burst into applause at the leading actor's fine purple cloak, before he has said a word.

Horace may well have underestimated the unruly behavior of theater audiences. Even during the reign of Augustus it had been necessary to introduce new seating regulations into the theater to protect rank and ensure order. Suetonius reports that Augustus was so upset when a senator was denied a seat in the crowded theater of fashionable Puteoli on the Campanian riviera that he required the front row of seats to be reserved for senators. The wealthier class of knights already had privileged seating in the next fourteen rows, and he set aside the range behind them for the married male citizens. As for those who were not male citizens, Augustus excluded foreign envoys from their previous seats in the orchestra, prohibited noncitizens and the poor from sitting in the mezzanine,[40] secluded young boys and their attendants in a separate segment of the auditorium, and relegated women to the rear range of seats, comparable to our upper balcony in distance from the stage.[41]

It is difficult to guess what Horace's inattentive audience was watching—perhaps revivals of Pacuvius or Accius.[42] But rather than straight tragedy and comedy, the theater would be most often filled for two less literary dramatic forms: the mime, which had largely displaced ancient comedy, and the performance of the pantomimes.[43]

Although Augustus was very fond of the old-style comedy, Plautus and Terence were probably presented infrequently, and Menander, the model writer of Greek New Comedy, had become an exercise for young students of rhetoric, who were trained by a comic actor to present their speeches with style and conviction.[44] Such comedy might be offered as entertainment in private parties. What the great Roman public loved were the mimes, based on a literary libretto but deriving most of their excitement from stage business and unscripted improvisation. Given the fixed nature of the mime plots, the role of the scriptwriter can never have been very important, and the fact that the only substantial fragments of mime authors to survive date from the age of Sulla and Julius Caesar suggests that subsequent scripts were being submerged by striptease, knockabout, and comic action.

Tragedy fared little better in the theater. The passion of the audience was devoted to the dancers, the pantomimes, for whom the singing itself was usually supplied by a chorus. Already in Augustus's time the feuds of pantomime artists like Bathyllus and Hylas caused public riots, and Tacitus's *Annals* trace the recurrence of the theatrical riot as a social phenomenon.[45] Tiberius did not have Augustus's authority or his love of the theater, and in A.D. 15, after the crowd had broken up into factions, abused the magistrates, and killed some soldiers and a centurion, not to mention some of their fellow spectators, he brought the situation before the Senate. The senatorial solution was to give praetors the right to flog the dancers,[46] but when they realized that Augustus had once officially forbidden this, they shifted to punishing the spectators.

Readers who assume something on the lines of the violent English football (soccer) fans, mostly underprivileged and unemployed, should think over the remedies announced. It was forbidden for any senator to visit a pantomime dancer's house, and for any Roman knight to escort one in public, or to watch the dancers except in the public theater. To crown it all, the magistrates were authorized to penalize the spectators with exile. Tacitus is talking about upper-class misbehavior and upper-class penalties. But the explanation for the riots was probably the same as for the modern football rioters. Fanatical support for public entertainers becomes a substitute satisfaction for a class that has lost its function and its self-respect.

Other notices of theatrical riots show that fans of rival artists were not the only trigger to violence. In A.D. 20 a noble woman accused of adultery and poisoning raised a claque of supporters who created a riot by their loud laments in the theater, provoking the spectators to boo and curse the aggrieved husband. Three years later the emperor himself brought before the senate the wanton behavior of the pantomime dancers (*Ann.* 4.14), who were riotous in public and created scandals in private homes. The time had come to make an example of them, and they were expelled from Italy. But ten years later, even without dancers to quarrel over, there was angry rioting in the theater over a shortage of the free corn supplied by the imperial administration to the city populace (*Ann.* 6.13). Tacitus's record is lost for the years of Caligula and early years of Claudius, but in 47 Claudius issued fierce edicts against theatrical rioting after an incident in which the crowd had insulted the dramatist Q. Pomponius. Tacitus adds that this man wrote tragedies for staging, the first and only definite evidence for a contemporary writer of stage drama since the *Thyestes* of Varius. Had new tragedies and comedies been staged all this time? Or were they brought back when the dancers were banned? This is the only evidence for a playwright being abused; perhaps it attracted imperial intervention because of Pomponius's exceptional distinction. He was a senator of praetorian rank and noble connections,[47] awarded triumphal regalia in A.D. 50 for his successful command in Germany.

To round off the account of theatrical rioting we should look ahead to what happened when Nero came to power. In his first year he decreed the removal of the customary military guard (mentioned in the affair of A.D. 15) to a distance to keep the soldiers free from joining in the rioting of spectators and to see whether the populace would behave more decently without a guard detachment. But the next year Nero himself fomented a renewal of the brawling among the fan groups of the performers, turning them into pitched battles by granting indulgence and rewards for rioting. At first he watched and reveled in the battles until he too was alarmed by their violence, and resorted to a new expulsion of the dancers from Italy and the restoration of the guard.[48] But another episode from this year shows that the upper classes were still contributing to the disorder; the praetor running the games had taken some riotous fans into custody, when a tribune overrode the praetor's orders and set them free. The Senate acquiesced but censured the tribune and removed the old established right of tribunes to intervene in the actions of other magistrates. The theater had become an outlet for the frustrations of all the classes.

In the republic young aristocrats had whiled away their leisure by translating or composing tragedies; from various sources we know of the tragedies of the magistrate Caesar Strabo, Julius Caesar the dictator's early *Oedipus*, Quintus Cicero's four tragedies composed in two weeks of winter quarters in Gaul, and young Octavian's *Ajax*. The prince Germanicus even wrote comedies in Greek, but there is no hint that these plays were performed in public.[49] Only one nobleman is known to have composed a tragedy in the time of Tiberius and it cost him dearly. Aemilius Mamercus Scaurus wrote an *Atreus*, on the theme of the tyrannical ruler of Argos who recalled his brother Thyestes and fed him a cannibal meal of his own sons. According to Dio, a character in the play declared that one must endure the follies of the reigning prince; Tacitus reports that the prefect of the guard Macro denounced Scaurus for verses that could be turned against Tiberius.[50] Scaurus, who was also accused of adultery and magical practices, anticipated condemnation by suicide.[51]

Scaurus's play does not seem to have been performed on the public stage, but for every verse tragedy (or, indeed, comedy) there were potentially four modes of presentation: it could be staged in the public theater like the ill-received drama of Pomponius; it could be staged in a private setting,[52] since many great houses had theatrical spaces, used for a variety of purposes; it could be recited by one or more performers; or it could be read aloud to an individual or a group at dinner. There was also plenty of opportunity for individual friends of the author to read a text in private.[53]

Pomponius was a literary dramatist; he cared about language and he recited his plays to his friends. We can deduce this from Pliny the Younger's story of Pomponius answering his friends' criticism at a recitation, with the retort that he would "appeal to the people"—this constitutional echo of the old republican legal procedure would neatly describe a public performance. But another piece of evidence also brings him into contact with the only extant tragic writer of our period, with the younger Seneca. Quintilian describes how Pomponius and Seneca exchanged critical views in the spoken introductions to recitations of their plays. They were disputing over the use of archaic language, which Seneca largely avoided in his tragedies, and over a particular phrase not found in Seneca.[54] C. Cichorius,[55] who was first to establish the context of this exchange, deduced that it was Pomponius who favored archaisms; no wonder the common people booed his tragedies! Unfortunately the only evidence for his actual writing is a single word cited from a play, *Aeneas.* He is also cited for his possession of an ancient manuscript of Gaius Gracchus—another mark of his interest in archaism—and for correspondence on theatrical matters with the Stoic Paetus Thrasea, who performed as an amateur tragic actor in the local games of Patavium. So Pomponius is shown to be a learned member of the senatorial intelligentsia.

But the report of his disagreement with Seneca also helps to date Seneca's own interest in drama. Since Quintilian says this happened when Seneca was already distinguished, the debate must be dated after Pomponius's return from his tour of duty in Germany and Seneca's return from exile in A.D. 49. This supports the assumption that Seneca wrote at least some of his tragedies before his restoration from exile. It is difficult to see how he would have leisure to write as Nero's tutor and counselor after 49, but recent opinion based on changes in his language and versification argues for the possibility that the last plays, *Thyestes* and the incomplete *Phoenissae*, were written considerably after the others, perhaps after Seneca's self-imposed retirement in 62.

Did Seneca's plays carry a contemporary political message? Several of the tragedies (*Oedipus*, and *Thyestes* in particular) deal with family scandals that had their equivalent in the life of Nero, and it has been a popular suggestion that the plays were allegories of the dynastic scandals of incest and murder, and were even written for the pleasure of informed friends who would delight in the loaded topical allusions of these plays. There is a particular tendency among those who enjoy the liberty of American democracy to suppose that Romans would risk their necks by composing heavily allusive political dramas even under suspicious and tyrannical emperors. Seneca would not have risked public knowledge of politically loaded scripts. He had suffered exile once, and was too near to the court and too experienced to expose himself to the fate of a Scaurus. Several of his tragedies would not have been safe for presentation even within his own household. Slaves had ears and were everywhere ready to inform.

I have argued elsewhere on the basis of the texts themselves that these were not stage plays.[56] The discontinuity of scenes within Senecan tragedy and other problems of hasty entrances and exits made them unsuitable for stage performance and show that Seneca did not intend them for this medium. It is true that any dramatic text can be staged with a change of conventions and with modern technology. Nor was ancient technology behind when it came to stage devices for public shows. But the very nature of these texts is literary rather than theatrical; it requires them to be heard or read as a tour de force of language and of verbal acting. Even in recitation it is likely that the continuous speeches rather than the swift exchange of dialogue or transitions between scenes would be chosen for presentation: such continuity of framework as Seneca provides would work best in written form.

These tragedies soon had imitators—at least one adaptation of the history of Nero's own time, the *Octavia*, was composed soon after the deaths of both Seneca and Nero, and includes Seneca himself in its cast, acting as an unsuccessful advocate of restraint. We may have evidence for another contemporary dramatist if *Hercules on Oeta*, another script preserved with the Senecan tragedies, is not by Seneca, but a pastiche of themes and ideas from his surviving plays.[57]

It is likely, then, that literary tragedy had ceased to appear on the public stage well before the time of Nero; the stage had been taken over by the pantomime artists, and tragedy had become another form of poetry to be recited among friends. But the separation of professional and amateur was unstable, and the turning point in stage history came when the young Nero first reached beyond the guidance of Seneca and his other adviser, Burrhus, prefect of the guard, and took the first tentative step toward his later theatrical extravagances.

In A.D. 60 Nero established a new Quinquennial Games, based on the Greek model. Tacitus accompanies this innovation with a kind of public critical debate, giving in paired chapters, *Annals* 14.20 and 21, the arguments of those approving and disapproving of the games. Despite the horror that will be shown by Tacitus and Suetonius as Nero cast off decorum to embark on an artificial career as a citharode and impose his singing on captive audiences, Tacitus is fair to the relatively sober and intellectually demanding Quinquennial Games—the *Neronia* as they would be called. He gives the advantage to the arguments of those accepting the games as a new contribution to the history of the theatre at Rome. These were to be contests in oratory and poetry,[58] both tests of the ability to compose and to perform. And as Tacitus relates, they passed off without disgrace, not even rousing mild partisanship from the common people, who probably stayed away, since the pantomime artists were no longer allowed in the public *ludi*.

No one won the prize for oratory, but Nero was pronounced the victor. It is probable that the prize for poetry was won by the first public performance of a new poet: the *Praises of Nero* by Annaeus Lucanus, the nephew of Seneca and an official "friend" of the young emperor.[59] In the next few years, before Nero met his end, first the private stage and then public theaters would be occupied by his extraordinary vocal performances in mythological roles such as *The Blinded Oedipus*, *Orestes in Chains*, *The Maddened Hercules*, or *Canace in Labor*.[60] The contests of Naples, Italy, and Greece would have their schedules changed and their victor predetermined as Nero pursued his artistic career. It is quite possible that he was a better singer than emperor. But the drama had left the stage, and poetry would find its voice in other, nondramatic genres.

Five

Between Nero and Domitian:
The Challenge to Poetry

During this forty-year period, poets experienced two significant external influences. Both represent the weight of authority, but of very different kinds: the temporal power and excessive expectations of Nero (55–68) and Domitian (81–97), two emperors preoccupied with literary culture (we must contrast here the indifference of Vespasian and the short-lived Titus); and the aesthetic power and cultural dominance of Rome's great poet, an influence that would extend beyond either this period or his own literary successors to later prose writers and poets of all kinds.

The Neronian Revival

Our investigation of Neronian poetry should begin with the most famous poet of Nero's reign—Nero himself. He was not born heir apparent, and may have reached his teens before he realized that his mother intended him to be emperor. Certainly the seventeen-year-old who accepted power after the murder of his adopted father Claudius in A.D. 55 was more interested in the arts than in his future responsibilities. But how genuine was his talent? There are some contradictions in the separate accounts given by Tacitus and Suetonius of Nero's interest in and practice of poetry.

Tacitus claims that Nero "from early boyhood turned his lively genius [away from oratory]; he carved, painted, and sang or practiced the management of horses, occasionally composing verses which showed that he had the rudiments of learning" (*Ann.* 13.3); later he adopts a similar tone of contempt for Nero's poetry sessions with his friends, arguing from surviving poems:

> Nero also affected a taste for poetry and drew round him persons also who had some skill in such compositions, but not yet generally recognized. They used to sit with him stringing together verse prepared at home or extemporized on the spot, and fill up his own expressions, such as they were, just as he threw them off. This is plainly shown by the very character of the poems, which have no vigour or inspiration or unity in their flow. (*Ann.* 14.16, trans. Church and Brodribb)

Now Suetonius agrees with Tacitus in showing the emperor as diverted into poetry because his mother discouraged him from philosophy and his tutor Seneca from classical oratory. But it seems as though Suetonius has heard or read Tacitus's criticisms and is responding to them:

> He wrote verses [*carmina*] with eagerness and without labor, and did not, as some think, publish the work of others as his own. There have come into my hands notebooks and papers with some well known verses of his written with his own hand, and in such wise that it was perfectly evident that they were not copied or taken down from dictation, but worked out exactly as one writes when thinking or creating. So many instances were there of words erased or struck through and written above the lines. (Suet. *Nero* 52, trans. Rolfe)

So the autograph gives proof of genuine creative effort. And it is not surprising that the emperor's recitation of his works was an outstanding success:

> He read his poems too, not only at home, but in the theater as well, so greatly to the delight of all that a thanksgiving was voted because of his recital, while that part of his poems was inscribed in letters of gold and dedicated to Jupiter on the Capitol. (Suet. *Nero* 10.2, trans. Rolfe)

But again there is a discrepancy with Tacitus, for this episode is set by Suetonius before Nero's establishment of the new Greek style Quinquennial Games, or Neronia, of A.D. 60, although Tacitus does not mention Nero reciting in public until the Neronia. The reader has the impression that Tacitus is writing from senatorial distaste, Suetonius in reaction and with access to more information. Certainly his account of Nero's triumph at these games is more circumstantial than Tacitus's brief report, quoted in the preceding chapter, and differs over Nero's success, claiming that he accepted the prizes for both Latin prose and verse "for which all the most eminent men contended, but which was given to him with their unanimous consent" (Suet. *Nero* 12.3, trans. Rolfe).

Suetonius' excursus into literary criticism shows the extraordinary interest that persisted in Nero as a poet, or at least as a composer of songs. The emperor's memory was officially obliterated after his death, but the evidence for his poetry and his songs persists and suggests that he was actually a better poet than some of the elite amateurs like Silius Italicus whose work has survived for our evaluation.

The word *carmina*, literally "songs," is ambiguous, covering the spoken poetry of Catullus and the lyrics of Horace, and tragedy, none of these set to music, as well as sung texts and magic spells. But a very strange thing can be observed in Tacitus's four books describing the years of Nero. Everyone either writes or performs *carmina*. To take the old and respectable, Seneca composes *carmina*—his tragedies;[1] indeed, his enemy Suillius Rufus claimed that he had taken to composing more *carmina* now that Nero affected an interest (*Ann.* 14.52). Poor young Britannicus, Nero's displaced half brother, was challenged to entertain the company at his last dinner and produced his own *carmen*, lamenting his loss of his inheritance (*Ann.* 13.15); the eminent Thrasea sang in tragic costume at the Founder's Games in Patavium (*Ann.* 16.21). Piso, the noble senator whom the conspiracy wished to appoint emperor in Nero's place, used to sing in tragic garb, so that the soldier Subrius Flavus saw no point in removing an imperial citharode to promote a tragic actor (*Ann.* 15.65).[2] Petronius may not have sung, but he spent his last evening listening to "trifling *carmina* and easy verses"

(*Ann.* 16.19). Sosianus wrote insulting *carmina* about Nero and died for it; Curtius Montanus did not write them but was wrongfully accused of it (*Ann.* 16.14, 28–29). And Nero wrote *carmina* (verse) and composed *carmina* (songs), which he performed in private and in Naples, on his domestic stage during the great fire and, ultimately, to the horror of senatorial traditionalists, on stage at Rome (*Ann.* 15.33–34, 39; 16.4.).[3] Finally, let me anticipate by noting that Nero's rival, the poet Lucan, broke with Nero because the emperor tried to suppress his *carmina* (*Ann.* 15.49) and died quoting verses from a soldier's heroic death in the same *carmen* (*Ann.* 15.70). Nero was exceptional, then, not in writing or performing *carmina*, but in being emperor.

Thus Nero was under pressure, at least for the first "good" years. If, as Suetonius tell us (*Nero* 20.1), he devoted himself as soon as he became emperor to the private study of singing with Terpnus the citharode, it seems very likely that he resorted to the poetry of recitation and the book only until he felt free to practice the less dignified and more exciting musical art of the singer.

The five chapters on Nero's career as a citharode in the Suetonian life concentrate on the emperor's voice production and physical technique in singing. This scandalized the orthodox Romans, but was no mean art, and was highly esteemed in Greece. Citharodes had always been poets and composers for their own performance with voice and lyre. There were four skills involved, of which poetry was only one. Whether or not Nero competed in conventional spoken verse at the first Neronia in 60, he competed as a citharode in the accelerated second Neronia[4] and must have composed the operatic *Scena ed Aria* for Niobe, which he sang as his competition piece. The role offered every scope for Nero's transvestism and love of melodrama, exploiting the favorite Roman theme of a woman distraught. Catullus's Ariadne had started a taste for female suffering, which persisted through Dido and Ovid's epistulary heroines to Senecan tragedy, and now Nero's dramatic roles. The desperate or maddened heroine was as fashionable as in Donizetti's day,[5] and we must acknowledge that none of the literature that has come down to us could have reached so vast an audience as the nonliterary theater, indeed the sheer spectacle, that fascinated both the juvenile emperor and the common people who shared his tastes.

The plebs seem to have loved Nero's performances. Even after Nero's death when Vitellius held funeral games in his memory to ingratiate himself with the Roman plebs, he shouted for the citharode to play "something from the master's work" and regaled them with *Neroniana* to loud applause. When a pretender appeared in 69 claiming to be Nero, he was an expert at the cithara and singing—this was his qualification.[6]

Songs require literary skill of a special kind and a simplicity far from the neoteric allusivity of the Latin poetry associated with Nero. What did he compose? The "Fall of Troy," performed in his stage costume when he watched the Great Fire of Rome from Maecenas's tower, suggests a citharodic song. But is it the same as his *Troica*, the tales of Troy that seems to have been an epic poem in several books? A three-line excerpt survives from this epic, lines ingeniously describing the disappearing watercourse of the Tigris that resurfaces far away, restoring its waters to men who no longer seek for them.[7] It seems likely that the "Fall of Troy" was a separate, lyric treatment; the Nero life of Suetonius quotes one phrase—on the "beauty of the flame" that is lyric in tone—but that is all we know.[8] Did Nero compose his tragic monodramas? Citharodes normally composed their own music and poetry, but the "masked tragedies" (*tragoediae personatae*) performed by Nero in his later years seem to have been another genre. Suetonius gives us titles: *Canace in Labor, Orestes Demented, The Blinded Oeodipus,* and *The Maddened Hercules.* Their subjects of madness and even childbirth called for violent dramatic action but must have stopped short of full pantomime dancing, because he was a poor dancer.[9] Even if Nero did not compose his own tragic libretti, he stooped to lighter verse. Suetonius mentions a lampoon, *The One-Eyed*, written by Nero against Clodius Pollio, and Tacitus knows of lampoons by the emperor against a man Quintianus (*Ann.* 15.49).

Some actual lines and themes of Nero's serious poetry seem to survive. The satirist Persius quotes some highly mannered verse that his ancient commentators ascribe to Nero, although they admit that other authorities said the lines were Persius's own pastiche—a snatch of "Berecynthine Attis" and four lines on Bacchanalian revels: "their grim horns they fill with Mimallonian boomings—the Bassarids ready to tear the scornful calf's head from his shoulders and the Maenads ready to rein in the lynx with ivy branches, shout Evoe! again and again, and the redeeming power of echo chimes in."[10] Another more sober line, "you would have thought it thundered under earth," was burlesqued by the poet Lucan to comment on a resounding fart in a public lavatory.[11]

Horace had warned his young friends that a patron who composed verses might not be willing to hear them recite, and would certainly require them to listen to his own verse; the rich patron knows that his own verse is magnificent and expects to be complimented.[12] Nero too, in the hostile Suetonian life, "offered his friendship or declared his enmity in proportion to men's enthusiasm or reluctance in applauding him" (*Nero* 25.3). But Nero's behavior in the last years has overshadowed his earlier enthusiasm for artistic activities and apparent enjoyment of evenings spent with other clever young noblemen in a friendly exchange of verse.

The greatest poet of Nero's age suffered from his very privileges and proximity to the emperor. Seneca's brilliant nephew Lucan, two years younger than Nero, had been recalled from Athens at the age of eighteen to be one of Nero's official friends and earned his first public honors when he performed a poem in praise of the emperor at the Neronia in A.D. 60. Lucan seems to have written a variety of poems even before that, and the earliest catalog of his works[13] shows the kind of topics that would suggest themselves to a bright young poet of this period: Priam's supplication to Achilles (perhaps a verse translation of *Iliad* 24?); an *Orpheus,* which may have been the same as the poem called the *Catachthonion* or *Underworld* (this must have emulated either the descent of Orpheus in *Georgics* 4 or perhaps that of Aeneas in book 6 of the *Aeneid,* or even the description of Hades in the *Culex,* a poem Lucan is known to have admired). Lucan had grown up with the legend of Virgil's early career as well as the love of his mature published work. The legends included the tradition that Virgil had composed the *Culex* at the age of twenty-six, and Lucan evidently felt himself working against time to match Virgil's achievement: the Suetonian life reports that he cried out in despair "how far I have to go to match [even] the *Culex!*"

Besides the Homeric and Virgilian tributes he also wrote a tragedy, *Medea*. In homage to Ovid? To his uncle Seneca's tragedy? Or was this now a requirement of Latin education? In his last years, again according to Statius, he composed a poem on the Great Fire and an *allocutio*, or personal address, to his wife Polla.[14]

But Lucan chose to give his art to an epic of the Caesarian civil war and make his hero the Stoic republican martyr, Cato of Utica. It must have been obvious that this was hazardous. The last poem about the civil wars had been Cornelius Severus's *Sicilian War*, written during the middle Augustan years—a safe topic, in that most Romans would have seen Octavian's victory as desirable, a triumph over the "degenerate" Sextus Pompeius and his pirate fleet, which cut off Rome's essential food supplies. Octavian had suppressed any tradition favorable to Sextus, and Cornelius, for all his known praise of the republican Cicero,[15] was free to compose a heroic narrative of sea battles interspersed with romantic Sicilian geography and legend. For Lucan, at this time, it may just possibly have seemed that Nero would not take the denunciation of Caesar and Caesarism as a comment on the legitimacy of his own power. Nero was still young and had been tutored by traditional upholders of senatorial liberty to see himself as under some moral or constitutional restraint. There was a five-year period in which he at least seemed to respect the facade of a public government, *res publica*, and live on equal terms with his peers. Lucan must surely have begun his epic of the civil war very soon after the first Neronia, since he had written nine and a half books when he involved himself in the conspiracy of 65 and was forced to commit suicide.

Extant lives of Lucan, like Tacitus's account of the poet, stress that Lucan was moved to join the conspiracy against Nero by a quarrel with the emperor, who banned the recitation or publication of Lucan's poetry. Our sources inevitably give different versions of the quarrel,[16] which can be construed either as imperial pique because of Lucan's success or in truly political terms. The motive of artistic jealousy should not be ruled out. Dewar has recently argued that the Neronian lines on the Tigris were probably written to outdo Lucan's treatment of the same theme in his third book (3.261–63), itself developed from an allusion in Senecan tragedy. On the other hand, even if Lucan had only recited (and perhaps issued) the first three books as we now have them, the republicanism of his loyalties must have offended.[17] The result of Nero's ban was a kind of internal exile for Lucan; his poetry silenced, it was inevitable that he would conspire to remove the imperial obstacle to his fame.

In the light of Lucan's republican principles both the quarrel and his subsequent suicide at Nero's orders seem inevitable, and have led modern readers to challenge the literal intent of Lucan's encomiastic dedication of his poem to Nero. At first sight it presents a palpable contradiction with the poet's political interpretation of the Caesarian victory as a loss of liberty that had left Lucan's own generation enslaved. It was common even among ancient critics to solve the problem by reinterpreting the eulogy as ironic mockery of the emperor's squint (55), his weight (56–57), and his dangerous driving (48–50), but that is not good enough.[18] Let us suppose that Lucan and other poets composed texts designed to make fun of their imperial addressee for those in the know. Why would this particular poet cancel his ironies by the outright fury of his denunciation in the great report of the battle of Pharsalia in the seventh book? "Of all the nations that bear domination, we are the last to be ashamed of our servitude. . . . the civil wars will make gods to match those above, and will adorn dead men with thunderbolts and stars and swear by human ghosts in the temples of the gods" (7.444–45, 457–59). Surely this republican idealist should have been ashamed to declare in his proems that the civil wars and human evil were worth the cost to bring Nero to power?

Modern scholars write with hindsight, but they should bear in mind the early promise of the emperor under Seneca's guidance and the reluctance his contemporaries would feel to see his character in individual acts of folly or vindictiveness. Could they have imagined the depraved and brutal figure that would emerge once Nero escaped from all external control? Lucan's dedication goes only a little further than Virgil's *Georgics* 1 in its panegyric, and his first three books damn Caesar, rather than the line of Caesars. He surely came to regret his dedication, but, once made public, the books could not be recalled or canceled out. The later books show increasing anger and defiance, and at some time before Lucan reached the composition of book 7, the emperor had passed beyond forgiveness.

At the same time horror at Nero's excesses should not blind us to the prejudices and arrogance of those who opposed him. No doubt Lucan was as arrogant as his ruler, and his attitudes as extreme; but the passion and the protest, added to his fantastic imagination and intimacy with the epic tradition, made brilliant poetry. The greatest poem of the Neronian era would not be heard or read until after the emperor's death.

Three other Neronian poets represent the variety of social origin, genre, and talent that flourished in the renewed cultural climate. One, Calpurnius Siculus, has recently been a battleground between scholars upholding his traditional dating to the Neronian period, and others who have advanced historical and metrical reasons for placing him much later.[19] The poet writes eclogues of shepherd life in obvious imitation of Virgil, but with rather more emphasis on his own dependency and the new hopes provided by the new god (*Ecl.* 4.30). I think we must accept that this Calpurnius is a humble client poet of the Neronian period. Whether he is a client of Piso, as has been suggested, or not, the new emperor, so young and strong, who Calpurnius hails as peace bringer in 1.84–85 and 4.82–86, and the godlike figure glimpsed in the fine new wooden amphitheater by the eager shepherds, is Nero, presiding over his great wooden construction erected for the animal hunts (*venationes*) of A.D. 57.

In contrast, the strange young satirist Persius had some access to literary circles but held himself aloof. A committed Stoic, he was schooled with Lucan under the philosopher and grammaticus Annaeus Cornutus, but avoided social life from ill health and from a deep puritanism. Misanthropy might not be too strong a word. Persius's language reflects his awareness of human ugliness, whether of the soul or body, and is gentle only by omission. At least he does not abuse women, or foreigners, or slaves, but writes with the distaste of man for man. His special importance in helping us to understand the poetry of his time lies in his repudiation and exposure of all the conventions. Thus he prefaces his satiric hexameters with a few deflating choliambics (the "limping" iambic trimeter used for invective):

> I never swilled my lips in the hack's spring, nor do I recollect having had
> a dream on the twin-peaked Parnassus, so as to burst upon the world at
> once as a full-blown poet. The daughters of Helicon and that cadaverous
> Pirene I leave to the gentlemen whose busts are caressed by the clinging
> ivy (*Prologus* 1–6)

The old Callimachean apparatus is cast off—the sacred spring Hippocrene, struck by the hoof of Pegasus, here downgraded to a riding
hack, the dream of Hesiod, and that of Callimachus after him, not to
mention Ennius at Rome some three hundred years back. These are,
he suggests, mere devices to exempt the poet from the proper toil of
preparation. Callimachus's muses and the rival inspirational fountain Pirene are mere programmatic fustian, like the poetic ivy
wreath celebrated by Propertius and Horace.

His other satire against contemporary literary forms is in some
ways more endearing because of his tribute of affection to Cornutus. It opens with an antifanfare: a rejection of the Homeric topos
"had I a hundred throats, I could not match." Quite right, says
Cornutus, "let those who mean to talk grandiose go and catch
vapors on Helicon, if there be any who are going to set Procne or
Thyestes' pot boiling to be the standing supper of poor stupid
Glycon" (*Sat.* 5). So tragedy is out, and Nero, who paid a prodigious
sum to set free the tragic actor Glycon, is cut down to size. What
Cornutus does advise is a new sanity of writing in the Horatian
tradition: "your line is to follow the language of common life with
dexterous nicety in your combinations." It is a fine ideal, but Persius's diction can never have been the *verba togae*, straight Roman
talk, that he aspired to.

Poetry and Parody in a New Setting

Straight Roman talk tended to have another reference, which
emerges from one of the more memorable sequences of the unique
novelist-satirist-poet Petronius. Petronius, whom Tacitus introduces as Nero's master of court entertainment, had held the consulship before relaxing into the life of the court. Tacitus himself presents Petronius only at the approach of his death, on the orders
of Nero, and uses the *arbiter elegantiae* as a contrast to the con-

sciously Stoic death scenes of Seneca before him and Paetus Thrasea soon after. But Petronius's death scene reflects two unique qualities of the great novel he left behind him: his choice of light songs—from the world of mime and burlesque—to pass his final night, and the brilliant malice with which he leaves behind him a catalog of Nero's sexual follies. Because of the picaresque content of the *Satyricon* and its easy oscillation between prose and verse forms, scholars have tended to identify Petronius's novel with the Menippean satire used, as far as we know, by no one since Varro, and not by Varro for narratives on any comparable scale (what survives is apparently only a small fraction of the at least sixteen books of the *Satyricon*.)[20] But recent papyrus discoveries have given reality to a genre far closer to Petronius's work: the Greek comic novel with its paratragic intrigues and hybrid form of verse and prose. Petronius's novel is infinitely more complex in its reflection of both the literary production and the literary attitudes of his generation than can be conveyed in summary; it could fairly be called the single most powerful demonstration of the literariness of Nero's age, caught between admiration and competition with the authority of the great literature of the past, with Homer, with tragedy, and now with Virgil.

Everything about Petronius's novel is hybrid, including its protagonist Encolpius, the bisexual Greco-Roman trained as a rhetorician but living as a petty adventurer. So when Encolpius in one of his many poems addresses his imaginary censors, his boast of plain speech need not speak for Petronius, and his words are belied by the insincerity and self-deception of his behavior as we have observed it:

> Why do you stare at me and frown, you Catos, and damn my work of fresh candor [*novae simplicitatis opus*]? No grim thanks are returned for pure speech, and the frank tongue only tells what the whole world does. For who doesn't know about bedding and the joy of love? Who forbids our limbs to grow heated in a warm bed? Even Epicurus the father of truth diverted himself with love and declared it produced the end of life. (132)

Petronius has always won audiences by his sexual content, but many read Encolpius's scandalous narrative without understanding its literary dimension, which incorporates both travesty of the Greek romantic novel and echoes of the great classical works Romans had been trained to admire and imitate, at least in their writings.[21] Encolpius goes further: he tries to imitate epic and tragic behavior in his otherwise disreputable life and the conflict of values creates pure farce. In Petronius's text there is as much literary as social satire, offering almost continuous delight for lovers of pastiche in the ironic contrast between the heroic self-image and the unheroic behavior of his raffish protagonists.

The surviving part of the novel takes place in southern Italy, first in the half-Greek communities of Puteoli, near Naples, then approaching Croton, on the instep of the peninsula. Petronius's figures of fun are chiefly "lowlife" Romans and former slaves, but Encolpius and his associates Ascyltos, Giton, and Eumolpus, whose fortunes we follow, are educated but disreputable Greeks. The best-known part of the narrative is Encolpius's account of the banquet given by the ignorant and wealthy Trimalchio, which some have suggested could be a parody of Nero's feasts. But the larger-than-life Trimalchio is his own parody, with his all-pork diet, his undisciplined slave household, his shrewish and tipsy wife, his elaborate tastelessness, and his lavish rehearsal of his own burial.

From the beginning of the surviving text Petronius parodies various types of contemporary literary criticism, and the themes and tendencies of this criticism offer a vivid reflection of the platitudes of Neronian literary culture. The rhetor Agamemnon serves up a stale diatribe (*Sat.* 3), already familiar from the previous generation, on the degeneracy and effeminacy of the young and its deplorable effect on style in oratory. We have read the same clichés in the elder Seneca's preface to his sons, but the ideas were too widespread for this Agamemnon to be specifically a takeoff on old Seneca.[22] The hero and his friends encounter a more colorful figure in the compulsive critic and poet, Eumolpus, who seizes the pretext of a picture gallery to improvise sixty-five lines of tragic senarii on the episodes of Laocoön and the horse in Virgil's fall of Troy (*Sat.* 89). It is not particularly awful, nor is it a reflection either on Virgil—who wrote in hexameters—or on Seneca the Younger, whose Trojan tragedy is very different in subject and diction. It may be a parody of the undramatic messenger speeches to which Seneca and other contemporary poets were inclined; for the paramount influence of Virgilian epic had weakened the struggling genre of drama.

But Eumolpus has more to offer. After a singularly unedifying story of pederastic seduction, he shifts gear to present a critical introduction to the problems of composing poetry, which is a key to the assumptions underlying contemporary aesthetics (*Sat.* 118). The miniature manual is less than a hundred words, but each sentence is replete with imagery and implications. "Poetry has frustrated many," Eumolpus begins, "for as soon as anyone has drawn up his verse arrayed with feet and woven a delicate thought into its wrapping of words, he thinks he has immediately reached Helicon." The mixture of imagery from military tactics and weaving reflects the discrepancy between technical versification and aesthetic striving. His composers are the familiar Roman gentlemen amateurs— men driven from the incessant drudgery of the lawcourts, who deceive themselves that poetry will be easier and more undisturbed. He insists that they must be saturated in culture—"flooded with a vast stream of reading"—and cultivate rare and refined diction, shunning the common herd. Their aphorisms must shine with the same sheen as the text in which they are imbedded, and they must follow the models of Homer and the lyric poets (!) and Roman Virgil, and the careful skill of Horace.[23] (Perhaps at this stage the would-be poets are not yet set to compose an epic.) From this general recommendation Eumolpus turns to a very specific ambition: composing an epic of civil war. This too required the poet to be loaded with culture (*plenus litteris*). It is not a matter of reporting events, which historians can do more successfully, but of "hurling the free inspiration through complications and the interventions of the gods, and mythological contortions of ideas."[24]

Whatever this last much disputed phrase means, Eumolpus can only be voicing the objections of contemporaries (not necessarily of Petronius himself) to the new secular epic of Lucan. It is not clear how much Petronius could have heard or read of Lucan's *Civil War* before he died (within a year of Lucan) but, once launched into his account of victorious Rome out of control from greed and overreach, Eumolpus rewrites the episodes of Lucan's opening book with all the post-Virgilian trappings of gods and forces of darkness, to leave his Caesar poised at the summit of the Alps, looking down on a Rome ready to fall. Since the chief absurdity of the three-hundred-line excerpt lies in the grotesque cast of demons and deities, which Lucan himself had avoided, it is difficult to see why this miniepic has been treated as a parody of Lucan. Better the interpretation of Erich Burck,[25] who sees it as improvised out of an almost Ovidian exuberance and delight in facility, to show how the poetic conflict could be started up in another way. But it is also significant that Eumolpus's two compositions represent the making and unmaking of Rome, and mirror in Virgilian terms the tragicomic escapades of Eumolpus and his interlocutors.[26]

In this period of increasing crossinfection of style between prose and poetry, Petronius the supreme prose artist earns a place among the poets for the sheer versatility and charm of his many short poems or snatches of poetry.[27] Apart from the few lines attributed to Trimalchio, the poems of the *Satyricon* are fresh even when their topics are stale. In the twelve chapters from 127 to 139, there are at least ten poetic insets. First, seven hexameters evoke an idyllic setting for lovemaking, modeled on Hera's famous seduction of Zeus in *Iliad* 14. Next come nine hexameters on the nature of dreams (128) and eight describing an ideal pleasant landscape (*locus amoenus*) of tree and stream (131). Chapter 132, the tragic débacle when Encolpius is struck impotent, excels itself with three poetic treatments: nine lines in a meter unprecedented in Latin, of thirteen syllables; then, after a paragraph of renewed effort and subsidence, a three-line description of his limp member pieced together from three separate Virgilian parts—Dido's rejection of Aeneas in Hades (*Aeneid* 6.469–70), the sagging willow tree of *Eclogues* 5.16, and the drooping poppy that represents the dying Euryalus in *Aeneid* 9.436. Finally Encolpius offers up a hexameter prayer to Priapus, which is answered by the appearance of the witch. She too switches into hexameters to enumerate her magic powers (134) and leads him to her humble hovel (more hexameters and the statutory allusion to Callimachus's *Hecale*, the first poem to romanticize simple hospitality).

But Petronius is not tired yet. On the next page comes a pseudo-epical simile of harpies, and on the next some flippant elegiacs on the power of money (136, 137). The last poem in this sequence (we do not know what followed it, because the text is damaged) rounds off the drama with eight lines comparing the hero's suffering with that of other offenders punished by angry gods (141). Petronius shows himself as easy a versifier as Ovid and master of all the traditional topoi of Latin poetry. The poetic variety of this short sequence suggests that we have in what survives of Neronian literature only a rather conservative sample from a dazzling range of poetry and song at all levels, going far beyond the orthodox definitions of genre. This is a brilliant writer, only prevented by a fundamental irreverence or disillusionment from making his name as a poet, and the loss of the rest of the *Satyricon* is a deprivation to literary historians as well as to the mass of delighted readers.

Vicissitudes of the Epic Muse

Nero's reaction to the Pisonian conspiracy of 65 brought the apolitical and urbane Petronius, along with Seneca, Lucan, and many others, to their deaths before he met his own. It may be that only the cautious and conventional survived. Among these were Valerius Flaccus and Silius Italicus, men of considerable technical skill saturated in the Virgilian tradition of Roman epic: together they represent in their mythological and historical epics the cramping conservatism of those overawed by Virgil and the limitations of commitment without talent or individuality.

C. Valerius Flaccus Setinus Balbus returned for his epic to a theme that had already been set to Latin epic verse: the *Argonautica*, which Varro of Atax had translated from Apollonius of Rhodes's Greek poem during the last years of the republic. But, after Virgil, Roman poets were no longer content merely to translate: even the princely amateur Germanicus had inserted material of his own into Aratus's astronomical poem. So Valerius's *Argonautica* is influenced by, but independent of, Apollonius, even to his division of the narrative into eight books, of which the last is incomplete. He probably died young, although he identifies himself as a *quindecim-*

vir, which implies the rank of senator; his poem can be dated by the formal dedication to Vespasian with its allusion to Titus's sack of Jerusalem in A.D. 70, and his death is reported as a recent loss by Quintilian in his survey of Roman epic.[28] Quintilian does not offer a critical assessment, perhaps because Valerius lacks distinctive features. Besides changing the proportions and emphases of the well-known Greek narrative, Valerius has given simpler and less passionate characters to Jason and Medea, making her less sinister and Jason less weak and ambiguous. Given the perpetuation of the witch aspects of Medea in Ovid and Seneca, we might see this as innovation, if it were not more easily explained as a return to Virgilian decorum. Valerius's language echoes Virgilian diction, but his epithets and similes are unimaginative and his speeches lack power or personality. He is perhaps the most colorless of the Flavian epic poets.

Unlike Valerius, T. Catius Asconius Silius Italicus was a public figure, with a successful, if compromised, political career. Because he died in his seventies, when the younger Pliny was composing his collection of *Letters*, we have from Pliny a complete obituary putting this gentleman in his political and social setting.[29] Although he was the first senator of his family, Silius rose to be *consul ordinarius*, the magistrate giving his name to the year, in A.D. 68, soon after the age of forty. But Pliny makes it clear that he had earned discredit as a prosecutor under Nero, and we might doubt whether any honest man would have been awarded the consulship in Nero's last year. Nor is it to his credit that Silius was a friend of the incompetent Vitellius, but Pliny sees him as recovering respectability after his governorship of Asia, and living a quiet and cultured life of retirement.

Silius seems to have been a fairly indiscriminate collector of books and statues, and apparently acquired country houses at random and without needing the new or selling the old.[30] His reverence for Virgil took the form of religiously observing his birthday and visiting his tomb,[31] but its most persistent manifestation was his epic (*carmina* again) "written with more care than talent" and tested by the usual recitations. The *Punica* reached seventeen books before Silius took his life (in the face of a painful illness) and he had probably planned to reach eighteen. This would have matched Ennius's eighteen books of *Annals*—the first great poetic account of the Hannibalic war—although Silius's historical source was not Ennius but Livy, and his poetic model not Ennius but Virgil.

Piety does not make for great art, but Silius had been well educated and his verses run clearly as he adapts the historical events of the three-hundred-year-old war to the format and set pieces conventional since Virgil. He motivates the war through the divine machinery of Juno's hatred of Rome and introduces Hannibal as the tool of her anger, trained by his father and sworn to hatred, before the tomb of Dido, which is of course described in an ecphrasis. Here we have the kind of theme that most appealed to the literary tastes of the day: the *locus horridus*, or place of doom and gloom, had become as much a favorite of poets after Seneca as the old pleasant landscape of the Augustans, mocked in Horace's *Ars Poetica*.[32] Similarly Silius's infernal ritual borrows from Lucan the priest's vision of the future contents of the poem—and course of the war—before Silius leads into the sequential historical narrative. In one way the poem adheres more strictly to the model of the *Aeneid*. In contrast with almost all post-Virgilian poetry, there is no proem dedicated to the current emperor, nothing except a simple Homeric appeal to the muse to give him strength to "tell of the ordeals of Italy and its warriors, when the descendants of Phoenician Cadmus broke the sacred treaty" (1.3–6). Silius reserves his loyalty for two internal panegyrics which combine praise of the emperor's martial and poetic gifts.[33] Silius's praise was appreciated and he lived to see his son Decianus receive the consulship from Domitian in 94.

We can see the consequences of Silius's faithful imitation of Virgil in many features and motifs of his epic; it could be incongruous as in one of the last sections of the poem, when Juno is made to rescue Hannibal from Scipio by the same device of the phantom adversary that she had used to rescue Turnus, however briefly, in *Aeneid* 10. The historical facts of Hannibal's survival and exile from Carthage were inconvenient for a poet who would expect to end with the death of the archenemy.

Romans who looked to the senatorial gentry for the continuance of poetry must have been discouraged by the predictability, the routine, of these epics, and wondered where the next poet of talent would come from. In fact the epic had not died, but it is an outsider from a mixed Greek and Roman cultural background who revives it and represents serious poetry under Domitian.

The Neapolitan Papinius Statius, son of a Greek grammaticus who had himself won prizes for poetry, published his major epic, the *Thebaid*, in 92, before he turned to the social poetry that tells us so much about himself and the society in which he moved. Statius claims that he had spent twelve years on the *Thebaid*—twelve years for twelve books (and one more year than was attributed to Virgil's work on the *Aeneid*). It will be best to take the *Thebaid* with its predecessors to round off the sequence, before considering at greater length the five books of *Silvae*, for these occasional poems are our best source for understanding the serious poet's changing role in society under Domitian and need separate treatment at some length.

The *Thebaid* differs from the work of Valerius and Silius in adding a new model to the Virgilian supermodel. Statius too was obviously educated on Virgil's poetry, and absorbed it into his own artistry. He constantly pays his homage both through the large-scale form of his narrative and in more local imitation of language and imagery, and he ends his twelfth and final book with confidence in the immortality of his epic, but a warning to his poem not to attempt competition with the "divine Aeneid." But the theme he chose, the war between the sons of Oedipus for the throne of Thebes, enabled him to add the colors of "worse than civil war"—a battle of brothers—to his epic, and the overt imitation of Lucan's angry tale of horror borrows many features of Lucan's language and his moral vehemence. Since the story of the "seven against Thebes" also involved a more conventional conflict between two cities, and a multiplicity of warrior heroes, Statius's epic can exploit the techniques and themes of the second, warlike, half of the *Aeneid*, and he makes full use of the divine motivation and interventions that Lucan had shunned. At its most mannered, Statius's work comes uncomfortably close to the epic of Eumolpus.

But in one respect this epic does credit to the growing humanization of ordinary society at Rome. Statius gives subtle and sympathetic treatment to the roles of women as wives and mothers. Lucan had made a start in depicting with sympathy the virtues of two Roman wives: Cato's austere Marcia and Pompey's tender and loving Cornelia. Statius creates a whole separate action in his fifth book around the bereaved Hypsipyle and the tragic death of the baby Opheltes left in her charge. The mourning of Hypsipyle and of the child's mother Eurydice is a foreshadowing of the mourning women who will gradually take over the action at the end of the epic: the other Eurydice, mother of Menoeceus, who voluntarily goes to his death; Jocasta, who tries in vain to reconcile her sons and dies in grief over their bodies; and Antigone, Argia, and Evadne, whose heroism is fully developed and honored in the final book.[34] This is not just a matter of volume, but of real insight into the emotions and needs of women, and it is more characteristic of the private world around Statius than of the inherited myths that he is reworking. Despite the horrendous portraits painted by Tacitus of debauched or domineering imperial women like Messalina or Agrippina, Roman authors from Seneca onward show a respect and sympathy for the good wife and mother, which can also be found in the slightly later writings of Plutarch about marriage.

Statius took twelve years to compose his *Thebaid*, but he had rather less time to compose two other epic poems. His *German War* composed to honor Domitian's campaigns of 89 renewed the old Roman tradition of celebrating important commanders, but as a competition poem for Domitian's Alban Games (to which we will return) it must have been short enough to be recited in one session.[35] Late in his life he returned to epic, starting an *Achilleid*, of which little more than the first book was written when Statius died. Statius may have been planning an Iliadic poem of siege and single combat, but the surviving first book achieves a quite different tone, one of playful comedy, divided between a shrewdly sympathetic portrait of Achilles's anxious mother Thetis and an equally vivid account of the young boy's discovery of his sexuality. The intrigue of Deidamia's seduction is characteristic of comedy and lends itself to Ovidian charm and naturalism.[36] This single book is closer to the Phaeacian books of the Odyssey than to any subsequent work, but achieves something new and different, showing that in the hands of this poet the genre was capable of further growth.

Statius's epic met with considerable success. The evidence comes from a hostile witness, Juvenal, who was a young man in the time of Domitian and perhaps already beginning his career as a satirist. When Juvenal wants to demonstrate the lack of economic support offered to serious poetry in his time, he chooses the *Thebaid* as his example. Yes, poetry brings glory, enough to keep the dead Lucan happy in his marble tomb, but what use is glory to the living and struggling Serranus and Saleius Bassus?[37]

> Men rushed to the pleasing voice and poem of the beloved *Thebaid*, when Statius made the city happy and promised it a date: such is the charm with which he beguiles men's infatuated hearts, and such the excited lust of the crowd who listen to him. But when he has brought the house down with his verse, he starves, unless he can sell his virgin *Agave* to Paris, the pantomime dancer. (7.82–87)

Juvenal's language is designed to turn Statius into a pimp, setting up a rendezvous for his meretricious epic, but forced to sell his virgin daughter if he is to make ends meet. Is this a judgment on the poetry or the poet? We shall see in the next chapter how Juvenal hated Greeks, and hated their success, and Statius, for all his citizenship and command of Latin poetry, was Greek by birth and training.

Professional Poets in the Time of Domitian

As a professional poet, Statius had to meet other demands on his time than the epic, which he probably saw as his poetic fulfillment. Indeed, the demands and expectations of patrons, especially the emperor, the supreme patron, would increase with Statius's first victory in an imperial competition and again with the publication of his completed *Thebaid* in 92.

The mention of an imperially sponsored competition suggests that Domitian was genuinely interested in the art of poetry, but Tacitus and Suetonius, in his *Life of Domitian*, claim that once he reached maturity the emperor only paid lip service to poetry— unless, of course, it celebrated himself and his achievements. Suetonius contrasts Domitian's affectation of interest in poetry as a young man, when he even gave recitations in public, with his behavior as emperor, when he made no effort "to become acquainted with history or poetry or even to acquire an ordinarily good style."[38] Whatever their date and quality, Domitian's epic compositions are given special praise at the end of Quintilian's survey of recent epic poets. Quintilian owed his professorship of Latin oratory to Domitian's father and was honored by Domitian with the ornaments of a consul. The grateful professor's compliment to his emperor is also an index of the heightened level of obsequiousness now required.

> We recently suffered a great loss in Valerius Flaccus. The talent of Saleius Bassus was passionate and poetic, but did not reach the ripeness of old age. Rabirius and Pedo are quite worth knowing, if there is time to spare.[39] Lucan is ardent and excited and brilliant in his aphorisms, and, to speak my mind, even more to be imitated by [us] orators than by poets.
>
> We mention these names because the supervision of the world has diverted Germanicus Augustus from the studies he began, and the gods have thought it beneath him to be merely the greatest of poets. But what is more lofty, learned, and distinguished in every variety of meter than the pieces on which he spent his leisure as a young man when he had already taken up imperial power? Who could sing wars more nobly than he who wages them so well? Whom would the muses hear more attentively as he presided over literature? To whom would Minerva, now an intimate, more gladly reveal her arts? Future ages will say this more copiously, but at present his glory in this field is eclipsed by the brilliance of his other virtues. But you will tolerate us, Caesar, who carry the sacred torch of literature, if we do not pass over this theme and at least bear witness with the Virgilian line: *that ivy winds around your victorious laurels.*[40]

Such language was now required, and no reader can miss the gearing up of rhetorical questions that it imposes on the sober and moderate Quintilian.

But Domitian's public acts show another and more beneficial side of the emperor: he gave his official care to literature as patron, not as poet. According to Suetonius he set out to restore the libraries that had recently been burned—perhaps that in the Porticus of Octavia, burned in 80, or libraries on the Capitoline.[41] Domitian sought out replacements for the holding of the great libraries and even sent scribes to Alexandria to make copies from the holdings of the Mouseion. Domitian, not his father or brother, founded the Alban Games, held in honor of the spring feast of Minerva (hence Quintilian's comment), at his villa in the Alban hills; he established a college of priests and provided stage performances and contests for orators and poets in both Latin and Greek. Coleman suggests that this personal festival may have served primarily as a talent contest enabling Domitian to find poets who would serve the imperial reputation in war and peace. In the city itself Domitian returned to the Neronian model and established the Quinquennial Capitoline Contest on the Greek pattern, in "music" (poetry and prose, both Greek and Latin, and performances by the citharodes), in equestrian events, and in athletics. Like any ruler or civic head of a Greek community, the emperor himself presided over these games as *agōnothetēs*.[42]

The senatorial writers (who will be the subject of the next chapter) hated Domitian for his suppression of their liberty, but professional poets like Statius and Martial praised him while he lived, and their work was not lost in the general abolition of his memory after his assassination. The Spanish epigrammatist Martial began to publish with a collection honoring the gladiatorial games and animal displays of Titus around A.D. 80. He is a fine source for social pretensions, but he mixes real and fictitious persons, and sees the wealthy and influential from outside. His is a bachelor, but not a celibate, world, and his short and glib epigrams are more informative on the public life of the streets and baths than on the domestic life of the court and governing classes.[43] But Statius wrote extended descriptive poems about the character and domestic life of a smaller number of acknowledged patrons, which enable us to recover both the private and the public worlds of this period and their values. And in Statius Domitian found a poet trained and ready to do him honor, whose poetry for and to the emperor shows how contemporary society wanted to see its ruler. His extraordinary treatment of imperial themes can be measured against the very different tone of poems for his wife, his father, and his friends.

It will be useful to move outward from one of Statius's most intimate poems, perhaps unpublished during his lifetime. This is *Silvae* 5.3, the lament for his father, both a biography and an autobiography, the most detailed portrait of a poet's education and his world since Ovid's explicit autobiography written in exile.

First, then, Statius's upbringing. The lament evokes the life of father and son and is designed to show their continuity. But for the modern reader it also sheds light on an important component of this society, the bicultural and bilingual Greeks who contributed so much to imperial education and culture. Naturally, as Greeks living overseas, both father and son were eager to confirm their Hellenic culture, and Statius's highest compliment for his father is to hope that in Elysium he will talk with Homer and Hesiod. Statius describes in his father's school of *grammatikē* a level of education that may have been quite exceptional in its time. Father Statius taught an advanced Greek syllabus; not merely Homer and Hesiod, but Pindar, Ibycus, Alcman, and Stesichorus (texts largely lost to us today), as well as Sappho and other lyric poets. He does not seem to have taught Greek tragedy; perhaps it was seen as too easy and omitted from his syllabus in the way that Livy and the elegists were omitted from the Oxford Latin syllabus forty years ago. But the father's specialty seems to have been Hellenistic poetry: "the poems of the learned Callimachus, the obscurities of compressed Lycophron, twisted Sophron and the mysteries of delicate Corinna" (*Silvae*. 5.3. 157–58).

Students came to this school from all southern and central Italy and, in due course, from the Roman senatorial class. Perhaps this is why Statius praises the institution, rather like nineteenth-century Oxbridge or an Ivy League university today, not for its academic products but for their present successes as public servants, governors, and generals in the far flung empire (170–90). Yet this itself is a mystery. At what age did these young Romans come to Statius's father, and with what intent? In the time of Cicero young men had gone to Athens to study rhetoric and philosophy and make their Greek more fluent; Virgil and other aspiring poets had spent time in Naples learning to know and understand Greek poetry with grammatici. Why then is this grammaticus teaching future administrators? Perhaps this was a preliminary before they embarked on the study of philosophy and advanced rhetoric, an alternative to the declamatory schools for teenagers? Perhaps Statius exaggerates the success of his father's school in producing administrators so as to appeal to materialist parents, but on the face of it such an education was only suited to future poets, such as Statius became himself.

Throughout the poem Statius celebrates his father's role as model for his own career. The father won an award for his poem on the Great Fire of the Capitol (in A.D. 69), and had planned to compose a poem on the eruption of Vesuvius, which took place in 79, but did not live to begin it, or to see any of his son's victories after his first successful contest at the Augustalia in Naples. He never knew Statius's career in the wider arena of Rome itself. The poem does not mention the language in which his father competed. Was it Greek, his own tongue, or Latin, in which Statius would write his poetry? It is difficult to imagine a modern analogy. The victorious bards of Welsh *Eistedfoddau* do not usually make a name for English poetry, and other bilingual poets such as Cavafy have chosen a single language even if it was not the language in which they conducted their daily life.

So Statius too must have chosen a single language, and chosen Latin. It was in Latin that he competed in the Alban Games of 90 and won the prize with his epic poem on Domitian's Dacian and German wars. It was in Latin, no doubt, that he competed in the Capitoline Games, perhaps the same year, and missed the prize.[44] But Statius lived between two cultures, and his wife, Claudia, who came from Rome and was so reluctant to return with him to Naples in his last years, may also have been of Greek origin.[45] The powerful and wealthy friends for whom he wrote, such as Claudius Etruscus, were mostly *equites*, gentlemen of leisure rather than senatorial administrators, and their culture was probably as Greek as his own. The poems that honor their mansions, their objets d'art, and their menageries show that these men had leisure and comfort.

Indeed Statius's descriptive poetry is more luxurious, more replete with textures and materials, words denoting luster and smoothness, than any Latin poet since the brief passages of Catullus's longer poems (61 and 64) describing the bridal chamber and couch. This is not the deliberately dissonant diction of the satirist who seeks to make the furniture and household goods of his poetry seem awkward or intrusive. Such poetry was always complimentary, always a response, often at short notice, to a request or invitation. Thanks to the investigations of Peter White and Alexander Hardie,[46] it is possible now to imagine how this professional poet lived, though not on what he lived, beyond his prize money and the villa given to him by Domitian.

Statius's occasional poems combine professional artistry with protestations of hasty improvisation—hence, the title *Silvae*, a name originally used for rough drafts. Four of these books were clearly organized by the poet to be artistic units, that paid tribute to the emperor and to his influential friends; they are introduced by dedicatory prose prefaces that are both tables of contents and expressions of homage. But the separate poems must have gone through two phases of life before Statius gathered them into these convenient volumes. These are mostly poems for or about specific occasions: indeed, many indicate the occasion on which they were first delivered. Some occasions in human life are foreseeable, and Statius has poems honoring births and marriages, journeys and new houses, or additions to the houses of the wealthy.

Sickness and death are less foreseeable, and the several poems of mourning and consolation[47] included in Statius's collection must have been either requested or volunteered on his own initiative after the event. But it is fair to assume that most of the poems included in the *Silvae* were, as Statius himself declares in his preface, a rapid or immediate response to a social situation, expected if not requested by those he honored. They would be performed for the patron at one of his public entertainments, or sent to him as soon as possible after the occasion they marked, perhaps gathered with others into a small *libellus*;[48] presumably they would only reach publication and sale with the patron's approval. Some indication of the form is provided by the apparent preface to book 5, a preface really only intended for the single lament offered to Abascantus. Even the *Thebaid* was apparently sent to Vibius Maximus (dedicatee of the Sapphic ode *Silvae* 4.7) with a prefatory letter, which Statius has suppressed as unworthy of publication.[49]

Thus in the first three books of *Silvae*, almost certainly published together as a group, Statius honors twelve patrons besides the emperor. Arruntius Stella, the dedicatee of book 1, is addressed only by poem 1.2, and White has shown that Stella, a senator of noble family, was chosen as poet in his own right rather than for any close acquaintance with Statius. The marriage of Stella provoked Statius's epithalamium, but it also provoked an epigram from Martial (6.21),[50] who knew Stella far better than Statius did. Statius himself speaks of other poets vying to do justice to the theme. The dedicatee of book 2 is Atedius Melior, an older man of leisured wealth, but it is significant that Martial again has epigrams covering the theme of Statius's first poem—a lament over Melior's dead boy favorite Glaucias (6.28–29)—and that both poets emphasize the same aspects of the dear departed. This was a standard occasion for poetry, as witness the Greek epigram of Lucilius, a poet of Neronian date, complaining to a Roman gentleman of his tedious laments for his dead favorite.[51] Statius would live to compose his own lament for the loss of a dear child, who was probably little more than a favorite slave.

Melior obviously had a luxurious estate, and the other two poems addressed to him in book 2 suggest that he invited Statius for a visit with a hint or outright request for a little poem on his plane tree, or the death of his parrot. A similar patron known to both Statius and Martial is Claudius Etruscus, whose new baths are praised by both men (*Silvae* 1.5, Martial 6.42) and for whom both composed poems of consolation on the death of his father (*Silvae* 3.3, Martial 7.40). Other epideictic poems describing treasures of wealthy friends are Statius's praise of the villa at Sorrento and statue of Hercules of Pollius Felix, to whom Statius dedicated his third book of *Silvae* (2.2 and 3.1), and a similar celebration of Novius Vindex's table-sized statuette of Hercules, which is also praised in epigrams of Martial (Statius *Silvae* 4.7, Martial 9.43–44). The three poems for Melior, dedicatee of book 2, are balanced by the two poems for Etruscus (1.5 and 3.3) and the two for Pollius (2.2 and 3.1), and their careful distribution across the three books is proof that all three were conceived and arranged for publication together.

Two other figures receive poems from both poets: Polla Argentaria, the widow of Lucan, is offered poems to honor her dead husband's birthday by both Statius (*Silvae* 2.7) and Martial (7. 21, 22, 23), and White has argued convincingly that Statius's hendecasyllables were planned in consultation with Polla for the special anniversary. In a later poem Martial will call her *regina* (queen) a rare equivalent of the name *rex* regularly applied to male patrons. White notes that she is one of several widows or wives addressed by Martial as dispensers of literary influence in their own right, and suggests that women were emerging not only as readers of poetry but as patrons and promoters of poets on a modest scale.[52]

Thus for these few patrons it seems Statius was in competition with Martial. He came on the scene after the epigrammatist, but his expansive descriptions of their way of life give the impression that he was perhaps more fully accepted into the patrons' private world. It is difficult to measure the many brief epigrams of Martial against the elaborate and more fulsome hexameters of Statius, and additional factors may intervene to explain a poem. The other common addressee of both poets, the eunuch Earinus, received six epigrams from Martial, of which the fourth and fifth (9.16, 17) commemorate the same occasion as Statius's *Silvae* 3. 4. According to Statius's preface, Earinus requested the poem when he cut and dedicated his first locks of adult hair to the shrine of Asclepios at Pergamum.

It seems to us an unworthy subject, but Earinus was Domitian's cupbearer and Statius would see it as an indirect tribute to his emperor. This is in fact the only poem related to Domitian in book 3, whereas the first book opens with a poem on the emperor's new equestrian statue and the second includes a poem (2.5) on the death of a tame lion in the arena, which provoked Domitian's concern.

The preface to Statius's fourth book implies that the poet had met some hostility; this has been interpreted by Ahl as a reaction against Statius's flattery of Domitian in the first three poems written to honor the emperor.[53] But as supreme universal patron, the emperor expected poems from all active poets, and these verses should not be seen as implying even a remote personal relationship such as Statius had with his ordinary patrons. Let two of these poems illustrate the appropriate adoration from a distance, and the proper form of *basilikos logos*, poetry for a king. The first celebrates the annual ceremonies performed by Domitian as consul for the seventeenth time (it would be his last) on January 1, 95. There was a traditional technique for describing rituals in process, derived from Callimachus's *Hymn to Apollo* and other Hellenistic poems. Tibullus and Ovid had used it freely, and Ovid provides a close precedent in the complimentary poem describing this very ritual to honor his friend Sextus Pompeius, inaugurated as consul in A.D. 16.[54] But with the emperor every appearance is an epiphany. Statius heralds Domitian like a bridegroom—shining more brightly than any dawn—and consigns to Janus the bulk of the poem, describing the new brilliance of the temples and the glad applause of Senate and knights and people. The tradition required a comparison with former emperors to show Domitian's preeminence, and one is provided. Only Augustus, and he was only consul thirteen times, has even approached Domitian's record—not to mention the honors that he has refused. Janus also offers the customary prayers and prophecies for the future, predicting Domitian's conquest of India and China. Since the emperor had recently renamed September and October Domitianus and Germanicus, it remains for Janus to suggest that future victories will give names to the other months. A predominant tone in these panegyrical poems is of amazement, and Statius ends with the admiration of the gods: "then all the gods were amazed and gave signs in the exultant sky, and Jupiter granted You years equal to his own" *Silvae* 4.1.45–47.

But the next poem reaches a higher level of devotion. Statius has been invited to one of Domitian's public feasts held in the new residence on the Palatine, and the poem is a thanksgiving (*eucharistikon* in Greek, which the Romans adapted as *gratiarum actio*.) It seems most likely that this poem, which purports to be written in recollection of the event, was composed in advance and even performed by the poet at the banquet. Whatever level of exaltation opens the poem must be maintained or increased: it is not easy. But Statius's literary culture keeps him supplied. He calls on the whole of Greek and Roman high epic, beginning with Virgil, who described the banquet of Dido, and Homer, who set out the feast of Alcinous: great poets indeed, but not with the poetic laurels of both Smyrna and Mantua could Statius rise to this occasion. Only Olympus will do, so he imagines that he is reclining with Jupiter and being served by Ganymede. His life has been barren until this day, and he cannot believe that he is now allowed to gaze on his emperor, "ruler of the nations, great father of the subject world, hope of mankind and concern of the gods" (4.2.14–15). The center of the poem evokes the size and beauty of the hall, so lofty it might be heaven, but only as a warm-up to the verbal portrait of the emperor, "tranquil in his expression, with serene majesty tempering his radiance and modestly dipping the standards of his eminence: yet the splendor that he tried to hide shone in his countenance" (41–44).

This language of moral and aesthetic praise is something new in Roman eulogy; after this the comparisons with Mars and Pollux, Bacchus and Hercules, are more conventional, but designed to lead up to the crescendo. "Such is the leader of the gods when . . . he bids the muses sing songs undivulged and Phoebus celebrate the triumph of Pallene" (53–56). If Domitian is like Jupiter, Statius himself can be imagined as the counterpart of both the muses and Apollo. The poem must end with good wishes, but it also contrives to reinsert the poet: for he compares the happiness of this day to the time long since when Domitian gave him the victor's prize for his poem on the Dacian and German wars. A nicely turned compliment, this also subliminally invites the emperor to call on his poet for further celebration.

In Ahl's persuasive study of the poets' relations with their emperors, he argues that such flattery went beyond the accepted limits even of its own time, and offers what I take to be two models for Statius's behavior. His first suggestion is that Statius flatters Domitian to such excess that "one must either conclude that this is mannerism gone mad, or that his purpose is to hold the emperor up for the ridicule of later generations." Ahl's rhetoric does not intend his reader to assume the first, but favors the second choice. But a little later in his argument Ahl offers a far subtler interpretation based on Czeslaw Milosz's *The Captive Mind*, which seems closer to Statius's exercise of ingenuity. In that novel a writer is described who controls his subtext: "because he constantly used exaggeration as his artistic tool, his opponents could prove nothing against him; he neither mocked nor spoke the truth; he performed tricks, he practiced art for art's sake."[55] I am grateful for this marvelous evocation of what Statius achieves.

The focus of this chapter, on the implication of poets in the taste and politics of the reigning emperor, has led me to emphasize an uncongenial side of Statius's poetry of occasion, but this should not blind readers to the extraordinary skill with which he found new words and new ways to express ideas now compulsory by the rules of the imperial game. The *Silvae* are composed of highly traditional themes, for which there were old established rules observed by both orators and poets, but Statius succeeds in escaping the formulas, in surprising the reader or listener, and in creating a genuine variety out of his supposedly improvised and hasty compositions. Some may deplore social poetry, and it is true that the best social poetry, like some of Horace's *Odes* and *Epistles*, conceals its occasion by its very originality; but if poetry is permitted to celebrate the unremarkable, this is how it should be done, with style and ingenuity. Statius's virtues were those of his class, and better attuned to the society around him than the irony of a Petronius or the Stoic indignation of a Seneca, a Persius, or a Lucan. But the external pressure of the overheated imperial cult required an extraordinary talent, and a sacrifice of pride few Romans were prepared to make. For high or even ceremonial poetry, those days would not return.

Six

Literature and the Governing Classes: From the Accession of Vespasian to the Death of Trajan

Equestrian and Senatorial Writers, a Changing Elite

Was the Roman governing class still so coherent and distinct a body in the Flavian and Trajanic periods that it justifies the socially restrictive title that I have imposed on this chapter?[1] We have seen that in the fifty years after the death of Augustus certain types of literature—predominantly history and moral philosophy—were read and composed by senators and members of senatorial families. But there was little difference in culture or interest between imperial senators and other men of established social prestige: landowners who might be content with purely local distinction, or pursue an equestrian administrative career or a military commission under imperial patronage, or even devote themselves to suitably dignified and indirect moneymaking. The same family might sponsor sons in both senatorial and equestrian careers. Seneca and his brother, the orator Gallio, became senators and consuls; their third brother, Annaeus Mela, stayed in private life but saw his son begin a senatorial career. Men of both classes might take up intellectual pursuits. The consular Seneca and the equestrian Musonius Rufus both wrote moral treatises; the chief difference between them is that Seneca directed his philosophical interests into writing for other members of his own class, whereas Musonius actually served as the teacher of moralists and philosophers and seems to have derived some of his income from this role.

In general, then, the equestrian and senatorial elites overlap, and we can expect them to have much in common as writers and as public. In Cicero's time the difference lies in the narrower orientation of the senatorial class toward oratory, history, biography— literary genres used in public life or in recording public careers. By the time of Vespasian, a class has begun to emerge of senatorial technocrats writing technical texts, including the military commander Sextus Julius Frontinus (suffect consul in 74?), whose books on land surveying, on aqueducts, and on military tactics survive to this day, and the jurists such as Pliny's friend Neratius Priscus (suffect consul in 97) whose work has been excerpted in the Digest. Other members of this social stratum who abstained from participation in public life turned their attention to antiquarian or quasi-scientific treatises on subjects of less interest to the career politician or provincial administrator.

Any approach to the literature and culture of this period has to take into account the ambiguous and fluctuating status of those who professed philosophy. Under Nero prominent adherents of Stoicism and those influenced by the more extreme Cynic teaching were suspect, and liable to prosecution for treason; senators tended to be condemned to death, but men of lesser rank like Musonius were merely exiled. Musonius had first left Rome to accompany the endangered imperial heir Rubellius Plautus into banishment in Asia Minor in 62, but returned after the assassination of his patron. In 65 he was incriminated in the Pisonian conspiracy against Nero, and exiled to the barren island of Gyaros, but must have returned after Nero's death, since he is found trying to advise the warring forces of Otho and Vitellius in 69.[2] With the accession of Vespasian, it seemed a new openness had dawned, and Tacitus records Musonius's prosecution of Publius Celer for his betrayal of his patron Barea Soranus under Nero (*Hist.* 4.10, 40), but the freedom of criticism proved short-lived, and at some time in the 70s, Vespasian was driven to expel philosophers by decree.[3] So we hear of no Latin philosopher or philosophical writing under the new dynasty. But the regime was more tolerant of the apolitical Greek philosophers and public lecturers that first begin to visit Rome under Vespasian. After his last restoration, Musonius, who taught in Greek, numbered among his pupils Dio of Prusa, nicknamed Chrysostom for his golden eloquence, Euphrates, and the ex-slave Epictetus.[4] Both Dio and Euphrates seem to have made contact with Vespasian before he was emperor,[5] and Dio at least was able to stay in Rome after Vespasian's ban on philosophers. But then Dio indeed saw himself not as a philosopher but as an orator who offered brilliant speeches on moral and political topics, speeches that inspired and took care not to offend. As a friend of Vespasian's son Titus and Titus's son-in-law Flavius Sabinus, he enjoyed imperial favor and esteem at Rome until he was exiled by Domitian, to be restored to favor and prominence soon after Domitian's assassination in 96.

Anyone who wishes to form a complete picture of the culture of Rome in the period from A.D. 70 to 120 must keep in mind the prominence of the Greek-speaking and Greek-writing lecturers at the beginning and end of this period. Some put most emphasis on their oral communication—whether private teaching like that of Musonius and Epictetus, or more public displays like those of Euphrates.[6] Others carefully recorded and published their lectures and sermons, like Dio, many of whose orations survived as models for future orators and declaimers. Another Greek sophist, Nicetes Sacerdos from Smyrna, is criticized for his Asianic intonation and loquacity by Messala, the conservative spokesman of Tacitus's *Dialogus* (15.3), but treated with respect by the younger Pliny, to whom he taught Greek rhetoric (*Ep.* 6.6.13). These figures of the so-called Second Sophistic[7] are difficult to classify, but whether we call them philosophers, sophists, or rhetors, their renewal of the Greek tradition of the oral *logos* was a glamorous component of the social and cultural life of Rome, a feature that would become even more prominent in the time of Hadrian.

But before considering the literary activities of those who involved themselves in public life at Rome itself, it would be appropriate to contrast two writers, one from the beginning of this period, the other toward its end, whose books in some ways come closer to our definition of scholarship than of literature. Each is known to us for a major work used throughout the Middle Ages and Renaissance as a source for knowledge of the Roman world, and one of them at least is still enthusiastically read in English today. I cannot claim credit for making the comparison between the elder Pliny and Suetonius Tranquillus, the encyclopedist author of the *Natural History* and the biographer of the Caesars. This is the helpful approach of Andrew Wallace-Hadrill, whose *Suetonius: The Scholar and His Caesars* is as informative about the literary culture of these years as it is about his central subject.

Neither Pliny the Elder nor Suetonius embarked on a senatorial career, and both seem to have been chiefly concerned with scholarly research and writing at an age when others would have been seeking administrative posts. Pliny was born around A.D. 23, Suetonius around 70. Each man can be found at the age of thirty-five engaged in research and living in apparent retirement. During the principate of Claudius (A.D. 41–54) Pliny had served as an officer in Germany under Corbulo and Pomponius Secundus (47–51) and as procurator in Roman Africa under Nero, with six years of service to Vespasian in Spain and Gallia Belgica[8] before accepting the position of admiral in command of the fleet at Misenum in Campania. We may think of him as the stout elderly uncle and adoptive father of young Pliny, his sister's son, or as an obsessive scholar who spent his day in annotating and listening to learned Greek and Roman treatises, and even used a litter so that he could read while in motion. But Pliny the Elder died a full-time officer of the emperor, and the *Natural History* was only the last of his compositions. Before he turned to this encyclopedia, he had composed a history of the German wars, a manual of javelin throwing, and a biography of his commander Pomponius Secundus.[9] He even took an interest in language and rhetoric, composing eight books "on doubtful idioms" (*De Dubio Sermone*) and a work of rhetoric in three double volumes that is criticized by Quintilian.[10] We will see that the elder Pliny also began a Roman history, continuing where his friend Aufidius Bassus had left off.[11] If we look at his output dispassionately, it would seem that his early writings were very much in the public domain—both military history and military technology—

and that his excursion into philology was encouraged by the hazards of life under Nero, while his encyclopedia itself was begun as the work of his old age.

Pliny's preface to the *Natural History* is surprising in several ways. First we discover that he is on close terms with Titus, the future emperor, and can invoke in nostalgic language their good times in camp together. He is probably the only Roman ever to address a future emperor as *iucundissime imperator*, "most gracious commander." But the English version is too formal to translate an adjective Catullus chose to address to his dearest friend. Apparently Pliny has written to Titus before, since he talks of an earlier "teasing letter" and he proceeds to a mock-serious account of the risks he takes in dedicating his book to Titus, since this robs him of the right to excuse its faults. He should quail before so expert a reader instead of inviting him to use the book.

The old soldier goes on to deprecate his task because it offers no scope to artistic rhetorical prose, or for the excitement of amazing events and diverse changes of fortune.[12] His material is scholarship—not new material but subjects often obscurely presented by the Greeks who are his sources, and in many cases plagiarized by his Roman predecessors (praef. 12–16). His excuse is that he prefers to make a legacy of useful works rather than writing what merely gives pleasure. Indeed, this work only occupies his moments of leisure, while he gives his days to the service of his emperor. Even so, he feels under pressure to explain why he is not dedicating a history of the Flavian family and their victories. The explanation is unexpected [Nat. Praef. 20]:

> As for your father, your brother, and yourself, we have spoken of you all in a formal work, the *History of Our Times,* that begins where Aufidius's history leaves off. Where is this work, you will ask? It was finished long ago and preserved safely: in any case I was determined to entrust it to my heir, so that my life would run no suspicion of having courted ambition.

Can this be true? Why didn't his devoted heir, who reports his adoptive father's work, also publish it? Given Domitian's jealousy of Titus it might have been dangerous until the death of Domitian, and then again perhaps it failed to meet the younger Pliny's critical standards. Perhaps he made a few copies for friends and left it at that.

But Pliny's *Natural History* survived, and it features an important editorial innovation: an analytical table listing the contents of each book and the sources he used, to save his readers from wasting time in finding the information they sought.[13] A work of reference, then, not to be read from end to end. Recent studies by Andrew Wallace-Hadrill and Gian Biagio Conte[14] have brought out the originality of this work, and the extent to which it reflects its author's personality and values: his admiration for nature, and detestation of luxury—always perceived as the result of foreign, that is Greek, influence on the natural and traditional Roman way of life—and, with it, his sheer delight in listing, counting, and making an inventory of the world and its wonders.

Before he died, asphyxiated by the eruption of Vesuvius in 79, this busy administrator had amassed the bare facts and details of Hellenistic and Roman knowledge of cosmology, astronomy, anthropology, zoology, botany, medecine, and metallurgy, not to mention a history of human culture and inventions (in book 7 on man) and the fullest surviving account of Greek and Roman art and artists known or represented at Rome in the first century. There is here more moral interpretation than scientific search for understanding, and the simple man's love of detail for its own sake, but his book would still be in use in the time of Erasmus after fifteen centuries.

In the years when Suetonius Tranquillus, born to an equestrian family around A.D. 70, was growing up, the dominant educational influence at Rome was that of Vespasian's professor of Latin literature, Quintilian (M. Fabius Quintilianus) from Calagurris in Spain. Quintilian's twelve books on the teaching of oratory give a vivid impression of his high standards for both elementary and advanced education. He may never have directed a school for the younger boys of the grammaticus, but he taught rhetoric both privately to the princes of Domitian's family and publicly to the Roman elite. Quintilian's books reflect the two goals of giving trainee orators a broad education in literature and other disciplines, and a realistic preparation for life in the courts. The younger Pliny studied with

Quintilian and scholars have argued that Suetonius did also, but he seems to have held aloof from public life until the time of Nerva. Although he could apparently afford a life of quiet scholarship until his thirties, the letters addressed to him by the more affluent Pliny suggest that Suetonius was then beginning to establish himself. They show him afraid to go into court because of a dream (*Ep.* 1.18); asking advice on buying an estate (1.24); seeking a commission to a military tribunate, which he apparently asked to transfer to a relative (3.8); and finally reaching the point where Pliny openly prods him to publish his first literary work (5.10, a letter written when Suetonius was about thirty-five). According to Pliny, this is a perfect and refined production, and needs only to be transferred to elegant scrolls and displayed for sale. But what was it? Pliny gives no hint.

Wallace-Hadrill classifies Suetonius's work into three categories:[15] the lexicographical studies, the essays on institutions, and the biographical writings, of which the *Lives of the Caesars* came last. The diversity of Suetonius's other recorded titles is quite extraordinary. For what readership would Suetonius compose *On Terms of Abuse* and *On Greek Games*, apparently written in Greek?[16] Did he see himself as a scholar in the Greek tradition writing treatises for other Greek-speaking scholars? The topics do not lack interest for Roman readers; but Suetonius may have used Greek simply because the core of these works was a Greek word list, compiled from Greek sources.[17] On the other hand his treatises— *On Names and Types of Clothes*, *On Physical Defects*, *On Weather Signs*, *On Names of Seas and Rivers*, and *On Names of Winds*—also coincide with topics worked on by Greeks, from Callimachus on rivers to, for example, Telephus of Pergamum writing on several of these subjects a generation after Suetonius. And in this next generation Romans too, like Aulus Gellius or Apuleius, will revel in collecting names—of winds, for example, or types of eye defect, or of dress.[18]

On Greek Games is concerned with private pastimes, but *On Roman Spectacles and Games* deals with the public festivals of Rome, following the Varronian model of antiquarian research into national institutions and their development. Wallace-Hadrill groups in the same category Suetonius's lost treatises *On the Roman Year*, *On Rome and Its Customs and Manners*, and *On the Institution of Offices* (that is, government administrative appointments). It must have been during his period of involvement with these antiquarian topics that Suetonius composed the treatise *On Cicero's Republic* apparently as a reply to a Greek grammarian.[19]

There remain the lives—not those of the Caesars, but the five books *On Distinguished Men* dealing with men of education and literary culture. They have already been cited repeatedly for evidence about grammatici and rhetores, grouped in one brief book that is still extant, and for the *Lives of the Poets*, many of which have been retrieved, at least in abridged form, from later sources like Donatus.[20] But the lives of orators, historians, and philosophers survived only as brief and arbitrary excerpts in Jerome's Christian-oriented imitation, *On Distinguished Men*.

Given this extraordinary output over and beyond the renowned *Lives of the Caesars*, there remains the further problem that Suetonius, like the elder Pliny, gave up his private studies to become an imperial official, probably after he returned from service in Bithynia with his friend Pliny the Younger[21]—perhaps in 113. Suetonius held three successive offices as director of research (*a studiis*) and of libraries (*a bibliothecis*) under Trajan, then as director of correspondence (*ab epistulis*) under Hadrian until his dismissal in or before 122.[22] He may have been a full-time private scholar in his twenties and thirties, but once scholarship won him imperial office, at least half of his time must have been absorbed by duties. In compensation these very duties, at least in his first two positions, increased Suetonius's access to the rare and learned works preserved in imperial libraries. The post *a biblothecis* will have been particularly important if, as Wallace-Hadrill surmises, Suetonius was appointed to supervise the establishment of the new Bibliothecae Ulpianae in Trajan's great forum complex: to equip the new libraries was no sinecure. At the same time, his appointment was obviously both a recognition and an encouragement of his scholarly activities.

Suetonius's access to the imperial archives gives his early *Lives of the Caesars* a level of documentation that is taken for granted in modern authorized biographies but is unprecedented in ancient literature. And even for Suetonius it did not last. Although he had at least begun the eight volumes of his *Caesars* under Trajan, they would not be finished until well into Hadrian's principate, and after the *Life of Tiberius* the biographies reflect the loss of access to the imperial correspondence that came with his dismissal by Hadrian. Both the imperial lives and the lives of grammatici and rhetores show a particular fascination with the intellectual last generation of the republic and renaissance under Augustus: hence Julio-Claudian lives continue to be rich in interest, but Suetonius writes much more briefly of the Flavian emperors, just as he skimps the poets and grammarians of the period, partly because they would be of less interest to his readers. These would be men of his own age or more, who recalled from their own youth both the political and cultural life of these years.

Suetonius's imperial biographies are not fully developed moral and political lives after the fashion of his contemporary Plutarch, nor is there any reason to think the two biographers knew of each other's work. With their focus on the private habits and tastes of the individual, the Suetonian lives have much to offer the modern historian of literary culture, but they would be a supplement to, not a substitute for, the representation of the emperors in serious history. And although they became immensely influential models for the imperial biographies of the *Historia Augusta* composed in the third and fourth centuries, Suetonius's *Caesars* is a product, not a factor, of the cultural life of Trajan's principate. Roman society before the accession of Hadrian would have known him only as a learned source on institutional and cultural history, and read him, as we have done, to reconstruct the society of past generations.

Choices of Literary Career: Fame or Survival

Perhaps the best access to the active society of the senatorial class and to its more public concerns is through a brief but unforgettable work by the historian Tacitus that enables his readers to eavesdrop on a literary discussion among cultured friends. The dramatic date is A.D. 75, in the sixth year of the emperor Vespasian, and the scene a private house, the home of the poet Curiatius Maternus. It is the morning after he has given a recitation of his tragedy *Cato*, and he has the text in hand as he reconsiders it for copying and publication. Guests include the orators Marcus Aper and Julius Secundus, accompanied by the observant young student Cornelius Tacitus.

The first words spoken are—somewhat surprisingly in that polite society—a reproach from Secundus to his host. "Hasn't malicious gossip deterred you at all" he asks "from cherishing the offensive material in your *Cato*? Or is that why you have returned to your text, to edit it more carefully and delete anything that gives scope for a hostile interpretation? If you did that you would be publishing not a better *Cato*, but certainly a safer one."

"No," his host replied, "you will read the sentiments that Maternus's self-respect requires, and recognize the same text that you heard. Anything that Cato forgot to say, Thyestes will say in the next recitation; for I have already planned this tragedy too and laid out its dialogue."

Thus the first words of Tacitus's report indicate that tragedy is a genre written, and interpreted, with political implications. Maternus's choice of a Roman historical theme, the death of the republican hero Cato, is a mark of opposition to the principate, but he feels equally able to express his disapproval of autocracy through the Greek myth of the exiled Thyestes and his tyrannical brother King Atreus of Mycenae. The poet is being advised to practice self-censorship, and it is assumed that criticism of autocracy is dangerous under the new emperor Vespasian, as it was for Mamercus Scaurus and others under Tiberius.

Although tragedy, even for recitation, was not the most significant public form of poetry, Tacitus has chosen this real-life figure, perhaps the same man as the senator and provincial governor of this name,[23] to represent the art of poetry in a debate that begins with the conventional antithesis of poet and orator. It is assumed that every educated man of this class has to make a choice of the literary form in which he will express his ideas: and Aper, at least, political animal as he is, assumes that Maternus ought to be devoting himself to *orationes*, political speeches, and *causae*, judicial speeches in the courts.

The discussion that follows, like Cicero's great dialogues *On the*

Orator and *Brutus*, should not be read as the historical record that Tacitus claims to offer. For one thing Tacitus has modeled his work both in style and content on Cicero's dialogues, and both genre and the fact of imitation imply at least a modification of the record. In addition, scholars agree that the *Dialogus* was written about a generation after its dramatic date. They may disagree about its precise year of composition, but it is certainly later than the reign of Domitian, and its political stance is bound to reflect the experiences of the senatorial class under that suspicious and unpopular ruler. Vespasian is generally thought to have been politically tolerant of all but the most open challenges,[24] but Domitian had exiled and condemned to death more than one republican idealist. Even biography could be an ideological weapon and bring on a political punishment. In the younger Pliny's generation his friend Arulenus Rusticus was condemned to death by Domitian for writing a biography of the Neronian Stoic senator Paetus Thrasea, and Herennius Senecio was condemned and the women of his family exiled for composing a memoir of Helvidius Priscus the Elder.[25]

Tacitus's *Dialogue on Orators* has in fact two topics, of which the first, though a mere preliminary to his main concern, is just as important for our interests. Ostensibly he presents the first question, whether a man of this class should become an orator or a poet, only because he wants to reopen the problem of the declining importance and quality of public oratory at Rome. But the alternative literary occupations raise questions about the uses of writing that return in different disguises in the personal letters of the younger Pliny and the *Satires* of Juvenal.

First, let us be clear that these are men with private wealth, whose lives will not be devoted exclusively to their chosen form of writing or speaking. They are probably landowners, certainly men with duties to friends and clients, if not to tenants, and as members of the Senate they were expected to give their time to its meetings and to holding administrative positions to which they were elected or nominated by the emperor. Even so, they have assumed that they should make their name through the artistic use of language, whether through the applied literary genre of oratory or the "pure" genre of poetry.

Curiatius's retort to Secundus shows that he at least feels even poetry should be applied to conveying his ideological values: he will boast later (11.2) that one of his plays caused the downfall of a vicious favorite of Nero. But in the ensuing discussion, he supports the value of poetry by the example of a pure poet—or at least one politically loyal to the regime, the example of Virgil himself.

Tacitus is a subtle writer, and he intimates in his introduction that his readers are not to believe everything that is said on either side in this debate. On the contrary, he follows Aper's eloquent advocacy of contemporary oratory against poetry and his preference for the current speakers over those of the past by the comment of Maternus that Aper himself does not believe what he has said. Aper has simply been playing the *advocatus diaboli* (24.2).[26]

So consider the first issue: oratory or poetry. In Aper's eyes oratory is the only art worthy of a man, whereas poetry is good enough for men like Saleius Bassus who have not the gifts for advocacy. Oratory enables you to protect your friends (Cicero had said the same), to make alliances, and to put whole provinces in your debt. It is the single activity that brings most profit, prestige, and glory both at Rome and across the empire. But Aper's examples jar. The notorious Eprius Marcellus and Vibius Priscus, men of low birth and bad character, as he admits, are cited for the power they exercised through oratory, not only to defend themselves against the attack of senatorial adversaries (5.6) but to become friends of the emperor. Indeed, he hints discreetly, even the emperor respects them because they alone owe nothing to him (8.3) and can help him by removing critics and potential adversaries.[27] It does not help the morality of Aper's argument that he stresses the pleasure eloquence can give the orator through his sense of power; power over other men comes before the more legitimate power over his art itself, and the ability to produce effective speech on the spot or with due preparation.

Aper himself is an established politician of praetorian status; he boasts of no prosecutions, only the speeches he has made as advocate in civil cases and as defending counsel—the more honorable role—before the emperor himself, on behalf of imperial freedmen and administrators. But these imperial officials were not loved, and his words would have been read with some skepticism by men of Tacitus's own class. As for poetry, Aper's picture of the hardships of contemporary poets, forced to pay for a recital hall and supplicate an indifferent audience,[28] is unfortunately more convincing than Maternus's appeal to the prestige and glory won by Virgil. We do not know whether Tacitus really thought the dead Pomponius Secundus and Saleius Bassus were poets of distinction who would be famous with posterity. But Maternus's need to cite the unique Virgil on behalf of his case shows its weakness. Perhaps his most convincing argument is for the innocence of his poetry and the pleasure it affords him—or would be if the works that he names were not all politically colored. He can legitimately argue that even leisure is his to enjoy only because he is not a popular advocate but a private poet who can offer no material benefit to greedy clients.

So far we have accepted the premises of Tacitus's speakers. But the record of Roman literature to date has made it clear that oratory and tragedy, or even post-Virgilian epic, were not the only literary forms practiced among men of this class. The regular poetic genres are briefly surveyed in order of importance by Aper at 10.4. Not only Maternus's tragedy and epic, but the lesser genres of lyric, elegy, iambi, and the diversion of epigrams earn his recognition, if only as superior to any of the nonliterary arts. Aper pretends respect for poetry, but his analogies show both his real attitude and his social values. In the same passage he compares the primacy of oratory to the superior prestige of wrestling over javelin throwing "at the games in Greece, where it is also honorable to practice sport [*ludicras artes*]." This is the only place in Aper's speeches where the word honorable is used, and there can be no doubt that Tacitus is signaling to his readers, by the very absence of *honestum*, the criterion of honor, from Aper's speech in support of modern oratory, that it is no longer honorable, nor, in many ways, is the society that he represents.

It is even more obvious that the speakers are not considering the full range of literary prose practiced at Rome in or before their own time. Secundus is praised for his work on the biography of the orator Julius Africanus (14.4), but there is no mention of composing moral treatises like Seneca's, or encyclopedias like that of the elder Pliny, whose work was contemporary with the dramatic date of the dialogue, or history, the very genre in which Tacitus himself would achieve distinction.[29] History might be problematic under the empire, but it had continued, composed by Aufidius Bassus, Pliny the Elder, Cluvius Rufus, Servilius Nonianus, and others (all recorded by Tacitus or by Quintilian's survey of 10.1) and it would produce the last great literary work from Rome itself. Why is Tacitus silent about the potential of composing history? Even if he had not yet formed his literary ambition when he composed the *Dialogue*, no one doubted the seriousness or moral value of writing history.

The answer may be suggested by a rather different and slightly later cultural survey—Juvenal's *Satires* 7, in which he considers the unprofitability of literature and rejects in turn each career option available to the educated Roman. Whatever the truth of Juvenal's economic status, he writes in the persona of a poor gentleman, by inclination a poet, but prepared to consider the full range of honorable occupations open to his education, yet driven to reject them all. The poem was probably composed twenty years after the *Dialogus* and almost fifty after its dramatic date, but the situation seems constant. Juvenal starts with a bald statement of the problem. All hope of reward for art will have to depend on the new emperor (Hadrian), since recently poets have been forced to work as bath attendants or bakers, or become auctioneers and gladiators.[30] While young men are urged to exert themselves and attract imperial generosity (*ducis indulgentia*, 7.21), it is made clear that the days of private patronage are gone, and unlike Horace or Virgil, or even Lucan, recent poets—exemplified by the popular Statius—can makes ends meet only by selling pantomime scripts. The two obstacles are the patron's stinginess—why, he will barely provide a miserable room for his poetic client's recital—and the low valuation he puts on poetry. Most patrons prefer to spend their money on suppliers of luxury or entertainment and are not impressed by poetry, since they all write verses and think their own work superlative.

Essentially Juvenal is prepared to consider five intellectual or discourse-related occupations. The educated man may aspire to be a poet or a historian, a lawyer or a teacher, either rhetor or grammaticus. History is given the least attention—only seven lines, because it was not a career or a living but generally an occupation for the retirement of men of leisure. Cicero had said many years back that he wanted to write history, but it demanded uninterrupted time, which he did not have.[31] Juvenal too stresses the time and toil and cost of the writing materials for this voluminous genre.[32] The writing of history would have suited the mature and wealthy men of the *Dialogus*, provided that they kept to the safe history of the remote past, but this probably brought little glory, while contemporary history was hazardous, and neither kind of writing brought income.

The next possibility for making a living is the role of lawyer. Martial expresses envy of lawyers: "you'll get rich if you plead lawsuits" (2.30.5), but Juvenal pictures a risky profession incurring great debts and requiring expensive display.[33] There is a better career to be made of acting the lawyer in Gaul or Africa—perhaps at Rome too many aspiring lawyers were competing for the cases in dispute. There is no word here of the literary aspect of advocacy, no hint that oratory in the lawcourts was still considered a form of high art and distinction, but we will see the reason for this when we draw on Pliny's evidence for the oratory on which he prided himself. A more likely possibility for the educated man with no inherited wealth was a career in teaching—honorable for some, and considered at length by Juvenal. Modern scholars have perhaps been too ready to assume that no gentleman would choose to teach.

The form of education practiced during the fifty years covered by this chapter has not substantially changed from the stages we met a century earlier (see Chapter 1). The child of a moneyed family would learn reading and writing at home, and at the age of ten to twelve, either have a grammaticus as private tutor or go to a school to study poetry and historical narratives and acquire basic skills in composition. In his teens, he would move on to the rhetor's school to learn declamatory rhetoric, passing from the study of literature to the elaboration of his own speeches. Where the grammaticus's class might study Homer or Virgil, Livy or Sallust collectively, the rhetorician's class meant labor-intensive individual performance and correction. The program outlined by Quintilian represents an ideal, and the most significant deviation from it lay in the tendency of grammatici to skimp the students' exposure to literature in order to accelerate their progress in composition: this could be designed to please impatient parents, or to claim a higher status for the teacher inasmuch as he was giving a more advanced training.[34]

Certainly the two professions of grammaticus and rhetor were not equal in respect or remuneration. Not only parents but other adults would visit the rhetor's school to hear declamations by teacher or pupil, and his teaching was seen as the path to success in the lawcourts.[35] Hence Juvenal moves by association from the lawcourts to the rhetorician's school (7.150–216) and gives it more attention than that of the grammaticus. Juvenal's portrait of the profession evokes the boredom of repetition, of hearing each pupil handle the same exercise, of the standard assignments in the historical *suasoria* and the legal *controversia*, but his chief grievance against the profession is once again the meanness of the wealthy—in this case, the unwillingness of the pupils' parents to pay out fees except after litigation or after all the tradesmen have been paid off. The trouble was that everyone knew the most famous rhetor, Quintilian, had received a good salary and honors as professor of Latin rhetoric from Vespasian and his successors, so that the satirist has to counteract his case by writing off the successful teachers as lucky. With typical pessimism Juvenal also relegates good pupils to the distant past. It was and still is a commonplace of the older generation, whether parents, satirists, or educational theorists, to condemn the corruption, indiscipline, and low standards of contemporary schooling, and we should not be misled by Juvenal or Vipstanus Messala, the Young Fogey in Tacitus's *Dialogus*, on the closing of the Roman mind.

Juvenal seems to have been unmarried and childless: what did he know of the rhetorician's school—unless he had once served as a rhetor or hypodidascalos (assistant master)? Along with Quintilian's good fortune, honored by the right of wearing consular dress (*ornamenta*), Juvenal invokes a tragic reversal of fortune that Pliny too describes in a lively letter: the senator who ended up as a teacher of rhetoric.[36] In A.D. 97 the ex-praetor Valerius Licinianus, who had been convicted of incest with a Vestal and disfranchised, was allowed by the emperor Nerva to reside in Sicily, and he set up school there as a rhetorician. Obviously he was a local attraction, and adult audiences for his displays must have spread the story found in Pliny of Valerius's favorite preambles on the vicissitudes of Fortune. The career of grammaticus is presented as the last and worst of the educated man's options. Was it a real possibility? Juvenal stresses the outlay on paying ushers and attendants, the hours of nocturnal study, the vulnerability to trivial questions out of school, and the burden of disciplining the young, but reserves as his final argument the same difficulty of recovering pay and the same low rate of remuneration that he had invoked in rejecting the life of the rhetorician.

Oddly, classical teachers themselves have usually taken this seriously. But isn't this a caricature? How often was the rhetor or grammaticus dependent on irregular private fees? Leaving aside the professorial grandeur of a Quintilian, Pliny's letters show that Italian municipalities had learned something from the regular Greek pattern, and started to hire at least public rhetors. A well-known letter to Tacitus (4.13) describes Pliny's offer to his fellow citizens in Como to provide sufficient capital for one-third of the cost of paying a schoolmaster. But readers often do not notice two details of more general interest. First, Pliny may treat his own proposal as a bold innovation, but he reports that teachers are publicly hired by many Italian communities, and that the competition for the job is often warped by canvassing: clearly the position was in demand.[37] Second, Pliny's overt motive in writing to Tacitus is to ask him to find a good candidate for this position from the crowd of studious men (*copia studiosorum*) who gather around him in admiration for his intellect. So the position of rhetor is likely to attract the sort of young men Tacitus knows.[38]

How do we read this? Is Pliny referring to cultured clients, hangers-on of the wellborn and consular Tacitus? Or are these more like actual students, young men whose families have arranged for them to be introduced to the ways and techniques of the courts with the distinguished advocate? In the *Dialogus* Tacitus's backward-looking Messala claims that young men of good family no longer observed the famous orators in the genteel apprenticeship of the

199

tirocinium fori, as they used to learn public life from observing Cicero. But apparently these *studiosi*—perhaps sons of the provincial aristocracy like Tacitus himself—were ready to take on the post of rhetor in a small north Italian *municipium*. And Pliny himself, asked to find a private teacher of Latin rhetoric for Corellia Hispulla's nephew, recommends a friend, Julius Genitor (*Ep.* 3.3). That Genitor is not just some client is shown by Pliny's inclusion in his published collection of two more letters to Genitor, one indeed provoked by the death of his pupil (*Ep.* 7.30). This is clear evidence for a cultural world beyond that of the elderly and the leisured rich, and for a class of educated men who expected to work for a living. It is fair to assume that the teaching profession was both commoner and more acceptable to Roman citizens of respectable family than Juvenal admits.[39]

Pliny's Letters and His Literary World

I have already drawn repeatedly on Pliny's *Letters*. These are not only the single most important contemporary source for the literary culture of the educated classes, they are a unique illustration of the changes in literary culture since the last generation of the republic, for which Cicero's letters were so precious a source. Unlike Cicero's collected correspondence, Pliny's *Letters* constitutes neither a collection nor a selection of actual dated messages and communications to friends. They were certainly written and sent to the friends named in the greeting, but as literary sketches or essays, not a communication determined by circumstances, giving news and making or answering current requests. Pliny does not conceal this: his opening letter, to Septicius Clarus, is more like a dedication.

> You have often urged me to collect and make public any letters of mine which were composed with some care. I have now made a collection, not keeping to the original order, as I was not writing history, but taking them as they came to my hand. It remains for you not to regret having made the suggestion and for me not to regret following it: for then I shall set about recovering any letters which have hitherto been put away and forgotten and I shall not suppress any which I may write in future. (*Ep.* 1.1., trans. Radice)

This letter is undated, and contains nothing that specifically relates to Clarus's interests, and such is the regular pattern of Pliny's letters. They bear no date, they are usually written on a single topic, and in most of them there is nothing that points to a particular addressee. If they were originally sent as communications, they were surely heavily edited for collection and publication. Otherwise the recipient might fairly have been disappointed and felt this could have been written to anyone. Alternatively we might suppose some of them were sent with a covering letter to contain the actual news and inquiries. Certainly Pliny openly encouraged his friends to practice the same art, for *Letters* 7.9 to Fuscus Salinator advises him to include artistic letters among his forms of literary exercise and one of the last letters of the collection, 9.28, shows that Voconius Romanus had written to announce that he in turn was sending one of these literary epistles (*litteras curiosius scriptas*).[40] Anne Marie Guillemin, in her superb book on Pliny's world of literature,[41] protests that modern readers wrong Pliny by measuring his literary letters against Cicero's correspondence, and suggests that it would be fairer to relate them to the poetic epistles of Horace or the quasi-epistolary epigrams of Martial. But this tells us something about the age as well as the individual. The sheer self-consciousness of these letters, the concern with self-representation, is itself characteristic of this postclassical phase of Roman culture.[42] These are more like autobiographical essays, composed, not merely selected, to create a picture of Pliny's world, and in this world literary activities are even more prominent than Pliny's public commitments as senator and advocate.

Since these letters have been so carefully chosen to provide a full representation of Pliny's life and world as he wished to display it, they are important not only for their own sake, as models of a new literary genre, midway between essay and autobiography, but as our best evidence for Pliny's literary milieu and its activities.

But in one respect their evidence is disappointing. For Pliny seems only interested in the public or performative context of literary activity. He indicates where and when he is writing only in exceptional circumstances—such as the occasion when he pens a letter sitting by the hunting nets, at his Tuscan villa (*Ep.* 1.6). For the same reason he does not describe his townhouse, where he spent the greater part of each year; nor does he describe his domestic routine in town, surely because his time in town was spent in public, consumed by public duties or social commitments. Two finely wrought essays describe in detail the contrasting architecture of his villa at Laurentum, which he could retreat to after the day's work in Rome (2.17), and the summer villa at Tifernum Tiberinum (5.6). To these essays correspond shorter letters, written toward the end of his private collection, describing his daily routine first at Tifernum (9.36; cf. 9.15), then at Laurentum (9.40), and these permit us to reconstruct what he meant by the pursuit of *litterae* in private.

The first thing to notice is the lack of emphasis on reading. Pliny seems to have no library in town, and certainly has none in Tuscany. The villa at Laurentum, Pliny's "private shrine of the muses" (1.9), contains a "room built round in an apse to let in the sun as it moves round and shines in each window in turn . . . with one wall fitted with shelves like a library to hold the books which I read and read again" (2.17.8). This is the nearest approach to a library in Pliny's epistolary self-portrait, though his friend the learned Herennius Severus has a library that includes both established and minor or specialist authors (4.28). Romans regularly set above the shelves of their libraries busts or portraits of the authors whose books they contained, and Pliny is asking the help of Vibius Severus to obtain portraits for Herennius of Cornelius Nepos and the Epicurean Catius.

Have we been too quick to assume that all educated Romans had libraries like those of Cicero, Lucullus, and Atticus? It has been shown recently that many of the large rooms in villas of Pliny's day identified by archaeologists as libraries were in fact designed not to hold bookshelves but wall-reliefs;[43] Roman bookshelves stood on their own legs, and required alcoves rather than the niches with raised ledges exemplified in these rooms. Seneca never speaks of a room used as a library in his letters, except to mock the illiterate Calvisius Sabinus and his like (Sen. *Ep.* 27), but Seneca's letters have an ideological focus quite separate from incidental description of his way of life. Given Pliny's concern for full portrayal of his world, it seems fair to assume that the apsed room at Laurentum was his only library space. The benefactor actively concerned to give to Novum Comum a public library (Como; Pliny *Ep.* 1.8) seems not to have had a formal library of his own.

We should of course allow for a certain modest understatement in the public man, who does not wish to boast, or to seem more erudite than is appropriate for a public man. After all Pliny describes the Laurentine villa as the place of study, "where I either read or write something and find time to take exercise . . . where I talk with myself and my books" (1.9 again), "[where] I do most of my writing . . . I cultivate myself [*me studiis excolo*, 4.6]." But what form does that study take? He mentions having a work of Asinius Gallus read aloud (7.6), and in his account of his routine at Tifernum he includes "reading a Greek or Latin speech aloud and with emphasis, not so much for the sake of my voice as for my digestion!" and later refers to a book "read aloud during the meal" (9.36). But let us contrast the evidence of these letters with Cicero's correspondence. Neither in these letters nor elsewhere does Pliny ever name any books he has read, outside two categories: his rhetorical models and the copious amateur compositions written by and for his friends. The rhetorical models, probably the "books which I read again and again" (2.17.8), Pliny cites for style, not content: his friends' compositions offered only the kind of light reading we obtain from journalism and offprints. With the exception of the Asinius Gallus memoirs, Pliny does not speak of reading any book; nor does he ask any friend to lend him or seek out a text, Latin or Greek. His emphasis is almost entirely on writing, not on reading, and the books with which Pliny converses at Laurentum are as likely to be his own current *libelli* as the works of historians or poets, living or dead.

It is possible, then, that Pliny had little use for literature in the sense we privilege. That he possessed only a specialized collection of the classic orators, and the account of the apsed room in Laurentum is quite accurate. Pliny's private life of study may have been one relatively starved of real literary nourishment, putting out more than he had time to take in.

The Public World of the Senator and Orator

What of Pliny's public use of *litterae*? What he most valued as a senator, imperial official, and consular was the public service of Senate and court—ostensibly a replica of the public world of Cicero. The oratory of Senate and lawcourt was in Pliny's eyes the real source of his dignity, one on which he prided himself and which he took pains to put on record even a decade after the events. Tacitus suggests in the *Dialogus* that oratory had become a tool in the hands of imperial cronies, exploited to prosecute the senatorial class for disloyalty or at best defend imperial administrators before the emperor himself. The picture conveyed by Pliny's cumulative correspondence is quite different. In his judgment his speeches were works of literary art, just like those of Cicero before him, and he did not hesitate to give private recitations of speeches after their delivery and to invite help from his friends in rewriting them.

But both the categories and the physical setting of public speeches had changed since the days of Cicero. In order to survey the varieties and contexts of Pliny's oratory we cannot divide it into the old genres and categories, grouping deliberative speeches before the Senate apart from judicial oratory in the courts, and ceremonial speeches in special public contexts. Pliny's speeches before the Senate were not just expressions of support or dissent from matters of policy or legislation. Because the Senate had become the primary court for the public and private offenses committed by senators, Pliny's speeches to that body included prosecution and defense of governors on trial before their peers and, on one occasion, his most ceremonial speech of all—the famous *Panegyric* of Trajan.

An example will indicate how much these senatorial performances mattered to Pliny's artistic ambitions. One of his earliest political speeches is recalled by Pliny in detail some ten years later in a letter to Ummidius Quadratus, who has been lent Pliny's written version of the speech (*Ep.* 9.13). The letter describes the political ferment after Domitian's assassination. Pliny is proud that he gave notice before the Senate of his intension to accuse Publicius Certus for his role in securing Domitian's condemnation of

Helvidius Priscus the Younger, proud that, despite opposition and warnings, he stood firm behind his motion, responding on the spot to the flurry of protest. But the letter also shows how he worked up the speech after delivery. It is characteristic that Pliny enlarged the speech for the written version, and proudly retained and circulated after more than ten years this almost historic document.[44] Another letter (6.29) recapitulates his record as prosecutor or advocate in the trials of provincial governors for offenses of extortion or abuse; the first of these, the showpiece trial of Marius Priscus in which Pliny spoke for the provincials of Africa, is described at length in 2.11.

The emperor was consul that month, so he presided at the trial, and Pliny shared the burden of prosecution with Tacitus. Despite his extreme anxiety, with one interruption, Pliny spoke for five hours, and that day there was time for only one defense speech. The length was not unusual; on another occasion Pliny spoke for seven hours. These trials were a matter of disgrace or survival for the defendant, and Pliny reports only two other accusations, related to each other, for the provincials of Baetica (southern Spain) against Caecilius Classicus and Baebius Massa with his dependents (3.4). As in Cicero's day, senior figures usually left the unpleasantness of prosecution to newcomers, and Pliny's later senatorial speeches were in defense, first of Iulius Bassus, governor of Bithynia, and then of Varenus, who had been the Bithynians' advocate against Bassus and was subsequently appointed to govern Bithynia himself. This last case involved many complexities and was ultimately referred to the emperor's decision.[45]

Pliny himself declares that he spoke most happily in the Senate, perhaps because it was rather like a gentleman's club, in which reputation and friendships counted as much if not more than legal or rhetorical rights and wrongs. But he was proudest of all of a speech that other senators may have heard with relative inattention: the *Panegyric*, technically a vote of thanks (*gratiarum actio*), which Pliny as consul for A.D. 100 was expected to address to the emperor Trajan, who had just returned to Rome for the first time since his elevation. The vote of thanks was routine, but the recent return of the emperor made the occasion special. Panegyric has little appeal to our age, and Pliny himself was conscious of the formulaic and predictable nature of its material, which he struggled to diversify in form and expression. But he keeps returning to the speech in other letters, first when enclosing samples of the best parts to Lupercus (2.5), then when he sends the whole text to Romanus (3.13), regretting that "in this genre everything has been said and made familiar" and "the reader is indifferent except to the diction."

The speech itself, more subtle and carefully thought out than many subsequent panegyrics, shows Pliny's real concern to work out a concept of imperial authority compatible with his belief in senatorial liberty;[46] it also takes pains to understand and express the impact of all the members of the imperial house as a model for the wider society. The senator also measures Trajan's role as emperor of the Roman people at large, in a way that is perhaps lacking in Tacitus's more aristocratic text. More important to our understanding of Roman ideology than of its literary history, the *Panegyricus* was the Roman ancestor of a persistent literary genre. It would become a blueprint not only for second-century encomium, sophistic and epigraphical, but for many centuries of "Mirrors for Princes," persuasive descriptions of princely virtue addressed to the princes of Europe in Latin, Italian, and all the vernaculars in turn.[47]

The letter to Romanus is typical of many in which Pliny first proudly describes his most recent composition, then begs his correspondent to criticize and mark what needs correcting. However, a third letter, to Vibius Severus (3.18), first describes the whole occasion of the speech anew, then balances it with an account of Pliny's recent recitation of the revised text on three successive days to specially invited friends.

Pliny is obsessed with style, and his chief interest in his audience's reaction is pleasure that they preferred his plainer and more sober passages. He sees this as an index of public good taste that portends an improvement in the theater also—and yet the friends so carefully selected as his audience can hardly have been representative of the much larger theater crowds.[48]

Compared with this imperial occasion, Pliny's other known ceremonial speeches are more modest: a funeral laudation on the son of his friend Spurinna (*Ep.* 3.10) and the speech made when he presented the library to the town council of Novum Comum. Although he calls it a *sermo* or talk, Pliny admits it is rather lofty at times and is troubled at the implied self-praise of showing it around. But this has not prevented him from asking Pompeius Saturninus to read a revised version for him before he decides whether to publish it (*Ep.* 1.8). We learn about his motives and principles of public benefaction, but nothing of the actual occasion.

For contemporary oratory in a more challenging context, one must turn to Pliny's accounts of the chief civil court at Rome, the Centumviral court, held in the main basilica of the Forum. Normally the jury panel of 180 was divided into four so that four cases could be heard simultaneously in different areas of the basilica. This procedure was open to the public and lent itself to grandstanding. A vivid letter (2.14) describes the decline in the standards of decorum and integrity of the court, with men openly paid to supply audience applause and fill the benches and standing room.[49] Since these paid supporters did not listen, there were signals (like the placards requesting laughter in recorded radio shows) to alert them when they must applaud. On the occasion that Pliny spoke for seven hours (4.16), he could only get into the court through the magistrates' rear entrance. In another testamentary case (6.33), Pliny spoke before the full four-panel jury of 180, with a throng downstairs crowding the tribunal, and an additional "public gallery" of men and women hanging over the balconies in the attempt to see and hear. This was a society scandal in which Pliny's client, wife of a praetor, was disputing the will of her eighty-year-old father who had disinherited her in favor of his new wife of two weeks. But despite a hung verdict with two of the jury units voting for his client and two against, the trial somehow ended in victory for his client. Pliny describes his performance as highly emotional, full of grief, indignation, and anger, and recommends the speech (which is, of course, enclosed for his correspondent) as the tour de force of his oratory, comparable with Demosthenes' *On the Crown*.

There was obviously additional interest in lawsuits involving both women and money, as in another case that Pliny won for two freedmen whose young master had died suddenly after making them coheirs with his mother. She had twice charged them before the emperor with poisoning and forgery, bringing notoriety to the hearings and the advocate (7.6.8–13). Although these causes célèbres may not be literature in the modern sense, they were clearly a major ingredient, both as text and as performance, in the verbal culture of Pliny's society.

Oratory always involved the double skills of composition and delivery, and Pliny's success makes it likely that he was a skilled performer, but at the same time his letters are obsessed with the verbal or textual aspect of his speeches, and his descriptions are of style or tone rather than argument. Indeed it is only in writing about oratory that Pliny parades his knowledge of critical theory and, in particular, of Greek models. Guillemin comments on the limitations of Pliny's knowledge of Greek literature, largely confined to Homer and Demosthenes.[50] Although Pliny names Demosthenes in the first letter after his dedicatory note, and often invokes Homer, the bulk of his quotations are to be found in two elaborate letters, set symmetrically in the first and the last books of the private collection (1.20 and 9.26).

These epistolary discussions have much in common. Each starts from an unnamed straw man. "I often dispute with a learned and expert man who loves nothing so much as brevity in court cases" (1.20). Compare 9.26: "I was right to say about an orator of our generation, who is correct and sound, but lacking in grandeur and richness 'he is faultless, except that he has no faults.'" Each letter then parades a series of excerpts and comments to justify Pliny's own stylistic preference for fullness (1.20) and extravagance of phrasing (9.26). For all that Pliny cites Homer, Eupolis, and Aristophanes in the first letter, and five different speeches of Demosthenes in the other, critics have noted that these are the standard examples of rhetoric, to be found in Cicero or Quintilian.[51] Pliny's principles are his own but his learning is revived from the training of his youth and, although his friends compared his speeches with Demosthenic masterpieces (*Ep.* 6.30, 7.30), they can have had little in common with Demosthenes' fierce bluntness and power.

Although Pliny lists the historical and biographical works of his uncle[52] and included among his friends Tacitus and Suetonius, the two best-known writers of prose in his own time, he did not himself attempt the writing of either history or biography. Pliny's temperament led him toward shorter literary forms, and the letter (5.8) inviting his friend Titinius Capito to advise him on choosing a historical topic is only a pretext to enable him to contrast the genres of oratory and history. His motives and critical assumptions are strange, and worth a moment's scrutiny. Pliny admits that he longs for fame, but claims that, whereas in oratory and poetry one must achieve greatness to become famous, he is considering history, since it appeals to the public, however it is written, because of human curiosity.[53] There is also the problem that he is still revising his speeches, and has barely time to attempt both genres. Can he really have thought his oratory less likely to earn immortality than inelegantly written history? His next argument shows that he is familiar with the artistic code established for history as early as Cicero,[54] for he sets out the traditional expectations of the historical style:

> Although both oratory and history are narrative in form the one is sordid and everyday, the other unfamiliar and grand, offering scope for rippling muscles, flowing and pleasing, with its own diction, rhythm and composition—like Thucydides' great work a long-term possession rather than a momentary prize piece.

But even if he finds the time, how can he find a topic? Past history already written up saves time on research but involves tedious comparison of different accounts, while recent history risks serious offense, since even praise can be reproached as too grudging. This is a letter about historical writing, not the inquiry of a would-be historian. But much is explained by the identity of his addressee. Titinius Capito is one of two contemporaries active in commemorating the deaths of political victims. Fannius too, probably a relative of the Helvidius family, was recording the deaths of Nero's victims and had completed three books when he died (*Ep.* 5.5). Capito's death scenes of distinguished men may have been set safely in the past: certainly he must have been discreet, since he rose to be prefect of the guard under Trajan. He was much respected by

Pliny as a patron of literature, but there is no hint that he was moved to reply to this letter or that Pliny ever returned to the option of composing history.

Pliny could have consulted a real historian: he was on good terms with Tacitus and has published many letters addressed to him. Two of them (6.16 and 20) provided Tacitus with Pliny's autopsy account of the eruption of Vesuvius and burial of Pompeii. They are followed by a series reflecting Pliny's growing pride in sharing Tacitus's distinction. One letter (7.20) expresses his delight that posterity will tell of their friendship and mutual support. Another written soon after (7.33) congratulates Tacitus on the brilliance of his *Histories* and invites him to include in them an anecdote from Pliny's youth.

This letter is revealing in several ways. Pliny has clearly modeled the letter on a very famous letter of Cicero, one of the few that Cicero intended to be made public and circulated. This was an elaborate request addressed to the senatorial historian Lucceius in 55 B.C. asking him either to work an account of Cicero's consular achievements into his continuous history, but to compose it ahead of time, or perhaps to dedicate to it a separate monograph.[55] Cicero raised the question of historical truth and favoritism and openly asked for an indulgent interpretation, but may have assumed that the conservative Lucceius saw things as he did. Pliny ends his request to Tacitus with the words: "You will make these actions more famous, glorious, and important, but of course I am not demanding that you exaggerate the event. For history should not exceed the truth and truth itself is quite enough for honorable deeds." The model is obvious; the occasion, however, is trivial—a mere anecdote, scarcely comparable with the events that Cicero took part in or Tacitus recorded.

We might include in this series a letter with a different addressee, one to Maximus (9.23), reporting Tacitus's splendid anecdote of his neighbor at the games who asked him, "Are you from Italy or the provinces?" (Did Tacitus have a regional accent?) When Tacitus answered "You must know me from your reading," the man instantly replied, "Then are you Tacitus, or Pliny?" By this date, near to 110, Tacitus had published not only his *Life of Agricola* and the ethnographic account of Germany, but his *Histories*. What published works of Pliny would be so well known? Is it not likely that the man had read his letters? Murgia has recently argued that Pliny deliberately shaped and issued the last two volumes of his nine books of letters to appear at the same time as Tacitus's *Histories*.[56] While scholars differ about the earliest publication of the letters, it is agreed that by 104–5 at the latest Pliny had compiled and published books 1 and 2, whether separately or together. There is also a common agreement that books 4, 5, and 6 were published, probably together, soon after 107.[57] So it is not surprising that the growing celebrity of the *Letters* is reflected in an early letter of book 9 (9.11). Pliny's addressee Geminus had written asking Pliny to write him a note for inclusion in his next book of letters and reported that they were selling well in Lyon, capital city of the Three Gauls. Pliny asks if this note will suffice and expresses a metropolitan surprise that there are booksellers in Lyon;[58] in any case, he is delighted that his work still finds the favor in the provinces that it has already won in the city of Rome.

The World of the Auditorium

Rome knew schools before there were lectures to adult audiences, and lectures and displays of improvisatorial declamation, before there were public recitations. For schools the setting might be a private room, an open balcony, or even a discreet corner of a public space, in a quiet street or an exedra beside a square or forum. An open setting made it easier for adults to "drop in" and attend lectures or declamatory performances, and accounts of the Augustan period use phrases like *auditio*, "a hearing or lecture," or *schola* "a school," that do not specify the situation of the activity in an open or closed space. When the form *auditorium* first occurs in a letter of Seneca (*Ep.* 52.11), he is criticizing any teacher of philosophy whose ignorant listeners send him away *ex auditorio* happy at their applause. This could be the occasion, rather than the space, but the word is used for the class or classroom by Quintilian and Tacitus as well as in Pliny's *Letters*.[59] At the same time the word *auditorium* began to denote a certain kind of room, particularly one used for public readings.[60] Aper, Tacitus's advocate of modern oratory in the *Dialogus*, imagines the poor poet obliged to organize and finance the recitation and publication of his poetry: "he must equip an *auditorium* and hire benches and distribute his slim volumes,"[61] and later calls him impatiently away "from the *auditoria* and theaters to the Forum and the real battles of the courts."

If even the real battles of the courts, as another of Tacitus's speakers points out (*Dialogus* 39), were often relegated to these same *auditoria* or to record offices (*tabularia*) away from the public ear, the primary association of the *auditorium* was now with cultural activities. Pliny regularly uses the term of the place or simply the occasion of other men's recitations.[62] Since any context of recitation can be called an *auditorium*, it would be misleading to assume without evidence some formal space with stage and semicircular seating, or even a spacious room with a raised dais for the speaker. This oscillation between physical and conceptual reference is most obvious in a passage of Apuleius describing his visit as a celebrity to a small town, which scheduled his performance in the public basilica:

> All those in town filled the basilica, which was the location of my *auditorium*, with a huge crowd and applauded me, unanimously shouting "brilliant!" and begging me to stay and become a citizen of Oea. So when the *auditorium* was over . . . " (*Apology* 7.5–9)

Associated with readings, recitals, improvised declamation, or crafted ceremonial speeches, the *auditorium* was the most characteristic literary milieu of Pliny's day and of the ensuing generation.

It is noticeable that nothing in Pliny or Tacitus himself suggests that Tacitus ever recited any of his works, although other writers chose this as their access to public attention. Pliny mentions Titinius Capito's readings from his memoirs of the deaths of great men (*Ep.* 8.12) and Regulus's obituary of his son (*Ep.* 4.7), but there are no indications that others besides himself gave readings of either history or oratory—except his statement in a key letter defending his own practice:

> I am all the more surprised to read in your letter that there were people who criticized me for giving any reading of my speeches at all: unless

they think that this is the only kind of writing which never needs correction. I should like to ask them why they allow (if they do allow) readings of history, whose authors aim at truth and accuracy rather than displaying their talents, and tragedy, which needs a stage and actors rather than a lecture room [*auditorium*], and lyric poetry, which calls for a chorus and a lyre instead of a reader. (*Ep.* 7.17, trans. Radice)

While recitation was the high point of literary culture for the Roman gentlemen of Pliny's circle, they would have to compete for public attention with the Greek visitors, orators, rhetoricians, and philosophers who dazzled large public audiences with their performances midway between sermon and lecture. These public speakers were not necessarily Greek in origin, coming most often from the flourishing urban society of Asia Minor or Syria, but Greek was the language of their education and their performance. Dio Chrysostom was welcomed by Trajan himself, and much of Dio's work is preserved, but we have only incidental descriptions of his performances. However we can compare two figures of whom Pliny gives complementary literary portraits: the philosopher Euphrates and the rhetor Isaeus. Seneca and Epictetus both condemn the Roman audiences for being more concerned with the style than the substance of the public moralists, and Pliny's reports fall into the same category; there is no hint of the topic expanded upon by either man, but much about their style and its impact. The letter devoted to Euphrates the Syrian praises him first for his almost Platonic loftiness of style; then Pliny broadens focus to describe his appearance—tall, handsome, bearded, well-groomed, and without grimness, but severe in aspect.

As a pupil of Musonius, and a man of public prestige in his own province, Euphrates could hardly have been a regular teacher, giving extended classes to continuing pupils. Pliny laments that he would like to spend the days listening to him, but Euphrates, clearly a diplomat, has reassured Pliny that his Martha-like distraction with public duties is the best form of philosophy.[63]

It is not clear to what extent Euphrates put on public performances, as opposed to lectures for afficionados, but Pliny's account of the declaimer Isaeus clearly describes a display. Isaeus is obviously a recent arrival in Rome and Pliny reports that the performances have exceeded his reputation. His method is to open with a preamble, sometimes designed to charm, sometimes to provoke serious attention; then to ask his audience for *controversiae* (the fictitious court cases of the declaimers) and let them choose from among the suggested cases and even impose the role of defender or accuser upon him. These are the improvisations of a veteran and testify to his culture and experience in formal composition.[64] But what interests Pliny in this sixty-year-old celebrity is Isaeus's preference for remaining a declaimer (*scholasticus*) and his abstention from the rhetoric of public life, which has preserved in him a kind of innocence. After an analytic rhetorical portrait, Pliny turns aside to urge his addressee to come and hear for himself: certainly one can read works just as eloquent, but nothing has the impact of the live performance, with its voice and gesture.[65]

For many of us it is harder to listen than to read; the eyes have it over the ears, as Horace declared (*Ars* 180–82), and most people are more easily distracted from construing an oral argument than one set out on pages that can be turned and re-turned. But since the Roman scroll was far less easy to unwind to track down a reference or the course of an argument, it is likely that many Romans obtained as much benefit from listening to a public reading as from their own perusal of a text, or the more common situation in which they listened to their own readers.[66]

How dominant, then, were these public or private readings in the life of cultured Romans? They form the subject of so many of Pliny's letters, whether his own readings to intimate dinner guests (3.18) or those hosted by Capito at his home (8.12) or the more public readings in a rented room or recital hall. The audience could be ill-mannered: one of Pliny's best-known letters (1.13) describes the reluctant and partial attendance at the height of the April poetry recital season—listeners turning up only for the last unit, or leaving in midrecital, in contrast with the days of Claudius when the emperor himself would go uninvited to hear Servilius Nonianus recite. It is noticeable that these readings are by amateurs—men whom Pliny calls his friends, men who have sent out personal invitations. This may be onerous, but Pliny prides himself on never letting friends down and on giving loyal attendance to Capito and others.

Another of these duty occasions provokes his indignation against apathetic members of the audience who paraded their boredom instead of providing polite enthusiasm: he sees it as a mark of generosity to applaud an inferior, and sheer folly to waste time alienating a friend in this way (*Ep.* 6.17).

Most of the evidence for readings other than Pliny's own private consultation of his friends seems to be for the reading of poetry, and virtually all genres are represented. Courtesy entails that Pliny never withholds praise or encouragement either in writing to his poetic friends or in describing their performances to others, and the same courtesy prevents us from assessing their level of skill or originality. But to the Roman audience originality of content was unimportant. Given the time that young Romans spent during their education in composing both prose and verse, they would be more interested in the technical problems and less bored by the repetition of age-old themes than postromantic or modern readers of poetry and literary prose.

No genre of poetry was unrepresented, even those that do not occur in the works of surviving imperial poets, like Sotadeans, Scazons, or the Palliata of republican times. But the longer and more demanding genres are certainly mentioned less often. Take epic. Silius Italicus and Statius both died with an epic in progress, Statius with only one and half books of the *Achilleid*, when he died in 95, and Silius with a perfunctory finale to the *Punica*.[67]

Statius and Domitian had both written epic narratives of contemporary wars, and at the time of Pliny's *Letters* Trajan was actively engaged in highly successful warfare in Dacia, so there was still room for Roman epic. And one of Pliny's friends, Caninius Rufus, is planning to write up Trajan's Dacian Wars. Like the letter to Titinius Capito, Pliny's letter of advice is an excuse for literary theorizing. Pliny can see it all, the descriptions of unfamiliar rivers and new bridges imposed by Roman engineering, castles on mountain heights, the king driven from his palace and to suicide, the double triumphs. The only challenge is to meet the glamour of the achievement—that and squeezing the Dacian names into Greek forms and classical meter. So this is to be a Greek epic! Undeterred, Pliny urges him on:

> So call the gods to your aid, as a poet may, without forgetting that divine hero (Trajan!) whose exploits, achievements, and wisdom you are going to celebrate, slacken your sheets, spread sail, and now, if ever, let the full tide of your genius carry you along. (*Ep.* 8.4)

And in case inspiration flags, Pliny is eager to see even the first draft of what Caninius writes and give his advice. Is Pliny so naive? Or is he indulging an old friend? For Pliny had already urged this country gentleman from Como to devote himself to *studia* some years earlier (*Ep.* 1.3). Perhaps then this is a merely a suitable proposal to fill his leisure.

This is the only time Pliny discusses hexameter poetry with a friend. For himself and his many correspondents the forms of poetry practised are otherwise always the short and social genres adapted to improvisation or limited leisure and application.

In a sense, then, epic does not feature in the world of recitation,[68] but it seems that every other genre, even those where recitation is not attested, must have done so. Pliny's friend Vergilius Romanus writes (or adapts?) New Comedies in Latin and is now trying his hand at Old Comedy (*Ep.* 6.21) ; Arrius Antoninus writes both epigrams and Mimiambi (literary mime) in Greek (4.3), and Pliny sets himself to compose translations of them into Latin.[69] Sentius Augurinus, a young friend of Arrius, composes *poematia*, which turn out to be hendecasyllables, and has been reciting them over a three-day period. One of them is in praise of Pliny, and so it reaches his pages, much as does the far superior poem of Martial cited by Pliny (*Ep.* 3.21). Pliny finds it pointed, neat, and expressive and threatens to send a copy of Sentius's collection to his correspondent as soon as Sentius has published it. This sample, one of only four excerpts from contemporary poetry quoted in the letters, can stand for the whole class:

> I sing my songs in dainty little verse,
> the same that once my dear Catullus used
> and Calvus and the classics. What do I care?
> Pliny alone is greater in my eyes.
> He scorns the Forum and prefers my verse,
> looking for love, he thinks himself beloved.

Pliny the great, a match for many Catos!
So lovers go now and don't dare to love him.[70]

Pliny backs up his enthusiasm for this quasi-erotic nonsense with a social recommendation of the lad and an apt quotation from Euripides (*Ep.* 4.27). The imitative element is sometimes triggered by family tradition; Pliny's acquaintance Passennus Paulus of Assisi has been reciting his elegies—the medium he chose because he is descended from Propertius himself. Unluckily Javolenus Priscus, an eccentric jurist, was in the audience and ruined the recitation by taking literally the opening words "Priscus, you ask me . . . " and interrupting with a denial (*Ep.* 6.15).

Elegy was a short and flexible medium. So it is not surprising that an aristocratic young poet, Calpurnius Piso, put on a recitation of his elegies about the mythological origins of the stars; since Cicero's translations from Aratus, budding poets had always cut their teeth on astronomical lore. Piso's performance pleased Pliny by its variety of tone, and the young gentleman's honorable stage fright, and he describes his effusive encouragement to the young man and congratulations to his family (*Ep.* 5.17).

Pliny's readings of his own work must have exhausted his friends' tact. He may, as he claims, have read his speeches only to a select few whose corrections he invited and even adopted, but the poetry readings that he began to give a few years later may have been more frequent and more embarrassing. A final brief case history of Pliny's own poetic activity may serve as the epitome of the role played by poetry in this class and time.

Pliny first mentions his hendecasyllables in the fourth book of his collection, when he has firmly established his own record as an orator, critic, and patron of young poets and even professionals like Martial. The key letter (4.14) comes after the account of his victory in the prosecution of Julius Bassus and the educational initiative at Como. Now he can let his hair down without loss of face. Pliny sends to Paternus a group of his hendecasyllables, deprecating them as trifles with which he passes the time in traveling, at the baths, or between courses at dinner. They are his relaxation, for joking and amusement, for expressing love and grief, complaint and anger, or again for a short or expansive description.[71] Apparently some of them are a bit raw, for he explains carefully to Paternus that, as he will know, being a well-read man, the classic poets in this genre spoke frankly of wanton topics; it is only his own age that has become mealy mouthed. As it is, he feels some anxiety about defining them by genre; metrically they are what he calls them— poems written in the eleven-syllable verse of Catullus or Martial. But in theme they could be called epigrams, idylls, eclogues, or simply *poematia*—short poems. He begs Paternus for a frank criticism, which will not pain him, since this is only a pastime, not his main profession.

Soon after this, however comes a much fuller letter to Titius Aristo (5.3). Apparently the frankness of Pliny's poems has not been appreciated and he is on the defensive, because some friends have felt that he should not write or recite this kind of poem. His immediate reply, like Ovid's defense of his poetry to Augustus, is to point out the greater explicitness of other genres; why, he hears comedies, he watches mimes, he reads lyric poetry, and he is familiar with Sotadean verse.[72] The answer, as Pliny surely knew, lay in the first-person format of these poems, one of which we have already sampled. To compose such personal statements suggested autobiography to the literal-minded. Catullus himself had felt the need to distinguish between his poetry and his practice, in famous verses, which Pliny quoted in the previous letter.

Obviously professions of pederastic infatuation hardly suited a consular like Pliny, but he has no difficulty mustering a roll call of republican statesmen and even a few figures from the early first century who wrote erotic verse.[73] Virgil, Nepos, Ennius, and Accius are mentioned more hesitantly because they were not senators, and they may not have given recitations. If they did not, it was because they were more confident of their own merit than he is. Pliny justifies his verse readings in the same way that he will justify reading his speeches (cf. *Ep.* 7.17): he needs to give readings to discipline his own work and to benefit from his friends' corrections.

The only hints at their subject matter will come from two later letters: 5.10, which reminds Suetonius that Pliny had announced Suetonius's forthcoming work in his verse, and 7.4, where he runs over the history of his career as a poet. Like other Romans we have met—Caesar, Augustus—Pliny began by composing a tragedy at the age of fourteen; later, as a young soldier, he composed elegiac poetry about the island of Icaria, where his ship was stranded by a storm and even tried heroic meter (hexameters). But it is only recently that he has turned to hendecasyllables, with the poems that his addressee has been reading. His excuse for taking up this idle amusement is an attack of insomnia in his Laurentine villa, when he distracted himself by composing twelve lines of hexameters. (The lines he quotes for his addressee lack point or wit and the subject is better suited to a shorter meter.) After this, Pliny tried elegiacs and other meters and read them to his friends, once he was back in town.

> Finally I decided to do as many authors have done and complete a separate volume of hendecasyllables, and I have never regretted this. My verses are read and copied, they are even sung, and set to the cithara or lyre by Greeks who have learned Latin out of liking for my little book.

Had people so little to occupy their time? Had these Greeks so much need to flatter a decent but influential man? Juvenal's Umbricius starved because he could not praise a patron's bad book and complained that Greeks would stop at nothing.[74]

Pliny renews the topic of his verse readings to Arrianus, an old friend whom he had consulted for correction of his oratory at the beginning of his correspondence (1.2). The letter accompanies the gift of a book of poetry, but Pliny again feels he must (8.21) excuse this use of his leisure. It turns out that the book is a record of a performance, for in July, the empty season for the courts, after a good dinner, he had arranged his friends in upright chairs to hear a miscellany of poems in mixed meters from his new book. He read on two days and decided not to omit any poems so as to enjoy the corrections of his friends. Here is the result: a brand new book, including some old poems that Arrianus will remember reading before, but mixed with newer poems, all freshly revised and corrected.[75]

The literary process is now complete, from composition, to recitation, to correction, to third thoughts, and finally to incorporation in the published text. The sad side of this story, however, emerges in a sort of epilogue—a letter almost at the end of the collection, written to Pliny's old protégé, Suetonius (9.34). Pliny has learned that he does not read poetry well, so he is planning to employ his freedman as reader in his next recitation, though the freedman himself is new to the art. Now he has a problem: how is he to behave sitting there as his poems are read? Should he sit still, or follow the word with gestures and expression? After all, he is no actor. Wouldn't it be better to read his work, however badly, rather than adopt either procedure?

The collection tells us no more of Pliny the poet or recitalist, but this sampling will make clear the seriousness with which he treated his occasional poetry and that of his friends as both a literary and a social commitment. Perhaps this was the major problem of the senatorial writer—that his social training was so thorough and his standards of courtesy so high, that they took precedence over genuine artistic values.

But if literature suffered from the attentions of the amateur, this chapter will have demonstrated its enormous social importance. Like bridge or golf, it served to provide a common activity for men of different ages and interests, men largely deprived of their original absorbing political life. Like crossword puzzles, it served the individual in times of waiting or distraction from his normal life. And like no modern equivalent, it gave a continuing and constructive occupation to men cut off by geographical remoteness, like Terentius Junior, or age, or both, like Vestricius Spurinna, or Arrianus. Let us leave aside the dedicated scholar or antiquarian, a minority then as now. For gentlemen of leisure, literature was not the passive pleasure it still gives to many of us, but their prime *activity*, for which they had been trained in school and to which they could devote their talents, composing memoirs or histories, personal poetry, or works of encyclopedic erudition and instruction. This was the model that Pliny's uncle had left to him, reading, annotating, listening, filing, and assembling his 20,000 memorable facts into the thirty-seven books of natural history. Pliny was more of a stylist, laboriously molding conventional content into brilliant form, but

the descriptions of his own rural days that end his private correspondence (9.36 and 40) differ in degree rather than in kind from
his account of his uncle's strenuous literary routine (3.5). For men
of culture in these fifty years, their traditionalist society might seem
to have undergone little change.

Seven

Literary Culture in Decline: The Antonine Years

Hadrian, the Philhellene

Reviewing the prospects for Latin poets and intellectuals, Juvenal opened *Satires* 7 with the declaration that "all hope and prospect for culture [*studiorum*] depend on Caesar" (*Sat.* 7.1). The new Caesar at this time was the forty-one-year-old Hadrian, who combined a long military career with considerable cultural pretensions, and the omens must have seemed good. But when Hadrian reached Rome in 118, after the eleven months required to achieve a settlement with Parthia, to escort Trajan's body and his household back to Antioch, and to organize affairs in the eastern provinces, Latin literary culture had few active representatives. Both Pliny and Tacitus were dead: of major Roman writers, only Juvenal and Suetonius survived. Suetonius was probably holding the second of his imperial appointments, as director of the research office (*a studiis*). Hadrian transferred him to the more powerful position of director of correspondence (*ab epistulis*), but would dismiss Suetonius, together with his patron Septicius Clarus, after only three years. Henceforward Suetonius worked without benefit of imperial support. As for Juvenal, whose reference to the consulship of Juncus

(*Sat.* 15.27) shows that he was still writing as late as 127, we may discount the later legend that he was exiled to Egypt, but there is no cause to believe there was any improvement in his circumstances. Yet Hadrian was generous in other ways. Skilled in the Greek arts of music, arithmetic, geometry, and painting, he was clearly an enthusiast for architecture, and he enriched both Rome and Athens with innovative private and public monuments. In Rome the mausoleum to which he devoted his last years has survived, transformed and reinforced as the papal stronghold of Castel Sant' Angelo on the right bank of the Tiber near Vatican City. Still more adventurous was the architectural complex of the magnificent pleasure palace he would erect at Tibur (Tivoli). Its innovative remodeling of space represented both new levels of building technology and a miniature concentration of the marvels of Near Eastern and Egyptian architecture, which he had visited before and after he became emperor. But these could not be considered benefactions to the Roman people.

Trajan had enriched public life at Rome with the whole magnificent complex of the Forum set around his commemorative column, with the two superb new libraries, the Basilica Ulpia, and the many-tiered market built, like the most sophisticated modern urban shopping mall, into the contours of the Quirinal hill. Dio reports that Trajan's architect Apollodorus had also built an odeum and a gymnasium (69.4.1), and "Spartianus," the pseudonymous biographer of Hadrian, claims that Hadrian actually demolished a theater that Trajan had built in the Campus Martius.[1] But it is most unlikely that Hadrian would have done such a thing. He loved the theater and gave privileges and an official headquarters in Rome to the guild of professional actors. He also used his own court theater company to revive public productions of tragic and comic drama.[2] In a later chapter, no doubt from a different source, the biographer lists Hadrian's benefactions to Rome. It seems he remodeled the city center on an Augustan scale. He erected a new temple—that of Venus and Roma overlooking the Sacred Way—and restored public areas and buildings like the Forum of Augustus and baths of Agrippa, and the "Saepta," the old voting enclosures in the Campus Martius. But Hadrian's most famous act of restoration was a radical remodeling of Agrippa's original, modest structure in the Campus Martius, to create the great domed temple that we still know today as the Pantheon. As Boatwright has argued, this must have become the new focus of the lower Campus Martius, and in it Hadrian held many of his tribunals for public business (Dio 69.7). Around it were other buildings such as the temple in honor of Matidia, Trajan's niece and Hadrian's mother-in-law, flanked by the basilicas named after Matidia and Trajan's sister Marciana.

But despite Hadrian's many acts of public generosity—the remission of debts to the imperial and public treasuries, commemorative games on the death and deification of Matidia, and other largesse to the people—despite his acts to conciliate the wealthy equestrian class and the Senate, Hadrian was, and felt himself, a stranger in Rome.

Although of a noble Italian family, he was born and received his early education in Baetica (the Spain of the Senecas) and was apparently trained primarily in Greek and from Greek instructors; the biographer notes that before Hadrian reached the age of fifteen he "immersed himself rather enthusiastically in Greek studies. In fact he was so attracted in that direction that some people called him 'the Little Greek.'" Soon after this Hadrian began his military service and can be found in the new provinces of the empire, in Lower Moesia (Bulgaria), in Upper Germany (Bavaria), and with Trajan in Dacia (Romania). Yet he seems to have acquired a highly sophisticated Greek-style education in the artistic and mathematical sciences not taught at Rome. Hadrian surely had a basic training in Latin rhetoric, but when the young man was sent to Rome as Trajan's quaestor to read an address from the emperor before the Senate, they laughed at his uncouth accent.[3] From this time, we are told, Hadrian paid special attention to gaining fluency in Latin oratory. But he must have seen himself as an outsider, and his discomfort in Rome will have been intensified when he returned as emperor, amid rumors that his nomination as successor had been engineered after Trajan's death, and the unpopularity caused by the hurried execution of four senior senators. It is not surprising that Hadrian left Rome after three years in the city, and spent the greater part of his remaining years in journeys of inspection around the empire.

A city that Hadrian greatly admired, and in which he felt at home, was Athens. We do not know when he had been able to visit Greece either for sightseeing or study, but it seems almost beyond doubt that he did so in his late teens. How else could he had have become attached to the elderly philosopher Epictetus, who taught at Nicopolis (the city founded by Augustus overlooking the site of Actium)? How else could he have won the goodwill of the Athenians, who honored him with the archonship, the chief titular magistracy, in 112–13? After this, Hadrian often visited Athens, certainly in 124–25, 128–29, and 131–32, and he bestowed his blessing in the form of a new city, whose triumphal gate still stands. He financed a great new library and saw through the completion of the extravagantly colossal temple of Olympian Zeus first begun by Pisistratus in the sixth century before Christ, which Hadrian inaugurated on his visit in 131–32.[4] By his example he also stimulated the lavish building program of the wealthy Athenian, Herodes Atticus, who in due course added the new stadium across the Ilissus and the great odeon under the slope of the Acropolis.[5]

Hadrian did more for Athens and, in so doing, he greatly affected the literary culture of Rome itself. In the last years of his life he brought the culture of Athens to Rome, creating an Athenaeum for the education of the Romans in Greek grammar and rhetoric.[6] Aurelius Victor groups this foundation with Hadrian's interest in Athenian cult, reporting that

> in the Greek way, or that of Numa Pompilius, he began to attend to religious rites, laws and the gymnasia and teachers, so much so that he even established a place of instruction actually for the liberal arts, which they call the Athenaeum, and devoted himself at Rome in the manner of the Athenians to the mysteries of Ceres and Libera, which are called the Eleusinian mysteries. (Victor, *Caesares* 14.2–4, trans. Boatwright)

The teachers that Hadrian imported from Athens to serve as its professors should not be confused with the independent sophists, to whom we will turn very shortly. Hadrian seems to have been

225

concerned for the earlier stages of education, which would require professional grammarians and rhetors. Thus his appointments expanded the program begun as early as Vespasian to foster education by endowing specific public professorships at Rome.[7] It is not clear, however, whether Hadrian provided a special building for this institution, or where it was situated. Braunert has argued that Hadrian installed this school in the Atrium Minervae,[8] adjacent to the Senate house. Other scholars have set it in the Schola Fori Traiani or in the Grecostadium.[9] However, since the institution is dated to Hadrian's last years, it seems most likely that it began operating in an existing building, whatever the claims of the writers of the *Historia Augusta* and others familiar with the Diocletianic Athenaeum.

Even if the Athenaeum was only modest in scope and limited to the teaching of Greek literature and rhetoric, it would soon become a natural magnet for the fashionable sophists that made their way to Rome. We need not go as far as Bardon[10] in blaming Hadrian's philhellenism for the decline of Latin culture at Rome, but this "center for the study of Greek in the heart of Rome" may well be compared to the Trojan horse. Admittedly it succeeded, like the Trojan horse, because of the folly of the citizens. A measure of Rome's cultural inferiority complex is given by Philostratus's account of the popular enthusiasm when the sophist Hadrian of Tyre, Marcus Aurelius's professor of Greek rhetoric at Rome, was scheduled to declaim at the Athenaeum:

> A messenger had only to announce in the theater that Hadrian was going to declaim when even the members of the senate would rise from their sitting, and the members of the equestrian order would rise, and not only those who were devoted to Hellenic culture, but also those who were studying the other language at Rome [i.e., Latin, the native tongue of Italy for many centuries past!]; and they would set out on the run to the Athenaeum, overflowing with enthusiasm and upbraiding those who were going there at a walking pace. (Philostr. *VS* 233 [LCL])

The sophists, who have already been foreshadowed by the popularity of figures like Dio and Euphrates at Rome, became increasingly frequent and honored visitors from now on and must be given extended attention in any account of the literary culture of Rome under Hadrian and his successors. But the emperor Hadrian must be distinguished from his successors, because his interest in Greek literature was not simply receptive but active, and went beyond rhetoric and philosophy to an enthusiasm for learned poetry. Dio's description of Hadrian as "a man of letters [*philologos*] in both languages" implies composition as well as appreciation in both tongues; he credits Hadrian with some prose works and all kinds of compositions in hexameter verse.[11] Besides the Greek memoirs (cited by Dio at 66.17), Hadrian left a strange composite poem called *Catachannae* (named after a type of artificially hybrid tree grafted with many fruits) in the manner of the learned Hellenistic poet Antimachus,[12] and he both composed and patronized shorter forms of Greek poetry.

A recent essay by Ewen Bowie has brought together examples of the new types of poetry surviving from the age of Hadrian, and it is informative to compare the poems attributed to the emperor himself with those of his friends and protégés.[13] Of the six epigrams attributed to Hadrian in the *Palatine Anthology*, two are particularly significant because they illustrate his conception of his role, and that of the Roman Empire, in the sum of Greco-Roman history.

The first was supposedly written by Hadrian for inscription at Antioch in 106 when he accompanied Trajan to his Parthian campaigns:

> To Casian Zeus did Trajan, the descendant of Aeneas, dedicate these ornaments, the king of Men, to the King of Gods: two curiously fashioned cups and the horns of a Urus mounted in shining gold, selected from his first booty when, tirelessly fighting, he had overthrown with his spear the insolent Getae. But Lord of the black clouds, entrust to him, too, the glorious accomplishment of this Persian War that the heart's joy may be doubled as thou lookest on the spoils of both foes, the Getae and the Arsacidae. (*Anth. Pal.* 6.332, trans. Paton)

The second was composed for the grave of Hector, to which honors were still paid at Troy, and offers consolation to the great hero:

> Hector of the race of Ares, if thou hearest wher'eer thou art under ground, hail! and stay a little thy sighs for thy country. Ilion is inhabited, and is a famous city containing men inferior to thee, but still lovers of

war, while the Myrmidons have perished. Stand by his side and tell Achilles that all Thessaly is subject to the sons of Aeneas. (*Anth. Pal.* 9.387, trans. Paton)[14]

What these poems have in common is the antiquarianism that exploits Homeric language and Homeric concepts to represent Rome's victories in the heroic terms that Greeks themselves would have used. A similar antiquarianism is shown by the more extraordinary poems of Julia Balbilla, sister of C. Iulius Antiochus Philopappus, the wealthy friend of Plutarch, who visited Egypt with Hadrian's party in November 130. In the tradition of wealthy Roman tourists, she had inscribed on the thigh of the great colossus of Memnon four poems in the old Aeolic Greek dialect of Sappho. This statue uttered musical sounds, which were treated as a kind of omen, and had performed first for Hadrian's wife Sabina, then for the emperor himself. The purpose of such poems is strictly egotistic: to specify the occasion, and the author's "I was there." The first six lines of Balbilla's longer poem specify Memnon's welcome to Sabina; the central section tells the history of the statue, and the last six lines give the poet's identity: "For pious were my parents and grandparents, Balbillus the wise and Antiochus the King, Balbillus the parent of my royal mother, and Antiochus the king, father of my father. From their line do I draw my noble blood, and these are the writings of Balbilla the pious." The second poem bears witness that Hadrian himself had composed verse to acknowledge Memnon's greeting: "then the lord Hadrian himself also offered ample greetings to Memnon, and on the monument left for posterity verses marking all that he had seen and all that he had heard. And it was made clear to all that the gods loved him."[15]

Not all Hadrianic poetry was quite so bound to the occasion, and Bowie has also discussed the surviving texts of Mesomedes the Citharode, Hadrian's freedman. Hadrian's biographer claims the emperor was himself an expert citharode, but if Mesomedes wrote a hymn to the memory of Hadrian's drowned favorite Antinoos, it is easy to imagine that this was the origin of Hadrian's favor and the official appointment of the composer and poet. Several of these texts, such as the proemia to Calliope and the hymns to the Sun and to Nemesis, are preserved with musical notation and can still be performed. They are in conspicuously short, at times choppy, rhythms, similar to the abrupt rhythms and short cola of Asianic prose rhetoric much favored in this period. Whether Mesomedes lost his skill, or Antoninus did not share his predecessor's taste for Greek lyric is not clear, but the biographer of Antoninus reports that he terminated the lyric composer's imperial pension.

It is perhaps typical of this period that it should have produced travel literature in both verse and prose. Thus, the historian Arrian dedicated to Hadrian his *Circumnavigation of the Black Sea* in Greek, and seems to have composed a parallel but slightly expanded Latin version.[16] Dionysius of Alexandria composed a *Guide to the Inhabited World*, in the form of a hexameter poem of over a thousand lines, including an acrostic clue that dates it to the age of Hadrian.[17] Pausanias certainly did not compose his guide to Greece until the time of Marcus Aurelius,[18] but both the last two works reflect the extraordinary globetrotting of the period, made easy and secure by the military calm of the Mediterranean before the onset of economic and military crisis toward the end of the century.

The Traveling Sophists

In the previous chapter, discussing the literary culture of the years from Vespasian to Hadrian, I mentioned the visits to Rome of the earliest figures of the Greek rhetorical renaissance known as the Second Sophistic: Dio, who died in the year of Hadrian's accession, Apollonius, and Euphrates, who petitioned Hadrian for the right to end his terminal illness by death in 119. But the full flowering of this widespread cultural movement was still to come when Hadrian entered power, and two generations of the most famous rhetors would coincide with the years of Hadrian, Antoninus, and Marcus Aurelius.

This book aims only to interpret Latin literary culture; however, the influence of these men through their relationship with successive emperors, and their glamour and notoriety among the educated classes at Rome and in the Greek-speaking empire, were so great that they dominate the cultural history of this period. They have been the subject of increasing study in recent years, and there is an extended bibliography treating them from several points of view. These are the sons of elite families, the leading men of their communities, who enjoyed the respect of both their fellow citizens and of Rome itself. Among them are holders of every kind of office, intellectual and priestly, civic and imperial, both professors and consuls. Bowersock's *Greek Sophists* has brought out their undoubted political and social prominence, and the network of their interaction across the *oecumenē*. Because the most prominent of these celebrities were accomplished declaimers, their themes and techniques provide the greater part of the account of Greek declamation that has been so admirably presented by Donald Russell.[19]

A puzzling aspect of this cultural movement is the difficulty of determining the common features binding these men, some of whom claimed to be philosophers, some rhetors,[20] but all of whom achieved fame through their command of the spoken word. Yet even this statement needs qualification, since their fame as wielders of rhetoric came less from their functional speeches as ambassadors of their community or its representatives in divine worship, than from their manipulation of words and ideas in pure display.

The extent to which their productions have survived varies considerably, from the well-preserved artistic prose pieces of Dio Chrysostom or Aelius Aristides, to the more fragmentary texts of a Favorinus or Polemo. But the contemporary fame of the sophists is almost in inverse relationship to the extent of their surviving texts, because its source was their oral performance, as much or more in their art of delivery as in their art of language. As Bowersock candidly observes at the opening of his influential study, the sophists' works "are often over-elaborated productions on unreal, unimportant or traditional themes." But their personalities were of the greatest importance as an index to the culture of their age. Their role as representatives of second-century Hellenic nostalgia, an archaism of both theme and diction, has been powerfully interpreted by both Bowie and Reardon.[21] It remains for me to convey their direct and indirect influence on Romans and on the Latin-speaking western empire.

Although our primary source for these celebrities is Philostratus's volume of collected biographies, the most famous of the sophists left their mark even in the histories and epitomes. The two figures that dominate the age of Hadrian are Favorinus of Arelate (Arles), the effeminate philosopher and polymath who chose to write and speak in Greek, and Polemon of Laodicea, who set up school in Smyrna and was the city's spokesman at Rome.

Both Cassius Dio and Hadrian's biographer speak of Favorinus's special closeness to the emperor, but they also record Hadrian's subsequent hostility. Favorinus is found everywhere, at Ephesus, in Athens, at Rome, and must have been prominent in Gaul too, to be offered the high priesthood of the imperial cult, which he tried to refuse. (Priesthoods were very expensive.) Although he withdrew his refusal, this was one early incident in which he was seen to offend Hadrian.

A flamboyant speaker, Favorinus used to end his declamations with a half-chanted epilogue he called his ode, and his success provoked fierce quarrels at Rome between the "consulars and sons of consulars" who favored him and those who favored his rival Polemon. Philostratus reports that he charmed even those at Rome who did not understand Greek. Although Favorinus's celebrity clearly came from his eloquence, he claimed to be a philosopher. We shall see that the young scholar Aulus Gellius cites Favorinus for matters of learning in philosophy, and in many other specialized fields, and Favorinus himself published a book of miscellaneous researches *Pantodape Historia*. Add to this the ten books discussing the skeptical theories of Pyrrho, his treatises on history and geography, a treatise on physiognomy which found its way into an Arabic translation, and speeches including "On the Untimely Dead," "For the Gladiators," and "For the Baths" (Philostr. *VS* 491 [LCL, 29]). Herodes Atticus, the Athenian so wealthy he could afford every teacher, was Favorinus's favorite pupil and received in Favorinus's will his library, his house in Rome, and his pet Indian slave.

But Favorinus was notorious for more than his gift of speech. He used to boast of exemplifying three paradoxes, that being a Gaul he spoke Greek, that as a eunuch (he was really a cryptorchid) he was accused of adultery, and that he quarreled with Hadrian and still lived (Philostr. *VS* 489 [LCL, 23]). Dio Cassius claims that Hadrian was jealous of him, as of so many intellectuals, and tried to boost the claims of rivals: certainly it seems that Favorinus was exiled.[22]

Philostratus gives much more attention to Polemon, and his very full biography can serve as a model for what Greeks wanted to know about their sophists. Besides the basic facts of his birth in the leading family of Laodicea in Caria and his early education, Philostratus tells us about Polemon's teachers, his travels, his relations with emperors, and the gifts and honors he won for himself and his city. Thanks to the enthusiastic reports given by Herodes, Philostratus is also able to describe Polemon's delivery, to rebut criticisms of his skills, to list his themes, and finally to record his death and place of burial.

It seems that Polemon, who studied with Dio Chrysostom in his youth, made Smyrna his home after he went to study with its leading orator Scopelian. He first came to public attention in Rome when he was delegated by the aged Scopelian to serve in his place as Smyrna's envoy to Trajan. On another occasion Polemon's embassy for Smyrna won over Hadrian, who had previously favored the rival city of Ephesus, and brought back to Smyrna an imperial bounty that paid for a grain market, gymnasium, and temple. Hadrian also gave him other funds, for which he refused to be accountable to the citizens, and was vindicated by the emperor. Both as a famous orator and as an aristocrat in his own community, Polemon was conspicuous for his arrogance: Philostratus remarks of him that "he conversed with cities as his inferiors, with emperors as not his superiors, and with the gods as his equals" (*VS* 535 [LCL, 115]). Polemon had already received from Trajan the privileges of free travel by land and sea: Hadrian extended these to include his descendants (but he died childless) and gave him dining rights in the Mouseion at Alexandria. He also enjoyed exemption from taxes and other imposts like billeting, and more than one source describes how the future emperor Antoninus, on an official visit to Smyrna, requisitioned Polemon's townhouse, until Polemon returned and had him thrown out of the house at midnight. Yet Hadrian reconciled the sophist with Antoninus: he singled out Polemon to give the ceremonial speech at the inauguration of his Temple of Olympian Zeus in Athens in 132, and he indicated in his will that he had followed Polemon's advice in making his dispositions of the empire. Herodes Atticus, born around A.D. 100, was already an experienced teacher of rhetoric and imperial procurator supervising the free cities of Asia when he went to Smyrna to study the art of impromptu speaking with Polemon. The rhetor treated him to an instant declamation, and followed it up with an encomium of Herodes himself (!) delivered to a different audience. And Herodes has recorded in a published letter to his friend Barbarus a description of Polemon's performance: he praises the sophist's confident expression and ringing voice, and notes that although Polemon was already crippled and spoke sitting down, he would rise from his seat at the climaxes of his argument. To command an audience's enthusiasm from a sitting position demands an extraordinaily dominant personality. Polemon's favorite topics as recorded by Herodes were typical of the nostalgic preoccupation with the free cities of Greece before the empire of Alexander: Demosthenes swearing that he had not taken Alexander's bribe, a proposal after the Peloponnesian War that the Greeks should take down the trophies of their victories against each other, and a speech urging the Athenians to return to their demes after the defeat of Aegospotami. No hint of Rome, and no historical event more recent than 450 years past.

We can form some idea of Polemon's wealth from an anecdote recorded by Philostratus. Herodes was so impressed by Polemon that he sent him a gift of 150,000 drachmae, which Polemon promptly returned. Luckily Munatius of Tralles, another of Herodes' many teachers, served as intermediary and set Herodes right: Polemon had been expecting 250,000 drachmae, and he did not refuse them when Herodes sent him the increased honorarium. It is a measure of Herodes' wealth that he could give Polemon as much as the sophist had asked from the emperor Hadrian after speaking before him in Rome (Philostr. *VS* 533 [LCL, 111] and 538 [LCL, 123]).

Herodes borrows a line from Homer to compare Polemon's voluble Asianic eloquence to "the sound of swift-footed horses." It is not clear whether Polemon served up the same historical and patriotic declamatory themes to Hadrian or to young Marcus Aurelius. Philostratus (*VS* 542 [LCL, 133]) lists a whole series of such topics, but only one, "The Adulterer Exposed," is forensic, like the *controversiae* that the Romans preferred. But we do have on record Marcus Aurelius's tactfully unenthusiastic report on Polemon to his tutor, the orator Cornelius Fronto; the heading of the letter dates this to 143, a chronological landmark that can be used to anchor three careers: Fronto was consul suffect, but Herodes was one of the two *ordinarii*, the opening consuls who gave their names to the year, and it is likely that Polemon visited Rome in part to honor his admirer. To Marcus, however, Polemon

> seems like a hardworking farmer of great expertise, who has laid out a large holding with nothing but wheat and vines, which certainly bring the finest harvest and the richest profit. But nowhere on his estate is there a Pompeian fig tree or Arician cabbage or rose of Tarentum, or a pleasant wood or thick grove or shady plane tree; everything is for utility rather than for pleasure, so that you ought to praise it, but do not feel inclined to love it.

It is possible that young Marcus is not only being patriotic, but willfully resisting Polemon's notoriety: "Do you think," he asks, "I am bold and rash enough in my opinion, to pass judgment on a man of such great glory?" (Fronto, *To Marcus* 2.5).

Either in this or the following year another famous but more retiring Greek rhetor, Aelius Aristides, visited Rome and delivered his great panegyric *To Rome*.[23] Aristides' work has survived because he disseminated it in writing. He was prevented by his ill health from a career as a popular speaker, and perhaps for that reason he is not included in Philostratus's parade of sophists. But unlike the better-known sophists he did not confine his eloquence to the Greek past, but found more than one occasion to visit and to praise Rome.

With Herodes Atticus and Aristides (born 117) comes the next generation, which made its name after the death of Hadrian. Different as they are, both men maintain their fame in the years after 170, although Aristides turned to composing prose hymns to the gods, while Herodes was involved in patriotic and pious benefactions. It is worth noting that Herodes' benefactions extended to Italy: he provided a new water supply to the Italian city of Canusium, and erected a lavish temple near Rome to his dead wife, the Roman lady Appia Annia Regilla (allegedly beaten at his orders when eight months pregnant). This generosity must have had some bearing on his ability to survive the enmity of the Athenian populace and accusations of treasonous conspiracy brought to Marcus Aurelius by prominent Greek and Roman enemies.

But we should not neglect two more academic aspects of these glamorous figures: the nature of their teaching, and the kinds of intellectual and official positions to which they were nominated by the emperors. A story in Philostratus describes Herodes' special class of favored pupils, the class of the clepsydrion. After his general public lecture these ten young men were welcomed to stay to dinner with Herodes for the time required to declaim a hundred verses; this was measured by the clepsydrion, the water clock used to control court procedure. Then Herodes would expound the verses in a continuous presentation. After that came the ceremonial drinking, over which more relaxed study continued.

On one of these occasions the brilliant Hadrian of Tyre demonstrated his intimate knowledge of all the recent sophists (except Herodes) by mimicking their style. Hadrian of Tyre was chosen to pronounce the funeral oration for Herodes, but at this stage he may already have been an established figure, for Philostratus marks three steps in his career, steps we may assume were also followed by other sophists. First, he was appointed to the chair of rhetoric that the emperor Hadrian had established at Athens.[24] Thus when Marcus Aurelius visited Athens to be initiated into the mysteries, he invited Hadrian of Tyre to give him a declamation about Hyperides' persistence in supporting Demosthenes in the face of Philip's imminent invasion. It delighted Marcus, who rewarded him with the customary Greek-style honors—dining at state expense, seats at the games, and immunity from taxes and priesthoods—but also promoted him soon after to the chair of (Greek) rhetoric at Rome. It was in this role that Hadrian drew the young Romans, even those without Greek, to the Athenaeum to hear his Greek eloquence, in that scene which I quoted earlier. As the final honor, when Hadrian lay dying at Rome, Marcus Aurelius' successor Commodus sent him a rescript appointing him imperial secretary.

In this case the appointment was no more than a gesture, but the gesture itself speaks for the pattern of imperial patronage to the sophists. Marcus Aurelius even endowed Athens with the funds to support directors for each of the four philosophical schools, and appointed Theodotus to the vacant chair of rhetoric. His successor under Commodus would be the learned lexicographer Julius Pollux. But Marcus also needed less congenial official services from Greek men of letters. As the emperor Hadrian had appointed Eudaemon and Heliodorus to be his secretaries for Greek correspondence, so Marcus Aurelius in turn summoned Alexander Peloplaton to Sirmium in Pannonia, where he was campaigning, and appointed him imperial secretary for Greek correspondence. Presumably his duties began on the spot: otherwise it seems a very long journey to be interviewed for even the highest appointment.[25]

The Provinces and Latin Culture

Not only sophists traveled across the empire, and not only those of primarily Greek culture became sophists or men of letters. The western provinces too sent their elite to Rome to receive and later to provide education. Spain had won prominence for its orators and poets since the turn of the era. The reign of Hadrian introduces the new prominence of Roman Africa (modern Tunisia), a province almost as old as Spain and with its own wealthy elite of Roman or Italian origin. One document can be dated slightly earlier. The incomplete introduction to P. Annius Florus's dialogue *Was Virgil More an Orator or a Poet?* seems to set a dramatic date after Trajan's first or second Dacian triumph in 102 or 107. It reflects the ambitions and travels of an African poet who sought fame in Rome as a competitor in one of Domitian's Capitoline contests, but was defeated, despite popular acclaim—according to the author, because Domitian was unwilling to give the victory to the province of Africa.

Scholars have understandably doubted this suggestion, seeing it as the excuse of a defeated competitor. It is more interesting to follow Florus's description of his own subsequent career. With some self-dramatization, he reports that the bitterness of defeat drove him far from Italy: he traveled to Sicily, then to Crete and the

Cyclades, then to Rhodes and Egypt to see the Nile Delta and the worshipers of Isis, endlessly wielding their sacred rattles. A tourist voyage, then, and not apparently one in search of further education. After returning to Italy, he decided to travel overland and visited Gaul and the pale peoples of the North (he seems to blame the wind, rather than lack of sun!). Changing direction he went west and crossed the soaring Pyrenees. I have tried to preserve in paraphrase the rather unreal and poetic coloring of Florus's language. But the travels to east and west are presented as fact, and so is Florus's present situation. He has become a grammaticus in Tarragona. His interlocutor (another traveler, who had made the journey from southern Spain to Rome for Trajan's triumph, only to be shipwrecked on this return voyage) expresses shock and pity, and this leads into Florus's defense of the schoolmaster's profession. Besides revealing the extent of travel in Trajan's empire, this provides a different perspective on education.

> I am not surprised you are of that opinion, since I suffered from it myself for some time. For all the five years that I worked in this profession I was utterly weary of it and thought no man had a more miserable life. Then I mulled it over, and compared my lot with all the chances and toils of life: gradually the nobility of the task I had undertaken became clear to me. You should know that no salary or administrative title or public office is as great as this profession. If the greatest of generals had given me a centurion's commission to command a hundred men, I would have felt this was a considerable honor; likewise if I had been given a cavalry command or a military tribunate: the honor would have been equal and the pay higher. But if Fortune, not the Emperor, has imposed this post on me in life, to command well-bred and respectable boys, don't you think I have won a noble and glorious position?
>
> I ask you, consider it more closely: which is more glorious, to command men in military cloaks or boys in the toga of purity? Brute barbarian hearts, or gentle innocent natures? Dear God, how like a King or commander it is to sit on the dais, teaching morality and the study of sacred literature, interpreting the poetry that forms their speech and minds. (*Vergilius Orator an Poeta* 3.)

The text breaks off soon after this, but the teacher's praise of his profession is clearly leading into the praise and scrutiny of Virgil, the dominant text of the schools. The lost work has a place in the tradition that began with Tacitus's *Dialogus*, with the dispute between Maternus and Aper over the respective value of the poet's and the orator's career: it will be continued in the much longer discussions of Macrobius's *Saturnalia* in the fourth century. But the story is more complicated, because it has long been recognized that this author may well be the historian Florus who composed two books on the wars of Rome not long after this time, and is even more likely to be the poet Florus who associated with Hadrian.

Paul Jal, in the recent Budé edition of the preface and the poetic fragments of Florus, reconstructs a life for the African poet in which he is born about A.D. 78, competes unsuccessfully at Rome in 94, travels and teaches until he decides to return to Rome under Hadrian, associates on good terms with the emperor, his contemporary, and in his last years composes the histories that have come down to us.[26] The least likely ingredient—his intimacy with Hadrian—is guaranteed by the exchange of poems in the biography of Hadrian, where Florus utters mock pity for the emperor's self-imposed travels, and Hadrian mocks Florus's imaginary debauchery in Rome:

> I would hate to be our Caesar
> making trips among the Britons
> suffering the Scythian hoarfrosts.
>
> I would hate to be our Florus,
> making trips among the taverns
> hiding out among the brothels
> suffering the rolling bedbugs.
>
> (*Hist. Aug. Hadr.* 1.16.3–4)

The likelihood of intimacy is reinforced by the phrases excerpted "from Annius Florus's letters to Hadrian" by the grammarian Charisius, stressing his delight in poetry and alluding to exotic triumphs over the Arabs and the Sarmatae (Ukrainians). Other poems reflect his pride in poetry ("only a king or a poet cannot be born just any year") and his irony about Roman conservatism:

> "Show contempt for foreign fashions, full of many thousand tricks
> no one lives in all the world more rightly than the men of Rome:

I would rather have one Cato than three hundred Socrates."
Everyone declares it's true, and by his actions proves it false.[27]

Marcus Aurelius and His Teachers

According to the biographer, Hadrian's taste in Latin literature, both prose and verse, was for the old republican writers, preferring the elder Cato to Cicero, Ennius to Virgil, and the historian Coelius Antipater to Sallust. If this was true, it may help to explain the appointment of M. Cornelius Fronto to be tutor to the young Marcus Aurelius.[28] Marcus was born in 121, and so he would have begun to need a tutor in rhetoric in or soon after 135 as he approached young manhood. The ample information provided by both Marcus and his biographer in the *Historia Augusta* is one of our best sources for the full process of elite education at this time. It will be useful to begin by examining, in the accompanying table, the sequence of teachers indicated for Marcus and for his very different coheir, the worldly prince Lucius Verus. Then we can consider more closely Fronto's correspondence with Marcus as evidence for both the personal and the working relationship of teacher and pupil.

Here we see the whole sequence from the child's education in reading and handwriting, elocution, mathematics, and music, through the years of the grammaticus to the adult teachers, the rhetors and philosophers. But some caution is needed in gauging the chronological relationship between study with the grammatici and with the rhetors. Given the increasing interest in sophisticated literary questions, given the professionalism of the grammatici, many of whom wrote learned books, it is hardly conceivable either that the sons of the elite ceased to study with their grammatici at fourteen, or that grammatici imparted their full weight of learning to obstreperous teenagers. Can we imagine that Gellius (see the next section) was less adult when he studied with Sulpicius Apollinaris than when he associated with Fronto? He often speaks of discussion shared with both the grammaticus and the orator. It seems to me more likely that there was an overlap during the years from fourteen to eighteen, in which the student spent his time between both disciplines.[29]

The Teachers of Marcus Aurelius and Lucius Verus

Subject	Marcus Aurelius	Lucius Verus
I Elementary		
Reading	Euphorion	
Elocution	Geminus	
Music/geom.	Andron	
Painting	Diognetus	
II Grammar		
Greek	Alexander of Cotiaeum	Telephus
		Hephaestion
		Harpocration
Latin	Trosius Aper of Pola	
Latin	Tuticius Proculus of Sicca	Scaurinus
IIIa Rhetoric		
Greek	Aninius Macer	Apollonius
Greek	Caninius Celer[1]	Caninius Celer
Greek	Herodes Atticus (ord. 143)	Herodes
Latin	Cornelius Fronto (suf. 143)	Fronto
IIIb Philosophy		
Stoic	Junius Rusticus (cos. 133)	
Stoic	Apollonius of Chalcedon	Apollonius
Stoic	Sextus of Chaeronea	Sextus
Stoic	Claudius Maximus (cos. 144)	
Stoic	Cinna Catulus	
Peripatetic	Claudius Severus (cos. 146)	
IIIc Jurisprudence		
	L. Volusius Maecianus[2]	

Source: The list of teachers for Marcus is combined from *Historia Augusta: Marcus Aurelius* 2–3 and *Meditations* 1.7–15 and 17. Verus's teachers are listed in *Historia Augusta: Verus* 2. See also E. J. Champlin, *Fronto and Antonine Rome* (Cambridge, Mass., 1980), 118–20.

[1] Champlin, *Fronto*, suggests this Celer is the same as the Greek secretary of Hadrian and Antoninus; see Philostratus *VS* 524.

[2] Maecianus is attested in an inscription as Antoninus's secretary during the reign of Hadrian; he would later be prefect of Egypt and become a senator.

The discrepancies between the teachers of the two princes reported by the *Historia Augusta* are particularly interesting. The biographer makes it clear that Marcus and Lucius received their elementary and grammatical training in their different families, and were only brought together at the tertiary level for rhetoric and philosophy. If Marcus had only one Greek grammaticus, whereas Verus had three, this may mean either that Verus's teachers left their positions more quickly or that he needed more teaching. In fact, the biographer says that Verus was weak in literature, and weaker in verse than in rhetoric—he seems to have spoken better than he wrote. For Latin Marcus is found with two instructors, Trosius and Tuticius: again these may be serial rather than simultaneous. Tuticius is conspicuous as a fellow African with Fronto and with that other contemporary grammaticus Sulpicius Apollinaris, who will reappear later in this chapter.

At the tertiary level, however, we should also distinguish between two kinds of teacher: the professional (and paid?) rhetor and philosopher, and the gentleman. Clearly the senators, those men whose consulships are listed, did not take money; they taught not on a regular basis but by association (*contubernium*), which could however be intense, as in the case of Junius Rusticus, Marcus's most revered instructor in philosophy, and of Fronto himself. Marcus's *Meditations* acknowledge his debts to all his sources of philosophical teaching but mention only his Greek *grammatikos* Alexander and Fronto among his other teachers.

But Marcus can hardly have spent equal time with all the philosophers. Sextus and Apollonius seem to have been official teachers of both princes, even the unphilosophical Verus. Marcus clearly deeply respected the Roman consular Rusticus, and appreciated the younger senators, who no doubt received their consulships in part as reward for their role in his adult education. He does not mention Herodes Atticus, who supposedly contributed to the education of both princes. Given Herodes' busy public career, this probably means very little: perhaps that he declaimed or gave epideictic speeches in their presence, and talked to them informally afterward. In view of Herodes' character, one would like to think that, even when young, Marcus found him rather uncongenial.

Much could be said about Marcus as a moralist and about the philosophical teachings he will have received from the five Stoics and the single but much respected Peripatetic (that is, Aristotelian) Claudius Severus Arabianus. But the philosophical culture of this period requires its own separate history. In contrast, Marcus Cornelius Fronto has to stand not only for the educational history of this generation but also for the Latin literary culture of the age of Hadrian and M. Antoninus. He is not just the only Latin writer on rhetoric and education from this period; he is the only datable Latin prose writer whose work in any genre has survived between the elusive Florus and Apuleius's early *Apologia*, his dramatic defense against the charge of witchcraft in 158.

But despite the limited appeal of Fronto's surviving works to modern readers, he is the right man to represent his age. He came from Cirta, in Roman North Africa, the city that had given Rome its first African consul, Q. Aurelius Pactumeius Fronto, consul in A.D. 80.[30] Fronto's year of birth is unknown, but he must have been born around 95, to have reached preeminence as an advocate in the 120s under Hadrian. An anecdote in Dio Cassius (69.18) shows him associating intimately with the Roman elite, including Hadrian's first prefect of the guard. It is a mark of his cosmopolitan associations—and that of this era—that Fronto's wife, called Gratia in our Latin texts, seems to have been Crateia, of Greek family. She was a close friend of Marcus's mother Domitia Lucilla, to whom Fronto writes in Greek. Perhaps Greek was the first language of both ladies. Fronto is known to have published four books of speeches, and letters in both Greek and Latin to his friends, to the imperial family, and to his pupil Marcus from their early years together until Fronto's death. Of his speeches, even the supposed denunciation of the Christians,[31] only echoes, excerpts, and titles survive, and before the nineteenth century Fronto was known only by reputation. But texts of many of his letters were recovered by Cardinal Mai from two palimpsest manuscripts in the Ambrosian Library in Milan. Luckily these include enough letters to Marcus to convey Fronto's principles and methods, and illustrate his stylistic range.

Their evidence can be amplified by the affectionate accounts of

Fronto as a teacher in the writings of Aulus Gellius some years after the event. Both sources show that Fronto suffered from arthritis and other ailments that hampered his mobility: one of Gellius's reminiscences is set at Fronto's home, where he is resting on a couch and presiding over a discussion among his young men at the same time as he is dealing with tenders from architects to supply him with a new suite of baths. Many of the letters to Marcus present Fronto's excuses because he cannot pay a duty call at court, or substitute written suggestions about rhetorical exercises for occasions when they had planned to work together. Together the teacher's ill health and the prince's royal commitments may explain why the letters virtually provide a correspondence course in rhetoric. It has recently been suggested that these letters were designed for publication.[32] It would be in keeping with Fronto's careful completeness, but it is difficult to imagine that Marcus wrote with that intent.

Both Fronto's letters and Marcus's replies often illustrate the various exercises he recommends, in writing natural descriptions, producing variations of a proverbial saying, reporting a story, or developing an extended comparison.[33] The last figure is Fronto's special favorite, and his stress on these *eikones* goes a long way to explain Marcus's rather odd report on Polemon's speech.

In another letter Fronto provides a model comparison, between Marcus's relationship to his "father" Antoninus and the protection enjoyed by a small island set in a lake within the larger island of Aenaria. Fronto even offers a kind of self-parody in his elegant Greek letter to Marcus's mother Domitia Lucilla (*Ep. Graec.* 1 [LCL, 1:131–37]). There three elaborate images compare Fronto's direct course in pursuing his argument to a hyena, the dart-snake, and a spear; they are backed by two more comparisons with a headwind and a straight line. But the letter is designed to entertain, and it would be a mistake to take it seriously and miss his humor. His self-description as a "Libyan of the Libyan nomads" is certainly humorous but may disguise some real insecurity about his command of Greek: he claims to be so anxious to write a model letter that he asks young Marcus, who has studied Greek more recently, to vet it for him.

Officially Fronto was Marcus's tutor only in Latin rhetoric, but his recommendations include a wide range of reading in Latin, from the archaic authors of the second century B.C., including the work of Ennius, the speeches and *On Agriculture* of Cato, speeches of Gaius Gracchus and Scipio Aemilianus, comedies by Plautus, and farces by Novius. How would he find such rare and ancient texts? Some of them were only available in the imperial libraries, and a revealing letter warns Marcus that Fronto has already borrowed the Palatine library copy (or copies) of two Cato speeches that Marcus needs to study, so Marcus will have to suborn a library official from the Tiberian library instead.[34] Fronto sent his pupil chasing through the ancient texts to find rare words and had Marcus compile lists of them for use in his own writing. There were no dictionaries in ancient Rome and each man had to form his own vocabulary in this way.

Fronto also prescribed Roman themes for declamation, set in the republican past, which Marcus gently challenges: he finds the theme of the consul who is censured for fighting as a gladiator and killing a lion "implausible" (*Ep.* 5.22, 23).

As Marcus grew older and teaching was replaced by friendship, Fronto still felt a professional need to advise his former pupil. A series of five longer letters have acquired the title *On Eloquence*, because in them Fronto concentrates the essence of his teaching and reaffirms the importance of rhetoric to the new emperor. And his imperial pupils expected other services of him. For Lucius Verus, the soldier prince, Fronto began to draft the presentation of an "encomiastic history" of his Parthian campaigns. But what has survived is more encomium than history; on this evidence, it was no longer possible to write serious history of any war conducted by the reigning emperor.[35] Despite the encomium, Fronto can still assert his sincere valuation of eloquence to Verus, and he uses the example of Marcus's eloquence to drive home his conviction that an emperor needed the arts of oratory even more than the arts of war:

> Therefore if you are aiming to be a true commander and emperor [*Imperator*] of mankind, it is your eloquence that commands, your eloquence that sways men's minds. It inspires awe, wins love, arouses energy, suppresses indiscipline, urges to virtue, dicredits vice, persuades, soothes, teaches, consoles. . . . ., a single speech by your brother

on you and your merits will be more glorious and more renowned with posterity than most princely triumphs. (*To Verus* 2.1.7)

While Fronto and Marcus were still teacher and pupil, they concerned themselves with Greek as well as Latin. Fronto sends to Marcus a Greek *Erotikos Logos* or "Lover's Courtship" (*Ep. Graec.* 8 [LCL, 1:20–30]), an exercise modeled on Socrates's famous speech in the *Phaedrus* and practiced by every Greek rhetor in this century.[36] Greek was an important part of their world, and another letter from Marcus reports a disappointing experience listening to Greek panegyrists:

> We have been listening to panegyrists here, Greeks of course, but wondrous creatures, so much so that I, who am as far removed from Greek literature as is my native Caelian hill from the land of Greece, could nevertheless hope, matched with them, to be able to rival even Theopompus, the most eloquent, as I hear, of all the Greeks. So I, who am all but a breathing barbarian, have been impelled to write in Greek by men, as Caecilius says, of "unimpaired ignorance." (*To Marcus* 2.6 [LCL, 1.143])

A revealing letter, with its awareness of Greek contempt for Roman culture, but reflecting Marcus's own doubts about the Greeks' automatic superiority. Some of his language—*litteratura* instead of the usual *litterae*, *Opicum animantem*[37]—mocks either himself or contemporary attitudes. But Marcus is a good pupil eager to make his teacher happy, and his sentiments here may serve the same purpose as the learned allusion to the old comic poet Caecilius. Ultimately Marcus's own inclinations and values led him away from rhetoric, and it was a sorrow to Fronto that, once Marcus reached manhood, he would devote himself only to philosophy—and naturally philosophy in Greek, the language of the discipline.

Despite Fronto's cultural loyalty to Latin, it is clear that he took his Greek studies seriously, and that he needed to use the language at every level of technicality to talk and write to his friends, who included the floridly eloquent Herodes Atticus. A letter of condolence has been preserved on Fronto's loss of a new-born child, one of his many bereavements (*Ep. Graec.* 3 [LCL, 1:168–70]). Fronto was also friendly with the sophist Favorinus (with whom he discusses Latin color adjectives in Gell. *NA* 2.26) and with Appian, the historian from Egypt who was also a high public official (*Ep. Graec.* 4, 5). Thus besides his letters of literary friendship, Fronto's correspondence includes letters of recommendation in both Latin and Greek to the leading public men of Rome, of his own region of Africa, and of the wider empire, with whom the ex-consul naturally associated.

Aulus Gellius, the Eternal Student in Rome and Greece

A different kind of evidence for the daily teaching of Fronto and other educators and men of letters in this period comes from the wonderful miscellany called the *Attic Nights* by Aulus Gellius, a combination of memoirs, encyclopedia, and commonplace book, which Gellius claims he put together during his evenings as a mature student at Athens. Gellius too seems to have come from a Roman family in Africa, and Fronto may have been his introduction to Roman life as well as his informal teacher. As with Pliny and Tacitus, we are talking of the great man's *contubernium* or social patronage, not of his formal teaching or of any material favors. Although Gellius does not seem to have sought a career in the courts or in imperial service, Fronto's sponsorship would have ensured the young man's acceptance in cultured circles.

Aulus Gellius was born between 125 and 128, and although he nowhere mentions his place of birth, he seems to have come from a Roman colony in Africa. We do not know when he began to write his leisurely collection of reminiscences, but since 19.21.1 implies that Herodes Atticus is no longer alive, Gellius was still writing after 177. This is the last datable reference in the *Attic Nights*.[38] Gellius's preface implies that he was busy enough managing his estate and supervising his children's education to have leisure only for his compilation, and there is no indication that he is still preoccupied by the work as an official empaneled judge that he mentions in *Attic Nights* 14.2.3.

The beginning of the preface (where we would look for a dedication) is lost, but Gellius explains in the first surviving sentences how he began to assemble his *commentarii*. He claims that the order is random (so did Pliny in introducing his *Letters!*) and he has simply set down what he fancied as he took up any Greek or Latin book, or heard anything worth recording, noting it down without classification and storing all the information up as a kind of larder from which he could easily take the knowledge of any thing or word he might forget. In explaining his title Gellius offers a fascinating survey of the many miscellanies known to him, largely with Greek names, but some more recent Roman names evoking specific authors: *A Natural History, Moral Letters, Epistolary Investigations* (these by his own teacher Sulpicius Apollinaris). This type of miscellany had become increasingly common, and it is illuminating to set alongside Gellius's preface the report given by Photius of the preface by a learned Alexandrian lady, Pamphile, who wrote in the time of Nero, and whose work Gellius actually cites more than once.

> She says that having lived with her husband for thirteen years since she was a child she began this composition of historical materials and recorded what she had learned from her husband during her thirteen years of living with him, departing from him neither by night nor day, and whatever she happened to hear from anyone else visiting him (for many men with a reputation for learning visited him) and in addition whatever she had read in books.
>
> She divided all this material as it seemed to her worthy of report and record, into mixed commentaries, not distinguished according to their individual content, but randomly as she came to record each item, since as she says it is not difficult to classify material, but she thought a miscellany would be more enjoyable and attractive, and variety more appealing than homogeneity. (Photius 175S 119b)

There are differences; the learned Greek lady is confined to her house and limited to the learning available there—luckily she could expect to listen to her husband's readers as well as beg access to his books. In contrast, the bilingual Latin student can travel and listen to whom he pleases in more than one cultural center. But the genre is defined, and Gellius is writing in an established and fashionable tradition, to which even Favorinus had contributed.[39] Of Gellius's twenty books, one (book 8) is lost, except for the section headings in his table of contents; the others each contain between twelve and twenty units, some strictly reports of knowledge that he has acquired, some brief dramatic dialogues between Gellius's various teachers and friends, or between Gellius and unidentified interlocutors. What mattered to Gellius was the knowledge itself, and the personalities of his teachers, rather than accurate recording of specific occasion or texts. And the reader should beware of thinking that Gellius actually heard, or his teachers said, the things he reports: the distinction between speech and text is arbitrary. He will represent as conversation what he found in a book, or represent as his own reading what is really reported at second hand by an intermediary. His motive is not deception but, like the clergyman appropriating anecdotes for his sermons, to add immediacy and personal interest to textbook information.

Gellius revered the archaic literature of Rome and is our source for a great deal of precious knowledge—or ancient lore—about the books and lives of the early poets, orators, and historians. Literary-historical details, information about customs, language, law, and moral debates are his main interest, reflecting his training in grammar, rhetoric, perhaps law, and philosophy. Of the Greek arts of science, mathematics, music, and architecture, we have only snippets and the occasional curiosity.

Gellius is proud to be associated with his masters, and they in turn show respect for earlier teachers. His first extended excerpt (1.2) carefully establishes Gellius's own status as a welcome guest of the great Herodes at his villa in Cephisia. Then it shows Herodes teaching a lesson in behavior to a forward (but anonymous) young man by quoting a rebuke once given by Epictetus. A similar episode in 1.10 describes Favorinus reproaching another nameless victim for his obscure vocabulary "as if he were talking to the mother of Evander" (the prehistoric king who supposedly first occupied the site of Rome).

Among Gellius's teachers Favorinus is found in the greatest number of encounters, discoursing in Greek or Latin on every kind of learned topic—but many of these topics may have been chapters in Favorinus's own written miscellany. In fact, Fronto, who might have been expected to feature in book 1, first appears in 2.26 when

Favorinus takes his student Gellius to Fronto's home, where he is laid up sick. There is no suggestion that it is Gellius's first visit, and the occasion is significant because Gellius shows that Favorinus's learning in Latin is as immense as in Greek: he can match Fronto's lovely quotation from the tragedian Pacuvius with an equally rich quotation from Ennius. But having held his own, Favorinus compliments Fronto on having vindicated the richness of Latin against the claims of Greek. It is a contest in learning and courtesy that does honor to both men and both cultures.

Gellius will have studied with his Latin teachers in Rome, and among his Greek teachers Favorinus at least lectured or taught him in the city. But Gellius spent years in Athens, which cannot be precisely dated.[40] Besides his stories of Herodes[41] many of Gellius's anecdotes and minilectures (real or fictional) honor his Greek teacher of philosophy, Calvenus Taurus, the Platonist from Berytus (Beirut) who wrote a learned commentary on Plato's *Gorgias*.[42] Platonists were probably the natural choice of teachers for unphilosophical or literary-minded students, and Taurus's complaints (17.20) against students who chose Plato only to read about Alcibiades or the erotic discourse of the *Phaedrus* suggest that these were many. Gellius introduces examples of Taurus's scientific knowledge and others of his ethical teaching. He warns against anger (1.26), he describes how Euclid of Megara during the war with Athens used to disguise himself as a woman and walk twenty miles each day to hear Plato (7.10), and he profits by the courtesy call of a Roman proconsul and his father to demonstrate the proper etiquette of seniority between age and official status (2.2). Two stories have a context: Taurus's dinner parties for his privileged students to which they brought problems instead of wine or delicacies (7.13) and an excursion with him to the Pythian Games, in which they turn aside to visit a dying friend at Lebada. Taurus fetches a doctor and talks to Gellius on the walk back to their vehicle about involuntary groaning and the battles fought between a philosopher and pain (12.5).

Taurus and Herodes were probably Gellius's only teachers during his stay in Athens, but, as in Athens, so in Rome he provides vivid vignettes of his teachers and his student life. He studied rhetoric with Antonius Julianus and recalls two summer excursions led by Julianus to Puteoli and to Naples. They might be called busman's holidays. At Puteoli they find out that a professional reciter will be reading Ennius publicly in the theater; Gellius uses the occasion to introduce his own report on an archaic form of *equus* that was mispronouned by the reader, thus violating the meter. At Naples they come across a rich young man practicing declamation with his Greek and Latin rhetors, in order to become an advocate at Rome. He asks them to come and hear him, and opens his performance with a boastful preamble. To pay him back, one of Gellius's fellow students offers him a difficult topic to handle and he makes a logical dog's breakfast of it. When they finally escape, the young man's friends insist on asking Julianus what he thought of the performance. The excerpt ends in his bon mot: "he certainly is an eloquent fellow, without any argument!" (9.15.11).

The encounter has its equivalent in Philostratus's *Lives of the Philosophers*,[43] and many of the stories in Gellius occur elsewhere— and will occur again in Macrobius, who lifts them unchanged from Gellius. Despite the fascinating anecdotes of his Greek mentors, most of Gellius's material reflects Latin rather than sophistic Greek culture. Besides the rhetor Julianus,[44] he also studied with two grammatici, the learned but severe Castricius[45] and the more affable Sulpicius Apollinaris of Carthage, who composed acrostic summaries of Terence's six plays and of the twelve books of the *Aeneid* for his pupils to memorize.

In one episode Sulpicius is featured sitting with Gellius in the library of the Domus Tiberiana on the Palatine, where they find a speech ascribed to Cato's grandson (*NA* 13.20). On another occasion he answers a query on augury from the city prefect Erucius Clarus (7.6), but it is more likely that Gellius drew this technical material from a literary epistle than from a remembered conversation. At 13.18 Gellius describes how Clarus wrote to Sulpicius to discover the meaning of *inter os et offam*, "twixt the cup and the lip," and quotes Sulpicius as writing back "in my presence, for this was when I was studying with him," that it had the same meaning as the Greek proverb "Many things arise between the cup and the tip of the lips." In another discussion at 11.15, Gellius artfully postpones reference to Sulpicius. First he reports how the Hadrianic scholar, Terentius Scaurus, wrote a book *On the Errors of Caesellius Vindex* correcting Vindex's *Collection of Ancient Readings*, about the meaning of adjectives ending in *-bundus*. Very impressive! Then Gellius adds as his own discovery a learned instance from the historian Sisenna. Only then does he allow Sulpicius credit for the final comment—"when I investigated what could be the significance and origin of this suffix . . . our Apollinaris said with a lucky shot . . . " What has been presented as an immediate oral reaction is surely the conclusion of one of Sulpicius's learned books, in which he had cited all Gellius's preceding material.

An excerpt deliberately placed late in the collection features Fronto and Sulpicius with Gellius and another student from Africa, Postumius Festus, waiting in the vestibule of the Palatine residence, no doubt to pay their respects to Hadrian. The scene epitomizes the Roman literary world at this time. Here in the heart of Rome public men and private scholars are debating word usage. Fronto has found an archaic word, *pumilio*, for "dwarf," which he would like to use instead of the current *nanus*, and seeks Sulpicius's authorization, adding that he thinks *nanus* is vulgar and barbaric. Sulpicius politely explains that *nanus* is not barbaric but Greek, and found in a little-known play of Aristophanes. "And surely the word would have been awarded citizenship by you, or settled in a Latin colony," he adds, "if you chose to use it, and it would be a great deal more approved than the low and shabby words that Laberius admitted into the usage of our Latin tongue" (19.13).

The emperor Tiberius was once told by the grammarian Pomponius Marcellus that he could not confer citizenship upon a word, but Favorinus more diplomatically acquiesced in Hadrian's language because "one cannot argue with the master of thirty legions."[46] Despite the extraordinary prominence of grammarians, despite the retarding tendency of the current fashion for archaism, Latin was still developing its descriptive and narrative vocabulary. The full diversity of the language is seen not in any poetic works— for there seem to have been none in this generation—but in a great and flamboyant writer of prose. Latin at its most exuberant would be heard and read in the speeches, treatises, and novel of the single

251

creative talent of this age—the African philosopher, orator, zoologist, perhaps also magician, Apuleius.

Apuleius, the Ultimate Word Artist

As we have seen in passing, the Roman provinces of North Africa had fully developed their own high urban culture by the time of the principate. Modern Tunisia, the peaceful senatorial province called Africa Proconsularis, had been Roman since 146 B.C., had received settlements of Marian veterans in the last century of the republic, and maintained influential *conventus* of Roman and Italian residents and traders. It was the richest source of grain for Italy, and large parts of the province were the estates of millionaire landowners. Numidia and Mauretania came into the Roman sphere of control after the defeats of Jugurtha (105 B.C.) and Juba (46 B.C.). By the time of Hadrian they had been provinces for a century, and the magnificent remains of their cities, with forums, temples, libraries, and theaters from the first two centuries of our era, attest the level of their culture.

W. V. Harris, in his survey *Ancient Literacy*, brings out some of the factors governing both the dissemination of the dominant nation's official languages and the survival of native or secondary tongues. A person whose mother tongue was neither Greek nor Latin might learn one or the other for "cultural prestige, commercial advantage, a wish to communicate with officials, social contact."[47] Slaves, especially domestics or overseers, would need to communicate in the language of their masters, but small or remote provincial communities would usually have little demand for more than a handful of people able to talk in Latin or Greek and it must have been difficult to learn either language beyond a basic level. Even so we might believe that public need would be countered by private ambition: "Learn Latin, young man, and get ahead and out of this dump!"

At least four languages were spoken and written in Roman Africa. Libyan and Punic are attested on inscribed tombstones from the first and second century of our era, three centuries after the destruction of independent Carthage. The long-established Italian and

Roman residents, perhaps like English residents of Harare or Cape Town, maintained their own society and language, which also remained the language of government. No other province has so high a density of Latin inscriptions, public and private, as Africa Proconsularis: indeed its nearest competitor is its neighbor, Numidia.[48] But persons of culture also learned Greek in elementary school and both heard and read it as the language of rhetoric and learning. There must have been intermarriage between urban speakers of Latin and Punic; there may have been members of the middle class who spoke only Punic, but it is more likely that they used both languages.

It is significant that Statius, addressing the wellborn Septimius Severus, ancestor of the emperor who would found a dynasty at the end of the second century, affirms his Latinity: "Your speech is not Punic, nor your dress, your mind is not alien: you are Italian, Italian, I say!" (*Silvae* 4.5). However, it is perhaps more significant that Statius has to insist on it. For Severus's imperial descendant spoke Punic fluently. Punic was used in conjunction with Latin on coinage from Leptis and Oea (the scene of Apuleius's marriage) in the first century, and in an inscription from Leptis as late as 180. A generation later the jurist Ulpian allows for the use of Punic in trusts, and Saint Augustine in the early fifth century writes of presbyters who spoke the language.[49]

Romani di Roma may not have fully acknowledged the cultural level of the elite in Carthage, Hippo, Leptis, or Cirta. We have already considered several products of this elite in action at Rome, but how representative of its society was this elite?

Lucius Apuleius of Madaura is best known for his wonderful novel the *Metamorphoses* or *Golden Ass*, a story that he is known to have adapted from a Hellenistic Greek novel, *Lucius, or the Ass* attributed to his Syrian contemporary Lucian. Although much of the novel is fantastic, it also reflects real life in both Thessaly and other more urbanized parts of provincial Greece, and has been used by a distinguished historian as evidence for the (rather ragged) economy and state of law and order in second-century Greece.[50] Now the novel reflects the cosmopolitan travel of its dramatis personae,[51] and the first-person narrator is a Corinthian who has

rhetoric at Rome and will return there at the end—an end
to Apuleius—as a convert to the cult of Isis and a successful
    While the Greek-speaking Eastern and Latin-speaking
western empire have little mutual contact, it seems that both Rome
itself and Africa were meeting places for both cultures.

It seems too that Lucius, the traveling comic-hero, is not so
unlike Apuleius himself. In his first datable work, the *Apologia*, or
Defense of Himself, Apuleius describes his family, origin, and education. The *Apologia* claims to be the speech delivered in his own
defense before the proconsul Claudius Maximus in 158. Apuleius
does deprecatingly call his homeland "half Numidian and half
Gaetulain," but in compensation he traces the history of Madaura
back to Syphax's defeat at the end of the Hannibalic war. Since then
it had acquired the honorable status of colony after it was settled
with Roman veterans and he is proud to report that he is a member
of its town council, following his father who had served as its mayor
(*duumvir*).

Although Apuleius reveals a great deal about his own culture in
this speech, it is fair to ask whether it was delivered to his audience
in the form we now read. The governor himself was a learned man
and had served as a teacher of philosophy to Marcus Aurelius, but it
is more than likely that even the educated Romans in his *consilium*
might have been alienated by the erudition paraded in the transmit-
ted speech.

First, however, something should be said of the circumstances. We
know only the defense version of the previous events. Apuleius
claims that he was traveling overland to Alexandria to continue his
pursuit of learning when he fell ill at Oea (Tripoli). There he stayed
with friends until Pontianus, who had been a fellow student of
Apuleius at Athens, urged him to transfer to his own home and
invited him to pay court to Pontianus's widowed mother, Pudentilla. Pudentilla, whose age is variously given as sixty and forty-five,
fell in love with Apuleius. But when Pontianus married soon after,
he was influenced by his father-in-law, who represented Apuleius as
a threat to the inheritance of Pontianus and his brother. According
to Apuleius, he was able to reassure Pontianus, but the young man

later fell ill and died. So it seems that Apuleius and Pudentilla married quietly—and hastily?—at her country estate, and now her younger son Sicinnius Pudens, with two older kinsmen, Tannonius Pudens and Aemilianus, have charged Apuleius with practicing magic, and perhaps also with using love philters and poisoning the dead Pontianus.

The case as we read it closely resembles Cicero's famous defenses of Cluentius and Caelius, and shares with those speeches its avoidance of the real issue and its preference for attack on the immorality of those behind the prosecution. The speech contains important evidence for masculine prejudices about female sexuality, which cannot be addressed here, but its opening sections in particular are extraordinarily revealing about the divergent levels of contemporary literary culture. Looking beyond the immediate occasion and audience, the literary showman Apuleius devotes the first half of his speech to parading his own cultural merits and mocking the limited education of his accusers. He must surely have shown more modesty and restraint in the original courtroom if he did not wish to alienate his local audience; but after his acquittal the written version aims at a wider public and can put the aim of advertising his learning ahead of conciliating the jurors who have served their part.

Apuleius always calls himself a philosopher, and opens with the claim that he wishes to defend himself before those ignorant of philosophy. This entails a defense of philosophy itself and a response to the charge that he is as eloquent in Greek as in Latin. His accusers had warned the audience against being seduced by his rhetoric and glib tongue, but they can see that he is no pomaded charmer; his neglected appearance bears witnesses to his dedication to scholarship (*literati laboris*). Not content with citing the *Iliad* and Plato's *Parmenides*, he calls on the old republican dramatist Caecilius Statius to vindicate the innocence of his eloquence; he can speak fluently because he has nothing to hide, nothing to be ashamed of, not even the supposedly shameful poems so mangled in recitation by his accuser.

Those in the audience who knew Apuleius as a lecturer or declaimer will have begun to sit back and enjoy themselves. Three poems are at issue, the elegiac recipe for toothpaste, which may have been used to mark him as a seducer, and two mawkishly sentimental elegies praising boys. The toothpaste poem, recited in full, enables Apuleius to quote Catullus,[52] and to utter a purple passage that uses a Homeric tag to stress the need to avoid bad breath in conversation, lecturing, and prayer (!) "since the mouth is vestibule of the mind, door of speech, and assembly place of thought" (7–8). The audience is told that Apuleius's so-called erotic verses (as insipid and innocent as Pliny's) were written as polite homage to the sons of his friend Scribonius Laetus under the Platonic pseudonyms Critias and Charinus: he has the precedents of Anacreon, Alcman, Simonides, Sappho, and the circle of Lutatius Catulus, not to mention the elegists and Virgil (9–10). This passage has a double interest, for his allusive learning in adducing Greek precedents (none of whom is actually named) and for the coincidence of the Latin excerpts with a passage of Aulus Gellius citing the same poems (*NA* 19.9). Holford-Strevens has recently argued that Apuleius was a fellow student of Gellius at Athens, and probably the unidentified "highly cultured youth" whose seventeen-line version of a two-line Platonic epigram Gellius praises at 19.11.[53] Certainly Apuleius did not need to borrow his material from Gellius, and Holford-Strevens's suggestion of a continuing friendship and exchange of cultural information between the two is an appealing explanation of the coincidence.

But Apuleius is not content with literary precedents, and after adducing both Plato[54] and Catullus, produces as his last character witness, the late emperor Hadrian's epitaph on Voconius Romanus —"wanton in verse, you were most pure in heart"[55]—and the emperor's own record of erotic verse.

As a self-styled "philosopher" Apuleius begins his sweep through Greco-Roman literary history with Diotima's *Erotikos Logos* from Plato's *Symposium*; as an antiquarian and archaizer, he includes two more archaic poets, Afranius and Ennius,[56] before he switches to Greek philosophical authorities, from Agesilaus and Socrates on the morality of mirrors to Epicurus, Archytas, and Archimedes on their optical qualities. It is with Archimedes, of all people, that Apuleius launches the refrain mocking his prosecutor, "if you only knew the book" (16), which he will repeat apropos of the elder Cato

(17), the story of Crates of Thebes (22), and finally even Virgil (30).

To complete the parade of his nonscientific knowledge, Apuleius appeals to history, with parallel Greek and Latin *exempla* in the tradition of Plutarch. He fields a team of Greek statesmen who shared his poverty and austere life-style—Aristides, Phocion, Epaminondas, and Socrates—then outmatches them with the Romans Fabricius, Cornelius Scipio, and Manius Curius, Valerius Publicola, Menenius Agrippa, and Atilius Regulus. Popular attitudes are again exploited as Apuleius expands on the noble Cynic tradition of Antisthenes and Diogenes, who lived simply traveling like himself with only a wallet and staff. On the other hand, Apuleius carefully reaffirms his respectable inheritance, which he has chosen to use for generosity to individual and community. By this time he has silenced the standard criticisms of a man's birth and behavior and can turn to the actual accusations of practicing magic. These too are turned into cultural ammunition as Apuleius cites *Eclogues* 8 ("If you had read your Virgil you would know without me telling you") on erotic magical practice.

But this is not enough. Apuleius also fancies himself as a scientist—perhaps the first writer in Latin to make a personal boast of such skills. In a display of bilingual learning, he calls for friends to bring into court both his Greek and his Latin *Natural Questions* and has excerpts from his own Greek text cited in court as if they were legal evidence. He claims to have rendered services to Latin science by his painstaking translation from the Greek zoological corpus of Aristotle and his followers; he has even created Latin names for these previously unidentifiable fishes, and he has his glossary cited as documentary evidence (31–41). If his accusers want to condemn his work as sorcery, will they drive the texts of Aristotle out of the public libraries (41)? Clearly he can presume on reverence for the name of Aristotle, but this study of Aristotle's scientific work is something new for a representative of Roman culture, far beyond the secondhand reportage of the elder Pliny. Should we assume that Apuleius is unique, or merely the most conspicuous representative of a submerged tradition?

In refuting the accusations of magic he is also able to vindicate his knowledge of medicine, discoursing on the epilepsy of a slave and of a freeborn woman brought to him for medical treatment (44–48).

Even religion has its turn as he vindicates his possession of secret objects wrapped in a linen cloth: as a devotee of Aesculapius[57] and an initiate into the mysteries, he naturally preserves the sacred objects wrapped only in linen (nonanimal fibers) at his home. But these sacred things were not concealed, but left in Pontianus's library where the slave who regularly fetched out his books could have exposed and examined them (53). The devotee and aesthete is equally confident that his possession of an ebony statuette of Hermes (61) is justified by Plato's recommendation in the *Laws* that images of the gods should be in simple natural materials; the climax in his submission of nonforensic exhibits comes when Apuleius offers up this statuette to the presiding magistrate Maximus for his examination and approval (63).

No wonder Apuleius calls himself a polymath! In an excerpt from one of his rhetorical prefaces, which we will consider shortly, he ventures to compare himself favorably with the fifth-century sophist Hippias. We know from Cicero and other Latin sources that Hippias had boasted of his mastery of handicrafts, by which he made everything he wore. But Apuleius boasts instead of his mastery of every intellectual craft. In the *Florida* excerpt he focuses on his command of rhetorical genres, but in the *Apology* there is no limit: poetry, philology, ethics, optics, zoology, history, medicine, and religion all have their turn.

The *Apology* offers some confusing evidence about the use and status of Latin and Greek and one significant discussion of translation. Three letters are quoted in the case. That of Pudentilla is in Greek (excerpts in 82–84) and that of Aemilianus in Latin (70), while the supposedly forged love letter of Apuleius to Pudentilla is also apparently Greek: "why would I have written in such faulty diction and such barbarous language, when the same accusers say I am far from unskilled in Greek? And why would I have wheedled her with such vulgar and commercial endearments when they say that I am quite neatly naughty in my love poetry?"

The prosecutor Aemilianus is mocked because he could not read Pudentilla's "too idiomatic Greek letter," whereas Pudentilla's younger son, the lazy student, "never speaks anything except Punic and the odd Greek he has picked up from his mother. He can't speak Latin and he will not try" (98). Which language did the educated locals speak in Oea? It looks as though they might learn Latin only as a school language, after being taught to read and write Greek. The system that worked for native Latin speakers would be more problematic for those who spoke primarily Greek. But Apuleius speaks to his audience as though Latin were its first language. In the very significant account of his work translating—or remodeling—Greek zoology into Latin, Apuleius has already introduced technical Latin words into his direct speech: *subent* and *suriunt* for the mating roles of female and male fish, and *viviparos/oviparos* for their types of reproduction. About his Latin text he notes the rarity of the subject matter and the words without Latin equivalent that he has laboriously created from the Greek so that they will pass as legitimate Latin coin.

After reading the Greek word list himself, Apuleius asks his reader to pronounce in Latin his own versions: these, however, are not part of his official speech. As Russell has pointed out,[58] Greek was so well known to the educated that they judged Latin versions by detailed comparison with the original, rather than depending on them to understand its meaning. And those who composed Latin versions did so to demonstrate their skill in matching language to language. More often indeed, the translator preferred to adapt freely, as a greater index of his own literary talent.

It looks then as though Apuleius's jury comprised Latin speakers who knew only some Greek, and would be grateful for discreet glossing: but Pudentilla was a Greek speaker, for whom Latin was an acquired language, while her former husband's Oean family may have spoken primarily Punic. No point is made of the double alphabet, and it is likely that this was no obstacle, just as modern Athenians easily read traffic directions in Roman letters.

To return to the highest level of society, it is not difficult to see in Apuleius's role as he describes it that of the Greek rhetor addressing a cultured audience with the lecture-going habit. Even at Oea when he gives a lecture, the people book the basilica, shout "bravo," and offer him citizenship (73). The picture is even more impressive at

Carthage. Here the twenty-three collected excerps from his declamations now called *Florida* provide a useful insight into his technique,
his milieu, and his public. Like Lucian's *Prolaliae*[59] they mix personal material, flattery of the audience, and anecdotes or marvelous
tales from other times or places. A few seem to have been preserved
complete, like *Florida* 9 on Hippias. It opens however with audience and artist.

> If any person of ill will among my detractors is sitting in this distin-
> guished gathering . . . or has infiltrated this most splendid audience, I
> would like him to cast his eyes briefly around this amazing crowd, and
> when he has taken in these numbers, greater than have ever been seen
> before at any philosopher's lecture, let him think how a man risks his
> reputation, who is not accustomed to contempt, since it is strenuous
> and difficult to satisfy even the moderate expectations of a small group.
>
> This is especially true for me, since the reputation I have already
> won, together with your kind expectations, does not allow me to utter
> any random or spontaneous thought. Who among you would allow me
> a single solecism? Who would let pass a single barbarously accented
> syllable? Who would let me blurt out rashly the sort of outlandish or
> faulty words that come to the lips of madmen? (9.29)

Apuleius goes on to comment on the versatile Greek sophist Hippias and contrast his own intellectual versatility:

> I put more value on composing with a single writer's pen poems of every
> kind, fit for the rhapsode's wand, the lyre, the comic slipper, the tragic
> boot, satires and riddles, a variety of scientific investigations, and
> speeches praised by the eloquent and dialogues praised by philosophers
> and every other kind of work, as much in Greek as in Latin, with double
> emulation, matching zeal and comparable style. (9.37)

Some of Apuleius's philosophical works—a translation of the
Phaedo and a discussion of Socrates's daemon—survive, but we
must deeply regret the loss of the debate that he promises in *Florida*
18 because it would be such a powerful symbol of the fusion and
indivisibility of the educated Greek and Latin tradition. To the
people of Carthage Apuleius offers his forthcoming performance as
his repayment for the education they have given him. He is about to
present a hymn to Aesculapius, who presides over their Carthagi-

nian citadel, a hymn in both Greek and Latin verse. But he has also devised a preliminary dialogue for this hymn in which the Carthaginian patriots and friends Sabidius Severus and Julius Persius converse. The only issue disputed between them is which of them loves Carthage most.

> At the beginning of the book I make one of my fellow students from Athens ask Persius in Greek what I had said in my discourse the day before in the Temple of Aesculapius. And gradually I add Severus to their conversation, giving him the role of the Roman tongue. For Persius, though he too can speak an excellent Latin, will play the Athenian for you today. (18.92)

Unfortunately, although the excerpt continues, it is with Aesculapius and not with the hybrid dialogue. Cicero thought it a solecism to include Greek words in his dialogues, and the only genre with any pretensions that admitted Greek was satire, whether the Lucilian verse form refined by Horace or the Menippean *prosimetrum*, the combination of prose and verse used in Varro's largely lost satires. But in this cosmopolitan African milieu both languages are equally valid.

Apuleius regularly praises the members of his Carthaginian audience for their erudition (so presumably did Polemon and Favorinus, but without interest in their linguistic abilities) and prided himself that he spoke to them in a lecturer's auditorium with a dignity worthy of their Senate house and a learning worthy of their library (*Florida* 18.29). In return they honored him like Asiatic Greeks, with a priesthood, and with at least the proposal of a statue, the last occasion that I shall describe. In Apuleius's version the story began when the ex-consul Aemilianus Strabo wrote to the Senate of Carthage requesting a prominent site for a statue of Apuleius. Aemilianus was an old friend, who studied under the same teachers with Apuleius, so his proposal is not surprising. And he uses the powerful arguments that other cities have already done this. Now Aemilianus has promised to erect the statue at his own expense— and Apuleius points out that Aemilianus deserves respect, for provinces all over the empire erect in his honor statues with four- and even six-horse chariots. When he made this proposal in the Senate

nanimously adopted, and some even proposed a second
show their own initiative.

␣ut it seems money is still needed for the bronze and the artist's
labor. Apuleius uses the strategy of shaming: since even second-
rank cities have always funded this kind of tribute, he can have no
doubt of the outcome in Carthage. For us it is instructive to have
even a one-sided view of this kind of "spontaneous" gesture of
respect for literary learning. Meanwhile Apuleius responds to the
Senate's promises with promises of his own. When the statue is
erected, he will compose a volume in praise of Aemilianus, "that
ennoblement of the senators, glory of the citizens, and prestige of
his friends." At the dedication ceremony he will give his thanks
more fully and "entrust to his book the duty of going through every
province and declaring in all the world and for all time the praise of
your benefaction, to all races and through all the years"
(16.76–77). Could the sophisticated Apuleius have spoken without his tongue in his cheek?

Neither Aemilianus Strabo's fame nor that of Apuleius would
have outlasted the century if he had not also written a masterwork,
the *Metamorphoses*. We saw that the novel is not original, but based
on a Greek narrative *Lucius: or the Ass*. In reworking this brief and
cynical picaresque novella, he kept both its realistic world of sex
and violence and its surrealistic world of magic. But he raised the
story to a new level by incorporating two major narratives: the
magnificent extended allegory of Cupid and Psyche, and the devo-
tional finale in which Lucius the Donkey is rescued from his self-imposed transformation by the grace of Isis, to end his adventures in
pious procession to her mysteries. Thus the novel, set in Greece and
based on a Greek fiction, honors an Egyptian goddess and was
composed in Latin by an African "philosopher." Probably the Car-
thaginians read it eagerly and thought it less meritorious than
Apuleius's Platonic philosophy, his zoology, and his exuberant lectures and dialogues. But its emotional and imaginative range, its
cosmopolitan scope, and its sophisticated narrative technique
make the *Metamorphoses* of Apuleius worthy of any number of
statues, even if they were of solid gold and driving six-horse
chariots.

Tacitus began his devastating account of the disintegration of authority at Rome after the death of Nero by speaking of the terrible secret that was revealed—that an emperor could be chosen elsewhere than at Rome (*Hist.* 1.4) What the achievements of Apuleius show even more clearly than those of Fronto or Gellius is that not only individual talent but also literary culture could flourish outside Rome. Indeed, from this generation on Rome itself has left no trace of literary creativity or culture for over a century: we have been looking at Latin, rather than Roman, literary culture—the flourishing Latin eloquence of North Africa, rather than the culture of Rome or even Italy. Another kind of transformation awaited that provides a closure to our cultural history.

Since the time of Nero, Christianity had been developing, first among humble, then among more educated people, earning itself increasing attention, then persecution during the last half of this second century by the administration of the otherwise enlightened Marcus Aurelius. All this time it was generating a new culture of texts and ideas, translating the scripture from Greek and expounding it in both tongues. In the time of Apuleius, cultured and eloquent advocates of Christianity are beginning to appear. From the third century onward, great men who write in Latin will be mighty with the pen like the Roman African Tertullian, born during Apuleius's lifetime, like Lactantius and the Christian fathers. By the end of the fourth century, Italians will again be eloquent with Ambrose and Jerome (who had nightmares reproaching him with his love of Cicero), and the greatest of all African writers, Augustine, will not only create but analyze and teach the principles of the new Christian Latin eloquence.

Latin itself still had a powerful future, but it would be some generations before the urge to write for pleasure or beauty broke free of this higher necessity. In contemplating the state of Latin literary culture, we might well be tempted to echo the despairing cry attributed to Julian, last of the pagan emperors: *Vicisti Galilaee*. The compelling power of Christianity would shape the literature of the Latin-speaking world for centuries to come.

Notes

Introduction. Toward a Social History of Latin Literature

1. What we know as Horace's *Ars Poetica* was not so called by Horace himself; this mode of reference (not necessarily a formal title) cannot be traced before its use by Quintilian (8.3.60), a century after Horace. The work is grouped by the manuscript tradition with the two major *Epistles* of Horace's second book, but scholars disagree as much about the purpose and nature of this work as on its date. See most recently B. Frischer's *Shifting Paradigms: New Approaches to the Ars Poetica* (Atlanta, 1991), which argues that Horace was parodying rather than following the traditional format of a manual of poetry.

2. The model here is Aristotle's method of distinguishing in *Rhetoric* 1.3.1–7 between the three genres of rhetoric: deliberative rhetoric and epideictic or display oratory differ from judicial rhetoric (the dominant model) not only in their subject matter and purpose, but in their setting, their audience, and the function exercised by the audience as judge or spectator.

3. See now J. Snyder, *The Woman and the Lyre: Woman Writers in Greece and Rome* (Carbondale, Ill., 1990), ch. 5, "Women Writers in Rome and Their Successors."

4. According to Suetonius (*Gramm.* 21), Melissus was freeborn but first kidnapped, then educated and presented as a gift to Maecenas. It is a measure of the comfortable circumstances that could attend high-level slavery that when his mother tried to claim his freeborn status,

Melissus preferred to remain Maecenas's slave. Later, however, he was given his freedom and became an intimate of Augustus.

5. On Tyrannio, Parthenius, and other possible captives from the war in Asia Minor, see E. Rawson, *Intellectual Life in the Later Roman Republic* (Baltimore, 1985), 8.

6. See David Armstrong, *Horace* (New Haven, Conn., 1989), argued in detail in *Horatius Eques et Scriba*: Satires 1.6 and 2.7," *TAPA* 116 (1986): 255–88. and on Horace's relationship with Maecenas, see the distinctive viewpoint of P. White, *Promised Verse: Poets in the Society of Augustan Rome* (Cambridge, Mass., 1993).

7. On Martial, Statius, and patronage, see the articles and books of Peter White and Alexander Hardie cited in the discussion of these poets in Chapter 5.

8. Cicero lists his studies with Molo and the philosophers Philo, Antiochus, and Diodotus in his survey of his education from *Brutus* 306–16. He also lists less known rhetors with whom he studied in Athens and Asia: Demetrius the Syrian, Menippus of Stratonice, Dionysius of Magnesia, Aeschylus of Cnidos, and Xenocles of Adramyttium.

9. Seneca comments on Ovid's talents and weaknesses both in declamation and in poetry in *Controv.* 2.2.8–12, 7.1.27; *Suas.* 3.7 (see Chapter 3).

10. Parthenius addresses his patron-pupil Gallus in the preface to his *Tales of Passion* composed to provide raw material for Gallus's poetry.

11. *Tristia* 4.10, written in exile.

12. The evidence for the syllabus of father Statius's school comes from the poet's eulogy (*Epikedion*) in *Silvae* 5.3 discussed in Chapter 5.

13. Cf. Cic. Att. 2.1: "when he read this sketch of mine, which I had sent him with the idea that he might compose something more elaborate on the same theme, so far from being stimulated to composition, he was effectively frightened away." The translation is adapted from D. R. Shackleton Bailey, *Cicero's Letters to Atticus* (Cambridge, 1964), 21.2. All references to Cicero's letters to Atticus, to his brother Quintus, or to his friends will be followed by the number of the letter in Shackleton Bailey's editions and translations (listed in the bibliography), under the designation SB.

14. On the very different cultural interests of Seneca, Lucan, and Nero, see Chapter 5.

15. Hor. *Epist.* 2.2.51; see below p. 77.

16. Horace supports his own profession of reluctance to write about Augustus's military campaigns by the bad example of Alexander who let his achievements be disfigured by the bad epic verse of Choerilus (*Epist.* 2.1.232–33).

17. Cf. Propertius's list of elegiac poets in 2.34.87–92.
18. Horace defines his own satires in relation to the form and content of Lucilius in the programmatic *Satires* (1.4, 1.10, 2.1).
19. Cf. Pliny *Ep.* 1.2, in which he applies the Greek term *zelos* to this stylistic emulation.
20. On Cicero's selected consular speeches, see *Att.* 2.1 (SB *Letters to Atticus* 21). In the late work *Orator* Cicero cites his speech *For Caecina* as a model for the plain style; but he also cites casually, as if obvious, the *For the Manilian Law*, *On Behalf of Rabirius*, and those for Cluentius and Cornelius (*Orat.* 102–3). For his use of Crassus's speech for the Servilian law as a model *quasi magistra*, see *Brut.* 164.
21. He explains his motives in the introduction to *On Moral Ends* (*Fin.* 1.1–10).
22. Compare Juvenal's comment (*Sat.* 10.122) that Cicero would not have need to fear Antony's assassins if his speeches had been as uninspired as the notorious jingle *O fortunatam natam me consule Romam* in his poem on the consulship. Even Quintilian (9.1.41) uses it as a bad example of sound play.
23. Utica and Ilerda (Hor. *Epist.* 1.20.13). Horace (*Ars* 345) speaks of a successful book earning money for the booksellers and crossing the sea, to prolong the life of a recognized poet.
24. "The Opportunities for Dramatic Performance in the Time of Plautus and Terence," *TAPA* 68 (1937): 284–304.
25. The college of scribes and poets is attested by a notice in Verrius Flaccus (Festus), *On the Significance of Words* (446–48L), datable to 207 B.C.; the Temple of Hercules and the Muses was financed and dedicated by Fulvius Nobilior in 187 B.C. from the spoils of his victory over the Aetolians (Cic. *Arch.* 27; Pliny *NH* 35.66).
26. Nepos's *Life of Cato* (1.4) makes Cato bring Ennius from Africa: but Silius Italicus (12.390) more plausibly has Ennius fighting in Sardinia where we know Cato served as Praetor in 198.
27. It was always easier for a Roman master to convert his slave into a citizen by emancipation, than for a patron of a foreign national to bestow citizenship upon him. This seems to have been a privilege limited to military commanders, who could give citizenship to individuals or units as a reward for active service.
28. The evidence comes from Cic. *Brut.* 65, but Cicero makes it clear that he had personally sought out these texts. It is not to be thought that they were commonly available.
29. The memoirs of Scaurus and Catulus are praised by Cic. *Brut.* 112, 132; the Greek memoirs of Rutilius and Sulla were available for consultation by Plutarch and Aulus Gellius (late second century), while

Rutilius at least was used as a source for the political life of his times by Cicero and Livy.

30. Cf. *Cat.* 95: "Zmyrna, my Cinna's, brought forth at last, nine harvests / and nine winters after her inception! . . . Zmyrna will travel far—to Satrachus's sunken waves: long will the white-haired centuries read Zmyrna" (trans. A. G. Lee).

31. This will be discussed at length in Chapter 2.

32. Cf. Tac. *Dial.* 21.2 (the *Verrines* in the hands of all students of oratory), Gell. *NA* 2.3.5, for a manuscript of Virgil *Aen.* 2, supposedly Virgil's own property, that fetched twenty aurei, and L. Holford-Strevens *Aulus Gellius* (London, 1989), 41, 51, 138–41, for Gellius's access to antiquarian manuscripts in bookshops and elsewhere. According to Pliny *Ep.* 3.7 the wealthy Silius Italicus had accumulated many books and Virgil memorabilia: such demand would create supply.

33. On Papirius, see Sen. *Controv.* 2. praef. 1–5 and 2.1.11–12, 2.5.7, Sen. *Ep.* 40.12, 52.11, 100.12. Seneca usually speaks of hearing Attalus or Demetrius: *Ep.* 20.9; 108.14. The older Sextius seems to have both taught (cf. *Ep.* 73.12) and published his work in book form (*Ep.* 59.7, 64.1–2). See V. T. Larson, "Seneca and the Schools of Philosophy," *ICS* 17 (1991): 49–56.

34. This is the criticism advanced by Plato in the discussion of the written word at the end of the *Phaedrus*. To us it seems a striking paradox, especially in view of Plato's extensive writing or rewriting of Socrates's teaching. But it need not have been so unusual a point of view.

35. Cf. 14.186 (a parchment codex of Virgil): "How neat a book enfolds the mighty Virgil! The poet's face adorns the frontispiece." But in view of 190 (a parchment Livy) "Confined by scanty skins is mighty Livy, though my whole library can't contain his work," realism suggests an anthology of favorite passages rather than 143 books even in microscopic hand.

36. On book format and booksellers, see P. Howell, *A Commentary on Book I of the Epigrams of Martial* (London, 1980), 105–8.

37. See Pliny *Ep.* 1.13, 7.17, and Juvenal's opening outburst "Must I always be stuck in the audience at these poetry readings, never / up on the platform itself, taking it out on Cordus / for the times he's bored me to death with ranting speeches?" (*Sat.* 1.1–3 trans. Green). This will be explored further in Chapter 6.

38. I have in mind Ovid's references in his literary apologia, *Tristia* 2.413, to the Milesian tales of Aristides, translated into Latin by an older contemporary of Cicero, Sisenna. The tale of the widow of Ephesus in Petron. *Sat.* 111–12 (adapted by the English playwright Christopher Fry in the 1940s as *The Lady's Not for Burning*) is the only Latin example of the genre.

Chapter 1. Rome at the End of the Republic

1. The actor Diphilus, quoted by Cic. *Att.* 2.19 (SB *Letter to Atticus* 39); cf. Cic. *Sest.* 123, for the allusive praise of Cicero as "Tullius, who established freedom for his citizens."
2. *aideomai Troas*, six times from Cic. *Att.* 2.5.1–13.24.1 (SB *Letters to Atticus* 25.1–332.1); Sophocles at Plut. *Pomp.*79.2; Eur. *Phoen.* 506 at Cic. *Att.* 7.11 = (SB 137).
3. The text can be read in quite diferent ways by those approaching it from its republican past and those more alert to the imperial future. It has recently been interpreted as a subtle exposure of Caesar's tyranny and a figured appeal for his assassination (R. R. Dyer, "Rhetoric and Intention in Cicero's *Pro Marcello*," *JRS* 80 [1990]: 17–30, but it is more simply taken as a skilled use of flattery to sweeten Cicero's advocacy of the return of constitutional government.
4. See A. D. Booth "*Litterator*," *Hermes* 109 (1981): 371–78, for the limitations of this type of teacher. According to Horace (*Sat.* 1.6.72) each boy paid Flavius eight asses a month, less than a day's pay for a soldier. He would need almost forty boys to make a soldier's wage.
5. Hor. *Epist.* 2.1.69–71 on the Latin *Odyssey* of Livius that he was required to study with "Orbilius the thrasher." Suet. *Gramm.* 9.
6. Quint. 1.1.13: "But I would not want this to be carried so far that the child only speaks and learns Greek for a long period, as is the usual practice. For this is how most faults arise, both of pronunciation, distorted with a foreign accent, and of speech: when Greek phrasing has become established by constant use, children persist obstinately in these different speech patterns."
7. Roman *H* has the same form as Greek *H* (long *e*); Roman *P* has the same form as Greek *P* (*r*), Roman *X* looks like Greek *X* (aspirated *K*).
8. A useful term for those whose native speech is neither of the official languages of the country.
9. M. H. Crawford, "Greek Intellectuals and the Roman Aristocracy," in *Imperialism in the Ancient World*, ed. P. Garnsey and J. W. Whittaker (Cambridge, 1978), 193–208.
10. J. Kaimio, *Romans and the Greek Language* (Helsinki, 1979). This detailed and well-documented study should be better known, both for its ancient and modern relevance.
11. For the careers of Greek *grammatikoi* at Rome and the contents of *grammatikē*, see the definitive study of E. Rawson, *Intellectual Life in the Later Roman Republic* (Baltimore, 1985).
12. Quint. 1.1.23.
13. For the argument that the teaching of the grammaticus was not practiced in Hellenistic Greece but introduced at Rome around 100 B.C.,

see A. D. Booth "The Appearance of the *Schola Grammatici*," *Hermes* 106 (1978): 117–25.

14. Cic. *De Or.* 1.187: poetarum pertractatio, historiarum cognitio, verborum interpretatio, pronuntiandi sonus.

15. The so-called *Hermeneumata Pseudo-Dositheana*, described by H. I. Marrou, *A History of Education in Antiquity*, trans. G. Lamb (New York, 1956), 355, 362, 365, 368; for an accessible text and discussion of one of these school books, see A. C. Dionisotti, "From Ausonius' Schooldays," *JRS* 72 (1982): 83–125.

16. Proclus's summaries can be found in the Loeb Classical Library (LCL) *Hesiod*, or in volume 5 of the Oxford Classical Text of Homer. Apollodorus and his epitome are combined in the LCL *Apollodorus*; Hyginus's *Fabulae* (probably not by the scholar Hyginus) have been edited by H. J. Rose (Leiden, 1934) but not translated.

17. N. Horsfall, "*Doctus sermones utriusque linguae?*" *EMC CV* 22 (1979): 85–95.

18. *Brut.* 310.

19. Commentators on the evidence for this decision given by Cic. *De Or.* 3.92–93 and Suet. *Gramm.* 25 assume that the motive was political conservatism, and the new schools would have enabled students from an outsider class to become skilled orators. It is also possible that the new school opened by Plotius Gallus, friend of the popular leader Marius, did teach a radical populist rhetoric.

20. Both survived because they were copied and handed down through the Middle Ages under the name of Cicero, but other works were undoubtedly written and displaced by later manuals.

21. For Cicero's study with Molon, see Cic. *Brut.* 307, 312, 316; for Caesar and Molon, Suet. *Iul.* 2.4, Rawson, *Intellectual Life,* 76–77; for Aristodemus, Strabo 14.650, Rawson, *Intellectual Life,* 68. On Pompey's daughter Rawson notes (46 n. 36) Plutarch's story in *Table Talk* (*Quaest. Conv.* 9.1.3) that Pompey's daughter quoted an ominous passage of Homer to him when he returned from the East.

22. Even if we discount Cicero's accounts of the presence of Crassus and Antonius at lectures by Athenian philosophers as tactful fictions like Lucullus's supposed presence when Antiochus reacted to his former teacher's new treatise in the earlier version of the *Academica*, there are the examples of Brutus and M. Marcellus, both of whom studied with Cratippus. The public attitude toward pure literature is best inferred from Cicero's justification of poetry in his *Pro Archia*, defending the poet Archias's claim to Roman citizenship.

23. For the excerpts from Accius's play *Brutus*, see Cic. *Div.* 1.44–45; there are two substantial quotations from the first book of Ennius's *Annals*, at 1.40 and 107.

24. Cic. *QFr.* 2.10.3 (SB *Letters to Quintus* 14): "Lucretius's poetry is all that you say; there is much inspiration and as much poetic skill."
25. According to Suet. *Gramm.* 18, the Augustan *grammaticus* L. Crassicius Pansa won fame for his expert commentary on the *Zmyrna*. It is characteristic of the "new poets" that this poem hailed by Catullus (see my Introduction) was known by the unconverted Greek form *Zmyrna* instead of the established Latin form *Myrrha*. Like other lurid tales of female lust, it was adapted by Ovid in the *Metamorphoses*.
26. *Bonae Litterae*, a war cry absent from Cicero, for whom *litterae* are so intrinsically good that he distinguishes only Greek from Latin literature, and everyday (*communes*) from erudite (*reconditae*) reading; the first discrimination (*liberales litterae*) comes only with the Latin panegyrics two centuries later.
27. See L. Canfora, *The Vanished Library* (Berkeley, Calif., 1989).
28. Plut. *Aem.* 28; Plutarch describes the boys as book lovers. On this and subsequent details of libraries at Rome, see A. J. Marshall, "Library Resources and Creative Writing at Rome," *Phoenix* 30 (1976): 252–64.
29. Rawson, *Intellectual Life,* 40, cites from the seventh-century Isidore of Seville the allegation that Lucullus got his library as booty from Pontus. Plut. *Luc.* 42 suggests a more deliberate process of commissioning and acquiring texts. It seems that the scholar Tyrannio may have helped to catalog them, if not also to correct them.
30. For the history of Aristotle's library, see Strabo 13C 609, and F. Grayeff, *Aristotle and His School* (Baltimore, 1974), 69–85. D. C. Earl, "Prologue Forms in Ancient Historiography," in *ANRW* 1.2 (1973): 850–52, and Rawson, *Intellectual Life,* 40 n. 4 and 43.
31. Cic. *Att.* 1.20.7, 2.1.12 (SB *Letters to Atticus* 20,7; 21.12).
32. The best survey of Atticus's role as a lover of books and patron of their publication is Rawson, *Intellectual Life,* 100–104; see also Horsfall, *Cornelius Nepos: A Selection from the Lives* (Oxford, 1989), on Nep. *Att.* 14.1.
33. Cic. *Att.* 13.27 (SB *Letters to Atticus* 326).
34. On the Roman book see E. J. Kenney, "Books and Readers in the Ancient World," in *The Cambridge History of Classical Literature*, vol. 2: *Latin Literature* (Cambridge, 1989), ed. E. J. Kenney and W. V. Clausen, ch. 1.
35. Can we judge from, for example, the Ambrosian palimpsest of Cicero's *On the Republic* whose columns vary between nine and fourteen letters to the line? The sheer brevity of the lines makes reading more difficult. But the works did have formal titles, despite arguments to the contrary; see N. Horsfall, "Some Problems of Titulature in Roman Literary History," *BICS* 28 (1981): 103–14.
36. Vitr. 6.4.1, 6.5.2.

37. On Theophanes, see W. S. Anderson, *Pompey, His Friends and the Literature of the 1st Century BC* (Berkeley, Calif., 1963), 35–41.
38. Cic. *Fam.* 5.12 (SB *Letters to his Friends* 22). It is a comment on Roman attitudes that Cicero was proud of the letter and sent copies to Atticus and other friends.
39. *Att.* 2.1.2 (SB *Letters to Atticus* 21). It is customary to mock Cicero's naiveté in expecting that Posidonius would write for him. Was he perhaps more disingenuous, and did he really hope to earn the compliments from Posidonius that were all he received?
40. For Parthenius's role in introducing Roman poets to Callimachus and other Hellenistic poetry, see W. V. Clausen "Callimachus and Latin Poetry," *GRBS* 5 (1964): 181–96, and my Chapter 2. Parthenius's dedication to Gallus is revealing: "the stories as they are found in the poets who treat this class of subject are not usually related with sufficient simplicity; I hope that in the way I have treated them you will have the summary of each and you will have at hand a storehouse from which to draw material, as may seem best to you, for either epic or elegiac verse." It suggests the need to placate an impatient and unsubtle soldier while discreetly spoonfeeding him.
41. See Rawson, *Intellectual Life*, 280–81; two obstacles have until now obstructed the reconstruction of Philodemus's theories: the intellectual problem of distinguishing views cited but rejected from his own positive assertions in the deciphered fragments, and the mistaken ordering of charred sections of scroll detached from their central core. The order of the sections has been restored and a new translation of Philodemus on poetry is being prepared by David Armstrong.
42. Nep., 14.1; Rawson, *Intellectual Life*, 51.
43. Trebonius, *Fam.* 15.21 (SB *Letters to His Friends* 207); Quintus's four tragedies, *QFr.* 3.5 (6) 7 (SB *Letters to Quintus* 25.2).
44. On Varro's research into Roman drama, see Rawson, *Intellectual Life*, 273–78.
45. On Varro's chronological disagreements with Accius, see Cic. *Brut.* 60 and 72–74 with Douglas's commentary, and Rawson, *Intellectual Life*, 271–73.
46. See Horsfall, *Nepos*, xvii–xviii, 31–32, and R. E. Fantham "The Chronological Chapter of Aulus Gellius 17.21," *LCM* 6 (1981): 17–27.
47. The *Oedipus*, Suet. *Jul.* 56; the comment on Terence, Suet. *Poet.*; reconciliation with Catullus, Suet. *Jul.* 73.
48. Cic. *Att.* 13.52 (SB *Letters to Atticus*) 353.12.
49. Varro *Ling.* 9.1.5 (LCL 2:445): "the orator ought not to regularize words, because he cannot do so without giving offence, but on the other hand the poet can with impunity leap all boundaries."
50. For the history of Cicero's attempt to honor Varro and the final version

of the *Academica*, see *Att.* 13.12–19.21a, 23–25, 35–36, 44, (SB *Letters to Atticus* 320–27, 331–34, 336), written between June 23 and July 28, 45.

51. Cicero himself coined several essential terms (one of them *essentia*) to represent Greek in Latin, but he could also decide that a Greek technical term like *sorites* was sufficiently used in Latin to stand in his elegant text (*Div.* 2.28).

52. On Aelius Stilo, see Rawson, *Intellectual Life*, 234–35, 269–70.

Chapter 2. The Coming of the Principate: "Augustan" Literary Culture

1. Calvus's death is implied by Cicero's commemorative assessment in *Brutus*, composed in spring 46 B.C.. According to Plut. *Brut.* 20, Cinna "the poet" was lynched by the mob after Caesar's murder. For the poet victim's identity with the tribune Helvius Cinna (cf. Val. Max. 9.9.1 and Suet. *Caesar* 85, and 52.3), see T. P. Wiseman, *Cinna the Poet and Other Essays* (Leicester, 1974), 44–46.

2. His birthplace near Mantua lay in the Po Valley and, despite its old established Latin culture, had only been incorporated into Roman citizenship by Julius Caesar in 49 B.C. This region was also the home of Catullus and Livy.

3. For extracts from Suetonius's life of Gallus, see *Suetonio: De poetis e biografi minori*, ed. A. Rostagni (Turin, 1944), 126–31.

4. Compare the unattributed epigram quoted by Suet. *Gramm.* 11: Cato grammaticus, Latina siren / qui solus legit ac facit poetas. "Legit" could mean either select or read (perhaps including the notion of public readings), and the latter sense, although weaker, cannot be ruled out. The author is probably Furius Bibaculus.

5. Parthenius himself offers Gallus material for either genre; for Gallus and Caecilius, cf. Suet. *Gramm.* 16 on Epirota.

6. Not Quintilius Varus the critic, poet, and friend of Horace. Alfenus Varus, the jurist, was an army officer in northern Italy at the time of the confiscations.

7. See Z. Stewart, "The Song of Silenus," *HSCP* 64 (1959): 179–205, and most recently J. Farrell, *Virgil's Georgics and the Traditions of Ancient Epic* (Oxford, 1991).

8. Lines 47–49 according to Servius; the same protests are addressed by Propertius to the departing Cynthia in his elegy 1.8.7–8.

9. Propertius's pretext is that Gallus's boy beloved may be stolen from him by young women, just as Herakles lost Hylas on the voyage of the Argonauts. The boy was pulled down into a pool by nymphs as he drew water in an unfamiliar land; Herakles lingered to search for him and was left behind by the others. For the identification of this addressee as

Cornelius Gallus, see F. Cairns, "Propertius 1.4 and 1.5 and the 'Gallus of the *Monobiblos*,'" *Papers of the Liverpool Latin Seminar* 4 (1983): 61–103.

10. See D. O. Ross's brilliant *Backgrounds to Augustan Poetry: Gallus, Elegy and Rome* (Cambridge, 1975).

11. For the form and content of this papyrus, see R. D. Anderson, R. A. Nisbet, and P. Parsons, "Elegiacs by Gallus from Qasr Ibrim," *JRS* 69 (1979): 125–55. It is reproduced as Plate 3 in *The Cambridge History of Classical Literature*, vol. 2: *Latin Literature*, ed. E. J. Kenney and W. V. Clausen (Cambridge, 1982), hereafter cited as *CHCL*.

12. Much has been made of the so-called Hellenistic arrangement of epithets in these fragments, but normal Roman practice would have maintained the tension of a sentence by separation of epithet and noun. See M. Putnam, "Propertius and the New Gallus Fragment," *ZPE* 39 (1980): 49–56, and for a good all-round assessment of the fragment and its poet, J. Whittaker, "Gallus and the Classical Augustans," *Papers of the Liverpool Latin Seminar* 4 (1983): 55–60.

13. The nearest parallel to this would be the two ten-line poems that end Propertius's first book, but neither these nor any other poem of Propertius is as short as four lines. For that we must go back to the shorter epigrams of Catullus, with their well-defined point in the final distich.

14. *uno tellures dividit amne duas*, quoted by Vibius Sequester of the river Hypanis (*Fragmenta Poetarum Latinorum*, ed. W. Morel [Stuttgart, 1927], 99–C. Cornelius fr. 1 Courtney).

15. See Macrob. *Sat.* 1.17.8; Gell. *NA* 13.27.

16. Most of the accepted biographical details of the great Augustan poets derive from Suetonius's lost volume *The Lives of the Poets* (*De Poetis*) (for surviving excerpts, see Suetonius in the Loeb Classical Library [LCL] edition, 2:465–83). However, even Suetonius, who was keeper of the imperial correspondence under Trajan, and is able to cite letters exchanged between Augustus and Virgil or Horace, was writing over a century after the poets' deaths. He too was influenced by popular romantic invention.

17. The Menalcas "quotations" are not actual lines from other poems in the *Eclogues* but are so closely related to them as to recall their content. Nor does Moeris say that Menalcas was attacked, only that he nearly died. In this reflexive technique Virgil is imitating the "self-quotations" in the *Idylls* 7 of his model Theocritus.

18. The story originates with Servius's comment on *Ecl.* 6.13; it was developed by Rostagni in his book on the young Virgil (*Virgilio Minore*) but see now G. D'Anna's skepticism in *Enciclopedia Virgiliana* 4 (1988), s. v. *Sirone*.

19. The ancient biographers attribute to Virgil the *Catalepton*, a collection

of short poems in lyric meters and hendecasyllables, short poems to Priapus, a collection of epigrams, and two miniature epics, the *Ciris*, which is certainly not by Virgil since it contains echoes of Ovid, and the *Culex*. Despite the merit of the latter, and the charm of the other poems that survived because they were ascribed to him, modern scholars do not believe he was the author of any of these poems.

20. This is hardly possible, since the events of book 3 are prior to those of book 1, but follow those of book 2 in time as in Aeneas's narrative. But some inconsistencies in book 3 suggest early composition or lack of revision.

21. See W. V. Clausen's discussion "Theocritus and Virgil," in *CHCL*, 2:301–19, here 313. Readers now have access to a definitive study of the Roman poetry book and its evolution from Hellenistic models: Nita Krevans, *The Poet as Editor: The Poetic Collection from Callimachus to Ovid* (Princeton, N.J., 1995).

22. Gallus is known to have published books of his elegies under the title *Amores* but nothing is known of their possible arrangement. The text of Catullus as it has survived in the tradition (ultimately depending on a single lost manuscript) comprises a sequence of three poetry collections, one of hendecasyllables, which Clausen believes was arranged and designed by the poet, and two posthumous groupings of *libelli*, one of longer poems (61–68) and one of elegiac and epigrammatic poetry. See W. V. Clausen "The New Direction in Poetry," *CHCL*, 2:193–97.

23. Thus Virgil originally dedicated *Ecl.* 4 (cf. lines 11–14) to Pollio, but the compliment to Pollio in *Ecl.* 3.80–95 was probably a later addition. Of Virgil's two other patrons, Varus is honored in *Ecl.* 6.6–12 (in second place to Gallus) and 9.26–29 (perhaps an addition?); Gallus in *Ecl.* 6 and 10. The unnamed addressee of *Ecl.* 8 is still in dispute. See note 33.

24. Horace actually composes the last poem of his first book of *Epistles* as an address to his new book, personified as a young slave boy, eager to leave his master for the wide world (of the booksellers) and win fame for himself.

25. This is the key to M. Santirocco's fine study *Unity and Design in Horace's Odes* (Chapel Hill, N.C., 1986).

26. See D. P. Fowler, "First Thoughts on Closure: Problems and Prospects," *Materiali e Discussioni* 22 (1989): 75–122.

27. Naming is nonetheless very significant for Propertius: his own name Propertius occurs in self-address at 2.8.17. Cf. 2.14.27 (he names himself in the third-person traditional form of votive dedication), 2.24.35 (where Cynthia his beloved addresses his grave "these are your bones, Propertius. Alas, you were true to me").

28. The honorific epithet Augustus (something like our "Reverend," or

"Venerable") was given to Octavian as his name by the grateful Senate and people of Rome after he formally restored the *res publica* to the control of the Senate on January 7, 27 B.C.

29. On poetic patronage by private citizen or emperor, see now P. White, *Promised Verse: Poets in the Society of Augustan Rome* (Cambridge, Mass., 1993). For a survey of private patronage of all kinds in Roman society, see R. P. Saller, *Personal Patronage under the Roman Empire* (Cambridge, 1982); see also the essays of Williams, Wiseman, White, and Zetzel in *Literary and Artistic Patronage in Ancient Rome*, ed. B. K. Gold (Austin, Tex., 1982).

30. I take the position of P. White, "*Amicitia* and the Profession of Poetry at Rome," *JRS* 68 (1978): 74–92, that patronage to poets was simply part of a wider system of support and favors extended by powerful Romans to many kinds of dependents. If some of these were poets, they would still perform many of the same services and receive the same rewards as others without literary talent.

31. Cf. White, *Promised Verse*, 24: "poetry had an authentic place in the cultural experience of adults in that it offered . . . the only literary means of exploring many realities of personal and social life. . . . the company of poets was particularly welcome to those among the elite who themselves wrote verse."

32. Pollio was still playing an important role as a political mediator at this time but the reference to his leadership surprises the modern reader.

33. For the debate see G. W. Bowersock, "A Date in the Eighth Eclogue," *HSCP* 75 (1971): 73–74, and 82 (1978): 201–2; R. J. Tarrant, "The Addressee of Virgil's Eighth Eclogue," *HSCP* 82 (1978): 197–99, and D. Mankin, "The Addressee of the Eighth Eclogue," *Hermes* 116 (1988): 63–76.

34. Cf. White, *Promised Verse*, 110: "from very early on the emperors held a monopoly over all new subjects that could be worked up in the venerable tradition of martial poetry."

35. Cf. Pliny *NH* 7.115, who rather strangely calls Pollio's library the first in the world. Perhaps he is distinguishing the privately owned public library from the royal libraries of Pergamum and Alexandria.

36. See A. Dalzell, "Asinius Pollio and the Introduction of Recitation at Rome," *Hermathena* 86 (1955): 20–28.

37. Sen. *Suas.* 6.27.

38. Tacitus's *Dialogue on Great Orators* is able to quote from and comment on Messala's speeches. For Messala's grammatical works, see *Grammaticorum Romanorum Fragmenta*, ed. H. Funaioli (Stuttgart, 1907), 1:503–4.

39. On poetic inadequacy compensated by goodwill, cf. Prop. 2.10.5–6, 21–26; on the availability of others, especially of hexameter poets, to

glorify campaigns, Virgil *Ecl.* 6.6–7, Prop. 3.1.15–16, Hor. *Epist.* 2.1.245–47.

40. For summaries of Ulysses's adventures, cf. Prop. 3.12.25–36, Hor. *Epist.* 1.2.17–26.

41. Tibullus uses the same device in praising Messala's campaigns at 1.7.10–11.

42. This patronymic of Melampus also turns up in Prop. 2.3.54, but in an oblique context that cannot have been the poet's model.

43. Horace in his letter to Augustus (*Epist.* 2.1.232–38) cites Choerilus as a dreadful warning of the discredit a bad epic poet can cast on his hero.

44. See now White, *Promised Verse*, 266–68, for a discussion of the problematic root *iubere/iussa* ("bid," "bidding") used by prose and verse writers alike of patrons' or dedicatees' requests.

45. Martial 1.107.3–4 and 8.55.5–6 respectively; see also Martial 7.29, 11.3, 12.4. Martial seems to have been convinced that Maecenas also provided Virgil with the slave-boy lover Alexander, whom Servius makes a gift from Pollio!

46. This would be in 39–38 B.C. What happened during those nine months? I would guess that Horace regularly appeared at the collective *salutatio* in Maecenas's public rooms each morning, but that it took nine months before he enjoyed the first one-to-one encounter or extended conversation.

47. On Horace's early life, see E. Fraenkel, *Horace* (Oxford, 1957), ch. 1, and for his relative wealth, D. Armstrong, *Horace* (New Haven, 1989).

48. Cf. *Odes* 2.17 (on Maecenas's hypochondria) and Epist. 1.7. The most sympathetic treatment of Horace's relationship with Maecenas is Fraenkel, *Horace*; see esp. 327–39 on *Epist.* 1.7.

49. I offer two samples: Fr. 1 "dear heart, I seek no glowing emeralds / no, Flaccus dear, nor gleaming berylstone / nor whitest pearls / nor rings nor jaspers yet / polished and honed by the Bithynian file." (*lucentes mea vita nec smaragdos / beryllos neque Flacce mi nitentes / nec percandida margarita quaero / nec quos Tunnica lima perpolivit / anellos nec iaspios lapillos*); and fr. 5 imitating Catullus's Galliambics: "come Cybebe," he cried, "wild goddess of the mountains / come and shake with jangling tambourine your tossing head" (*ades, inquit O Cybebe fera montium dea / ades et sonante tympano quate flexibile caput*).

50. Cf. Hor. *Epist.* 2.1.109–10, 117, *Ars P.* 416–36; Juv. *Sat.* 7; and Chapter 6.

51. Cf. White, *Promised Verse*, 135–36.

52. But the term "old comedy" may be used nontechnically by Suetonius to describe the old *Roman* comedies of Plautus and Terence.

53. Suet. *Poet.* (Virgil) 31 (*On Poets*, LCL, 2:475).

54. Pliny *NH* 7.114 reports that he forbade the burning of the poems of Virgil, despite the poet's will.

55. Composers since the fifteenth century have avoided the problems of hearing and following choral works by setting a simple text with repetition of phrases; this does not seem to have been part of the Greek or Roman tradition, but Horace has grasped the need for simplicity and for immediately intelligible short phrases.

56. For a translation of the inscription, see N. Lewis and M. Reinhold, *Roman Civilisation*, vol. 1: *The Republic and the Augustan Age*, 2d ed. (New York, 1990), 612–17; K. Chisholm and J. Ferguson, *Rome: The Augustan Age* (Oxford, 1981), 152–57.

57. Suet. *Poet.* (Horace) (*On Poets*, LCL, 2:487).

58. It should be pointed out that this letter was addressed to Maecenas and not to Horace; Augustus recognized the rights of friendship established by his old adviser.

59. Cf. Suet. *Poet.* (LCL, 2:487–89); Rolfe's translation is too formal; I have substituted one more in the intimate style of the letter.

60. Ibid., 2:485, cites Maecenas's words *Horati Flacci, ut mei, memor esto*. In fact Horace survived Maecenas by only a few months.

61. Here I differ from the eloquent interpretation of F. M. Ahl, "The Rider and the Horse: Politics and Power in Roman Poetry," in *ANRW* 2.32.1 (Berlin, 1984), 40–108, who argues that Virgil and Horace were ambivalent about Augustus's achievements and encoded their misgivings into their poetry. Ahl seems to me to reread back into this period the masked disaffection of later poets toward a Nero or a Domitian.

62. The title of this subsection is borrowed from C. O. Brink, *Horace on Poetry* (Cambridge, 1963), and is his heading for discussion of *Ep.* 2.1.93–176.

63. Fannius *Sat.* 1.4.21–22; 1.10.80; Crispinus *Sat.* 1.3.139, 1.4.14–15, 2.7.45. In *Sat.* 1.4 Horace envisages a challenge from Crispinus: "accept the match, please do; I'll take a notebook—let us choose a place and time and supervisors [*custodes*]. Let's see who can write more verses."

64. Hor. *Ep.*14.9–10 alludes obliquely to Maecenas's infatuation through the like-named Bathyllus loved by the archaic Greek poet Anacreon.

65. This is the implication of *Epist.* 2.1.110, *fronde comas vincti cenant et carmina dictant*; see Brink's comments on writing at the dinner table and Cic. *Fam.* 9.25 (SB *Letters to His Friends* 197) and *Att.* 14.21 (SB *Letters to Atticus* 375).

66. Suet. *Aug.* 85: "a poetic book in hexameters whose theme and title is Sicily" suggests a poetic tour or *periegesis*, rather than, for example, a narrative of the Sicilian war. He mostly takes for granted Augustus's

book of casual epigrams composed while bathing (*quae fere tempore balnei meditabatur*).

67. Quint. 8.3.60 cites Horace's opening vignette of a visual monster as in *prima parte libri de arte poetica*, "from the first part of the book on the art of poetry."

68. Hor. *Ars* 416–76.

69. The locus classicus for the unfavorable reception of the *Odes* by grammatici and fashionable public is *Epist.* 1.19.35–47, which I paraphrase here.

70. See J. Griffin, "Augustan Poetry and the Life of Luxury," in *Latin Poets and Roman Life* (Baltimore, 1985), 1–31.

71. *Odes* 2.9 seems to make fun of the genre's prevailing melancholy, but 1.31 and *Epist.* 1.4 show he was on good terms with Tibullus. The *Letter to the Pisos* studiously ignores Roman love elegy, assigning to the metrical genre of elegiacs only laments and votive epigrams, and diverting from the current scene by a dismissive allusion to the critics' dispute over the origins of the genre (75–78).

72. See N. Horsfall, "The *Collegium Poetarum*," *BICS* 23 (1976): 79–95. My interpretation of the association of readings with the Palatine temple and libraries depends on his arguments.

73. For the Greek society of Naples, and Augustus's enjoyment of its culture in his old age, see Strabo 5.4.7 (LCL, 2:448–50) and Suet. *Aug.* 98.

74. He alludes to the works accepted into the library canon at *Tristia* 3.1.65–68 and notes that the independent library of Pollio in the Hall of Liberty was also closed to his compositions of exile.

75. He was nicknamed "Parthenias" (the virgin) as a pun upon his name and his character.

76. Cic. *Att.* 9.4 (SB *Letters to Atticus* 173).

77. See Sen. *Controv.* 9.1.14, 9.2.26; Seneca has preserved from Livy's *History* the death notice of Cic. *Suas.* 6.16–17, 21–22.

78. He declares in the preface of *Controv.* 3 that "the felicity of Virgil's touch deserted him in prose."

79. Respectively "interpretation," "expertise," "mauvais gout." We might render the last phrase in the manner of Agatha Christie's Hercule Poirot as "a digression philosophique."

80. This is apparent from the discussion he puts into the mouth of his brother Quintus and Atticus in *Leg.* 1.1–12.

81. His rhetorical and critical works were dedicated to Romans, so it is reasonable to suppose they were read and had some influence.

82. See Strabo 1.2.3–6 (LCL, 1:62–66); there is a good translation in D. A. Russell and M. Winterbottom, *Ancient Literary Criticism* (Oxford, 1971), 300–305.

83. See *Res Gestae* chs. 2 and 25, and Chisholm and Ferguson, *Rome: The Augustan Age*, 4–9; but Antony is suppressed in *Res Gestae* 27 and the official version has to be gleaned from Hor. *Odes* 1.37, Virgil *Aen.* 8.685–88, and Prop. 3.11.

84. Preserved by Sen. *Suas.* 6.24–25. Seneca also preserves a passage from Pollio's speech for Lamia at *Suas.* 6.15.

85. Sen. *Controv.* 9.2.26, 9.1.15, and for his son-in-law Lucius Magius *Controv.* 10 praef. 2.

86. Abridgments begin with Florus in the second century (who also seems to have used Lucan) and include the *Periochae*, Eutropius, Julius Obsequens (who cared only for prodigies and portents), and the Christian Orosius.

87. "Livy, Augustus, and the *forum Augustum*," in *Between Republic and Empire*, ed. K. A. Raaflaub and M. Toher (Berkeley, Calif., 1990) 123–38.

88. For the decorative program of the Forum Augustum, see P. Zanker, *The Power of Images in the Age of Augustus*, trans. H. A. Shapiro (Ann Arbor, Mich., 1988), 210–15.

89. For the Ara Pacis and other monuments, see Zanker, *Power of Images*, chs. 4 ("The Augustan Program of Cultural Renewal") and 5. The ideological associations of the monuments are too rich and complex to be summarized here.

Chapter 3. Un-Augustan Activities

1. Little would be expected from daughters except the passive virtues of obedience and chastity and a good and fertile marriage. If the family had no son, it would be essential that the daughter provide the family line with grandsons.

2. Xenophon's *Cyropaedia* was simultaneously a romanticized account of aristocratic education and an idealization of the old Persian nobility and the life of hunting and warfare. Like his *Oeconomicus*, a more sedate model of the life of a gentleman landowner, this was favorite reading at Rome. Xenophon also wrote manuals of hunting and horsemanship, which must have been in regular use.

3. "The wicked perverts, Mamurra the queer and Caesar, fit each other beautifully" (Cat. 57); "I don't in the least bit care to please you, Caesar, or find out whether you are a white man or a blackguard" (93); Caesar visited Catullus's father in Verona and officially forgave the young man (Suet. *Jul.* 56).

4. Compare Cat. 28 to Veranius and Fabullus, "Piso's companions, that empty band with light and easy luggage." Catullus apostrophizes his

own propraetor Memmius "you really laid me flat and buggered me!" and commiserates with his friends for being victims of "no less a prick."

5. A light meter of eleven syllables (- - - U U -, U - U - X) suitable for occasional poems, much favored by Catullus and Martial.

6. The epigram was preserved by Martial, who incorporated it into a framework of his own (11.20).

7. Prop. 2.15.41–44. For the romantic image of Antony, see, J. Griffin, *Latin Poets and Roman Life* (Baltimore, 1985), ch 2.

8. For Juventius, cf. Cat. 24, 48, 81, 99. For courtesans and prostitutes, cf. Cat. 10 (Varus's girlfriend), 32 (Ipsithilla), 41 (Ameaena), 45 (Septimius's girlfriend Acme).

9. Much has been written on Clodia, almost certainly the wife, later widow, of Metellus Celer; the best studies are by T. P. Wiseman, *Catullan Questions* (Leicester, 1969), and *Catullus and His World* (Cambridge, 1985).

10. In Latin the single word *stuprum* must cover all extramarital sex with respectable women, both forced and consensual, regardless of whether the woman was an unmarried virgin, wife, or widow. Such intercourse was an offense against the family, but not a matter of public law before the legislation of Augustus. See R. E. Fantham, "*Stuprum*," *EMC* 10 (1992): 267–92.

11. Prop. 2.5.28: Cynthia, forma potens: Cynthia, verba levis. I have not been able to keep the elegant syntactical wordplay in the false parallelism of nominative *forma* and *verba*, accusative of respect.

12. Already in 1.7 when Propertius speaks of men praising him as Cynthia's accepted lover, he is thinking of those who know him from his book, for the next couplet urges neglected lovers to read "him" (1.7.11–14). Compare the reader of 2.34.81, 3.2.15–18, and 3.3.19–20 where the girl reads his poetry as she awaits her man. References to books and pages become common in book 2: cf. 2.3.4, 2.13.25, 2.25.3.

13. Hymn 5, to Pallas Athene, is a narrative of her punishment of Teiresias, who inadvertently saw her bathing.

14. The couplet, containing alternate lines of six and five feet, might permit a maximum of seventeen plus fourteen syllables (though this would be unusual), say eleven to thirteen words; in addition the sharply defined binary nature of the pentameter encouraged poets to include several short sense units within the metrical unit.

15. Prop. 1.6.29: Non ego sum laudi, non natus idoneus armis; 2.7.14: nullus de nostro sanguine miles erit.

16. Too much has been written about the Callimachean ideal of refinement, expressed in Greek by *leptos*, and translated by Romans as *tenuis*.

But the epithet was part of a manifesto; Aratus even created an acrostic on the word *lepte* in his serious poem on the constellations.

17. Tib. 1.10.2. The Latin entails a pun: quam ferus et vere ferreus ille fuit.

18. Tib. 1.1.53–56: *te bellare decet terra, Messala marique, / ut domus hostiles praeferat exuvias. / me retinent vinctum formosae vincla puellae / et sedeo duras ianitor ante fores.*

19. For the Augustan legislation, see N. Lewis and M. Reinhold, *Roman Civilization*, vol. 1: *The Republic and the Augustan Age*, 2d ed. (New York, 1990), 603–4; K. Chisholm and I. Ferguson, *Rome: The Augustan Age* (Oxford, 1981), 168, 176. The Lex Iulia de Adulteriis (18 B.C.) prescribed criminal penalties for proven adultery, but under the Lex Iulia de Maritandis Ordinibus (18 B.C.) and the later Lex Papia Poppaea (A.D. 9) the penalties for remaining unmarried or failing to have children only affected the speed of career in public service and the right of inheritance outside the immediate family. None of these laws was published until Virgil and Tibullus were dead and Propertius had almost abandoned love poetry.

20. *Stuprum*, unlawful intercourse, was defined by the protected status of the partner, and by nothing else.

21. Prop. 2.1.29: eversosque focos antiquae gentis Etruscae. and 3.9.1: eques Etrusco de sanguine regum. Contrast Horace who invokes Maecenas's royal blood but not his Etruscan race (*Odes* 1.1.1).

22. This programmatic language develops as part of his close adhesion to Callimachus and redirection away from amatory elegy toward the learned and allusive poetry of book 4.

23. *Tristia* 4.10.6, discussed subsequently.

24. The number of letters in the first collection is disputed because the fifteenth, impersonating Sappho, and several others have been suspected of being spurious, written in emulation of Ovid or in an attempt to pass work off as his. Ovid reports that his friend Sabinus composed answers to his own, but the three pairs of letters exchanged between Helen and Paris, Hero and Leander, and Acontius and Cydippe, whoever their author, must have been written later. See E. J. Kenney, "Love and Legalism," *Arion* 9 (1970): 388–414, and his edition of *Heroides* XVI–XXI (Cambridge, 1995).

25. On the influence of popular mime (not silent, but with a proper libretto permitting improvisation), see J. C. McKeown, "Augustan Elegy and Mime," *PCPS* 205 (1979): 70–80, note 73–74 on *Amores* 3.4, the only poem in the collection where Ovid uses the word *adultera*, and uses it more than once. *Amores* 2.19 makes the same assumptions. McKeown (76) argues that the elegist's sexual persona depends on the genre from which he is adapting; this is usually comedy or epigram, presupposing

a freedwoman living by her body, but when mime is the basis, the elegist assumes the role of adulterer.

26. For the role of dynastic problems as a cause of Ovid's exile, see J. Thibault, *The Mystery of Ovid's Exile* (Berkeley, Calif., 1964), and P. Green, "*Carmen et Error*," *Class. Ant.* 1.2 (1982):202–20. On the fate of the Julias, see B. M. Levick, "Julians and Claudians," *Greece and Rome* 22 (1975): 29–38; "The Fall of Julia the Younger," *Latomus* 35 (1976) 301–39.

27. Ovid claims that it was unsafe to name his male addressees in the five volumes of the *Tristia*; only Augustus himself is named. But Ovid's wife is named, as is the young woman poet Perilla, and in the *Letters from Pontus* Ovid returns to naming each addressee.

28. On Ovid's exile poetry, see E. J. Kenney, "The Poetry of Ovid's Exile," *PCPS* 191 (1965): 37–49; Kenney cites with approval A. G. Lee's description of these poems as "an Ovidian invention without parallel in Greek or Latin literature."

29. On this play of statement against implication, see Georgia Nugent, "*Tristia* 2: Ovid and Augustus," in *Between Republic and Empire*, ed. K. A. Raaflaub and M. Toher (Berkeley, Calif., 1990), 239–57.

30. Cat. 16, contrasting his naughty poems with his virtuous life, becomes a classic model, and will be echoed in due course by Martial and Pliny.

31. It is significant that he omits Horace, despite the many odes on amatory themes; Horace's writing was too discreet and his language too indirect to be interpreted as immoral.

32. Both Lucan and Statius in the next generation would support themselves by composing libretti for pantomime. On the adultery mime see note 25. Besides this passage Ovid refers to its plot in *Ars* 1.501–2, 3.605–8; *Rem.* 755, and *Tristia* 5.7.23–30.

33. The citation from the first line of the *Aeneid* permits a double entendre, since the Romans often used *arma* of male genitals.

34. Ovid does not mention the *Aeneid* in the *Metamorphoses*, but skirts around its action in his marginal tales of Aeneas's associates on the voyage to Italy. Later epic writers will be explicit; Statius ends his *Thebaid* with a confident prediction of its immortality and a caution to his departing poem: "do not challenge the divine *Aeneid*, but follow it at a respectful distance and ever adore its tracks" (*Theb.* 12.816–7).

35. Hor. *Odes* 3.30 celebrates the achievement of the *Odes* with confidence that he shall last as long as Rome and the Capitol, not in spite of its ruler.

36. Cf. *Tristia* 3.14.

37. *Tristia* 3.14, mentioned earlier, is addressed to one of these men, left unnamed. *Ex Ponto* 2.10 is addressed to Pompeius Macer; both Macer

and Melissus are listed among Ovid's poet friends in *Ex Ponto* 4.16.6, 30.

38. On this coincidence and other affinities between Horace's *Letter to Augustus* and Ovid's *Tristia* 2, see now A. Barchiesi, "Insegnare ad Augusto," in *Mega Nepios: Il destinatario, Materiali e Discussioni* 31 (1994): 149–84.

39. Cf. *Ex Ponto* 4.13.19–20, where Ovid reads his hymn to the Getae, announcing that Caesar's soul had gone to heaven.

40. See *Controv.* 10, praef. 7 (LCL, 2:358, with Winterbottom's note 2). Cf. Tac. *Ann.* 1.72; "Augustus had instituted court procedure against scandalous pamphlets under the pretext of this law, because he was shocked by the wantonness of Cassius Severus who had slandered noble men and women in abusive writings."

41. Sen. *Controv.* 10 in praef. 4: in tanta pace; and 7: di melius quod eo saeculo ista ingeniorum supplicia coeperunt quo ingenia desierant!

Chapter 4. An Inhibited Generation: Suppression and Survival

1. Cf. R. Syme, "History or Biography," *Historia* 23 (1974): 484: "Not A.D. 14 but A.D. 4, that was the decisive year." In *History in Ovid* (Oxford, 1978), 205 he speaks of "the atmosphere of gloom and repression that clouded the last decade of the reign."

2. These were still known and would remain known into the second century; compare the reference in Ovid's *Tristia* cited in Chapter 3 and the excerpts quoted by Suetonius in his *Life of Augustus*.

3. For the trial of Cremutius and his speech, see Tac. *Ann.* 4.34–35, Dio 57.24.1. For the restoration of his books, see Sen. *Ad Marciam* 1.3; Seneca speaks not only of preserving her father Cremutius's eloquence and liberty for posterity, but of Marcia's service to *Romana studia* (the knowledge of Roman history) "a great part of which had been burned." Suet. *Calig.* 16 reports that Caligula restored the work of all three authors, declaring that it was in his interest that these books should be known.

4. See A. J. Woodman, "Questions of Date, Genre and Style in Velleius: Some Literary Answers," *CQ* 25 (1975): 272–306, and the introduction to *Velleius Paterculus: The Tiberian Narrative* (Cambridge, 1977), 28–56.

5. See K. Heldmann, *Zur Theorie der Entwicklung und Verfall der griechischen und römischen Rhetorik* (Wiesbaden 1978). The issue is discussed briefly by R. E. Fantham, "Latin Criticism of the Early Empire," in *The Cambridge History of Literary Criticism*, ed. G. A. Kennedy (Cambridge, 1988), 274–96.

6. The *Controversiae* and *Suasoriae*, cited in the previous chapter. These

are translated with helpful annotations by Michael Winterbottom in two volumes from the Loeb Classical Library (LCL).

7. *Sermo*, "conversation," implies both personal address and informality. Letters were often thought of as conversations at a distance (*sermo absentis*). Hence Horace refers to his *Satires* as *Sermones* and sees his *Epistles* as in the same genre.

8. *Cornelius Nepos and Ancient Political Biography, Historia* Einzelschrift 47 (Wiesbaden, 1985).

9. Despite their ancient title, these were in fact essays; only one, the essay on leisure (*De Otio*) to Annaeus Serenus, includes speech by the addressee.

10. The "verse letters" were sent by Spurius Mummius from Corinth to his friends at Rome according to Cic. *Att.* 13.6.4 (SB *Letters to Atticus* 310).

11. Examples are Cicero's letter to Lucceius on celebrating him in a monograph *Fam.* 5.12 (SB *Letters to His Friends* 22), the long self-justification to Spinther in Cilicia (*Fam.* 1.9 [SB *Letters to His Friends* 20]), Cicero's dispatches from Cilicia to the Senate (*Fam.* 15.1), and almost certainly the disingenuous letters requesting Cato the Younger to support Cicero's request for a triumph (*Fam.* 15.3–4), clearly written to impress others than Cato.

12. Cf. the letter to Tiro *Fam.* 16.5.4 (SB *Letters to His Friends* 124) and D. R. Shackleton Bailey, *Cicero Epistulae ad Familiares*, vol. 1 (Cambridge, 1977), 23–24.

13. Seneca quotes only the *Letters to Atticus* (1.12, 16), and these not until his own later *Moral Letters* (*Ep.* 97, 118).

14. F. M. Ahl, "The Rider and the Horse: Politics and Power in Roman Poetry," in *ANRW* 2.32.1. (Berlin, 1984), 61. Ahl's focus is on poetry, and the manifestation or disguise of poetic dissent. He finds dissent where others, myself included, would not, but we are agreed on the absence of political implications in the poetry of the Julio-Claudian years before Nero.

15. In the absence of explicit testimony to the composition of *Aratea* by Germanicus, the evidence for its authorship must be taken from the manuscripts themselves. D. B. Gain, *The Aratea Attributed to Germanicus Caesar* (London, 1976), examines the evidence for Germanicus as author of this text, and allows for the possibility that it was in fact composed by Tiberius himself; in this case the "Father" addressed in the proem would be Augustus, as Tiberius's adoptive father, and the reference to Augustus inserted later.

16. Cf. Manilius 2.49–59, belittling pastoral and didactic poems on purely earthborn matters, and 3.1–25, rejecting at length heroic or national epic themes. M. Citroni "Produzione Letteraria e forma del potere," in *Storia di Roma*, ed. E. Gabba and A. Schiavoni (Turin, 1992) 2:383–

479, notes that Manilius is not simply echoing Virgil's claim in *Georg.* 3.3–6 but is moved by a commitment as strong as that of Lucretius (p. 395).

17. See G. Goold's superb introduction to the LCL *Manilius* (Cambridge, Mass., 1977), and Manilius 1.385–86, 800–925, 2.508; note the references to the deified Augustus in 4.552 and 934. The repetition in the second line of Germanicus's proem (quoted earlier) of the striking phrase *maximus auctor*, addressed to Augustus by Manilius at 1.385 may be coincidental. It is less likely that the *Aratea* is deliberately varying Manilius's rather different use of the phrase.

18. See Ovid *Ex Ponto* 4.16 for Grattius, who seems also to have written pastoral. But the bulk of the poems alluded to in Ovid's list are epic or mythological.

19. Note that despite the author's claim of novelty for the poem, F. R. D. Goodyear, "Tiberius and Gaius: Their Influence and Views on Literature," in *ANRW* 2.32.1 (Berlin, 1986), 603–10, argues dependence on the *Natural Questions*, which would date the *Aetna* to 65 or thereafter.

20. *Georg.* 4.147–48. But Virgil's complaint of lack of space is only a figure disguising his artistic choice; he has conveyed all the promise and beauty of the flower garden in his idyllic description of the old Corycian gardener.

21. This is the name adapted from Virgil's own words (Georg. 2.138) already given by Romans of the day to *Georg.* 2.138–76.

22. For Asconius's "Defense against the Belittlers of Virgil," see Suetonius *On Poets* (LCL, 2:481–83); Asconius concentrated on the historical references and Virgil's alleged borrowings from Homer.

23. Gell. *NA* 2.6. cites criticisms of propriety of diction in *Ecl.* 6.75–76, *Georg.* 3.4–5, and *Aen.* 10.314.

24. For the Palaemon anecdote, see Suet. *Gram.* 23 (LCL, 2:429–31), and for Probus and his editorial methods, *Gram.* 24 (LCL, 2:431–33). Probus is cited by Gell. *NA* 9.9.12 for criticism of *Aen.* 1.498–99 in relation to a model passage in the *Odyssey*, and at 13.21 for discussion of Virgilian euphony; but it is clear from other material reproduced in Gellius that Probus's learned commentaries also dealt with the language of Varro, Sallust, the historian Tubero, Plautus, and other early Latin texts. His work should probably be dated after A.D. 75.

25. On Tiberius's cultural associates in his youth see Chapter 2. Citroni, "Produzione Letteraria," 383–90, 392–93, has a good discussion of Tiberius's neoteric literary tastes and influence on contemporary writing.

26. *Tib.* 70, a comment interesting not only for Suetonius's own indifference to these Alexandrian poets, but because it implies that they had

not been included in the Augustan collections presided over by the grammatici Hyginus and Melissus.

27. Had Tiberius been reading Didymus Chalcenteros? Seneca (*Ep.* 88) reports that Didymus's four thousand books [*sic*] investigated the native land of Homer, the real mother of Aeneas, whether Anacreon was more prone to lust or drink, whether Sappho was a prostitute, and so on. The same letter shows familiarity (if some impatience) with the critical work of the great third-century Alexandrian Aristarchus, the first editor of Homer, and mentions the pretentious Apion, who toured all Greece in the time of Caligula airing his theories about the composition of the opening of the *Iliad*.

28. According to Suetonius (*Calig.* 34), he wanted to abolish the works of Homer and declared that Virgil was uneducated and untalented and Livy was prolix and careless in writing history; he openly despised Seneca's work as "mere interludes" and "sand without mortar." This shows that his restoration of the works of Cremutius and Labienus was motivated by political spite, not literary interest.

29. It is however likely that the emperor's patronage was self-serving, and the themes set for such displays were encomia of Rome or the emperor, as in the *Neronia*.

30. Suetonius reports that Claudius answered Greek envoys with speeches in Greek. These were probably composed on the spot, implying considerable fluency.

31. Sen. *Ep.* 56.12–14, citing *Aen.* 2.726–27.

32. *Georg.* 3.75–78, 83–85, cited at Sen. *Ep.* 95.68–70. This is no distortion of Virgil's thought, which implied the character of a heroic warrior in the description of his gallant young horse.

33. Sen. *Ep.* 108.23: *propositum non animum excolendi sed ingenium* (the contrast between character and intellect) precedes 24–27, citing *Georg.* 3.284 and 66–68.

34. The word first occurs in Cicero's intimate letters to Atticus, *Att.* 13.12.3 (SB *Letters to Atticus* 320), and Quintus, *QFr* 2.9.3 (SB *Letters to Quintus* 12). Vitruvius uses it in his preface written under Greek influence, then Seneca, but only in this letter, in Claudius's comment in the *Apocolocuntosis* (5.4) and perhaps at *Natural Questions* 6.26. It was already applied as a nickname to the learned Ateius, in Cicero's day, and Suetonius explains it as a compliment to his erudition. But the word is more adjective than noun; unlike grammaticus it did not imply a profession, and its use by Seneca for antiquarian learning may be by default, as a contrast to the dominant studies of the grammaticus and philosopher.

287

35. This was the annual salary of the third grade of administrative civil servants under Augustus.

36. N. Horsfall, "Stesichorus at Bovillae?" *JHS* 99 (1979): 26–48.

37. I am not persuaded by the eloquent arguments of T. P. Wiseman, "Satyrs in Rome? The Background to Horace's *Ars Poetica*," *JRS* 68 (1988): 1–13.

38. See R. J. Tarrant, "Senecan Drama and Its Antecedents," *HSCP* 82 (1978): 258–61, on the common characteristics that can be predicated of Varius's and Ovid's plays. Ten fragments have survived in various ancient sources; for a speculative reconstruction, see E. Lefèvre, "Der Thyestes des Lucius Varius Rufus," *Abh. d. Mainzer Akad. d. Wiss.* (Wiesbaden) 9 (1976): 1–48.

39. Quint. 10.1.98 (immediately after praising the *Thyestes*): Ovidi Medea videtur mihi ostendere quantum ille vir praestare potuerit, si ingenio suo imperare quam indulgere maluisset.

40. Men in unbleached working clothes were called *pullati*. Compare the comment of the shepherd in Calpurnius Siculus, *Ecl.* 7.26. Without the toga, dressed in his unbleached tunic, he can only sit among the shabby plebs high up in the amphitheater, near the women's seats.

41. See Suet. *Aug.* 44.

42. The sixty- or seventy-year-old plays of Accius were the theatrical fare served up by Brutus and his replacement (who substituted the *Tereus* for the too tendentious *Brutus*) at the games in 44 B.C.

43. The word "mime" can describe both the actors and the entertainment, but "pantomime" is used only for the star artists who were themselves the show.

44. See R. E. Fantham, "The Performance of Menander in the Late Republic and Early Empire," *TAPA* 114 (1984): 199–210.

45. For Bathyllus and Hylas, see Suet. *Aug.* 45.4. But like Roscius and Aesopus, the famous actors of Cicero's day, pantomimes could be both wealthy and respectable; Dio describes how the elderly Pylades financed and presided over games in A.D. 6. For the theater riots (*theatralis licentia*), see Tac. *Ann.* 1.77; 3.23; 6.13; 11.13; 13.24, 25, 28.

46. I shall use the word "dancer" for the Latin *histrio*, since these are the pantomime artists called *orchestai* (dancers) by Dio's parallel Greek narrative.

47. For Pomponius's prestige, cf. *Ann.* 11 13; compare the first notice of Pomponius, *Ann.* 5.8, where he is described as very refined in his lifestyle and of distinguished talent (*multa morum elegantia et ingenio inlustri*), and 12.28, where Tacitus, perhaps ironically rates the triumphal ornaments voted to him in A.D. 50 as contributing less to his posthumous reputation than the glory of his tragedies (*carmina*). He

was related to Mamercus Scaurus, condemned to death by Tiberius (see note 50).

48. Tac. *Ann.* 13.25.4, confirmed with lurid detail by Suet. *Nero* 26.
49. For the Latin tragedies of Caesar Strabo, see Cic. *Brut.* 177; Julius Caesar's *Oedipus*, Suet. *Jul.* 56.7; the tragedies of Quintus Cicero, Cic. *QFr.* 3.5.7 (SB *Letters to Quintus* 25.7); Octavian's *Ajax*, Suet. *Aug.* 85.2. On Germanicus's Greek comedies, see Suet. *Calig.* 3.2.
50. Dio 58.24.1; Tac. *Ann.* 6.29. Suet. *Tib.* 61 speaks more vaguely of Tiberius condemning a poet who abused Agamemnon. It should be noted that only members of the ruling classes suffered in this way. Suetonius is able to retail a series of abusive comments on Tiberius (*Tib.* 45), Claudius, and even Nero (*Nero* 39) in the improvised scripts of the Atellane farces as well as in anonymous epigrams.
51. It could be dangerous to write even loyal poetry, if it was mistimed. Tacitus reports in *Ann.* 3.49 (cf. Dio. 57.20.1) the blunder of Clutorius Priscus, who had written a fine funeral elegy for the prince Germanicus and been rewarded for it. In A.D. 21, when Drusus, the other princely heir, was sick, Clutorius composed a new elegy and read it to a domestic audience. He too was denounced for treason and condemned to death.
52. Ahl, "The Rider and the Horse," 105 cites Tac. *Ann.* 16.7 (on performances by *histriones . . . intra domum*) as evidence for the performance of Senecan tragedy in domestic theaters. This was certainly a possibility, but the Tacitean passage is discussing the shows of the pantomime dancers, not real drama.
53. Such texts were given, or lent, not sold. The authors did not need money and there was probably no general demand for such works.
54. Pliny *Ep.* 7.17.11; Quint. 8.3.31.
55. C. Cichorius, *Römische Studien* (1922; repr. Darmstadt, 1961), 423–29. The disputed phrase was *gradus eliminare*, "to unthreshold one's steps!"
56. In the introduction to my edition of *Seneca's Troades* (Princeton, 1982). For arguments in favor of stage performance, see D. F. Sutton, *Seneca on the Stage* (Leiden, 1986), and A. J. Boyle, "Senecan Tragedy: Twelve Propositions," in *The Imperial Muse: To Juvenal through Ovid*, ed. A. J. Boyle, (Melbourne, 1988), 88–89.
57. If it is by Seneca it does him no credit, since it is an inflated, repetitious, and hysterical apotheosis of Hercules, whom Seneca in the genuine *Hercules Furens* treated far more subtly.
58. Similar contests would be sponsored by Domitian a generation later under the name *Quinquennalia*.
59. See Suet. *Vita Luc.* (LCL, 2:500).

60. Suet. *Nero* 21: the Hercules and Oedipus scenes correspond to scenes in the Senecan tragedies; for Canace I know of no precedent outside Ovid's nondramatic *Heroides*. Despite Suetonius's use of the standard verb *cantare*, "to sing," these performances may well have been highly mimetic, closer to our concept of dancing than operatic acting.

Chapter 5. Between Nero and Domitian

1. Compare *carmina* of Pomponius's tragedies in *Ann.* 11.13 and 12.28.
2. On the theatrical preoccupations and self-dramatization of the Pisonian conspirators, see now A. J. Woodman, "Amateur Dramatics at the Court of Nero: *Annals* 15.48–74," in *Tacitus and the Tacitean Tradition*, ed. T. J. Luce and A. J. Woodman (Princeton, 1993), 104–28. Woodman makes clear, however, my wider claim that all court society around Nero was stagestruck; he shows that Tacitus himself has found in this an apt metaphor for the vanity and incompetence of the conspiracy.
3. Tacitus's wording seems to cover Nero's first recitation of poetry on stage, *carmen in scaena recitat*, and his first performance as a citharode, *mox . . . ingreditur theatrum, cunctis citharae legibus obtemperans.* As in *Ann.* 15.33, Tacitus cannot bring himself to say outright that the emperor sang but swerves aside to the circumstances and aftermath of the occasion.
4. Suet. *Nero* 21 indicates that Nero advanced the date of the second Neronia, but we can only guess by how many years. The earliest possible date appears to be 62, which would coincide with his escape from the restraints of Agrippina (murdered), Burrus (dead), and Seneca (cowed and in unofficial retirement).
5. Add to Niobe, Nero's role as the incestuous Canace in labor and, looking ahead to the age of Domitian, the libretto composed by Statius for an unknown pantomime, on Agave, the mother of Pentheus, who in Euripides's *Bacchae* was driven by Dionysus to kill her own son, and then was punished by the horrified realization of her deed.
6. See Suet. *Vit.* 11; Tac. *Hist.* 2.8.
7. Fr. 1 Morel: Quique pererratam subductus Persida Tigris / deserit et longo terrarum tractus hiatu / reddit quaesitas iam non quaerentibus undas. On Nero's originality or indebtedness for this conceit, see M. J. Dewar, "Nero on the Disappearing Tigris," *CQ* 41 (1991): 269–72.
8. Lovers of the cinema will recall the superb impersonation of Nero by Peter Ustinov in the film *Quo Vadis*, singing the lyric "O lambent flame! O force divine! O omnipotent fire, Hail!"
9. Being overweight, Nero would certainly lack agility and grace. Dio (in Epitome) 62.18, dealing with the year A.D. 67, claims Nero had the

pantomime Paris executed because he could not teach Nero to dance—the emperor was unable to learn. Suet. *Nero* 54 offers the alternative and more likely motive that Nero was jealous of Paris's success. The emperor had actually exploited the lawcourts to declare Paris, the former slave of his aunt Domitia, a freeborn Roman (Tac. *Ann.* 13.27).

10. Persius *Sat.* 1.93, 99–102 with scholia. Dio 61.20 says that Nero composed songs to the cithara about Attis and the Bacchantes.

11. *Sub terris tonuisse putes* (a metrically skillful half line); see Suet. *Vita Luc.* (LCL, 2:503).

12. Cf. Hor. *Epist.* 1.18.39–40; 2.2.106–8; *Ars* 382–84, 416–33.

13. This is not a formal list, but an allusive survey in Statius's poem *Silvae* 2.7, composed for Lucan's widow Polla to commemorate the fiftieth anniversary of Lucan's birth.

14. This sounds like a poem of advice or affection—for which we have no precedent in Latin poetry beyond Licinius Calvus's poem of remorse to his dead wife or the exiled Ovid's letters seeking his wife's help in Rome. Perhaps this was a poem of affectionate persuasion like Statius's address to his wife justifying his wish to retire to Naples (*Silvae* 3.5), perhaps indeed it was in some sense the model or inspiration for Statius's *Ad Uxorem*. The name *allocutio* does not help much: the word is used of a commander addressing his troops, and sometimes of a consolation, but both seem excluded by Statius's description of the poem as "pleasant" (*iucunda*).

15. The only excerpt of Cornelius's "Civil War" that survives is his eulogy of Cicero, quoted by Seneca the Elder, in *Suas.* 6.

16. Besides Tacitus (15.49) and the life attributed to Suetonius, there is a fuller life by an unknown grammarian called Vacca, which seems to have inside information from the family of Lucan. According to Vacca, Nero forbade Lucan to publish or recite his work or appear as a lawyer. Suetonius, whose version is generally more hostile to the poet, reports that Lucan was aggrieved over an interrupted recitation, and took the inevitable revenge, lashing Nero with an abusive *carmen* (Suet. *Vita Luc.* [*Ann.* LCL, 2:503]).

17. See Dewar's convincing argument, in "Nero on the Disappearing Tigris." "Three books as we now have them" comes from Vacca's account; he adds that when Lucan died he left the rest of the poem unfinished "like Ovid's *Metamorphoses*."

18. This is the explanation of F. M. Ahl, *Lucan: An Introduction* (Ithaca, N.Y., 1969), and "The Rider and the Horse: Politics and Power in Roman Poetry," in *ANRW* 2.32.1 (Berlin, 1984). See also the persuasive essay of S. Hinds, "Generalizing about Ovid," in *The Imperial Muse: To Juvenal through Ovid*, ed. A. J. Boyle, (Melbourne, 1988), 4–31 for comments

291

on the hazardous Phaethon comparison of Lucan's proem. My own defense of panegyric intent is reinforced by the arguments and parallels of M. J. Dewar, "Laying It on with a Trowel: The Proem to Lucan and Related Texts," *CQ* 44 (1994): 199–211.

19. See E. J. Champlin, "The Life and Times of Calpurnius Siculus," *JRS* 68 (1978): 95–110, answered by G. B. Townend, "Calpurnius Siculus and the *Munus Neronis*," *JRS* 70 (1980): 166–74, and R. Mayer, "Calpurnius Siculus: Technique and Date," *JRS* 70 (1980): 175–76.

20. The form *Satyricon* has nothing to do with the genre of satire and is a genitive plural, "[The books] of satyrlike adventures," not a neuter singular. The name is designed to suggest the irresponsible and randy activities typical of those half men, half beasts in the Greek satyr dramas composed about them.

21. My argument here depends entirely on the reinterpretation of the *Satyricon* and its protagonist offered by Gian Biagio Conte in the 1995 Sather Lectures at the University of California at Berkeley. To say more would be to anticipate the publication of those lectures.

22. Petron. *Sat.* 3; cf. Sen. *Controv.* praef. 1–10 (LCL, 1:3–11).

23. Horace is quoted by Eumolpus only for his priestlike exclusion of the mob *odi profanum vulgus et arceo* (*Odes* 3.1.1) and for his *curiosa felicitas*. It is this Horatian blend of care and happy success, perhaps the same skillful combination of language cherished by Persius in *Sat.* 5, which I have tried to translate here.

24. I take *fabulosum sententiarum tormentum* as a hypallage for *fabulosarum sententiarum tormentum*, "a distortion of mythological allusions."

25. E. Burck, "Das *Bellum Civile* Petrons," in *Das Römische Epos* (Darmstadt, 1979), 200–207.

26. Cf. F. I. Zeitlin, "Romanus Petronius," *Latomus* 30 (1971): 56–82. J. P. Sullivan, *Roman Literature in the Age of Nero* (Ithaca, N.Y., 1985), seems to be writing out of hostility toward Seneca and Lucan rather than with his eye on the actual style and content of Eumolpus's improvisations.

27. See now the study by E. J. Courtney, *The Poems of Petronius* (Atlanta, 1991).

28. Cf. *Argonautica* 1.5–6: "the cauldron witness of the Cumaean priestess stands in my chaste home and the laurel thrives on a worthy brow"; 1.7–14: "Do you, reverend father whose fame is made greater by the mastery of the Caledonian sea . . . give favor to me as I sing the marvelous deeds of men of old. Your son [young Domitian] will tell of overthrown Idume [Judaea] and his brother [Titus] black with the ashes of Jerusalem." Valerius probably died before Vespasian (in 79) despite Quintilian's reference to his death as recent (*nuper amisimus*, 10.1.90), since otherwise he would have changed this dedication when Vespasian died.

29. Pliny *Ep*.3.7. Its general tone is confirmed by the complimentary epigrams addressed to Silius by Martial (4.14; 6.64; 7.63; 11.48, 50).

30. Pliny's verdict may be confirmed by Martial's epigram 11.48 celebrating the fact that Silius owned one of Cicero's villas.

31. Cf. Martial 11.48, 50; 12.67.

32. Hor. *Ars* 17–18.

33. Sil. *Punica* 3.607–29, 14.686–88; see W. C. McDermott and A. E. Orentzel, "Silius Italicus and Domitian," *AJP* 98 (1977) 24–34, and F. M. Ahl, M. A. Davis, and A. Pomeroy, "Silius Italicus," in *ANRW* 2.32.4 (Berlin, 1986), 2493–94.

34. We should also mention the semidivine mothers Atalanta and Ismene, whose mourning for their sons is featured in book 9 of the *Thebaid*.

35. Only one excerpt survives, three lines quoted in distaste by Juvenal in *Satires* 4, parodying the Domitianic court.

36. As in Ovid *Ars* 1.681–704, the seduction is actually a rape, but ancient notions of female chastity compelled love poets to represent any honest woman as unwilling before the event; such rapes were treated as proceeding from love and therefore causing love (however unlikely) in the innocent victim.

37. The poetry of these men is unknown; not even a title has survived. But Quintilian (10.1.89, 91) praises them both, and Tacitus (*Dial.* 4.3) speaks warmly of Bassus, who was honored by a subvention from Vespasian.

38. On Domitian as poet and patron, see now K. M. Coleman, "The Emperor Domitian and Literature," in *ANRW* 2.32.5 (Berlin, 1986), 3087–114. Tac. *Hist.* 4.86 calls Domitian's youthful pursuit of *litterae* hypocrisy; cf. Suet. *Dom.* 2.2, but as Coleman notes, Suet. *Dom.* 20 suggests that Domitian ceased to compose after he became emperor from pressure of work. From the elder Pliny's address to Titus in *NH* praef. 5 ("how great you are in the poet's art! O mighty fertility of genius—you have contrived a way to imitate your brother also"), she deduces that Domitian was actually a more established poet than his elder brother. We saw (note 28) that Valerius Flaccus's proem alludes to Domitian as a poet, apparently of an epic on the capture of Jerusalem with a panegyric of Titus and his victory.

39. Quint. 10.1.90. He has gone back to poets of the late Augustan age, proof that recent talent is slight. There is no mention of Silius and Statius, presumably because he is following the regular practice of not judging the living.

40. The quotation is from Virgil *Ecl.* 8.13, which may have been addressed to Octavian himself (see chapter 2, note 33).

41. Coleman ("Emperor Domitian," 3095–96) notes that although the Capitoline was burnt in both 69 and 80, it is not clear that it contained

any libraries; Martial (12.2.7–8) speaks of the restoration of a library in the Tiberian Temple of Augustus, but there may have been more than one library in need of attention.

42. Suetonius, who had made a special study of the games at Rome, provides considerable detail, including comment on those events like the girls' footrace that were subsequently withdrawn. See Suet. *Dom*. 4.4 (LCL, 2:347–49).

43. For a more sympathetic analysis of Martial's themes and talent, see J. P. Sullivan, *Martial: The Unexpected Classic* (Cambridge, 1991).

44. For the Alban victory, see *Silvae* 3.5.28–31, 4.2.63–67, 4.5.22–28. For the Capitoline defeat, see 3.5.31–35; Statius mentions both in the lament for his father at 5.3.227–30 (success) and 5.3.231–33 (defeat).

45. She was the widow of a citharode, which suggests Greek origin. In addition the name Claudia often came from enfranchisement, or Roman citizenship, since besides imperial slaves like the father of Claudius Etruscus, many Greeks and Greek-speaking Levantines were made Roman citizens by the Claudian emperors.

46. P. White, "The Friends of Statius, Martial and Pliny," *HSCP* 79 (1975): 265–300; A. Hardie, *Statius's Silvae: An Exercise in Epideixis* (Liverpool, 1983). Cf. S. Newmyer, *The Silvae of Statius: Structure and Theme*, *Mnemosyne* suppl. 53 (Leiden, 1979).

47. There are two surprising aspects of Statius's poems for the bereaved; his avoidance of the metrical form of elegy, which must have lost its association with mourning and was perhaps also less adapted to the full expression of impressive sentiments, and his undifferentiated use of the Greek title *Epikedion* (properly a funeral speech) and the Latin *Consolatio* for these poems.

48. More will be said on these *libelli* in the next chapter.

49. T. Janson, *Latin Prose Prefaces: Studies in Literary Conventions* (Stockholm, 1964), thought this a prose letter; Newmyer argues for a verse introduction, but this would have survived with the *Thebaid*, and K. M. Coleman, *Statius: Silvae IV* (Oxford, 1988), 58, rightly argues that it was in prose. This could have served to introduce the first book alone before further books were published.

50. White, "Friends," 267–70, cites some twenty-one epigrams addressed by Martial to Stella, which bear witness to Stella's pride in his amatory elegiac poetry.

51. *Anth. Pal.* 11.135: "No longer, no longer, Marcus, lament the boy, but me who am much more dead than that child of yours. Make elegies, make dirges now for me, executioner, victim of death by poetry." Perhaps this is the explanation of Horace's mocking address to Valgius in *Odes* 2.9.

52. See White, "Friends," 281–82, on the implication of advance planning in the preface to book 2, and 284 on the category of female patrons.

53. See Ahl, "The Rider and the Horse," in *ANRW* 2.32.1 (Berlin, 1984), 40–108. But I am more persuaded by Coleman (*Statius*, 60) who suspects that Martial had criticized Statius for poaching on his preserves. Perhaps Statius took this to heart. Although there are six non-imperial addressees in *Silvae* 4, only Novius Vindex is also one of Martial's patrons.

54. *Ex Ponto* 4. 4. A miniature version is provided by Martial 8.66 for Silius Italicus on the inauguration of his son's consulship: "Muses, give pious incense and victims to Caesar for your Silius. Lo, Caesar, the first and only salvation of the world, bids the twelve *fasces* to return, as Silius's son is consul, and bids the Castalian home of his poet resound with the noble wand. Silius rejoices, happy in the purple and three times consul; this is the only wish remaining to him."

55. C. Milosz, *The Captive Mind*, trans. J. Zielonko (New York, 1951), 181, quoted by Ahl, "The Rider and the Horse," 91–92.

Chapter 6. Literature and the Governing Classes: From the Accession of Vespasian to the Death of Trajan

1. Senators, like modern politicians, used their leisure only to write on their own lives, or subjects with a political or historical significance. On "Senatorial Literature" see R. Syme, "Biographers of the Caesars," *Mus. Helv.* 37 (1980): 104–28 = *Roman Papers* 3 (Oxford, 1984), 1251–75.

2. Tac. *Hist.* 3.81.

3. See Suet. *Vesp.* 3. Musonius may have been exempted from Vespasian's first decree (Dio. *Epit.* 66.13) but was later exiled, to be restored under Titus. The senatorial Helvidius Priscus was not so lucky. He fell under Vespasian's displeasure and was executed by the emperor about A.D. 75, as his son would be executed by Vespasian's son Domitian twenty years later.

4. On Epictetus's memories of life at the Roman court, see F. Millar, "Epictetus and the Imperial Court," *JRS* 55 (1965): 41–48. Epictetus's master Epaphroditus had been a freedman of Nero, but lived on until A.D. 95. Thus Epictetus himself may not have known the court of Nero, but he preserves stories of conversations between Musonius and Thrasea Paetus from that period (*Disc.* 1.1.26–27). He withdrew to Apollonia in Epirus, and kept his school there. As an ex-slave he is a complete anomaly among these wellborn Asian Greeks. It is not clear where or how he had acquired his education, but his oral teaching was

recorded early in the second century by Arrian (see *Epictetus*, Loeb Classical Library [LCL], vols. 1 and 2).

5. This seems agreed, even if Philostratus's account of the meeting of Dio and Euphrates with Vespasian in Alexandria cannot be confirmed.

6. His speaking is praised by both Epictetus (*Disc.* 3.15.8, 4.8.17–18) and Pliny (*Ep.* 1.10).

7. See *Approaches to the Second Sophistic*, ed. G. W. Bowersock (University Park, Pa., 1974), and Bowersock's *Greek Sophists in the Roman Empire* (Oxford 1969). On Dio see C. P. Jones, *The Roman World of Dio Chrysostom* (Cambridge, Mass., 1978), and for both Dio and Euphrates, his translation of *Philostratus: Life of Apollonius of Tyana*, introd. G. W. Bowersock (Harmondsworth, 1970). The next chapter will treat at more length the next generation of sophists, and their influence on Roman culture.

8. See R. Syme, "Pliny the Procurator," *HSCP* 73 (1969): 201–36 = *Roman Papers* 2 (Oxford, 1979), 742–73.

9. This is the tragic poet, discussed in Chapter 4, and recalled by Tacitus, Quintilian, and Pliny the Younger.

10. Quintilian lists it with other rhetorical manuals at 3.1.21, and criticizes its comments on deportment at 11.3.143 and 148. Gellius on the other hand describes it as including "many assorted matters to delight the ears of learned men," suggesting a much more miscellaneous work. The excerpt (*NA* 9.16) praising a witty but rhetorically vulnerable *sententia* suggests something more like the memoirs of Seneca the Elder than a proper manual.

11. Aufidius was frail but still living in A.D. 64–65 (Sen. *Ep.* 30); his histories may not have gone beyond 47. No identifiable fragment of Pliny the Elder's *Histories* remains, but he is thought to have dealt with the reign of Claudius.

12. The LCL translator with his "marvellous accidents or unusual occurrences" misses the generic allusion of *casus mirabiles, eventus varios*, the novelistic attractions cultivated by Hellenistic and Roman writers of history.

13. I call it an innovation because the precedent he cites, Soranus's *Epoptides*, was written (probably in Greek) over 150 years earlier.

14. A. Wallace-Hadrill, "Pliny's Unnatural History" *Greece and Rome* 37 (1990): 80–96; G. B. Conte, "Pliny's Encyclopedia," in *Genres and Readers*, trans. G. Most (Baltimore, 1994), 95–144.

15. For the lost works, cf. A. Wallace-Hadrill, *Suetonius: The Scholar and His Caesars* (London, 1983), 43–49, 50–59.

16. These texts are known only from the excerpts made in the Byzantine period and found in a monastery on Mount Athos. They have been

edited as *Suetonius Peri Blasphemion / Peri Paidion* by Jean Taillardat (Paris, 1967).

17. Wallace-Hadrill, *Suetonius*, 45, naturally compares the Alexandrian lexicon of Pamphilus, now lost, and the surviving lexicon of Pollux, which lists names of items by topics.

18. Cf. Gell. *NA* 2.2. on names of winds (later plagiarized by Macrobius), 4.2 on types of physical defect, and 6.12 on Greek names for types of clothing.

19. Suetonius's interest may have been grammatical, not antiquarian. Compare Seneca's discussion of different academic approaches to Cicero's *On the Republic* in *Ep.* 108.30–31, discussed in Chapter 5.

20. For their surviving text and similar lives of the poets from other sources, see *Suetonio: De poetis e biografi minori*, ed. A Rostagni (Turin, 1944), and the LCL *Suetonius*, vol. 2.

21. His service to Pliny in Bithynia is deduced from Pliny *Ep.* 10.94, a letter to Trajan requesting the privileges of a father of three for Suetonius and stressing Pliny's recent observation of Suetonius's merits at close quarters.

22. On the chronology, see G. B. Townend, "The Hippo Inscription and the Career of Suetonius," and "The Post *Ab Epistulis* in the Second Century," *Historia* 10 (1961): 99–109, 375–81.

23. T. D. Barnes, "Curiatius Maternus," *Hermes* 109 (1981): 382–84, identifies Tacitus's host with M. Cornelius Nigrinus Curiatius Maternus, of Liria in Spain, with the status of a praetor under Vespasian and Titus, who rose to be governor of Moesia and proconsular governor of Syria around A.D. 90. He argues that this Maternus is also the "sophist" Maternus condemned to death by Domitian in 91 or 92 according to Dio 67.12.5. See also note 29.

24. Helvidius Priscus the Elder opposed Vespasian on principle and was first exiled, then condemned, about the dramatic date (A.D. 75) of Tacitus's *Dialogus*. It is not clear how this is related to Vespasian's undated expulsion of philosophers from Rome.

25. See Pliny *Ep.* 3.11.3, listing as executed Senecio, Rusticus, and Helvidius the Younger, as relegated Iunius Mauricus, and the women Gratilla, Arria, and Fannia; cf. 7.19.5 and R. MacMullen, *Enemies of the Roman Order* (Cambridge, Mass., 1966), ch. 2.

26. Compare the wording of *Dial.* 1.4: "We even had someone to support the other side, and give preference to modern eloquence over the speakers of the past, persecuting and making fun of antiquity."

27. On the bad memories left by these and other *Delatores*, see M. Winterbottom, "Quintilian and the *Vir Bonus*," *JRS* 54 (1964): 90–97. These men were at the height of their powers in 75; Eprius Marcellus held his

second consulship in 74, while Vibius had lucrative governorships of Africa and eastern Spain. Later, in the fourth book of the *Histories*, Tacitus demonstrates how they made their names by provoking and exploiting Vespasian's ill will against Stoic or republican idealists like Helvidius Priscus and Curtius Montanus.

28. These hardships are confirmed by both Pliny's letter on the current surfeit of recitations at Rome (*Ep.* 1.13) and Juvenal's lament for the poet's lot in *Sat.* 7.40–48.

29. T. D. Barnes, "The Significance of Tacitus's *Dialogus de Oratoribus*," *HSCP* 90 (1986): 225–44, argues persuasively that Tacitus composed the *Dialogus* in 97, as his first work, before the *Agricola*, when he had not yet started to write history; Barnes raises the possibility (232–33) that at this time Tacitus, with a promising future in oratory, was contemplating abandoning the courts to compose tragedy.

30. A. Hardie "Juvenal and the Condition of Letters: The Seventh Satire," *Sixth Papers of the Leeds Latin Seminar* (Liverpool, 1990), 145–209, argues that the opening statement is an act of thanks for support given by Hadrian to poetry, and may even have been performed at a ceremonial in the Temple of Hercules and the Muses (mentioned in 7.2 and 37). The Satire would then be a contrast between the new emperor's wise patronage of poetry and the follies of poets seeking support from private patrons.

31. Cic. *Leg.* 1.9: "there are some incidental moments which I don't waste, so that if I am granted a few days to spend in the country I adjust my writings to them. But a history cannot be planned and outlined without ensuring a period of leisure, or finished in a short time, and I usually feel tense if I am distracted from something I have begun to another task. Nor is it as easy to compose something once interrupted as to finish a work that has been drafted."

32. His point, according to Courtney's commentary, is not that papyrus or ink was expensive, but that the large scale of the genre raised costs. However there seems to be an implication that the cost of history is high because it can be written fast without the labor of refinement associated with poetry.

33. Under legislation of Claudius (Tac. *Ann.* 11.5–7) and of Nero (Tac. *Ann.* 13.42.1; see Courtney on Juv. *Sat.* 7.106), lawyers were allowed to receive fees of up to ten thousand sesterces, but these were at the discretion of the client.

34. On the state of education in first-century Rome and the distortion presented by our moralist sources, see S. F. Bonner, *Education in Ancient Rome* (London, 1977), ch. 9, "Education in a Decadent Society." On the tendency of *grammatici* to anticipate the rhetoric program under parental pressure, cf. Quint. 1.10 and Petron. *Sat.* 4.

35. Compare Pliny's report of the mature Julius Naso's attendance on Quintilian and Nicetes Sacerdos in *Ep.* 6.6.3.
36. Juv. *Sat.* 7.197–98: Si Fortuna volet, fiet de rhetore consul; / si volet haec eadem fiet de consule rhetor. His generalization exaggerates the actual example quoted by Pliny *Ep.* 4.11.1 and 14, but such success stories were not unparalleled. Suetonius *On Rhetors* cites Julius Tiro from Spain who rose to be senator and then praetor.
37. In a hyperbolic update on his own pessimistic assessment, Juvenal notes (*Sat.* 15.110–12), "Now our whole world has the culture of Greek Athens, eloquent Gaul has trained British pleaders, now Thule [a far western island beyond Ireland, perhaps Iceland] is talking of hiring a rhetoric teacher."
38. See the comments of Bonner, *Education in Ancient Rome*, 109 and n. 80.
39. For more evidence, see Wallace-Hadrill, *Suetonius*, 38–39.
40. Book 9 is the last book of the private letters; the tenth book of letters to and from Trajan has a different status, since these are records of official correspondence. C. Murgia, "Pliny's Letters and the *Dialogus*," *HSCP* 89 (1985): 171–206, has shown that Pliny both composed and arranged letters such as 9.28 to form a coda rounding off the nine-volume collection.
41. *Pline et la vie littéraire de son temps* (Paris, 1929), ch. 3.
42. On Pliny's embarrassed blend of modesty and pride in his own work, see N. Rudd, "Strategies of Vanity," in *Author and Audience*, ed. J. Powell and T. Woodman (Cambridge, 1992), 18–32.
43. See N. B. Kampen, "Observations on the Ancient Use of the Spada Reliefs," *Antiquité Classique* 48 (1979): 597–98, citing M. E. Blake, *Roman Construction in Italy from Nerva through the Antonines* (Philadelphia, 1973).
44. The books also seem to have contained the speeches of other supporters of Helvidius (cf. *Ep.* 9.13.14). Pliny tells his correspondent that he used the same opening that is in the written text (9.13.18) and subsequently reconstructed his speech as best he could, adding much (9.13.24).
45. See *Ep.* 5.20, 6.5, 6.29, 7.10.
46. See now M. Morford, "*Iubes esse Liberos*: Pliny's *Panegyricus* and Liberty," *AJP* 113 (1992): 575–93.
47. Compare the English *Eikon Basilike* composed for James I of England (James VI of Scotland) in the great decade of the Authorized Version.
48. In a later letter (*Ep.* 6.27), Pliny uses the occasion when a friend is to deliver the same formal speech of thanks to recapitulate his principles and his approach to the task.
49. This was not new. Pliny admits that his teachers Quintilian and Domitius Afer traced this decline to more than a generation before his time.

50. Guillemin, *Vie littéraire*, 78. Pliny twice quotes Euripides (*Ep.* 4.11.9, 4.27.6), and in an early letter to Suetonius on dreams he supports his arguments with well-known tags from the *Iliad*. See also A. M. Guillemin, "La culture de Pline le Jeune," in *Mélanges Felix Grat* 1 (Paris, 1946), 77–88.

51. The quotations from Homer and Greek comedy in *Ep.* 1.20 are also alluded to by Cic. *Brut.* 38, 40, 50; the Homeric examples and many of the Demosthenic citations in *Ep.* 9.26 (from *On the Crown, Against Aristogeiton, On the False Embassy, Olynthiac II,* and *Philippic I*) are found in the criticism of Dionysius of Halicarnassus and *On the Sublime,* now thought to be a work of the first century of our era.

52. See Pliny *Ep.* 3.5.

53. He may share Juvenal's belief that it is easy to write history, if not to write history well.

54. In Cic. *De Or.* 2.40–64 and *Orat.* 66.

55. On this letter, *Fam.* 5.12 (SB *Letters to His Friends* 22), and its influence on some of Pliny's letters, see Rudd, "Strategies of Vanity," 18–32.

56. See Murgia, "Pliny's Letters and the *Dialogus*," 171–206.

57. For the probable dates of compilation and publication of Pliny's letters, see A. N. Sherwin-White, ed., *The Letters of Pliny* (Oxford, 1968), 50–56, P. Cugusi, *Evoluzione e Forma dell' Epistolografia Latina* (Rome, 1983), 207–19.

58. Sherwin-White, *The Letters of Pliny,* 490, notes that whereas there were no booksellers in Verona in Catullus's day, Martial (7.88) knew his verses were read in Vienne and the spread of Roman literary education to Gaul and Spain is documented for two or three generations before this letter.

59. Cf. Quint. 2.11.3, 5.12.20; Tac. *Dial.* 29, 34; Pliny *Ep.* 2.3.6, contrasting the Forum as site of real oratory with *schola et auditorium et ficta causa,* and 2.18.2, where *auditorium* denotes the class rather than its location. See Sherwin-White, *The Letters of Pliny,* 200, and Funaioli, *RE* s.v. *recitatio,* 442.

60. One auditorium has been preserved complete from the time of Augustus, the Auditorium of Maecenas. But its form does not help us to understand the context of recitations, for it is equipped with a shell-shaped raised stage, whose tiers could contain a chorus of twenty to thirty, but whose central space could hold only one person: it might suit a conductor, if the ancient *symphoniae* used conductors, but the space as a whole would cramp a reciter. This surely was designed not for the single speaker but for (nondramatic) musical entertainment.

61. Tac. *Dial.* 9. Güngerich's *Kommentar* (Göttingen, 1980) notes that Tacitus's phrase *auditorium extruere* is unique, and suggests it might mean 'equip with benches'; it could also refer to providing a rostrum. Here

we should compare Juvenal's bitter and probably derivative account in *Sat.* 7.39–47. Meter prevents Juvenal from using the word *auditorium*, but the rented benches are there, together with raised wooden seating and chairs for the front row to be carried back after the reading. Courtney believes the recitation auditorium was arranged like a theater, reserving the *orchestra* for senators, fourteen rows of *subsellia* for the class of equites, and assigning the *plebs* to the *cunei* or rear wedges of seat, but this surely presupposes a very large auditorium and an indiscriminate, rather than invited, audience.

62. Cf. *Ep.* 5.3.11, where public recitation in the auditorium is contrasted with private reading in his home, 5.17.1, 5; 6.2.3; 6.17.1; 7.17.3.

63. Philostratus has left a less favorable picture of Euphrates, who apparently slandered Apollonius to Domitian when they were both jockeying for influence. Sherwin-White, *Letters*, 108, cites Philostratus's *Life of Apollonius* 7.36, 8.3, 8.7.11.

64. "Wide reading and much practice in writing shines through his improvisations" (*multa lectio in subitis multa scriptio elucet, Ep.* 2.3.3).

65. Juvenal is more negative, speaking with distaste of Greeks as "fast talkers, more voluble than Isaeus" (*Sat.* 3.74).

66. Pliny himself probably heard more literature at home than he read with his own eyes: his slave or freedmen readers were obviously very important to him and he writes solicitously of both the ailing Zosimus (5.19) and Encolpius (8.1).

67. On Silius see Chapter 5, and Pliny's necrology (*Ep.* 3.7) with its brief and slighting reference to Silius's *carmina*.

68. Though Juvenal's complaints suggest amateur epic persisted: the imaginary *Theseid* of Codrus (*Juv. Sat.* 1.3), and the unknown adapters of the traditional epic *topoi* listed in 1.7–11.

69. *Ep.* 4.18: Pliny is still trying in 5.15.

70. This version is my own. Although Radice's version is deliberately banal, it gains momentum from its meter and is not sufficiently repetitious to convey the tedium of Sentius's oeuvre. See also Rudd, "Strategies of Vanity," 29, on this and Pliny's own verse.

71. Pliny *Ep.* 4.14.3: His *iocamur ludimus amamus dolemus querimur irascimur, describimus aliquid modo pressius modo elatius.*

72. "Sotadean" in this excerpt is a correction of the manuscript reading. The Hellenistic genre invented by Sotades was apparently very coarse but was still known in Quintilian's time. In advising against letting young students read hendecasyllables, Quintilian mentions the related Sotadean verses as even more improper (Quint. 1.8.6; cf. Sherwin-White, *The Letters of Pliny*).

73. The numbers are significant; after Augustus the only names he can cite are Tiberius (whose reputation suffered from more than his poetry),

Lentulus Gaetulicus, Seneca, and Verginius Rufus. Pliny audibly passes over Nero.

74. Juv. *Sat.* 3.41–42, 100–108: cf. *Sat.* 7.38–39.
75. Pliny uses the metaphorical epithet *musteus,* referring to unfermented or very young wine.

Chapter 7. Literary Culture in Decline: The Antonine Years

1. *Hist. Aug., Hadr.* 7. While public and private epigraphical material is increasingly rich for the age of the Antonines, literary sources are poor. For lack of any serious historian, scholars must use with due skepticism this collection of biographies attributed to six different authors, but probably composed by one man. Modeled to some extent on Suetonius, they share his taste for scandal without his merit of access to primary sources of information.
2. Cf. *Hist. Aug., Hadr.* 19. For Hadrian's building program in Rome, see M. T. Boatwright, *Hadrian and the City of Rome* (Princeton, 1987). On his patronage of the guild of actors (*Dionysotechnitae*), see Boatwright, 206–7. For the speculation that he also revived recitations of poetry in the Temple of Hercules and the Muses, see Chapter 6, note 30.
3. *Hist. Aug., Hadr.* 3.1: Cum orationem imperatoris in senatu agrestius pronuntians risus esset, usque ad summum peritiam et facundiam Latinis operam dedit.
4. For the new Hadrianic city and its great entrance arch, see J. Travlos, *Pictorial Dictionary of Ancient Athens* (London, 1971), 161, 253–57; for the library, 244–52; for the Temple of Olympian Zeus, 403. Hadrian also built an aqueduct and (inevitably) a gymnasium. In return the Athenians made him a citizen, named after him a new tribe Hadrianis, and accepted a cult statue of Zeus Olympios with the features of their mortal emperor. See also D. S. Geagan, "Roman Athens: Some Aspects of Life and Culture I. 86 B.C.–A.D. 267," in *ANRW* 2.7.1 (Berlin, 1979), 389–99, and for Hadrian's architectural scheme linking the Roman forum to the New Athens, M. T. Boatwright, "Further Thoughts on Hadrianic Athens," *Hesperia* 52 (1983): 173–76.
5. On Herodes' benefactions, see Geagan, "Roman Athens," 403–4.
6. The best recent discussion is Boatwright, *Hadrian,* 202–12, "The Athenaeum and Other Manifestations in Rome of Hadrian's Panhellenism."
7. Hadrian also confirmed the privileges of exemption from taxes and local services granted by Trajan to grammarians, rhetoricians, doctors, and philosophers throughout the empire. See the letter of Antoninus cited by Modestinus in *Digest* 27.1.6.8 (translated in *The Digest of*

Justinian, ed. T. Mommsen, P. Krueger, and A. Watson, [Philadelphia, 1985], 2:783).

8. "Das Athenaeum zu Rom bei den Scriptores Historiae Augustae," *Historia Augusta Colloquium 1963*, ed. J. Straub and A. Alföldi (Bonn, 1964), 9–42.

9. Boatwright, *Hadrian*, 208 n. 81, citing H. I. Marrou, "La vie intellectuelle au Forum de Trajan et au Forum d'Auguste," *Memoirs de l'Ecole française de Rome* 49 (1932): 109–10, and S. B. Platner and T. Ashby, *A Topographical Dictionary of Ancient Rome* (Oxford, 1929), s. v. Athenaeum. F. Coarelli, *Guida Archeologica di Roma* (Bari, 1980), assigns it to the vestibule of Domitian.

10. Henri Bardon, *Les empereurs et la littérature latine d'Auguste à Hadrien* (Paris, 1940), chs. 14 (on Hadrian) and 15, "L' appauvrissement des lettres latines." Bardon is exceptional in relating his discussion of Hadrian's Greek and Roman culture to the decline in the Latin literature of Italy. He goes perhaps further than most modern critics in attributing this decline to Hadrian's example and his policies.

11. Dio 69.3. The Loeb Classical Library (LCL) translator is less than precise in two respects, in suggesting that Hadrian's prose compositions were varied but not his verse, and in passing over the implications of *en epesi*, that is, in hexameters or perhaps elegiacs.

12. For the meaning of Catachanna, see Fronto *To Marcus* 2.11 (LCL, 1:141); for Hadrian 's interest in the learned and now lost Antimachus, see besides *Hist. Aug., Hadr.* 15, the allegation by Dio that Hadrian was so jealous of Homer that he tried to have him suppressed (from the imperial libraries?) in favor of Antimachus (Dio 69.4.6).

13. "Greek poetry in the Antonine Age," in *Antonine Literature*, ed. D. A. Russell (Oxford, 1989), 53–90.

14. The authorship of this poem is disputed; it has also been attributed to Germanicus. But the language fits Hadrian as does the attention to Troy, also attested by Philostratus's story of Hadrian's commission to Herodes Atticus to provide Troy with an extravagant water system (Philostr. *VS* 548 [LCL, 143]).

15. A. and E. Bernard, *Les inscriptions du Colosse de Memnon* (Paris, 1960), 29.13–18, 28.

16. *Periplous* 6.2 and 10.1 refer to explanations of the fort found by Arrian at Apsarus and the site of Chobos in the *Romaika grammata:* could these have been dispatches sent by Arrian as commanding officer to the emperor or Senate?

17. See Bowie, "Greek Poetry," 77: one acrostic names the author as Dionysius "from inside the Pharos basin," the other honors the god Hermes and dates itself to "the time of Hadrian."

18. See now C. Habicht, *Pausanias' Guide to Ancient Greece* (Berkeley, Calif., 1985).
19. D. A. Russell, *Greek Declamation* (Cambridge, 1983). See especially ch. 4, "Performers and Occasions," and ch. 6, "Declamation and History."
20. Is it significant that Antoninus's letter granting exemptions, cited by Modestinus (see note 7) refers to the teachers of oratory as *sophistae*, then later as *rhetores*?
21. See E. Bowie, "Greeks and their Past in the Second Sophistic," *Past and Present* 46 (1970): 2–41, and "Greek Sophists and Greek Poetry in the Second Sophistic," *ANRW* 2.33.1 (Berlin, 1994), 209–58; and B. Reardon, *Les courants littéraires grecs des II et III siècles après J.-C.* (Paris, 1971); also discussions by G. R. Stanton, "Sophists and Philosophers: Problems of Classification," *AJP* 94 (1973): 350–64, and G. Anderson, "The Second Sophistic: Some Problems of Perspective," in Russell, *Antonine Literature*, 91–110, and "The *Pepaideumenos* in Action: Greek Sophists and Their Outlook in the Early Roman Empire." *ANRW* 2.33.1 (Berlin, 1994), 79–208.
22. This is implicitly denied by Philostratus but see C. P. Jones, "The Reliability of Philostratus," in *Approaches to the Second Sophistic*, ed. G. W. Bowersock (University Park, Pa., 1974), 14 and n. 30. Philostratus similarly denies the exile of Dio under Vespasian and of Herodes under Marcus Aurelius.
23. On the date, summer 144, rather than 143, see C. P. Jones "Aelius Aristides *Eis Basilea*," *JRS* 62 (1972) 150 n. 159.
24. Hadrian had appointed Lollianus of Ephesus, presumably in the days before he transferred his support to the school of Smyrna. Philostratus notes in the next section, (*VS* 588 (LCL, 231), that Marcus appointed Hadrian on his reputation without hearing him declaim.
25. On the creation of the separate post *ab epistulis Graecis* during this century, see G. B. Townend, *Historia* 10 (1961) 375–81. Syme has argued in connection with the dismissal of Suetonius, that the emperor took his chief secretaries with him on campaign, because he needed them with him for diplomatic correspondence.
26. P. Jal, ed., *Florus* 2 (Paris, 1967), appendix, 131–36. Note that the poem attributed to Florus by the biographer is one line short of Hadrian's reply; it almost certainly had an extra line including another province and its hardships before line 4.
27. "Sperne mores transmarinos, mille habent offucias
    cive Romano per orbem nemo vivit rectius.
    Quippe malim unum Catonem quam trecentos Socratas"
    Nemo non haec vera dicit; nemo non contra facit.
    Jal, *Florus*, 126.8 (*Anth. Lat.* 250). The poem is in the old Roman rhythm of the trochaic septenarius.

28. Which emperor made this appointment? E. J. Champlin, *Fronto and Antonine Rome* (Cambridge, Mass., 1980), who believes Fronto had a bad relationship with Hadrian and was even victimized by him, argues (97 and n. 20) that Fronto was appointed by Antoninus when Marcus Aurelius (born 121) was seventeen or eighteen. Syme assumes a more neutral relationship, and proposes an earlier date, more appropriate to the prince's level of education.

29. A. Birley, *Marcus Aurelius: A Biography* (London, 1987), 60, argues that Marcus must have begun rhetoric at fourteen, but makes no comment on his study of *grammatike*.

30. The common *cognomen* is no indication of common family. I have drawn for this and other information about Fronto's origins on Champlin's authoritative study. See *Fronto*, ch. 1, and app. 1, on Fronto's date of birth.

31. On this speech and its possible date, see Champlin, *Fronto*, 64–66. One letter (*To Marcus* 1.6.2–7; see Champlin, 61–63) includes an extended excerpt from a more technical speech on the validity of overseas wills; the emperor Antoninus had been unable to hear the speech delivered and so Marcus had read it to him. Fronto, in reply, is overjoyed that "my speech has had Marcus Caesar for its actor and declaimer" (*To Marcus* 1.7).

32. By Russell in the introductory essay to *Antonine Literature*.

33. Fronto learned this technique from his teacher Athenodotus, as he proudly tells his pupil in *To Marcus* 4.12.

34. Fronto *To Marcus* 4.5 (LCL, 1:179). Surely this does not mean that these libraries let manuscripts circulate: only that the crown prince and his tutor enjoyed special privileges.

35. Lucian would make fun of the encomiastic histories of Verus's Parthian Wars in his *On the Art of Writing History*, written around 166. On the other hand Arrian's lost history of Parthia was surely superior and truly professional historical writing; if it included contemporary events they would be properly treated.

36. Favorinus is known to have written *On Socrates and His Art of Love*, and Plutarch wrote a treatise *Peri philias* (this would include both affection and friendship). On Greek declamations in imitation of Plato's theories of *Eros*, see now M. B. Trapp, "Plato's *Phaedrus* in Second Century Greek Literature," in Russell, *Antonine Literature*, 141–73.

37. *Opicus* is particularly interesting because it mimics a Greek pejorative reference to Italians. Verrius Flaccus (Festus) explains that the word is a Greek distortion of Oscus, from the local peoples of Campania; it is used by Cicero's freedman Tiro, by Juvenal, by Fronto himself to Marcus, about correcting his Greek letter ("I don't want your mother to think me an ignorant *Opicus*"), and by Gellius.

38. Our understanding of Aulus Gellius's biography and cultural life has been greatly enriched by the definitive study *Aulus Gellius* by L. Holford-Strevens (Chapel Hill, N.C., 1989). The details of his biography are based on his opening chapter.

39. On the miscellany, see Holford-Strevens, *Aulus Gellius*, 21–22, 81. Favorinus's *Pantodape Historia* has the same title as the miscellany offered to Gellius by an unidentified friend in *NA* 14.6, but it is unlikely that Gellius would have been so negative about his respected teacher's work.

40. W. Ameling, "Aulus Gellius in Athens," *Hermes* 112 (1984): 484–90, sets these as late at 165–67, when Gellius was in his forties; Holford-Strevens, *Aulus Gellius*, 12, rejects this as incompatible with Gellius's responsibilities as a paterfamilias (see praef. 23), and sets the years in Greece early, before 147, to which he dates Gellius's visit to the Pythian Games.

41. Gellius, who proudly reports his visits to Herodes's villa at Cephisia, was almost certainly part of the *Clepsydrion*, Herodes's privileged elite to whom he spoke separately over dinner.

42. On Taurus, see Holford-Strevens, *Aulus Gellius*, 66–71.

43. Cf. Polemo and Varus, *VS* 541–42 (LCL, 129, 131).

44. Also featured in episodes at *NA* 1.4 and 15.1, where his pupils escort him back after declaiming to his home on the Mons Cispius.

45. Cf. Holford-Strevens, *Aulus Gellius*, 64–66.

46. The anecdote is reported in Suetonius's account of Pomponius (*Gram.* 22), while Favorinus's witticism, reported in SHA *Hadrian* 15, is itself a variation on Asinius Pollio's comment that he would not write (*scribere*) against Octavian (Augustus) since Octavian could outlaw (*proscribere*) him in return.

47. W. V. Harris, *Ancient Literacy* (Cambridge, Mass., 1989), ch. 7, "The Late Republic and High Empire, Literacy and Illiteracy in the Roman World," quotations are from 176.

48. On both the survival of native languages and the diffusion of Latin, see ibid., 179–81; on the high density of Latin inscriptions, 267–68, 272, and 287. But there are well over a thousand Punic incriptions, almost all private sepulchral *tituli*; for a detailed study of the persistance of native languages in Roman Africa, see F. Millar, "Local Cultures of the Roman Empire: Libyan, Punic and Latin in Roman Africa," *JRS* 58 (1968): 126–34. The evidence of Apuleius is adduced for the linguistic and literary culture of Africa and Libya in N. Fick, "Le milieu culturel africain à l'époque antonine et le témoignage d' Apulée," *Bull. Assoc. G. Budé* (1986): 285–96.

49. Harris, *Ancient Literacy*, 179, 180 nn. 18, 21, and 24.

50. See F. Millar, "The World of the *Golden Ass*," *JRS* 71 (1981): 63–75.

51. Cf. ibid., 66: "A Chaldean soothsayer plies his trade in Corinth (II.12–14); a young man has come from Miletus to see the Olympic Games (II.21); an Egyptian prophet displays his magical skills in Larissa (II.28); a group of Syrian priests journeys from village to village (VIII.24–IX.10). Travel between different regions of the Empire is simply presumed as an aspect of the wider context."

52. Apul. *Apol.* 6.10, citing Cat. 39, addressed to Egnatius the Spaniard, who cleans his teeth in urine.

53. Holford-Strevens, *Aulus Gellius*, 16–19.

54. At *Apol.* 65 Apuleius hails Plato as "my Counsel in this case, as he is my teacher in life." In this text alone he cites Plato's *Parmenides*, 4; *Symposium* 12 and 43; *Alcibiades*, 25; *Charmides*, 26; *Timaeus*, 15, 42, and 50; *Phaedrus*, 64; the probably spurious *Epistle II*, 64, and *Laws* 65.

55. *Lascivus versu, mente pudicus eras (Hadrian* fr. 2 Morel-*Apology* 11). Hadrianus Imp. 2 Courtney.

56. Not content with the standard citation from Ennian tragedy of Neoptolemus's argument for limiting the study of philosophy (Ennius Sc. 340V in 13), he provides a unique citation of Ennius's translation of the gastronomic poem *Hedyphagetica* (39) listing exotic edible fishes.

57. The cult of Aesculapius had increased its importance in this century and Apuleius had composed an epideictic speech in praise of the god, probably an official commission. At *Apol.* 55 he is so confident that the text is commonly available that he invites the audience to quote his opening words. But this speech is a separate work from the double hymn to Aesculapius in Greek and Latin announced by *Flor.* 19.

58. See the introduction by Russell to *Antonine Literature*, 1–3, 5 and G. Sandy, *The Greek World of Apuleius: Apuleius and the Second Sophistic*, Leiden-New-York-Cologne 1997 (*Mnemosyne* Suppl. 74) 9–12, 71F, 230f.

59. On these see now H. G. Nesselrath, "Lucian's Introductions," in Russell, *Antonine Literature*, 111–40.

Page 64: But as Denis Feeney pointed out in his generous review (*Times Literary Supplement*, August 1997) I should have noted that already in the last quarter of the second century B.C.E. poets thought in terms of being read. Lucilius names the readers he prefers from among his own circle (635 *Remains of Old Latin* III ed. Warmington) and both Lucilius (366–400) and his contemporary Accius (cf. R.O.L. II, xxii–xiv) lay down proposals to reform the spelling of texts.

Bibliography

Ahl, F. M. *Lucan: An Introduction.* Ithaca, N.Y., 1969.

————. "The Rider and the Horse: Politics and Power in Roman Poetry" in *ANRW* 2.32.1, 40–108. Berlin, 1984.

————. Davis, M. A., and Pomeroy, A. "Silius Italicus." In *ANRW* 2.32.4, 2492–556. Berlin, 1986.

Ameling, W. "Aulus Gellius in Athen." *Hermes* 112 (1984): 484–90.

Anderson, G. "The Second Sophistic: Some Problems of Perspective." In *Antonine Literature*, edited by D. A. Russell, 91–110. Oxford, 1990.

Anderson, R. D., Nisbet, R. A., and Parsons, P. "Elegiacs by Gallus from Qasr Ibrim." *JRS* 69 (1979): 125–55.

Armstrong, D. *Horace.* New Haven, Conn., 1989.

Bardon, H. *Les empereurs et la littérature latine d'Auguste à Hadrien.* Paris, 1940.

Barnes, T. D. "Curiatius Maternus." *Hermes* 109 (1981): 382–84.

————. "The Significance of Tacitus' *Dialogus de Oratoribus*." *HSCP* 90 (1986): 225–44.

Birley, A. *Marcus Aurelius: A Biography.* London, 1987.

Blake, M. E. *Roman Construction in Italy from Nerva through the Antonines.* Philadelphia, 1973.

Boatwright, M. T. "Further Thoughts on Hadrianic Athens." *Hesperia* 52 (1983): 173–76.

————. *Hadrian and the City of Rome.* Princeton, 1987.

Bonner, S. F. *Education in Ancient Rome.* London, 1977.

Booth, A. D. "The Appearance of the *Schola Grammatici.*" *Hermes* 106, (1978): 117–25.

———. "*Litterator.*" *Hermes* 109 (1981): 371–78.

Bowersock, G. W. *Greek Sophists in the Roman Empire.* Oxford, 1969.

———. "A Date in the Eighth Eclogue." *HSCP* 75 (1971): 73–80.

———, ed. *Approaches to the Second Sophistic.* University Park, Pa., 1974.

Bowie, E. "Greeks and Their Past in the Second Sophistic." *Past and Present* 46 (1970): 2–41.

———. "Greek Poetry in the Antonine Age." In *Antonine Literature*, edited by D. A. Russell, 53–90. Oxford, 1990.

Boyle, A. J. "Senecan Tragedy: Twelve Propositions." In *The Imperial Muse: To Juvenal through Ovid*, edited by A. S. Boyle, 78–101. Melbourne, 1988.

Bowman, A. K. "Literacy in the Roman Empire: Mass and Mode." In *Literacy in the Ancient World. JRA* Suppl. 3. Ann Arbor, Mich., 1991.

Braunert, H. "Das Athenaeum zu Rom bei den Scriptores Historiae Augustae." In *Historia Augusta Colloquium 1963*, 9–42. Bonn, 1964.

Brink, C. O. *Horace on Poetry.* Cambridge, 1963.

Burck, E. "Das *Bellum Civile* Petrons." In *Das Römische Epos*, 200–207. Darmstadt, 1979.

Cairns, F. "Propertius 1.4 and 1.5 and the 'Gallus' of the *Monobiblos.*" *Papers of the Liverpool Latin Seminar* 4 (1983): 61–103.

Canfora, L. *The Vanished Library.* Berkeley, Calif., 1989.

Champlin E. J. "The Life and Times of Calpurnius Siculus." *JRS* 68 (1978): 95–110.

———. *Fronto and Antonine Rome.* Cambridge, Mass., 1980.

Chisholm, K., and Ferguson J. *Rome: The Augustan Age.* Oxford, 1981.

Cichorius, C. *Römische Studien.* 1922. Reprint, Darmstadt, 1961.

Citroni, M. "Produzione letteraria e forme del potere." In *Storia di Roma* 2.3, edited by E. Gabba and A. Schiavoni, 383–479. Turin, 1992.

Clausen, W. V. "Callimachus and Latin Poetry." *GRBS* 5 (1964): 181–96.

———. "The New Direction in Poetry," and "Theocritus and Virgil." In *The Cambridge History of Classical Literature*, vol 2: *Latin Literature*, edited by E. J. Kenney and W. V. Clausen, 178–206, 301–19. Cambridge, 1982.

Coarelli, F. *Guida archeologica di Roma.* Bari, 1980.

Coleman, K. M. "The Emperor Domitian and Literature." In *ANRW* 2.32.5, 3087–114. Berlin, 1986.

———. *Statius: Silvae IV.* Oxford, 1988.

Conte, G. B. *Genres and Readers.* Translated by G. Most. Baltimore, 1994.

———. *Latin Literature.* Translated by J. Solodow. Baltimore, 1994.

Courtney, E. J. *A Commentary on the Satires of Juvenal.* London, 1980.

———. *The Poems of Petronius.* Atlanta, 1991.

Crawford, M. H. "Greek Intellectuals and the Roman Aristocracy." In *Impe-*

rialism in the Ancient World, edited by P. Garnsey and J. W. Whittaker, 193–208. Cambridge, 1978.

Dalzell, A. "Asinius Pollio and the Introduction of Recitation at Rome." *Hermathena* 86 (1955): 20–28.

D'Anna, G. "*Sirone.*" In *Enciclopedia Virgiliana* 4:893–95. Rome, 1988.

Dewar, M. J. "Nero on the Disappearing Tigris." *CQ* 41 (1991): 269–72.

Dionisotti, A. C. "From Ausonius' Schooldays." *JRS* 72 (1982): 83–125.

Douglas, A. E., ed. *M. Tulli Ciceronis Brutus.* Oxford, 1966.

Earl, D. C. "Prologue Forms in Ancient Historiography." In *ANRW* 1.2, 842–56. Berlin, 1973.

Fantham, R. E. "The Chronological Chapter of Aulus Gellius 17.21." *LCM* 6 (1981): 17–27.

———. *Seneca's Troades.* Princeton, 1982.

———. "The Performance of Menander in the Late Republic and Early Empire." *TAPA* 114 (1984): 199–210.

———. "The Growth of Literature and Criticism at Rome," and "Latin Criticism of the Early Empire." In *The Cambridge History of Literary Criticism,* edited by G. A. Kennedy, 220–44, 274–96. Cambridge, 1988.

———. "Mime: The Missing Link in Roman Literary History." *CW* 82 (1989): 153–66.

Feeney, D. C. "Ovid's *Fasti* and the Problem of Free Speech under the Principate." In *Augustan Poetry and Propaganda,* edited by A. Powell, Bristol, 1992.

Fick, N. "Le milieu culturel africain à l'epoque antonine et le témoignage d' Apulée." *Bull. Ass. G. Budé* (1986): 285–96.

Fowler, D. P. "First Thoughts on Closure: Problems and Prospects." *Materiali e Discussioni* 22 (1989): 75–122.

Fraenkel, E. *Horace.* Oxford, 1957.

Frischer, B. *Shifting Paradigms: New Approaches to the Ars Poetica.* Atlanta, 1991.

Gain, D. B. *The Aratea attributed to Germanicus Caesar.* London, 1976.

Geagan, D. J. "Roman Athens: Some Aspects of Life and Culture I. 86 B.C.– A.D. 267." In *ANRW* 2.7, 1 371–437. Berlin, 1979.

Gold, B. K., ed. *Literary and Artistic Patronage in Ancient Rome.* Austin, Tex., 1982.

Goodyear, F. R. D. "Tiberius and Gaius: Their Influence and Views on Literature." *ANRW* 2.32.1, 603–10. Berlin, 1986.

Green, P. "*Carmen et Error.*" *Class. Ant.* 1.2 (1982): 202–20.

Griffin, J. *Latin Poets and Roman Life.* Baltimore, 1985.

Griffin, M. *Nero: The End of a Dynasty.* New Haven, Conn., 1984.

Güngerich, R. *Kommentar zum Dialogus des Tacitus.* Göttingen, 1980.

Guillemin, A. M. *Pline et la vie littéraire de son temps.* Paris, 1929.

———. *Le public et la vie littéraire à Rome.* Paris, 1937.

————. "La culture de Pline le Jeune." In *Mélanges Felix Grat*, 1:77–88. Paris, 1946.

Habicht, C. *Pausanias' Guide to Ancient Greece*. Berkeley, Calif., 1985.

Hardie, A. *Statius' Silvae: An Exercise in Epideixis*. Liverpool, 1983.

————. "Juvenal and the Condition of Letters: The Seventh Satire." *Papers of the Liverpool Latin Seminar* 6 (1990): 145–210.

Harris, W. V. *Ancient Literacy*. Cambridge, Mass., 1989.

Heldmann, K. *Antike Theorien über Entwicklung und Verfall der Griechischen und Römischen Rhetorik*. Munich, 1982.

Hinds, S. "Generalizing about Ovid." In *The Imperial Muse: To Juvenal through Ovid*, edited by A. J. Boyle, Chapel Hill, N.C., Melbourne, 1988.

Holford-Strevens, L. *Aulus Gellius*. Chapel Hill, N.C., 1989.

Horsfall, N. "The *Collegium Poetarum*." *BICS* 23 (1976): 79–95.

————. "*Doctus sermones utriusque linguae*." *EMC/CV* 22 (1979): 85–95.

————. "Stesichorus at Bovillae." *JHS* 99 (1979): 26–48.

————. "Some problems of Titulature in Roman Literary History." *BICS* 28 (1981): 103–14.

————. trans. and ed. *Cornelius Nepos: A Selection from the Lives*. Oxford, 1989.

Howell, P. *A Commentary on Book I of the Epigrams of Martial*. London, 1980.

Hutchinson, G. O. *Latin Literature from Seneca to Juvenal: A Critical Study*. Oxford, 1993.

Jal, P., ed. *Florus*. Vols. 1–2. Paris, 1967.

Janson, T. *Latin Prose Prefaces: Studies in Literary Conventions*. Stockholm 1964.

Jones, C. P. *Philostratus: Life of Apollonius of Tyana*. Introduction by G. W. Bowersock. Harmondsworth, 1970.

————. "Aelius Aristides *Eis Basilea*." *JRS* 62 (1972): 134–52.

————. "The Reliability of Philostratus." In *Approaches to the Second Sophistic*, edited by G. W. Bowersock. University Park, Pa., 1974.

————. *The Roman World of Dio Chrysostom*. Cambridge, Mass., 1978.

Kaimio, J. *Romans and the Greek Language*. Helsinki, 1979.

Kampen, N. B. "Observations on the Ancient Use of the Spada Reliefs." *Antiquité Classique* 48 (1979): 583–600.

Kenney, E. J., "The Poetry of Ovid's Exile." *PCPS* 191 (1965): 37–49.

————. "Books and Readers in the Ancient World." In *The Cambridge History of Classical Literature* 2:3–32. Cambridge, 1982.

Larson, V. T. "Seneca and the Schools of Philosophy." *ICS* 17 (1991): 49–56.

Lefèvre, E. "*Der Thyestes von L. Varius Rufus*." Abh. d. Mainzer Akad. d. Wiss. (Wiesbaden). 9 (1976): 1–48.

Levick, B. M. "Julians and Claudians." *Greece and Rome* 22 (1975): 29–38.

————. "The Fall of Julia the Younger." *Latomus* 35 (1976). 301–39.

Lewis, N., and Reinhold, M., eds. *Roman Civilization*. Vol 1: *The Republic and the Augustan Age*. 3rd ed. New York, 1990.

Luce, T. J. "Livy, Augustus and the *forum Augustum*." In *Between Republic and Empire*, edited by K. A. Rafflaub and M. Toher, 123–38. Berkeley, Calif., 1990.

———. "Reading and Response in the *Dialogus*." In *Tacitus and the Tacitean Tradition*, edited by T. J. Luce and A. J. Woodman, 11–38. Princeton, 1993.

MacMullen, R. *Enemies of the Roman Order*. Cambridge, Mass., 1966.

Mankin, D. "The Addressee of the Eighth Eclogue." *Hermes* 116 (1988): 63–76.

Marrou, H. I. *A History of Education in Antiquity*. Translated by G. Lamb. New York, 1956.

Marshall, A. J. "Library Resources and Creative Writing at Rome." *Phoenix* 30 (1976): 252–64.

Mayer, R. "Calpurnius Siculus: Technique and Date." *JRS* 70 (1980): 175–76.

McDermott, W. C., and Orentzel, A. E. "Silius Italicus and Domitian." *AJP* 98 (1977): 24–34.

McKeown, J. C. "Augustan Elegy and Mime." *PCPS* 205 (1979): 70–80.

Millar, F. "Epictetus and the Imperial Court." *JRS* 55 (1965): 41–48.

———. "Local Cultures of the Roman Empire: Libyan, Punic and Latin in Roman Africa." *JRS* 58 (1968): 126–34.

———. "The World of the *Golden Ass*." *JRS* 71 (1981): 63–75.

Morford, M. "*Iubes esse Liberos*: Pliny's *Panegyricus* and Liberty." *AJP* 113 (1992): 575–93.

Murgia, C. "Pliny's Letters and the *Dialogus*." *HSCP* 89 (1985): 171–206.

Nesselrath, H. G. "Lucian's Introductions." In *Antonine Literature*, edited by D. A. Russell, 111–40. Oxford, 1990.

Platner, S. B., and Ashby, T. *A Topographical Dictionary of Ancient Rome*. London, 1929.

Putnam, M. "Propertius and the New Gallus Fragment." *ZPE* 39 (1980): 49–56.

Raaflaub, K. A. and Toher, M., eds. *Between Republic and Empire*. Berkeley, Calif., 1990.

Rawson, E. *Intellectual Life in the Later Roman Republic*. Baltimore, 1985.

Reardon, B. *Les courants litteraires grecs des IIe et IIIe siècle aprés J.-C*. Paris, 1971.

Ross, D. O. *Backgrounds to Augustan Poetry: Gallus, Elegy and Rome*. Cambridge, 1975.

Rostagni, A. *Virgilio Minore: Saggio sullo svolgimento della poesia virgiliana*. 2d ed. Rome, 1961.

————. ed. *Suetonio: De poetis e biografi minori*. Turin, 1944.

Rudd, N. "Strategies of Vanity." In *Author and Audience*, edited by J. Powell and T. Woodman, 18–32. Cambridge, 1992.

Russell, D. A. *Greek Declamation*. Cambridge, 1983.

————, ed. *Antonine Literature* Oxford, 1990.

Russell, D. A., and Winterbottom, M. *Ancient Literary Criticism*. Oxford, 1971.

Saller, R. P. *Personal Patronage under the Roman Empire*. Cambridge, 1982.

Santirocco, M. *Unity and Design in Horace's Odes*. Chapel Hill, N.C., 1986.

Shackleton Bailey, D. R., ed. *Cicero's Letters to Atticus*. Vols. 1–6 (with translation). Cambridge, 1965–72.

————. *Cicero: Epistulae ad Familiares*. Vols. 1–2. Cambridge, 1977.

————. *Cicero: Epistulae ad Quintum Fratrem et M. Brutum*. Cambridge, 1980.

————. trans. *Cicero's Letters to His Friends*. Vols. 1–2. Harmondsworth, 1978.

Sherwin-White, A. N., ed. *The Letters of Pliny*. Oxford, 1968.

Snyder, J. *The Woman and the Lyre: Women Writers in Greece and Rome*. Carbondale, Ill., 1990.

Stanton, G. R. "Sophists and Philosophers: Problems of Classification." *AJP* 94 (1963): 350–64.

Stewart, Z. "The Song of Silenus." *HSCP* 64 (1959): 179–205.

Sullivan, J. P. *Roman Literature and Politics in the Age of Nero*. Ithaca, N.Y., 1985.

————. *Martial: The Unexpected Classic*. Cambridge, 1991.

Sutton, D. F. *Seneca on the Stage*. Leiden, 1986.

Syme, R. *The Roman Revolution*. Oxford, 1939.

————. *History in Ovid*. Oxford, 1978.

————. "Pliny the Procurator." *HSCP* 73 (1969): 201–36 = *Roman Papers* 2:742–73. Oxford, 1979.

————. "Biographers of the Caesars." *Mus. Helv.* 37 (1980): 104–28. = *Roman Papers* 3:1251–75. Oxford, 1984.

————. "Hadrian the Intellectual." In *Les empereurs romains d'Espagne*, 243–53. Paris, 1965. = *Roman Papers* 4:103–4. Oxford, 1991.

Tarrant, R. J. "The Addressee of Virgil's Eighth Eclogue." *HSCP* 82 (1978): 197–99.

Taylor, L. R. "The Opportunities for Dramatic Performance in the Time of Plautus and Terence." *TAPA* 68 (1937): 284–304.

Thibault, J. *The Mystery of Ovid's Exile*. Berkeley, Calif., 1964.

Townend, G. B. "The Hippo Inscription and the Career of Suetonius." *Historia* 10 (1961): 99–109.

————. "The Post *Ab Epistulis* in the Second Century." *Historia* 10 (1961): 375–81.

———. "The Literary Substratum to Juvenal's Satires." *JRS* 63 (1973): 148–60.

———. "Calpurnius Siculus and the *Munus Neronis*." *JRS* 70 (1980): 166–74.

Wallace-Hadrill, A. *Suetonius: The Scholar and His Caesars*. London, 1983.

———. "Pliny's Unnatural History." *Greece and Rome* 37 (1990): 80–96.

White, P. "The Friends of Statius, Martial and Pliny." *HSCP* 79 (1975): 265–300.

———. "*Amicitia* and the Profession of Poetry at Rome." *JRS* 68 (1978): 74–92.

———. *Promised Verse: Poets in the Society of Augustan Rome*. Cambridge, Mass., 1993.

Winterbottom, M. "Quintilian and the *Vir Bonus*." *JRS* 54 (1964): 90–97.

Winterbottom, M. "Literary Criticism." In *The Cambridge History of Classical Literature* 2:33–52. Cambridge, 1982.

Wiseman, T. P. *Cinna the Poet and Other Essays*. Leicester, 1974.

———. *Catullus and His World*. Cambridge 1985.

———. "Satyrs in Rome? The Background to Horace's *Ars Poetica*." *JRS* 68 (1988): 1–13.

Woodman, A. J. "Questions of Date, Genre, and Style in Velleius: Some Literary Answers," *CQ* 25 (1975): 272–306.

———. *Velleius Paterculus: the Tiberian Narrative*. Cambridge, 1977.

———. "Amateur Dramatics at the Court of Nero: Annals 15.48–74," in *Tacitus and the Tacitean Tradition* edited by T. J. Luce and A. J. Woodman, 104–28. Princeton, 1993.

Woodman, T., and West, D. A., eds. *Poetry and Propaganda in the Age of Augustus*. Cambridge, 1984.

Zanker, P., *The Power of Images in the Age of Augustus*. Translated by H. A. Shapiro. Ann Arbor, Mich., 1988.

Zeitlin, F. I. "Romanus Petronius." *Latomus* 30 (1971): 56–82.

Index

General literary rubrics are in bold; titles are italicized. Major authors and political figures are listed in their familiar form, minor figures by gentile name: e.g. "Agrippa, M. Vipstanius" but "Domitius Afer." Titles of works are translated or simply given in English where the Greek or Latin will be problematic.

317

ANCIENT SOCIETY AND HISTORY

The series Ancient Society and History offers books, relatively brief in compass, on selected topics in the history of ancient Greece and Rome, broadly conceived, with a special emphasis on comparative and other nontraditional approaches and methods. The series, which includes both works of synthesis and works of original scholarship, is aimed at the widest possible range of specialist and nonspecialist readers.

Published in the Series:
Eva Cantarella, *Pandora's Daughters: The Role and Status of Women in Greek and Roman Antiquity*
Alan Watson, *Roman Slave Law*
John E. Stambaugh, *The Ancient Roman City*
Géza Alföldy, *The Social History of Rome*
Giovanni Comotti, *Music in Greek and Roman Culture*
Christian Habicht, *Cicero the Politician*
Mark Golden, *Children and Childhood in Classical Athens*
Thomas Cole, *The Origins of Rhetoric in Ancient Greece*
Maurizio Bettini, *Anthropology and Roman Culture: Kinship, Time, Images of the Soul*
Suzanne Dixon, *The Roman Family*
Stephen L. Dyson, *Community and Society in Roman Italy*
Tim G. Parkin, *Demography and Roman Society*
Alison Burford, *Land and Labor in the Greek World*
Alan Watson, *International Law in Archaic Rome: War and Religion*
Stephen H. Lonsdale, *Dance and Ritual Play in Greek Religion*
J. Donald Hughes, *Pan's Travail: Environmental Problems of the Ancient Greeks and Romans*
C. R. Whittaker, *Frontiers of the Roman Empire: A Social and Economic Study*
Pericles Georges, *Barbarian Asia and the Greek Experience*
Nancy Demand, *Birth, Death, and Motherhood in Classical Greece*
Elaine Fantham, *Roman Literary Culture: From Cicero to Apuleius*